EXAMPLES & EXPLANATION

Conflict of Laws

Conflict of Laws

Fourth Edition

Michael H. Hoffheimer
Professor of Law
Jamie L. Whitten Chair of Law and Government
University of Mississippi School of Law

Cover image: Kamaga/iStock

To contact Customer Service, e-mail customer.service@wolterskluwer.com, call 1-800-234-1660, fax 1-800-901-9075, or mail correspondence to:

Wolters Kluwer
Attn: Order Department
PO Box 990
Frederick, MD 21705

Printed in the United States of America.

1 2 3 4 5 6 7 8 9 0

ISBN 978-1-5438-0230-6

Library of Congress Cataloging-in-Publication Data

Names: Hoffheimer, Michael H., 1954- author.
Title: Conflict of laws / Michael H. Hoffheimer, Professor of Law, Jamie L.
   Whitten Chair of Law and Government, University of Mississippi School of Law.
Description: Fourth edition. | New York : Wolters Kluwer, [2019] | Includes index.
Identifiers: LCCN 2018058521 | ISBN 9781543802306
Subjects: LCSH: Conflict of laws—United States.
Classification: LCC KF412 .H64 2019 | DDC 342.73/042—dc23
LC record available at https://lccn.loc.gov/2018058521

SUSTAINABLE FORESTRY INITIATIVE   Certified Sourcing   www.sfiprogram.org   SFI-00756

About Wolters Kluwer Legal & Regulatory U.S.

Wolters Kluwer Legal & Regulatory U.S. delivers expert content and solutions in the areas of law, corporate compliance, health compliance, reimbursement, and legal education. Its practical solutions help customers successfully navigate the demands of a changing environment to drive their daily activities, enhance decision quality and inspire confident outcomes.

Serving customers worldwide, its legal and regulatory portfolio includes products under the Aspen Publishers, CCH Incorporated, Kluwer Law International, ftwilliam.com and MediRegs names. They are regarded as exceptional and trusted resources for general legal and practice-specific knowledge, compliance and risk management, dynamic workflow solutions, and expert commentary.

Contents

Preface

The world does not need another lofty theory for how to resolve disputes with ingredients in more than one state. But there is room in the market for a user-friendly guide to Conflict of Laws.

I first took Conflicts because my dad said it was fun. He was right. Conflicts should be fun. Parts of it are even easy. But way too many students feel like the law student in *Les Misérables* whose mind went blank while reading about Conflict of Laws.[1]

Part of the problem is that most Conflicts books do not keep it real. They don't give enough examples of how the different rules apply. Even worse, when they do give examples, they give them for the purpose of showing how hard—or even impossible—it is to apply the rules.

This book takes a different approach. Its chapters begin with no-nonsense summaries of the applicable law. Its aim is not to score scholarly points but to show what is easy and hard about the material. It then provides examples of fact patterns that test your understanding of the rules. Explanations show how the law applies to the facts and explore difficulties and uncertainties that arise in specific situations.

This book includes the basic material covered in standard Conflict of Laws courses. It begins with an overview (Chapter 1) that describes the topics and introduces the jargon. It covers domicile, personal jurisdiction, and forum selection (Part I); choice of law approaches (Parts II-VI); constitutional limits on choice of law (Part VII); rules for enforcing judgments (Part VIII); and proving foreign law (Part IX). The book's organization follows the sequence in most casebooks, but you can read the parts in any order.

I hope this book will provide a useful supplement to any casebook or treatise studied in Conflicts. But (warning!) this book is not a substitute for casebooks. Nor is it designed as an alternative to treatises that provide more complete, reliable coverage of specific laws.

This fourth edition updates several chapters and revises the coverage of personal jurisdiction to keep up with the U.S. Supreme Court.

---

1. OK, Hugo doesn't say that the law student was reading about Conflicts, but he *was* reading Savigny, the Conflicts guru of the day. *See* Victor Hugo, *Les Misérables* 754 (Charles E. Wilbour trans. Modern Library 1992) (1862). You can skip most of the footnotes in this book.

NOTE ON TERMINOLOGY

This book uses the word "state" to mean a state of the United States. Most Conflicts scholars and the Restatements on Conflicts use the word "state" to mean a sovereign political entity, including both states of the United States and foreign countries.

DISCLAIMER

Laws of specific jurisdictions are given hypothetically and for the purpose of illustration. Such laws are not necessarily valid today. In some cases, they are most definitely *not* valid.

I have tried to avoid disseminating legal disinformation by situating fictional laws in fictional jurisdictions. This can be annoying, but it is a traditional part of Conflicts discussions. No resemblance to any real jurisdiction, living or dead, is intended. Ditto for the fictional parties. Paris and Brittany are not who you think they are.

In contrast, errors in the description and application of relevant Conflicts principles are unintended. Editors, colleagues, and students have helped eliminate some real blunders. They also helped remove some bad jokes and obscure Beatles references. But errors remain, and I would appreciate it if you would contact me and bring them to my attention. Email me at mhoffhei@olemiss.edu.

CITATIONS

To reduce deforestation, citations are kept to a minimum. The two Restatements of Conflict of Laws are referred to as the "First Restatement" and "Second Restatement." Full citations for them and for treatises are given at the end of the Introduction (Chapter 1).

Acknowledgments

Joseph W. Glannon's *Civil Procedure: Examples & Explanations* provided a model for this book. I thank Professor Glannon for early encouragement and for continuing helpful feedback. Special thanks to Keith H. Beyler, Andrea K. Bjorklund, Charles H. Brower, II, Deborah J. Challener, Benjamin P. Cooper, Laura E. Little, Michael E. Solomine, and Michael Vitiello for detailed, substantive critiques; to Gary Myers for legal advice; to Peter Skagstad, Carol McGeehan, Jessica Barmack, Lee Jackson, and Frances Andersen for expert editorial help; and to Jennifer Kirby-McLemore, Matthew Love, Susanna Moore, Marcus Murphy, Jordan Redmon, Trevor Rockstad, and Lauren Stickland for research assistance. Thanks also to readers of earlier editions for identifying errors and suggesting improvements: Matt Barlety, David W. Bunt, Navi Dhillon, and Tyler Joseph Domino.

I thank the American Law Institute for permission to reprint material. Restatement of the Law, First, Conflict of Laws, copyright 1934 by The American Law Institute. Restatement of the Law, Second, Conflict of Laws, copyright 1971 by The American Law Institute. All rights reserved. Reprinted with permission.

Conflict of Laws

Introduction

CHAPTER 1

OH, THE PLACES WE'LL GO!

Conflict of Laws is the body of law that applies to legal relationships and disputes that have connections to more than one state or country. It is also called Private International Law, mostly in civil law countries.

Conflicts courses and treatises traditionally cover three topic areas: (1) personal jurisdiction (the power of courts to bind parties by their judgments), (2) choice of law (the law that courts apply in disputes where more than one law might apply), and (3) enforcement of judgments, including judgments from other court systems. The law governing these three areas is distinct but interrelated, and the areas overlap hugely in life . . . and on final exams.

Personal Jurisdiction

Personal jurisdiction defines the permissible scope of a court's authority to bind parties to its judgments. If a court has personal jurisdiction, a party must appear and defend, because a default judgment against the party will be valid. Valid judgments are generally enforceable even in the court systems of other states and countries except under a narrow range of circumstances.

Courts have personal jurisdiction over persons who have a fixed legal relationship (the status of being domiciled) with the state or country where the court sits. Domicile is treated at the outset (Chapter 2), because of its importance for personal jurisdiction, but we will see that it also plays a starring role in choice of law.

The Due Process Clause establishes outer limits to the exercise of personal jurisdiction. In general, a defendant must be served in a court's territory, be a domiciliary of the state or country where the court sits, or have "minimum contacts" in order for the court to exercise personal jurisdiction over the person (Chapters 3-4).

The Case of Carmen's Corpse

Don José, a lifelong resident of New York, gets an official looking envelope in the mail from Spain. The envelope encloses legal papers that charge Don with the wrongful death of Carmen in Seville, Spain. Don knows nothing about the alleged death. He has never been to Spain or known anyone named Carmen. Don comes to you for legal advice and asks whether he must respond to the legal papers from Spain.

It seems as though they have the wrong man. If Don is not a citizen of Spain, has never been to Spain (or any Spanish territory), and has done no acts directed at persons in Spain, then the Spanish courts lack personal jurisdiction. Although the U.S. Constitution does not apply directly to Spain, any attempt to enforce a Spanish judgment against Don in U.S. courts could be resisted on the ground that Don had no minimum contacts in Spain and enforcing the judgment would be unconstitutional.

The result would be different if Don had killed someone during a visit to Spain or if he sent some poison candy to someone in Spain. Then Spain could have valid personal jurisdiction.

Choice of Law

Courts usually apply the law of the country or state in which they sit. The law of the country or state in which a court sits is called forum law. The law of other countries and states is foreign law.

In some cases with connections with another state or country, a court does not apply its own forum law. For example, courts may honor the parties' agreement that some other place's law should govern. Under some circumstances, where disputes involve foreign parties or have other contacts with a foreign state, the application of forum law may be unfair because it might surprise or disadvantage people who have relied on the law of some other place. The application of forum law might interfere with the administration of law in a foreign country or state. In extreme cases, applying forum law might even be so unfair that it is unconstitutional (Chapters 27-28).

The law that courts apply in deciding whether to apply forum or foreign law is called "choice of law." A forum always applies its own forum choice of law rules, but under its choice of rules it may select another jurisdiction's law.

Conflicts in U.S. law schools is taught by studying selected examples of the main approaches followed by the courts. Each country and state has its own choice of law rules. In a real case, a lawyer would hit the books—tap the computers—to carefully research the applicable choice of law rules in potential forums to determine what law they would choose to apply.

As Much History as You Need In the good old days, all jurisdictions adopted similar traditional choice of law principles. These jurisdictions tended to look to the law of the place where some critical event occurred, such as the place of an accident for torts claims. Traditional rules were designed to promote the same outcome in all courts. During the past century, most but not all courts in the United States and courts in many foreign countries have abandoned the traditional rules. They have adopted a variety of alternative "modern" approaches (Chapters 17-23, 25). The modern approaches are more flexible, avoid privileging any single event, and avoid giving overwhelming importance to outcome uniformity.

Restatements Restatements are scholarly writings published by the American Law Institute. They are unofficial formulations of black letter rules written by committees of lawyers, judges, and professors. Sometimes Restatements accurately summarize the rules that are actually applied by the courts. Sometimes they have their own law reform agenda. They are the official "law" only when a court in a particular jurisdiction says so.

There are two Restatements of Conflicts. The first Restatement (1934) formulated one version of the traditional choice of law doctrines as black letter (Chapters 6-16). The second Restatement (1969) formulated one version of the alternative modern approaches (Chapters 21-22).

The Case of the Bad Spring Break Brake

Denzel and Dinah Washington, husband and wife, travel from their home in Washington state to the foreign country of Genovia for spring vacation. At the airport in Genovia, Denzel and Dinah rent a car. While Denzel is driving out of the parking lot, the car's brakes fail. He smashes into a brick wall, and Dinah suffers a broken arm.

Washington does not recognize spousal immunity, and husbands are liable for damages that they negligently cause to their wives. At the time of the accident, Denzel was driving carefully, so the facts would not support recovery on a theory of negligence if the accident happened back home. But suppose that under the law of Genovia, the operator of a motor vehicle is strictly liable for maintaining the safe operating condition of the vehicle. Under the tort law in Genovia, Dinah has a claim against Denzel for damages caused by the defective brake.

It is not clear what law will govern the claims and defenses in this case for two reasons. First, we don't know where the case is filed. The court where it is filed will employ forum choice of law rules to decide what law to apply. Second, we don't know what choice of law rules are applicable in the states where it might be filed. Each state and country has its own choice of law rules, so different courts can and will decide this case differently.

For now, it is enough to know that courts following the traditional rules would probably permit Dinah's claim against her husband by applying the law of the place where the accident occurred. Courts applying more modern approaches would probably split over whether the claim was governed by negligence or strict liability, and their resolution would be influenced by their understanding of the underlying objectives of the tort laws that were in conflict.

Depeçage   An entire case is not necessarily governed by one jurisdiction's law. American courts tend to make separate choice of law decisions for each legal issue. For example, in Dinah's lawsuit against Denzel, a court might choose to apply the strict liability law of the place of the accident. But if Genovia recognized a defense of spousal immunity, the same court might decide to apply Denzel and Dinah's home state law and reject the defense. This issue-by-issue analysis is called depeçage. In contrast, European courts tend to apply the same law to the entire case.

Reasons for Choice of Law   There is longstanding debate over the real reason for choice of law rules. This kind of debate is not unique to Conflicts. Law professors still argue about the reasons for torts, contracts, and property. Respect for the law of other jurisdictions is called comity. Comity is not exactly a rule or law; it is a value that courts acknowledge, and it provided one of the first explanations for choosing foreign law and for recognizing foreign judgments. In the Case of the Bad Spring Break Brake, the courts of either country might explain their application of the other country's law by referring to comity.

Choice of law rules can also be explained as a way of allocating spheres of lawmaking authority. By applying foreign laws in certain cases, courts recognize that another jurisdiction has exclusive or primary control over the regulated conduct. In deciding whose law applies, courts consider at least three different kinds of factors—territoriality, personal status, and justice.

A sovereign country or state has an interest in controlling behavior within its territory. For example, a country that makes drivers strictly liable for defective brakes has an interest in ensuring that people drive safe cars in the country.

Countries and states also have an interest in controlling the legal status and rights of persons who have a fixed legal relationship with the jurisdiction. For example, the home state of a husband and wife has an interest in assuring the recognition and protection of the legal relationship of their marriage that is established under its law.

Courts consider the content of the laws they apply. A forum that considers spousal immunity to be a bad law would be more reluctant to apply it. There is debate over whether this is a good or bad thing, whether it is a legitimate legal principle or a regrettable fact of life.

Foreign vs. Domestic   For most purposes, courts in the United States apply the same choice of law rules whether the foreign law comes from a foreign country or from a sister state. The international application of federal laws is governed by federal rules (Chapter 25).

Erie Doctrine   The Erie doctrine addresses special problems of choice of law when cases are brought in federal court based on diversity of citizenship subject matter jurisdiction. The Erie doctrine requires federal courts to apply state law to certain matters but permits them to apply federal law in some situations (Chapter 24). It is helpful to know in advance that federal courts in diversity cases usually must apply the choice of law rules of the state in which they are sitting.

Coverage Varies   The amount of coverage in Conflicts courses varies. Some Conflicts instructors skip personal jurisdiction and the Erie doctrine because they are covered in Civil Procedure. Others conduct an in-depth study of personal jurisdiction and Erie.

Recognition of Judgments

The third big topic area in Conflict of Laws is the law that governs the recognition and enforcement of judgments from other countries and states. A valid judgment from another country will be recognized and enforced even if the foreign country's courts applied a different law to the dispute. There are some restrictions, including a public policy exception to the recognition of foreign country judgments (Chapter 30). In contrast, the Full Faith and Credit Clause requires states to give sister state judgments the same effect that they would be given by the state where they were rendered, and there is no policy exception (Chapter 31).

The Case of the Bite Worse Than the Bark

Barbie, a citizen of California, was visiting the country of Barataria. While she was traveling on a bus in Barataria City, she was carrying her miniature dog Oodles in her purse. Seated across from her was Ken, also a citizen of California. When Ken saw Oodles's head sticking out of the purse, Ken began to make barking noises and to gesture at Oodles. Oodles responded by jumping from the purse to the floor of the bus. Ken then kicked Oodles, and Oodles bit Ken's ankle.

After Barbie and Oodles return to California, Ken sues Barbie in Barataria court. Under the law of Barataria the owner of a dog is strictly liable for its conduct. There are no defenses or exceptions. Moreover, a person who is the victim of a dog bite may recover $5,000 in place of actual damages, and prevailing parties are entitled to recover attorney's fees in civil actions.

This case raises three separate and overlapping issues. First is the question of whether Baratarian courts have personal jurisdiction over Barbie so that a judgment against her will be valid and enforceable anywhere. This will be a matter of Baratarian law in the first instance, and Baratarian courts will apply Baratarian jurisdictional law. Even if Baratarian law authorizes jurisdiction, enforcement of the foreign judgment in a U.S. court will require that Barbie have minimum contacts with Barataria because she was neither domiciled nor served with process there. Such jurisdiction must also be reasonable. It is enough for now to see the issue and to see that if Barataria authorizes its courts to hear the case and if there are minimum contacts, then Barbie cannot safely ignore the lawsuit. If the foreign court has personal jurisdiction, then its judgment will be valid and potentially enforceable even in California. In contrast, if there are no minimum contacts or jurisdiction was so unreasonable as to violate due process, then the judgment will be void and unenforceable in a U.S. court.

Second is the problem of choice of law. Baratarian courts might normally be expected to apply Baratarian tort law. But under that country's choice of law rules, its courts might not apply their own tort law to conduct by a California citizen that injures a fellow California citizen. (See Chapter 26.) What law the foreign court will apply will depend on the choice of law approach employed by its courts.

Third is the problem of enforcement of a foreign country judgment in the United States. Even if there are minimum contacts and the Baratarian court has personal jurisdiction, courts will not enforce a foreign country's judgment that is contrary to their own public policy. In this case, the Baratarian strict liability, exclusion of defenses, statutory damages, and award of fees might be found to be repugnant to the public policy of U.S. courts that would be asked to enforce it.

The important thing to see at the start is that the three big problem areas are related. The law regulating each area is distinct, but the analyses are linked. For example, if there is no personal jurisdiction, then the judgment is not enforceable. If Barataria applies California law, then there would be no public policy objection to California enforcing the Barataria court's judgment.

Easy Cases   Conflicts teachers are mean. They like to focus on hard cases. There are also easy cases with clear answers. For example, everything changes if Ken does not sue in Barataria but instead sues Barbie in California. The California court definitely has personal jurisdiction because Barbie is domiciled there (Chapters 2-3). The California court would apply a modern choice of law theory—a version of "interest analysis" (Chapters 18-19) and conclude that California tort law applies. Finally, the California judgment would be recognized everywhere.

LEGAL BIBLIOGRAPHY AND CITATIONS USED

First Restatement: Restatement of the Law of Conflict of Laws (1934)
Second Restatement: Restatement (Second) of Conflict of Laws (1969)
Richman et al., Understanding Conflict of Laws: William M. Richman et al., Understanding Conflict of Laws (4th ed. 2013)
Hay et al., Conflict of Laws: Peter Hay et al., Conflict of Laws (6th ed. 2018)
Weintraub, Commentary on the Conflict of Laws: Russell J. Weintraub, Commentary on the Conflict of Laws (6th ed. 2010)

PART I

Status and Power of Courts over Persons

CHAPTER 2

Domicile

INTRODUCTION

Domicile is a person's legal home.[1] A person who is domiciled in a jurisdiction is a "domiciliary" of that jurisdiction. Domicile is important for many legal purposes, including personal jurisdiction and choice of law.

JUST THE RULES

One and Only One   All natural persons (human beings) have one and only one domicile. First Restatement §11. This means that a person is born with a domicile and can lose it only by getting a new domicile.

Home, Sweet Home   General definitions of domicile are less than helpful for figuring out domicile. The First Restatement defines domicile as "the place with which a person has a settled connection for certain legal purposes, either because his home is there, or because that place is assigned to him by the law." Id. §9. The Second Restatement says, "Domicil is a place, usually a person's home, which the rules of Conflict of Laws sometimes accord determinative significance. . . ." Second Restatement §11.

---

1. The Restatements prefer the spelling "domicil" for reasons no one knows. I told you: You can skip the footnotes.

"Home" is defined as a dwelling place. But making a home in a particular building is not absolutely required. All that is really required is what is required for change of domicile—presence in the jurisdiction and intent to remain.

Most jurisdictions adopt similar definitions of domicile. But they may vary in details. A forum will apply its own definitions, not the definitions of the place where a person may be domiciled.

The law everywhere insists that a person can have only one domicile at a time. But different courts may reach different conclusions about where a person is domiciled. This could happen either because they apply the same rule but evaluate the facts differently or because they apply slightly different definitions of domicile.

To make matters more confusing, courts may in fact determine domicile differently for different issues. For example, federal courts define a natural person's citizenship as his or her place of domicile for purposes of diversity of citizenship jurisdiction. One federal court held that an 18-year-old had the capacity to change his domicile even though his (former) place of domicile required a domiciliary to be 21. Rodriguez-Diaz v. Sierra-Martinez, 853 F.2d 1027 (1st Cir. 1998).

Presumptions

Carry It Back Because a person always has a domicile, the law will trace domicile back to a person's last known domicile unless the person has acquired a new domicile. This means you can figure out a person's domicile by using a few key presumptions and mastering the rules governing change of domicile. These rules apply mechanically, and sometimes a person's domicile is not the place where the person is living. Someone's domicile might even be a place the person has left forever when he or she hasn't gotten a new domicile yet.

Domicile at Birth A person's domicile at birth is the domicile of the parents if they have the same domicile.

Spouses The law used to presume that spouses shared the same domicile—the husband's. Today courts will separately analyze the domicile of each spouse in an appropriate case. Second Restatement §21 (1988 revision).

Change of Domicile

Presence Plus Intent A competent person can voluntarily change domicile. Two ingredients are required in order to acquire a new domicile: (1)

a person must be physically present in the new jurisdiction, and (2) the person must have the subjective intent of making the new jurisdiction his or her home.

Presence means actual physical presence in the new jurisdiction. This means when someone is moving to a new jurisdiction, the person must physically enter the new state or country in order to establish domicile there. Cases have split over whether a spouse can satisfy the physical presence for the other spouse for purposes of changing the domicile for both.

Older authorities required the person to have the subjective intent to remain permanently or indefinitely in the new jurisdiction. The Second Restatement requires only that the person have the intention to make the place "his home for the time at least." Second Restatement §18. Cases have held that the subjective intent can be satisfied by an intent to remain in the jurisdiction for an indefinite time even though a person is thinking of moving elsewhere. E.g., Hawkins v. Masters Farms, Inc., 2003 WL 21555767 (D. Kan. 2003).

For example, a student from New York who enrolls in Cal Tech but intends to return to New York does not acquire a domicile in California. But the student from New York who intends to remain in California indefinitely and make it home for the time being acquires a new domicile in California. Courts evaluating a person's intent will consider all relevant facts, including self-serving testimony. But they will use common sense.

Soldiers and Prisoners The intent to remain must be voluntary. Older cases held that a soldier or prisoner could not acquire a new domicile in a jurisdiction where he or she was stationed or incarcerated. More recent decisions reject an absolute prohibition against such persons changing domicile, but it will not be easy to persuade many judges that the person voluntarily decided to remain indefinitely in the new jurisdiction without additional facts, such as the presence of other family members or property in the jurisdiction. The Second Restatement was revised to change the absolute prohibition into a recognition that a party does not "usually" change domicile when presence in the jurisdiction is compelled. Second Restatement §17 (1988 revision).

Time

The time for determining a person's domicile depends on the legal question for which domicile is important. For personal jurisdiction, courts look to a party's domicile at the time the action is commenced. For choice of law rules, the time varies with the rule.

Examples

Into the Sunset

1. For 20 years Ms. Miner lived in the state of West Virginia, where she owned a house and worked in the coal mines. In 2009 Ms. Miner decided to retire and move to Tucson, Arizona. On April 1, 2009, she loaded most of her personal property onto a rented trailer and drove to Arizona. She decided to stay at the Fleabag Hotel in Tucson until she found a house or apartment that she liked.

   As of April 2, 2009, Ms. Miner considered Arizona her home state, but she still owned the house in West Virginia, which she planned to sell. Her car was still in West Virginia and was still registered there, and she planned to return to West Virginia to get the car. She was still registered to vote in West Virginia and still held a valid library card at the public library in West Virginia. In contrast, Ms. Miner had some personal property in Tucson, Arizona, where she had a reservation for one night at the Fleabag Hotel. Where is Ms. Miner domiciled on April 2?

Footloose

2. Freddy Footloose was born and raised in Maine. He enlisted in the army and served for four years, from 1999 to 2003. From 2003 to 2006 he worked on an oil rig in the Gulf of Mexico. During those years he lived on the rig in international waters for four months at a time. While ashore, he resided alternately in hotels in Louisiana and Florida. In 2005 Footloose married Jane Doe, a resident of Louisiana. He and Jane Doe lived in a hotel room in Louisiana for three months.

   In 2006, without divorcing Jane Doe, Footloose went through a marriage ceremony in Florida with Barbara Roe, a resident of Florida. In 2007 Footloose moved most of his clothes and other personal property from the hotel in Louisiana where he had been living with Jane Doe to Barbara Roe's apartment in Florida. Since 2007 Footloose has spent most of his time working on the oil rig. He has divided his time ashore between Florida and Louisiana.

   Where is Footloose domiciled?

College Daze

3. Danny Farmer attends Vassar College in Poughkeepsie, New York. He lives in Cushing Hall, a dorm, and spends nine months of the year in New York and eats and sleeps during that time in New York. But he returns to his mother's home in Boston, Massachusetts, for weekends and occasional vacations and is partly dependent on his mother for support. Where is Danny domiciled?

4. Same facts. Danny graduates from college and works in New York City for two years. He then enrolls in the Culinary Institute of America in Poughkeepsie, New York. Danny rents an apartment in Poughkeepsie and plans to make his home in the city while attending the Culinary Institute. Where is Danny domiciled?

Going Home

5. Michael White lived his entire life in West Virginia until the year 1885, when he and his wife Lucinda decided to move into a new building across the state line in Pennsylvania. The building that they were moving to was part of a multi-building complex whose main building was located in West Virginia.

   On April 2, 1886, the Whites loaded up a cart with all their property and set off for the new house with the purpose of making it their home. They arrived by sundown and unloaded their goods. But the new house was cold and damp, and Lucinda White did not feel well, so they spent the night at the main building in West Virginia. Michael White contracted typhoid fever and died without ever returning to the house in Pennsylvania.

   Michael White died without a will, and the laws of intestate succession in West Virginia and Pennsylvania differed. Suit was brought in West Virginia challenging the distribution of the estate. According to the choice of law rule followed in West Virginia, the distribution of the decedent's personal property was governed by the law of the state where he died domiciled. Where did Michael White die domiciled?

6. Same facts. But suppose Michael White was killed in an accident while moving on April 2. He died in West Virginia, just one foot short of the Pennsylvania state line. Where did he die domiciled?

Over the Rainbow

7. Dorothy, a 12-year-old, lived with her guardians Aunt Em and Uncle Henry in Kansas. Dorothy ran away from home after her guardians threatened to take away her little dog. After a somewhat bumpy journey, Dorothy landed in the country of Oz, where she immediately decided to live forever.

   Suppose that under the law of Kansas a 12-year-old does not have the capacity to acquire a domicile of choice separate from her parents or guardians without going through a legal proceeding. In contrast, under the law of Oz, persons above the age of ten have the capacity to change their domicile. Is Dorothy a domiciliary of Kansas or Oz?

Explanations

Into the Sunset

1. Ms. Miner is domiciled in Arizona. She is physically present in the new jurisdiction and has the present intent to make this jurisdiction her home by having the subjective intent to remain in Arizona indefinitely. The fact that she will return temporarily to West Virginia to sell her house and get the rest of her property does not change the result.

   The other facts are irrelevant in this scenario because the example says that Ms. Miner had the intent to make Arizona her home. Ownership of a house is not required, and a person can acquire a new domicile by abandoning an old domicile and entering a new jurisdiction with the intent of making a home there. First Restatement §§11 illus. 4, 16 illus. 4-5.

   But three observations about objective facts evidencing physical relationship to a jurisdiction may help avoid confusion. First, other facts evidencing a person's relationship to a jurisdiction by themselves do not establish or prevent the establishment of domicile. Second, such facts may provide important evidence about a person's subjective intent. Courts are never required to accept a person's own claims about his or her intent, and factfinders will use common sense and reject self-serving claims about intent when they are inconsistent with objective evidence. Third, such facts may be necessary to satisfy other requirements imposed by law in addition to domicile. For example, Ms. Miner's recent departure from West Virginia would prevent her from qualifying for a tuition reduction available to a state "resident," if Arizona defined "resident" for purposes of in-state tuition as requiring both domicile plus residence in the state for one year.

Footloose

2. I am not sure where Footloose is domiciled, but I know he has one and only one domicile. In the absence of an effective acquisition of a new domicile, he will still be domiciled in Maine, where he was domiciled with his parents or guardians at birth.

   The example illustrates three important points. First, determination of domicile is fact-specific, and courts can and do reach different conclusions about domicile under the same facts. Much depends on Footloose's subjective intent, and the outcome may also depend on who has the burden of proof. One court might find no adequate evidence of his intent to make either Louisiana or Florida his home, and would thus trace his domicile back to Maine. But another court might find that marrying and residing with his wife in Louisiana established a new domicile in that state. Still another court might find that his physical move and ongoing bigamous cohabitation in Florida coincided with the necessary intent to remain indefinitely so as to establish a change of domicile to Florida. Note that the quantity of time spent in any particular place is unimportant: what matters is the person's subjective intent.

Second, motive (including bad motive) is not important. The fact that a person establishes a home for immoral or illegal reasons does not prevent the jurisdiction from becoming a domicile. However, a motive that is inconsistent with the intent to remain will prevent a change of domicile. For example, if a person moves to Nevada and stays just long enough to get a divorce, then the person's motive of getting a divorce will not be consistent with a finding that he or she really intended to stay and make a home in Nevada. In contrast, Footloose's dubious motives for moving to Florida will not prevent a finding that he in fact intended to remain and regarded the state as his home.

Third, although a person always has one and only one domicile, the reality is that courts may find different domiciles for different legal purposes. For example, you probably would not be shocked to find Louisiana courts finding that Footloose is domiciled in Louisiana for purposes of establishing personal jurisdiction over him in an action for child custody. Applying the same formal rules, you probably would not be shocked to find Florida courts similarly finding that Footloose was domiciled in that state for purposes of administering his estate at death.

This example thus shows how a person in theory has one and only one domicile. But applying the rules is fact-specific and permits some flexibility. As a result, different courts can and will reach different results for different purposes.

College Daze

3. Based on an illustration in both the First and Second Restatements, the right answer is that these facts "tend to show" that Danny is not domiciled in New York and thus remains domiciled in Massachusetts. Second Restatement §18 illus. 4.

The reason is, despite Danny's lengthy physical presence in New York, the absence of his intent to make the New York his home or to remain indefinitely means that he is not domiciled there. A student's intent to remain only for the purpose of completing an education is not an intent to make a home. In contrast, a person's intent to live temporarily in a state only so long as there are good work opportunities is sufficient to change domicile if the person abandons his previous domicile.

Danny's continuing visits to his previous home show his intent to return when he was away, which is one of the criteria of intent to make a place one's home. That, together with the limited purpose of his residence at the college, convinced the Restatements' drafters that the college student had no intent to make a home in the new state.

The Restatement position is reasonable in most situations, but the domiciliary's intent is always a matter of fact. Some students may in fact intend to make their legal home in the town where they move to attend college. A finding of such intent will, of course, be boosted by additional facts — such as the clear abandonment of the previous home or acquisition of a more permanent dwelling in the new state.

Because domicile comes down to the student's subjective intent, state universities often impose additional requirements on out-of-state students seeking to qualify for in-state tuition. For example, they may require that a student both establish domicile in the state and actually reside in the state for a certain period of time.

4. Also a variation on a Restatement illustration, the right answer is that Danny is now domiciled in Poughkeepsie. Second Restatement illus. 5 & 6. This is an easy one, because the question contains the answer: the example states that Danny is physically present in the city and plans to make his home there, and that is all that is required to establish domicile.

Going Home

5. Michael White died domiciled in Pennsylvania. The example — names, facts, and law — is stolen shamelessly from the famous case of White v. Tenant, 8 S.E. 596 (W. Va. 1888). The court concluded that Michael White's arrival at his new home in Pennsylvania on April 2 coincided with the intention to make that place his home for an indefinite time. This is all that is required to acquire a new domicile. The fact that he never lived in the house and in fact never returned to the state did not alter the result because he did not, while dying in West Virginia, reestablish domicile there. Consequently, the property was distributed according to the laws of Pennsylvania.

6. In the variation where Michael White died before entering Pennsylvania, he died domiciled in West Virginia. Even though he planned to leave the state and establish a domicile elsewhere, his physical presence did not coincide with the intention. Hence he did not yet establish a new domicile, and his old domicile of West Virginia would remain his legal domicile at death.

Over the Rainbow

7. It is uncertain where Dorothy is domiciled, and different jurisdictions may even find that she is domiciled in different places. The example illustrates the confusion that can result when different courts apply their own standards of domicile. Kansas, applying its rules, would conclude

that Dorothy is still domiciled in Kansas. Oz, applying its rules, would conclude that Dorothy is domiciled in Oz.

For Dinky, a 12-year-old Oz domiciliary, who wanted to change her domicile while present in Kansas, different problems would arise. The Oz courts would find that Dinky is domiciled in Kansas, but the Kansas courts would find that she is still domiciled in Oz.

Such possible inconsistent results really bothered the drafters of both the First and Second Restatements. They added comments suggesting clever ways to avoid inconsistency — not always supported by any legal authority. The important thing is to see how applying forum law leads to the problem of different determinations of domicile.

An *Erie* twist on the problem was presented by the facts in Rodriguez Diaz v. Sierra Martinez, 853 F.2d 1027 (1st Cir. 1988). A Puerto Rican plaintiff moved to New York after turning 18 and intended to make New York his permanent home. Under New York law, a person had capacity to change domicile at age 18, but under Puerto Rican law a person could not acquire a new domicile separate from his or her parents until age 21. The federal trial court sitting in Puerto Rico applied Puerto Rican law as the law of the forum and found that the plaintiff remained domiciled in Puerto Rico and, consequently, that there was no diversity of citizenship. The First Circuit reversed, holding that the capacity to change domicile in diversity cases should be governed by a uniform federal common law rule — and opted for the age of consent of the state in which the party is currently residing.

Personal Jurisdiction: Constitutional Foundations and Traditional Bases

INTRODUCTION

In order for a judgment to be valid and enforceable against a defendant, the judgment must be entered by a court that has personal jurisdiction. Valid personal jurisdiction requires three things: (1) strict compliance with the technical requirements for service of process, (2) a method of notice reasonably calculated to apprise the defendant of the proceedings in time to appear and object, and (3) an exercise of power by the court over the defendant that is authorized by state (or federal) law and not prohibited by due process.

Terminology   Older sources equated good service of process with good personal jurisdiction. More modern sources and the Federal Rules of Civil Procedure distinguish defects in service or notice from limits on the power of the court to bind parties to a judgment. The trend, especially in law schools, is to reserve the name "personal jurisdiction" for limits on judicial power over the defendant.

Coverage   This book follows the lead of most Civ Pro and Conflicts courses and focuses heavily on the constitutional requirements for personal jurisdiction. This chapter discusses the evolution of the traditional bases for personal jurisdiction and considers the division of personal jurisdiction into general and specific jurisdiction. It also discusses the constitutional requirement of reasonable notice. Chapter 4 discusses the expansion of personal jurisdiction under the theory of minimum contacts. Chapter 4 also discusses state long-arm statutes authorizing the exercise of personal jurisdiction over nonresidents served outside the state.

Like most casebooks, this book's coverage of personal jurisdiction skips important technical details, such as the requirement under federal rules that a person serving process must be a nonparty age 18 or older. Fed. R. Civ. P. 4(c)(2). Lawyers can look up the details in practice. But it is crucial for lawyers to master the constitutional principles so they will understand why following a particular statute or procedure does not guarantee constitutionally valid jurisdiction.

The Big Picture — Why You're Not the Only One Who's Confused

The Hard Part   Even when personal jurisdiction is authorized by state law, the judgment will be void when the exercise of state judicial power over the defendant offends due process. The main source of the confusion is the fact that constitutional limits on personal jurisdiction have changed since the 1800s. Trust me, your teachers are often as confused as you.

The Bad News — and the Good News   The bad news is that the Supreme Court is divided over the exact limits due process imposes on personal jurisdiction. Members of the Court even disagree about the theory of personal jurisdiction. Cases up to 1945 regarded due process limits on state court personal jurisdiction as based on territorial limits of a state court to control people and things outside the state.

After 1945 cases emphasized that due process protects defendants from being forced to litigate in a state court that is too inconvenient. Current constitutional doctrine combines parts of both theories. Cases in the 1970s and 1980s combined an evaluation of limits on sovereign authority with a consideration of fairness and reasonableness. And cases since 2011 have given less weight to fairness and reasonableness.

The good news is that there is substantial agreement on the Supreme Court about the outcomes in many cases. True, the Court divides in certain kinds of cases. But even where the members of the Court apply different constitutional tests, they sometimes end up reaching the same conclusion about whether a state's attempt to exercise personal jurisdiction violates due process.

What You Need to Do   To master personal jurisdiction, you will need to be able to do three things. First, you will need to know and apply the general constitutional requirements for due process. Second, you will need to know which types of cases the Court differs over in applying such requirements. Third, you will need to know the holdings of leading Supreme Court decisions and be prepared to apply them to analogous fact situations.

CONSTITUTIONAL FRAMEWORK: POWER

The Mother Case In Pennoyer v. Neff, 95 U.S. 714 (1877), a plaintiff sued Neff in Oregon state court. Neff did not consent to the court's jurisdiction or appear, and he was not a resident of Oregon. The plaintiff did not personally serve process on Neff in Oregon. Instead the plaintiff arranged for constructive service, as authorized by an Oregon statute, by publishing notice in an Oregon newspaper. When Neff failed to appear and answer, the Oregon court entered a default judgment against Neff.

The Supreme Court held that the Oregon state court judgment was void and unenforceable. The Court reasoned that states have exclusive sovereignty over the persons and things within their territorial limits. In contrast, states lack jurisdiction over persons or things beyond their borders. The Court concluded that the attempt by Oregon to bind a nonresident defendant who was not served personally in the state's territory was an impermissible attempt to control persons and things beyond the limits of the state.

What Was Unconstitutional in *Pennoyer*?

Pennoyer's actual holding is negative: a default judgment in an action in personam obtained by constructive service on a nonresident who does not appear is void.[1] Each of these factors was crucial to the holding:

```
+ default (no appearance or consent)
+ action in personam
+ constructive service
+ nonresident defendant
= VOID
```

Pennoyer held for the first time that requiring a nonresident to respond to litigation in a state where the defendant was not served and where the

---

1. An action in personam is the common kind of civil lawsuit where a plaintiff sues a defendant personally and seeks to recover a judgment binding on the named defendant. It contrasts with in rem actions.

defendant did not own property when the lawsuit began constituted a taking of a liberty interest in violation of the U.S. Constitution. This means no state law can authorize such judgments and that their enforcement is prohibited even in the court system that rendered the judgment.[2]

Pennoyer's *Philosophy* The Court's reasoning in *Pennoyer* can be hard to follow. Justice Field's opinion asserted two principles from international law: (1) sovereigns (and their courts) have full power over persons and things in their territory, and (2) sovereigns (and their courts) may not exert power over persons and things outside their territory. Justice Field reasoned that a sovereign's authority must be limited to its territory partly to avoid interfering with the full sovereignty of other courts in their own territories.

But Justice Field did not rely exclusively on territorial limits. He recognized that a state has power over both residents and nonresidents who are outside the state for some purposes. For example, a court might grant a valid divorce to a stay-at-home spouse, and the divorce decree could be binding on a runaway spouse who left the state. Similarly, he approved of state laws subjecting nonresidents doing business in a state to personal jurisdiction either by requiring the nonresidents to appoint an in-state agent to receive service of process or by constructively appointing an agent in their behalf.

What Was Constitutional in *Pennoyer*?

Pennoyer's territorial vision of power taught that personal jurisdiction could be constitutional in four situations: (1) when the defendant was personally served in the state where the defendant was sued; (2) when the defendant was a resident of the state; (3) when the defendant appeared in response to the summons and submitted himself or herself to the sovereign power of the state court; and (4) when the action was in rem and commenced by the judicial seizure of property located in the state. *Pennoyer* also broadly hinted that state courts could exercise personal jurisdiction to determine the status of state residents and to require nonresident businesses doing certain forms of business in the state to answer lawsuits against them.

---

2. Justice Ward Hunt wrote only five dissenting opinions during his career on the Court. One was in *Pennoyer*.

EXPANSION WITHIN THE TRADITIONAL CONSTITUTIONAL FRAMEWORK

For over 50 years after *Pennoyer*, state courts worked to expand the reach of their personal jurisdiction by creatively applying the categories of personal jurisdiction permitted by *Pennoyer*.

Nonresidents Doing Business in the State   States passed laws that required nonresident corporations doing business in state to appoint agents located in the state where they could be served. If a corporation failed to make such an appointment, state laws declared that the nonresident was present in the state or consented to jurisdiction, and the state laws then designated an agent (such as the secretary of state) upon whom personal delivery could be made within the state.

Nonresident Motorists   States passed laws that authorized personal jurisdiction over nonresident drivers who caused accidents in the state. The statutes declared that driving in the state was equivalent to the appointment of a designated state official as an agent to whom service could be delivered in the state. The nonresident business and nonresident motorists statutes both tried to satisfy *Pennoyer*'s requirement that the nonresident (or the nonresident's agent) be located in the state or consent to jurisdiction. The Supreme Court upheld the constitutionality of these creative ways of extending jurisdiction. E.g., Hess v. Pawloski, 274 U.S. 352 (1927).

MINIMUM CONTACTS

International Shoe *Test*   The Supreme Court grew weary of all the fictions adopted to establish a defendant's "presence" in a state's territory. In International Shoe Co. v. Washington, 326 U.S. 310 (1945), a shoe manufacturing company was incorporated in Delaware and had its principal place of business in St. Louis. The company had factories in several states and sold shoes all over the country. It sold enough shoes in the state of Washington to employ a dozen full-time salespeople in the state. But when Washington wanted to collect unemployment tax, the company claimed that it was not present in the state, did no business in the state, and was not subject to personal jurisdiction. The company carefully structured its legal affairs so that it did not directly own or even rent any property in the state. It had no inventory available for purchase in state. And it required buyers to send "offers" to St. Louis where the company would "accept" the offers and send the shoes to Washington.

Although *International Shoe* presented an easy case for the Supreme Court to find that the company was "present" in Washington, the Court adopted a new standard:

> [D]ue process requires only that in order to subject a defendant to a judgment in personam, if he be not present within the territory of the forum, he have certain minimum contacts with it such that the maintenance of the suit does not offend "traditional notions of fair play and substantial justice."

The Court's opinion in *International Shoe* emphasized that the new minimum contacts test was intended to look beyond the legal forms adopted by a defendant and to consider the defendant's real, economic relationship to a state. *International Shoe* did not overrule *Pennoyer*, but it offered a new flexible test that directed courts to consider both the quantity of contacts and the relationship of the contacts to the issues being litigated. For example, the opinion explained that a corporate agent's casual presence in a state and isolated contacts unrelated to the cause of action would not be enough for personal jurisdiction. In contrast, the shoe company's extensive marketing and sales to state residents established ample contacts when the legal claims arose out of those contacts. In applying the test, the Court added that "an 'estimate of the inconveniences' which would result to the corporation from a trial away from its 'home' or principal place of business is relevant...."

Justice Black penned a separate opinion in *International Shoe*. He had no problem with expanding personal jurisdiction. But he expressed concern that the flexible "fair play and substantial justice" standard might lead future courts to apply the standard to invalidate jurisdiction.

IN REM

Pure in Rem

In rem actions are civil lawsuits that are commenced by "suing" the property or thing and joining persons who have an interest in the property as parties. Examples are condemnation proceedings, mortgage foreclosures, and lawsuits against ships in admiralty cases. Execution and garnishment procedures used to satisfy judgments are also actions in rem.

Actions in rem are distinguished by the way they are commenced. An officer of the court actually or constructively seizes the property. For example, the sheriff posts notice on the front door of a house being condemned. The court's personal jurisdiction in actions in rem is limited to the thing that is seized. The court can dispose of the thing and decide who owns it, but it cannot impose greater liability on people who claim an interest in the thing.

Civ Pro gurus subdivide in rem actions into pure in rem actions (where the legal claims in the lawsuit concern the thing that is seized) and quasi in rem actions (where the legal claims are unrelated to the thing that is seized).

Pure in rem jurisdiction over property located in the state does not violate due process in most situations.[3] According to the reasoning in *Pennoyer*, a state has sovereign power over persons and things located in the state. Consequently, it has personal jurisdiction over actions in rem over property located in the state. Even if minimum contacts are required, the location of the property in the state establishes minimum contacts for claims that concern the property.

Quasi in Rem

In the days before *International Shoe*, quasi in rem jurisdiction became a popular device used to satisfy the fiction of "presence" in the state. To understand the beauty of the creative fiction, imagine a case where Tex, a tortfeasor from Texas, injured Penn, a plaintiff from Pennsylvania, in the state of Kansas. Penn could not get in personam jurisdiction over Tex in New York, but Penn could get in rem jurisdiction over any assets that Tex had in New York. If Tex had a home, bank account, or safe deposit box in New York, Penn could commence an action there by seizing the "thing" and asserting a claim based on the tort that occurred in Kansas.

Even if Tex did not actually own anything in New York, Penn might still get quasi in rem jurisdiction if Tex was insured by an insurance company that did business in New York. Penn would commence an in rem action in New York on the theory that one of Tex's assets was the right to recover money from the insurance company (if Tex was liable to Penn). The insurance company's obligation was considered a thing located wherever the debtor was subject to personal jurisdiction, including New York. If the company did business in Pennsylvania and Kansas, filing his case in those states would also be good options for Penn.

Plaintiffs loved quasi in rem jurisdiction because it allowed them to get personal jurisdiction over nonresident defendants in the days when the Supreme Court required the presence of some person or thing in the sovereign's territory. But quasi in rem jurisdiction also permitted personal

---

3. There is uncertainty about whether presence of property alone is enough when the property is taken to the state against the will of the owner. Abernathy v. Abernathy, 482 S.E.2d 265 (Ga. 1997) (holding state court had in rem jurisdiction to decide ownership of marital property taken to state by one spouse).

jurisdiction over a claim when the real defendant had absolutely no connection with the state where the action was brought.

In Shaffer v. Heitner, 433 U.S. 186 (1977), the Court declared that "all assertions of state-court jurisdiction must be evaluated according to the standards set forth in International Shoe and its progeny." This meant that quasi in rem jurisdiction would not be constitutionally permissible when there were no minimum contacts related to the claims being litigated.

Shaffer did not ban quasi in rem jurisdiction as a procedure. But it reduced its utility. After Shaffer a court would not have greater personal jurisdiction in an action quasi in rem than in an action in personam because both require minimum contacts. The decision thus eliminated the special benefits of quasi in rem.

CURRENT STATUS OF TRADITIONAL CATEGORIES OF PERSONAL JURISDICTION

Pennoyer: *Not Quite Dead* Pennoyer's core holding that due process limits state personal jurisdiction is still valid constitutional doctrine. But Pennoyer's framework has been bent and reshaped by over a century of constitutional decisions. Pennoyer's negative lesson that a court lacks personal jurisdiction over a nonresident served constructively (outside the state) has long been abandoned. The Supreme Court permits states to exercise personal jurisdiction over nonresident defendants served outside the state so long as there are minimum contacts. The expansion of state jurisdiction supported by minimum contacts is treated in Chapter 4.

***Viability of Forms of Jurisdiction Permitted by* Pennoyer** The viability of Pennoyer's positive lessons is more uncertain. The Court announced in Shaffer v. Heitner that all forms of personal jurisdiction must satisfy the modern minimum contacts test. One group on the Court has concluded that all forms of jurisdiction, even the traditional forms permitted by Pennoyer such as personal service in the forum state and in rem jurisdiction, must meet the standards of minimum contacts and reasonableness in order to be constitutional. In contrast, a more conservative group on the Court has limited Shaffer to quasi in rem cases and concluded that other traditional forms of personal jurisdiction permitted by Pennoyer remain constitutional. Some of the traditional forms have also been expanded by analogy to apply to different kinds of defendants.

Tagging "Tagging" or "transient jurisdiction" is the term used for personal jurisdiction based only on personal service of process on the defendant while the defendant is located in the state. Members of the Supreme Court agree that most tagging is constitutional, but they divide over the reason why.

In Burnham v. Superior Court, 495 U.S. 604 (1990), the Court unanimously affirmed the exercise of personal jurisdiction when a New Jersey resident was tagged while visiting California. Justice Scalia and three other Justices insisted that "jurisdiction based on physical presence alone constitutes due process because it is one of the continuing traditions of our legal system." These four Justices concluded that such traditional service need not be supported by minimum contacts. In contrast, Justice Brennan and three other Justices agreed that personal delivery of process in the state is usually constitutional. They also agreed that the duration of the historical practice was relevant. But they insisted that all forms of personal jurisdiction, including personal service, must satisfy the modern minimum contacts test. They concluded that minimum contacts were established by the defendant's voluntary presence in the state. The ninth Justice (Justice Stevens) agreed that personal jurisdiction was constitutional but rejected both opinions as unnecessarily broad.

Domicile The Supreme Court has approved the exercise of personal jurisdiction over an individual based on domicile even when the individual is served outside the state. Over time, the Court's rationale for this shifted from recognizing the state's de facto power over its domiciliaries to a consideration of fairness. See Milliken v. Meyer, 311 U.S. 457 (1940) (observing "[t]he state which accords [domiciliary] privileges and affords protection to him and his property by virtue of his domicile may also exact reciprocal duties.").

Corporate "Home" By analogy to personal jurisdiction based on domicile of individuals, the Supreme Court has said that a corporation is subject to jurisdiction in the courts of a place where a corporation "is fairly regarded as at home." Goodyear Dunlop Tires Operations, S.A. v. Brown, 131 S. Ct. 2846 (2011). Such places include the corporation's place of incorporation, principal place of business, and possibly other places where the corporate affiliations are so continuous and systematic as to render them "essentially at home."

Consent and Waiver A court can acquire valid personal jurisdiction if a defendant consents to personal jurisdiction. It can also get personal jurisdiction if a defendant appears and does not properly object to personal jurisdiction. Under federal rules and in many states, a defendant is required to raise the defense of lack of personal jurisdiction either in an answer or a pre-answer motion to dismiss. If the defendant files a pre-answer motion to dismiss for lack of subject matter jurisdiction, improper venue, insufficient process, or insufficient service of process, the motion must also raise the defense of personal jurisdiction or the defense is waived. Fed. R. Civ. P. 12(b) & (h).

Consent in Advance to Jurisdiction The Supreme Court has held that parties may agree in advance to the personal jurisdiction of a court that would not otherwise have personal jurisdiction. National Equipment Rental v. Szukhent, 375 U.S. 311 (1964). Courts also enforce mandatory forum selection clauses, agreements that require that litigation take place in a particular court. This is a different issue. (See Chapter 5.)

SYSTEMATIC AND CONTINUOUS CONTACTS AND GENERAL JURISDICTION

The Case Everyone Loves Everyone on the Supreme Court claims to love the "pathmarking" case of International Shoe. But members of the Court disagree about the historical significance and scope of the decision's minimum contacts test. Some like Justice Marshall in Shaffer see minimum contacts as a new test that replaces Pennoyer. For them, the requirement of "minimum contacts" and "fair play and substantial justice" can both expand and constrict personal jurisdiction. Others like Justice Scalia in Burnham see minimum contacts as a new test that applies only to newfangled forms of jurisdiction (like long-arm and quasi in rem jurisdiction) and that is limited to claims that arise out of or relate to the defendant's contacts in the forum state.

The Problem Everyone Hates In International Shoe Chief Justice Stone discussed the range of contacts that a defendant corporation might have with a state. He seemed to use "minimum contacts" as a conclusory formula. In deciding whether contacts were sufficient, he required a consideration of the defendant's ties to the forum state and also a consideration of the relationship between the contacts and the claims in litigation. For example, minimum contacts could be established by just one contact when the claim arose from the contact. But he thought minimum contacts could also be established by more contacts when the claim was not related to the contact. He referred approvingly to cases where "continuous corporate operations within a state were thought so substantial and of such a nature as to justify suit against [the corporation] on causes of action arising from dealings entirely distinct from those activities." Lower courts followed this hint for many years and found personal jurisdiction for any and all claims based on systematic and continuous corporate activity. The lower courts also required that personal jurisdiction in such cases was fair and reasonable.

Specific vs. General or All-purpose Jurisdiction   In Goodyear Tires Operations, S.A. v. Brown, 131 S. Ct. 2846 (2011), the Supreme Court held that foreign tire manufacturers were not subject to personal jurisdiction in North Carolina for wrongful deaths of North Carolina residents in France even though the defendants' tires were sold in North Carolina. In previous cases, the Court had required more contacts for personal jurisdiction when claims did not arise out of or relate to the contacts. In Goodyear, the Court read the decisions to support a distinction between specific jurisdiction and general jurisdiction. Specific jurisdiction (also called case-linked jurisdiction) requires that the claims in the lawsuit arise out of or relate to the defendant's contacts in the state. (Chapter 4 discusses specific jurisdiction.) General jurisdiction (also called all-purpose jurisdiction) does not require any link between the claims and the defendant's contacts.

No Hybrid Types of Jurisdiction   Goodyear established that a case must satisfy the requirements for either specific or general jurisdiction. There are no hybrid or intermediary forms of personal jurisdiction. If a case does not arise from or relate to the contacts in the forum state, then personal jurisdiction must rest on some form of general jurisdiction.

Valid General Jurisdiction   Individuals are subject to general jurisdiction in any state where they are served with process or in the state where they are domiciled. Corporations are subject to general jurisdiction (1) where they are incorporated, (2) where they maintain a principal place of business, and *maybe* in a third place (3) where "their affiliations with the State are so 'continuous and systematic' as to render them essentially at home in the forum State."

The Uncertain Status of Systematic and Continuous Contacts   Goodyear signaled that the requirements for general jurisdiction over corporations will be applied strictly. Because the wrongful death claims did not arise out of or relate to the foreign defendants' contacts in North Carolina, specific jurisdiction was not available. And general jurisdiction was also not available because the defendant tire manufacturers were not incorporated in North Carolina and did not have their principal places of business in North Carolina. The Court acknowledged that in theory continuous and systematic contacts might make a corporation "at home" and subject to general jurisdiction. In a previous case, the Court had decided that purchases of millions of dollars worth of equipment and related trips and in-state training did not establish general jurisdiction over claims unrelated to those purchases and trips. Helicopteros Nacionales de Colombia SA v. Hall, 466 U.S. 408 (1983). Goodyear decided that the fact that tens of thousands of defendants' tires reached North Carolina fell "far short of the 'continuous and systematic general business contacts' " required for general jurisdiction.

Recent Cases In two later opinions, the Court rejected a broad interpretation of continuous and systematic contacts that might support general jurisdiction in many states where corporations have extensive activity. In Daimler AG v. Baumann, 134 S. Ct. 746 (2014), foreign plaintiffs sued a German corporation in California state court alleging that the corporation's subsidiary in Argentina collaborated with a dictatorship in torturing and killing plaintiffs and their relatives. Because the claims did not arise out of or relate to the defendant's contacts in California, specific jurisdiction was not available. The Court held that general jurisdiction was also not available even though the defendant maintained permanent sales facilities in California and engaged in billions of dollars of sales in the state.

Daimler evaluated the sufficiency of the corporation's in-state contacts by comparing them to the corporation's contacts outside California. Given the international volume of the defendant's business, the Court concluded that its in-state contacts did not make it "at home" in California. The Court rejected the idea that a large corporation might be subject to general jurisdiction in every state where it engages in substantial, continuous, and systematic business. It was concerned that this would make large corporations amenable to general jurisdiction in too many places. 134 S. Ct. at 761.

While *Daimler* involved international litigation, its lesson applies equally to U.S. corporations. BNSF Railway Co. owns and operates over 2,000 miles of track in Montana and employs more than 2,000 workers in the state. In BNSF Railway Co. v. Tyrrell, 137 S. Ct. 1549 (2017), two BNSF employees sued the railroad in Montana for work-related injuries suffered in other states. Because the injuries were not related to the railroad's activity in Montana, specific jurisdiction was not available. BNSF was not incorporated in Montana and did not have its principal place of business in Montana. But the Montana courts found that general jurisdiction was proper based on the volume of BNSF's business in Montana and on the scope of its permanent physical presence in the Montana.

The Supreme Court reversed. True, a corporation is subject to general jurisdiction where its affiliations are so continuous and systematic as to render it "at home." But wait! The Court explains that the "paradigm" places where a corporation is at home are its place of incorporation and principal place of business. Perhaps out of respect for *International Shoe*, the Court still pays lip service to the possibility of jurisdiction based on continuous and systematic activity. But the Court makes clear that a corporate legal home based on contacts in a third place other than the place of incorporation and principal place of business will exist only in "an exceptional case." BNSF's volume of business did not make it at home in Montana because it also had extensive business in other states.

The Court's approach in BNSF and Daimler comes close to making continuous and systematic contacts the functional equivalent of principal place of business. So far the only case where the Court permitted general jurisdiction over a corporation based on contacts is Perkins v. Benguet Consolidated Mining Co., 342 U.S. 437 (1952). That case arose during World War II, after a Philippine mining company was forced to close its mining operations. The company's president returned to his hometown in Ohio where he moved the company's records, opened bank accounts, employed staff, maintained an office, and conducted limited business for the company. The Supreme Court held that the Due Process Clause did not prevent Ohio from exercising personal jurisdiction over the corporation. The Court reasoned that a state could exercise personal jurisdiction over a corporation that had continuous and systematic contacts with the state. In later opinions, the Court looked back on the facts in Perkins and reasoned that jurisdiction was proper because Ohio was the corporation's de facto principal place of business.

Service on Agents Appointed to Receive Service of Process

The validity of service on an agent appointed to receive service of process will depend on how the appointment was made. If one person voluntarily appointed an agent and gave the agent authority to receive process in his, her, or its behalf, then the service on that agent would be valid both because the principal's voluntary presence in the territory was established through the agent and because the principal consented to the resulting jurisdiction.

In contrast, some statutes appoint agents to receive process as a matter of law. Such statutes are often older legislative devices that employed legal fictions to establish a person's presence in the territory back when presence was required. For example, nonresident motorists statute might appoint the secretary of state as a nonresident's agent for purpose of service of process for lawsuits stemming from the nonresident's driving on the state's roads. Or a statute might appoint a state official as the agent for service of process for claims against nonresident corporations doing business in the state.

Statutory designations of agents do not manifest any real consent to jurisdiction, and they do not provide any additional presence or contacts by the target defendant in the state. Consequently, service on statutory agents will not establish valid jurisdiction by themselves. But they may provide a valid procedure for commencing an action, and the court may have personal jurisdiction in such cases so long as there is another basis for valid jurisdiction. For example, a nonresident motorist who is served by service on a statutory agent would be subject to personal jurisdiction for claims arising from accidents he caused in the state. The state court would have specific personal jurisdiction because the claims arose from the defendant's acts in the state, and the defendant had minimum contacts with the state.

All states require nonresident corporations that want to do business in the state to appoint agents located in the state for purposes of service of process. When corporations appoint such agents, service on the agents establishes valid specific personal jurisdiction for claims related to the corporation's activity in the state. It is doubtful whether service on such agents establishes valid general jurisdiction for claims unrelated to the corporation's activity in the state. The Supreme Court has not expressly addressed the issue. But when Montana's statute authorized jurisdiction over businesses "found" in the state in BNSF, the Court still required that personal jurisdiction satisfy the requirements for general jurisdiction when the claims did not arise out of the business conducted in the state.

CONSTITUTIONAL NOTICE REQUIREMENT

Notice is a legal term of art. Notice serves ritual functions and is different from notification and knowledge, even though giving knowledge is one of its goals. Due process requires "notice reasonably calculated, under all the circumstances, to apprise interested parties of the pendency of the action and afford them an opportunity to present their objections." Mullane v. Central Hanover Bank & Trust Co., 339 U.S. 306 (1950). A party is entitled to a constitutionally adequate form of notice even if the party actually knows about the lawsuit.

The standard is flexible and takes into account the real-life costs of notice. A method is constitutionally valid if it is "reasonably certain to inform" interested parties. Personal service will be constitutionally adequate except in unusual cases, such as service on an infant or on an insane person. When circumstances do not permit notice reasonably certain to inform, a method of notice will be constitutionally permissible if it is "not substantially less likely to bring home notice" than traditional substitutes.

The Court demonstrated its flexible approach in Mullane. It held that persons whose residences were known and who had a present interest in a trust were entitled to notice by ordinary mail. In contrast, those persons whose addresses were unknown and had future interests did not require notice by mail. Their constitutional right to notice was satisfied by publication notice.

Publication notice was traditionally used in actions in rem. Later cases made clear that publication notice was not constitutionally sufficient when the names and addresses of interested persons were listed in public records or were known to the plaintiff. Walker v. City of Hutchinson, 352 U.S. 112 (1956), Tulsa Professional Collection Services, Inc. v. Pope, 485 U.S. 478 (1988). In other words, whether an action is in personam or in rem, the Constitution requires something more than publication notice for known individual defendants.

Examples

First Contacts

1. Jodi, a citizen of California, collided with Foster, a citizen of New York, on the Massachusetts Turnpike. Foster sues Jodi in California. Is there personal jurisdiction?

2. Foster sues Jodi in New York for a claim that has absolutely nothing to do with New York. She arranges for personal service on Jodi in New York while Jodi is attending a Trekkie Convention in New York City. Is there valid personal jurisdiction?

Suitless in Seattle

3. Allie, a citizen of Alaska sues Wally, a citizen of the state of Washington in federal court in Alaska. Allie claims Wally trespassed on her land in Alaska. Wally has never been to Alaska. Wally files a motion to dismiss on the ground that the court lacks subject matter jurisdiction. The court denies the motion. Then Wally moves to dismiss for lack of personal jurisdiction on the ground that he has never been to Alaska and has no other minimum contact with the state. Rule on the motion.

From Real Test Files . . .

4. Explain whether the following is an accurate quote from Justice Brennan: "The Due Process Clause generally does not permit a state court to exercise jurisdiction over a defendant if he is served with process while voluntarily present in the forum State."

Tagged

5. One winter day, Snidely Whiplash assaulted and injured Dudley Dooright in the Yukon Territory of Canada. Both Whiplash and Dooright were citizens of Canada. On April 1, Whiplash boarded a commercial airliner bound for Cancun, Mexico. At exactly 2:30 PM, the pilot announced to the passengers that it was Whiplash's birthday. Whiplash was surprised because it was not his birthday.

   The flight attendant then delivered an envelope addressed to Whiplash covered with "surprise" stickers. Whiplash opened the envelope and was truly surprised to find he had been handed a summons and complaint naming him as a defendant in a lawsuit filed in California. He asked the flight attendant where they were. The flight attendant pointed to San Francisco, directly below the plane.

   Whiplash calls you and asks whether he will need to answer the lawsuit. He swears that he has never been to California before. Please advise.

6. Kumar was misidentified as a terrorist by U.S. Special Forces in Afghanistan. Ten years later he was brought against his will to Kansas to face charges of murder and other crimes. Kumar was found not guilty of all charges. While leaving the courthouse, Kumar was served with process in a wrongful death action commenced in Kansas state court by the survivors of terrorism victims. Does the Kansas state court have personal jurisdiction?

Purely in Rem

7. Doug Deadbeat, domiciliary of Delaware, is a year behind in the payments on his Dodge. While driving cross country, the car is seized in Oklahoma in a repossession action commenced in Oklahoma state court by Friendly Finance Corporation, a Delaware corporation, which owns a security interest in the Dodge. Does the Oklahoma court have valid jurisdiction?

8. Elvis Parsley, a citizen of Tennessee, was driving his gold-plated diamond encrusted Cadillac convertible through Alabama on his way to a car show in Florida. The sheriff stopped Elvis and informed him that the car had been attached in a lawsuit. The sheriff delivered a copy of the complaint to Elvis. The complaint alleged that Elvis had breached a contract in Tennessee with Arkie, a resident of Arkansas. It alleged damages of $1 million and attached the car to establish jurisdiction and satisfy the judgment. Does the court have good in rem jurisdiction?

Parting Is Such Sweet Sorrow

9. Earle was born and raised in Lubbock, Texas. One day he decided he would leave the state and never return. He loaded all his worldly goods into the back of his pickup and drove out of town. He sang softly to himself as he watched Lubbock recede into the distance in his rear view mirror. When he crossed the border, he pulled off the road, got out of the truck, and shook the dust off his feet.

   Earle soon joined a traveling circus in Oklahoma and moved in and out of seven states without settling down in any of them. He never returned to Texas. One year later, he was involved in a car accident in Utah. A person injured in the accident sued Earle in Texas state court. Do the Texas courts have personal jurisdiction?

The Case of the Wrong Woman

10. Persephone Pennywise, resident of Lakeville, Connecticut, was surprised to receive a certified letter from San Francisco, California. She has heard of San Francisco but never visited the state of California. She

was even more surprised to open the letter and find a summons and complaint naming her as defendant in a libel action filed in California.

Pennywise wrote a nice letter to the judge explaining that they had sued the wrong person and that she had not done the things in the complaint. Two weeks later, she received an envelope from the court clerk containing a stamped photocopy of her letter to the judge. Pennywise brings the papers to your office and asks what it all means. Please explain.

Home Again

11. Jerry from New Jersey went to California to go surfing. While waxing his board on the beach, he was run over by a delivery truck. The truck was owned and operated by DeliverCorp, a Delaware corporation with its principal place of business in New York City. What states will have personal jurisdiction in a civil action against DeliverCorp?

Big Box Slipup

12. While George from Georgia is vacationing in Florida, he goes to the Big Mart Store to buy sunscreen. While leaving the store, George slips on a banana peel and is injured. Big Mart is incorporated in Delaware and has its executive offices, training facilities, and other administrative offices in Bentonia, Arkansas. It has at least one large sales facility in every state and maintains warehouse facilities in several states. Big Mart owns and operates ten large retail facilities and a warehouse in Georgia where it employs over 1,000 people and generates millions of dollars in income annually. Can George get general (all-purpose) personal jurisdiction over Big Mart in Georgia for the slip and fall in Florida?

Explanations

First Contacts

1. This is sort of a trick question. Many lawyers would observe there is no personal jurisdiction until there is good service of process, and the validity of personal jurisdiction can depend on the form(s) of service that are employed. But the short answer is that California definitely will have valid personal jurisdiction in the sense of judicial power over the defendant because she is a citizen of the state. Domiciliaries or citizens are subject to general personal jurisdiction in their home states.

General personal jurisdiction means the court can validly exercise personal jurisdiction over all kinds of lawsuits no matter where the claims arise. Chapter 4 considers personal jurisdiction based on minimum contacts. Specific personal jurisdiction means the court can exercise jurisdiction only over claims that arise from or are related to the defendant's minimum contacts in the state.

General personal jurisdiction over persons domiciled in a state was recognized in the days of *Pennoyer* as the consequence of the state's authority over persons with a fixed status relationship. This power extended over such persons even when they were temporarily absent from the state. Cases rationalized this rule by observing that a defendant's home state court would not be inconvenient and that citizens derive benefits from their relationship with their state that give rise to a reciprocal duty to answer lawsuits commenced in their state courts.

2. Yes, there is valid personal jurisdiction based on personal service of process in the state. Such service automatically established personal jurisdiction under the rationale of *Pennoyer*, and such service is still good today according to the unanimous decision of *Burnham*. The Court today is somewhat divided over the reason for the rule, with about half the Court grounding it on longstanding practice and half the Court finding that voluntary presence plus longstanding practice normally satisfies *International Shoe*'s requirement of minimum contacts and fairness.

Although the individual defendant is probably surprised to be served with process, such personal delivery in the state is reasonably foreseeable given the established law, and it is thus foreseeable that a person who is voluntarily in the state will be required to respond to litigation in the state when served in the state.

Suitless in Seattle

3. Motion to dismiss denied. Even though Wally had no minimum contacts, his second motion to dismiss for lack of personal jurisdiction is waived because he filed a pre-answer motion to dismiss for lack of subject matter jurisdiction and did not include the defense of personal jurisdiction. In this case the defense would have been a winner.

From Real Test Files . . .

4. This is an inaccurate quote. It inserts a *not* into Justice Brennan's concurring opinion in *Burnham*, reversing his meaning. Although *Burnham* produced divided opinions on the reasons, the Court was unanimous in the result: personal service of process established constitutionally valid personal jurisdiction. According to Justice Scalia's opinion, personal jurisdiction resulting from such service was automatically valid. Justice Brennan agreed that such service was *usually* valid and also agreed that the long history of tagging jurisdiction made it reasonable for parties voluntarily present in a state to anticipate being haled before the state's courts.

Tagged

5. Personal jurisdiction was upheld in an older case where a defendant was personally served in the state's airspace. *See* Grace v. MacArthur, 170 F. Supp. 442 (E.D. Ark. 1959). But these extreme facts may produce a split on the Court. Justice Scalia's opinion in *Burnham* suggests that tagging establishes good personal jurisdiction because tagging is a traditional method of service that comports with due process. Of course, conservative Justices might find a ground for differentiating tagging when it takes place aboard a vehicle not contemplated by the drafters of the Due Process Clause, but air travel by balloon was known by the time the Fourteenth Amendment was drafted.

   Justice Brennan's opinion in *Burnham* may suggest a different result. While acknowledging that tagging during voluntary presence in a state usually establishes valid personal jurisdiction, his opinion required that such personal jurisdiction be supported by minimum contacts and fairness. The fleeting journey through the state's airspace may not satisfy such contacts. Moreover, while presence in the state may normally make the exercise of tagging jurisdiction reasonably foreseeable, such jurisdiction may not be foreseeable to persons in transit through a state's airspace.

   Tagging the international traveler presents an additional twist. Most foreign countries do not share the fondness for personal jurisdiction resulting from personal service in the territory of the court that is so widespread in the United States. They might well refuse to enforce a judgment resulting from tagging jurisdiction even if it is found not to violate due process. *See generally* Hay et al., Conflict of Laws §6.2 at 365 (noting that transient jurisdiction is "disfavored internationally"). But if it is valid in the United States, then all state courts must recognize and enforce the judgment (Chapter 29).

6. This almost sounds like a bad movie. The short answer is that I don't know for sure whether there is personal jurisdiction, but there is a strong argument that there is not. What distinguishes this example from the last is the important fact that Kumar was not physically present in the jurisdiction voluntarily. On the contrary, he was brought into the state against his will.

   It is useful to consider how such tagging would fare under the two different opinions in *Burnham*. According to the reasoning in Justice Brennan's opinion, the tagging jurisdiction would not be valid. Minimum contacts require purposeful activity directed toward the forum state. Such purposeful acts may be present when a defendant is voluntarily in the state, but they would not seem to be present when a defendant is brought into the state against his will.

California and attempt damage control. A timely motion to dismiss for lack of personal jurisdiction (and any other available grounds) may still be possible.

Home Again

11. The corporation is subject to personal jurisdiction in the state where it is incorporated, Delaware, and in the state where it maintains its principal place of business, New York.

    The answer is easy because the question tells you where the corporation's principal place of business is located. The Supreme Court has not yet explained how to define principal place of business for purposes of personal jurisdiction. You may remember from Civ Pro that the Supreme Court adopted the "nerve center" test and declared that in diversity of citizenship cases a corporation's principal place of business is typically its headquarters. See Hertz v. Friend, 559 U.S. 77 (2010). But scholars have cautioned against assuming that the "nerve center" test should apply to the question of where corporation is "at home" for purposes of general jurisdiction.

    The nerve center test focuses on administrative decisionmaking. For example, if DeliverCorp's corporate offices were in New York City, then New York is its principal place of business under the nerve center test. The nerve center test may be inappropriate when a corporation has a small administrative operation in one state but extensive business operations in another place. For example, DeliverCorp might rent a small office for its headquarters in New York where it employs three people. This could fix its nerve center in New York. But the corporation might also own a $500 million warehouse in New Jersey, own a fleet of 200 trucks licensed in New Jersey, and employ hundreds of drivers and other workers who work from its New Jersey facility. Under such facts, there is a strong argument that New Jersey should be the corporation's principal place of business for purposes of personal jurisdiction. Alternatively, courts may find that personal jurisdiction is proper in New Jersey under these facts because the corporation has systematic and continuous contacts in New Jersey. Under either approach, New Jersey would be a place where the corporation could be regarded as "at home" and subject to general (all-purpose) personal jurisdiction for all claims.

    Finally, DeliverCorp will be subject to personal jurisdiction in California for Jerry's claims arising out of the corporation's activity in the state based on minimum contacts (Chapter 4).

Big Box Slipup

12. George cannot get general (all-purpose) jurisdiction over Big Mart in Georgia based on the theory that the corporation has continuous and systematic business activity in the state. Prior to BNSF and *Daimler* there was room to argue that a large volume of business could establish general jurisdiction in a number of states. But the Court rejected that theory and requires a level of activity that establishes a legal home. Big Mart's activity in Georgia does not meet the test because the corporation is so large and engaged in so much activity elsewhere, and the Court reasons it cannot be at home everywhere. Justice Sotomayor disagreed with this approach. She concurred in *Daimler* and dissented in BNSF, arguing that the majority's reasoning leads to the largest corporations with the greatest level of in-state activity escaping general jurisdiction based on the level of their activity outside the state.

    George will be able to get general personal jurisdiction over Big Mart in its place of incorporation (Delaware) and principal place of business (Arkansas). We return to this example at the end of Chapter 4 and see that George will also be able to get specific (case-linked) personal jurisdiction in Florida but not in Georgia.

Personal Jurisdiction: Pushing the Envelope

CHAPTER

4

INTRODUCTION

Chapter 3 covered constitutional foundations of personal jurisdiction and traditional forms of personal jurisdiction based on consent, domicile, and the presence of persons and property in a state's territory. This chapter covers the expansion of personal jurisdiction over persons based on activity in or directed at a state. The personal jurisdiction covered in this chapter is called specific jurisdiction (or case-linked jurisdiction). It is available only when the claims in the lawsuit arise out of or are related to the defendant's minimum contacts in the forum state.

MANY LONG ARMS OF THE LAW

The Due Process Clause limits states' exercise of personal jurisdiction. But the U.S. Constitution does not directly require or authorize states to exercise personal jurisdiction, so any authority for the exercise of personal jurisdiction for state courts must come from state law. State statutes that try to exert jurisdiction on parties outside the state are called "long-arm statutes" because the statutes try to reach beyond the state borders.

State long-arm statutes (or state court rules) may literally authorize service of process outside the state, perhaps by certified mail or even personal delivery. But the procedure for service need not actually occur outside the

the state, and the claims arose out of the in-state conduct.) The issue was the harder question of whether there was specific jurisdiction over the writer and editor. In holding that both the writer and editor were subject to personal jurisdiction in California, the Supreme Court emphasized that the story concerned a California resident, impugned the professionalism of a person whose film career was centered in California, was drawn from California sources, and caused harm that was felt mostly in California. The Court noted that the writer and editor also did research involving California sources and that the editor had called the star's husband and read him the alleged lies.

Calder found purposeful availment based on the injurious effects of conduct in California and based on the defendant's awareness that their acts would cause effects in the forum. But it did so in a case where the writer and editor contributed to and benefited indirectly from the sales of the paper in California.

In Walden v. Fiore, 571 U.S. 277 (2014), plaintiffs were professional gamblers flying home to Nevada after visiting Puerto Rico. At the Atlanta airport a law enforcement agent seized their cash, believing it was drug money. The cash was eventually returned, but the plaintiffs claimed the agent deliberately delayed the return by swearing out a false affidavit. They sued the agent in Nevada, claiming he knew he was injuring them in Nevada and was thus subject to personal jurisdiction there. The Supreme Court unanimously held that due process prohibited personal jurisdiction in Nevada. The Court clarified that knowledge of an injury based solely on the plaintiffs' presence in the state does not satisfy minimum contacts. "[T]he plaintiff cannot be the only link between the defendant and the forum. Rather, it is the defendant's conduct that must form the necessary connection with the forum State that is the basis for its jurisdiction over him." In other words, even for intentional torts, some activity by the defendant is required that targets the forum state other than knowing that the activity outside the state will cause harm to the plaintiffs and knowing that the plaintiffs will suffer in the harm in the forum state.

RELATEDNESS

For specific (or case-linked) personal jurisdiction, the issues in the lawsuit must arise out of or relate to the minimum contacts that form the basis for jurisdiction. It is easy to see how this requirement is met when the defendant's forum-related activity directly gives rise to the cause of action. For example, suppose nonresident Nancy enters New Jersey and sells a boot or drives on the New Jersey roads. If plaintiffs sue Nancy in New Jersey for breaching the boot-sale contract or for injuring them while she was driving in New Jersey, then the plaintiffs' claims arise out of Nancy's forum activity. In contrast, if plaintiffs sue Nancy in New Jersey for an assault and battery she committed in Florida, then their claims do not arise out of or relate to her forum activity.

It becomes harder to imagine kinds of cases that might not arise out of the defendant's forum conduct but might still be related to it. What if Nancy sold a shoe to Frankie in New Jersey and Sammy brings an action against Nancy in New Jersey for an injury he suffered when she sold him the same kind of shoe in Nevada?

World-Wide Volkswagen held that the New York retailer who sold an allegedly defective car had no contacts in Oklahoma when the buyer drove it there. But in that case the importer that sold the product to the New York dealer also imported and sold the same allegedly defective product to retailers in Oklahoma. Unlike the New York retailer, the importer purposefully availed itself of the Oklahoma market. The claims did not arise out of the importer's activity in Oklahoma, but some law professors think the importer's conduct in Oklahoma "related to" the New Yorker's claims so as to support specific jurisdiction. After all, the importer profited from selling the same defective product in Oklahoma.[2]

My advice is to be afraid. The Supreme Court talks about arising out of or relating to. But recent decisions indicate that related-to will be hard to establish when claims do not arise out of the defendant's forum activity. In Bristol-Myers Squibb Co. v. Superior Court, 137 S. Ct. 1773 (2017), people alleging injuries from a nationally distributed drug brought their claims against the drug manufacturer in California state court. Some of the plaintiffs were California residents or were injured from sales of the drug in California. Others were nonresidents injured outside of California. The California court had personal jurisdiction over claims for injuries from products sold in California because those claims arose from the company's activity in the forum state. But the Supreme Court held that California could not exercise jurisdiction over claims by nonresidents for injuries outside of California. Similarity of claims, litigation connectedness, and efficiency were not enough. The Court required purposeful acts directed towards the forum state for each plaintiff's claim, and this effectively meant that each claim needed to arise out of the defendant's conduct in California.

No Sliding Scale for Contacts or Relatedness   Because minimum contacts support personal jurisdiction over a claim arising from the contacts, it might seem logical and in keeping with the ghost of *International Shoe* that with more contacts comes jurisdiction over more claims. Over the years many lower courts reasoned that with more contacts, a looser

2. Joseph W. Glannon, Civil Procedure Examples and Explanations 22 n.4 (8th ed. 2018).

relatedness would be sufficient. The Supreme Court has now made clear that due process does not authorize a sliding scale for contacts or relatedness. For actions in personam, the Court recognizes only specific and general personal jurisdiction, not hybrid or intermediary or mixed types of personal jurisdiction. Goodyear Dunlop Tires Operations, S.A. v. Brown, 131 S. Ct. 2846, 2851 (2011). And Bristol-Myers now makes clear that the Court rejects any sliding scale approach to relatedness. This means that if the cause of action does not arise from or relate to the contacts, narrowly defined, then personal jurisdiction must rest on some form of general jurisdiction (Chapter 3).

MULTI-PART TEST

In the 1980s the Supreme Court adopted a multi-part test for personal jurisdiction that looked to the defendant's conduct directed towards the forum, the relationship between that conduct and the claims, and the potential inconvenience to the defendant. See World-Wide Volkswagen Corp. v. Woodson, 444 U.S. 286 (1980). Drawing on language from International Shoe, the Court separately required:

    I. There must be minimum contacts based on the defendant's purposeful acts.
    II. These contacts must be considered in light of factors to determine whether the exercise of personal jurisdiction satisfies fair play and substantial justice.

The Fairness or Reasonableness factors listed by the Supreme Court are:

    1. burden on the defendant
    2. forum state's interest in adjudicating the dispute
    3. plaintiff's interest in convenient and effective relief
    4. interstate or international judicial system's interest in most efficient resolution of controversies
    5. shared interest of the several states or countries in furthering fundamental substantive social policies

Presumption When a defendant has established minimum contacts by directing activities at forum state residents, then the defendant must present a compelling case that other factors would make personal jurisdiction unreasonable. See Burger King Corp. v. Rudzewicz, 471 U.S. 462 (1985).

Applying the Fairness-Reasonableness Factors

The Supreme Court applied the Fairness-Reasonableness factors in Asahi Metal Industry Co. v. Superior Court, 480 U.S. 102 (1987). A California resident was killed and another seriously injured when their motorcycle tire had a blowout. The plaintiffs settled their claims against the tire manufacturer, a Taiwanese corporation, but the Taiwanese manufacturer wanted to prosecute its claim for indemnification in the California court against the Japanese corporation that had manufactured the tire valve component that allegedly caused the blowout.

The Supreme Court concluded unanimously that due process prohibited California from exercising personal jurisdiction over the Taiwanese manufacturer's claim against the Japanese component manufacturer. The Court applied the two-part test. First, the Court was divided over whether there were minimum contacts. (A majority concluded that the defendant had minimum contacts either due to placing its item in the stream of commerce or due to the quantity of the sale of its products in California.)

Second, the Court concluded that the exercise of personal jurisdiction was so unreasonable that it offended traditional notions of fair play and substantial justice. The Court considered the five fairness factors. The burden on the defendant was severe because the Japanese corporation was being forced to travel half-way around the world and submit to a foreign legal system. The interests of the plaintiff and the forum state in personal jurisdiction in California were slight. The underlying relationship that gave rise to the claim for indemnification was centered in East Asia, and California did not seem to be more convenient for the plaintiff than either Taiwan or Japan. The state of California had no interest in distributing the loss between the manufacturers and no interest in providing the Taiwanese manufacturer with a forum.

The Court emphasized that the fact that the plaintiff was not a California resident reduced California's interest in the dispute. Finally, emphasizing the international context, the Court found that the international judicial system's interest in efficient resolution of disputes and the shared interests of different states or foreign countries also weighed against exercising personal jurisdiction.

Asahi is an extreme case. First, the claims had little to do with California. (In fact four Justices found there were no minimum contacts.) Second, the plaintiff was not a forum resident; there was no need to litigate in the state, and the state's interest in providing a forum was reduced. Moreover, there appeared to be alternative courts available in other countries. Third, the burden on the defendant was extreme because of the international context.

But the Supreme Court remains divided over exactly what is wrong with stream of commerce. Four members of the Court took the occasion to announce a new submission theory of personal jurisdiction. They found that purposeful availment normally requires activities within the state or directed at the state "where the defendant can be said to have targeted the forum." 131 S. Ct. at 2788. They emphasized that foreseeing or predicting that its product will enter the state is not enough.

Two Justices concurred. They emphasized that only one defective product may ever have entered New Jersey. They concluded there was no personal jurisdiction but on the ground that a single isolated sale of a defective product through an intermediary does not support personal jurisdiction over the manufacturer. The concurring opinion also expressed doubts about the new submission theory of personal jurisdiction. 131 S. Ct. at 2792 (concurring opinion). Three Justices dissented and sharply criticized the new submission theory.

Bottom line: the Court was divided 4-4-1 about stream of commerce in 1987. It is still divided 4-2-3 in 2011. Stream of commerce alone does not establish personal jurisdiction — at least not where only one product entered the state. But a plaintiff can strengthen his or her case by showing additional sales of comparable products. (Additional sales would have satisfied the concurrence in 1987 and might satisfy the concurrence in 2011.) A plaintiff will satisfy all members of the Court by showing purposeful availment based on additional acts by the defendant targeting the forum state when the defendant's product is delivered in the forum state through a stream of commerce and causes injury there. But the conduct of legally separate intermediaries will not be attributed to the defendant.

Intentional Torts Members of the Supreme Court have sometimes hinted that different rules may be necessary for intentional torts. The classic purposeful availment formula requires a defendant to avail itself "of the privilege of conducting activities within the forum State, thus invoking the benefits and protections of its laws." This formula is awkward to apply in most specific jurisdiction cases, but it seems uniquely inapplicable when someone aims at a victim and shoots over the state line. It is not much easier to apply purposeful availment to the Florida writer whose libelous words were distributed in California in Calder v. Jones. The new not-yet-approved submission-theory also does not explain how a person volitionally submits to a state's jurisdiction just by purposefully causing an injury in the state when they took care to stay outside the state.

Given the theoretical confusion, the good news is that the law governing personal jurisdiction in intentional tort cases is more straightforward.

Knowingly causing harm in a state establishes a firm basis for personal jurisdiction when the harm is expressly aimed at residents in the state (and probably when aimed at anybody in the state). For example, the newspaper company that published the libel in Calder v. Jones was obviously entering the California market, targeting California purchasers with knowledge that the harm of any lies would affect the reputation of people it knew had a particularly strong personal and professional connection to California. Even though the editor and writer did not directly profit from selling in California, they benefitted indirectly from the sales, and they knew that their published words would reach a large number of California readers, knew that the person they wrote about was a California resident, and knew that her reputation as a movie star had a particularly strong affiliation with California. The editor and writer also did some research for the story by contacting California sources, though the importance of that additional conduct is not clear.

Walden v. Fiore clarifies that knowledge that conduct outside a state will cause harm in the state is not enough. In *Walden* the law enforcement officer allegedly made false statements in Georgia. But even though the defendant knew the plaintiffs were in Nevada, the Court rejected Nevada jurisdiction. *Walden* instructs that contacts must be based on defendant's conduct directed towards the forum.

Newer forms of communication raise some new issues. First, it may be harder to determine as a matter of fact whether a defendant knowingly aimed conduct at a particular state. Sending snail mail required the sender to identify where she was sending a letter. Email and cellphones do not require the same awareness. Second, it is not clear how courts should handle Internet postings that may be accessible everywhere. Knowledge that a posting can be viewed everywhere does not seem like purposeful availment anywhere. Courts have reached this result in two ways. Some have required a higher level of intent to target the state. In Pavolvich v. Superior Court, 58 P.3d 2 (Cal. 2002), the defendant posted a trade secret that allowed users to illegally pirate encrypted dvds. The plaintiff, representing interests of the film industry, sued the defendant in California. The California Supreme Court held that posting a trade secret on the Internet did not establish personal jurisdiction in California even though the defendant knew of the computer industry's strong affiliation with California. A slim majority announced that purposeful availment requires that "the defendant purposefully and voluntarily directs his activities toward the forum so that he should expect, by virtue of the benefit he receives, to be subject to the court's jurisdiction based on his contacts with the forum." Other courts have interpreted *Calder* as requiring (1) the acts were intentional, (2) they were uniquely or expressly aimed at the forum state, and (3) the defendant knew the brunt of the harm would be suffered in the forum state. Abdouch v. Lopez, 829 N.W.2d 662 (Nev. 2013).

Contracts

The Supreme Court's approach to contracts contacts is illustrated by Burger King Corp. v. Rudzewicz, 471 U.S. 462 (1985). Two residents of Michigan opened a Burger King restaurant in Michigan and entered into a franchise agreement with Burger King. Burger King's headquarters was in Florida, but most of the Michigan residents' dealings were with Burger King's regional office in Michigan. Burger King sued the Michigan defendants in Florida.

The Supreme Court applied its two-part test and found that (1) the Michigan residents had minimum contacts in Florida and (2) personal jurisdiction was reasonable and fair. The most important lesson was that the Court rejected any easy black letter rules for contracts and required a consideration of the entire course of negotiations, terms of the contract, performance, and breach. This makes clear that minimum contacts are not automatically established just by entering into a contract with a person in another state, agreeing to do something in another state, or even breaching a contract that causes loss of profits or damages in another state.

In finding minimum contacts, the Court emphasized that the contract dispute arose out of a franchise agreement with a substantial connection to Florida. It found that the Michigan residents deliberately reached out to deal with a Florida corporation engaged in nationwide business. It noted that they knowingly committed themselves to a 20-year relationship in which they submitted to close supervision and control from the corporation's office in Miami, Florida. Finally, the Court emphasized that the contract included a choice of law provision specifying that the contract would be governed by Florida law. This provided additional evidence that the Michigan residents knew they were entering into a relationship in which they should reasonably foresee being subject to personal jurisdiction in Florida.

HANDLING THE HOT POTATO

The Supreme Court's personal jurisdiction decisions give definite answers for those cases and for other cases where there are *more* contacts than the Court found to be minimum — and for cases where there are *fewer* contacts than the court found to be insufficient. For example, a writer who has even more contacts with California than the defendant in Calder v. Jones will have minimum contacts. A franchisee with even more contacts with Florida than the defendant in Burger King will have minimum contacts. But the Court's decisions leave many open questions.

When in doubt, apply the right rules and identify areas of uncertainty. There can be uncertainty about whether the personal jurisdiction is specific or general. When in doubt, consider both possibilities.

For specific personal jurisdiction, the cause of action must arise out of (or be closely related to) defendant's minimum contacts in the state. First consider whether the issues arise out of or relate to the claims. If they do not, then specific jurisdiction is not available. If they do (or if you are not sure), then consider both (1) whether the defendant established minimum contacts by purposeful availment and (2) whether the exercise of personal jurisdiction would be fair and reasonable by evaluating the five fairness-reasonableness factors.

Finally, keep in mind the big picture. If you fail to get personal jurisdiction on one theory, you may well get it on another. A defendant might not have either continuous and systematic or minimum contacts. But he or she might still be subjected to constitutionally valid personal jurisdiction because he or she is a citizen of the state or personally served with process in the state.

Examples

Minimum Contacts

1. John Donson, a citizen of Florida, told Elle Bean, a citizen of Maine, to meet him at the state line between North and South Carolina. While Bean stood on the North Carolina side of the state line, Donson reached across the state line and twisted Bean's nose.

   Bean sues Donson in North Carolina for assault and gets service on Bean under a North Carolina long-arm statute by mailing the summons and complaint to Donson at his residence in Florida. Is there good personal jurisdiction?

2. Same facts. Bean responded to the nose twist by throwing a rock at Donson, which struck him in South Carolina. Does South Carolina have valid personal jurisdiction over Bean if Donson sues him there for assault?

Getting Specific

3. Fred is a resident of Gary, Indiana, and sells flowers from a cart on the street and at public events in his hometown. He drives to Chicago, Illinois, once or twice a week to buy flowers from Ginger.

   One day while Fred is selling flowers in Indiana, he carelessly bumps into Bojangles and injures him. Bojangles is a resident of Chicago who was visiting Indiana at the time of the injury. As a result of the injury, he was unable to work at his job in Chicago and has lost income in the amount of $7,000. Bojangles sues Fred in Illinois state court. Instead of serving Fred personally while he is in the state of Illinois, Bojangles gets long-arm service on Fred by serving him with process by certified mail to his residence in Indiana. Does the Illinois court have valid personal jurisdiction?

4. Suppose Fred fails to pay his bill to Ginger, and Ginger sues him in Illinois for the amount he owes. Can she get valid personal jurisdiction if she serves Fred by long-arm in Indiana?

5. Fred sues Ginger in Indiana when the flowers turn out to be bad and his business suffers in Indiana. Is there valid personal jurisdiction over Ginger, who has never set foot in Indiana?

6. Suppose Fred is driving on the Dan Ryan Expressway in Chicago transporting flowers back to Indiana. It begins to rain heavily and Fred injures Gene, a pedestrian who is dancing in the street. Gene is an Indiana resident but hires an Illinois lawyer who sues Fred in Illinois state court under a long-arm statute that authorizes personal jurisdiction over persons who cause torts in the state. Is there good personal jurisdiction?

Bad Burgers

7. Robert Burgermeister decided to open a burger joint in South Dakota on the interstate one mile from the North Dakota state line. Robert knew that virtually all his customers were driving into North Dakota, and he knew that almost all customers buying carryout burgers would eat them on the road in North Dakota. When Robert served some bad burgers, ten customers ate them in North Dakota and became ill. They sue Robert in North Dakota for the personal injuries and he moved to dismiss for lack of personal jurisdiction. How should the trial court rule?

Empty Promise

8. John Bull, a resident of London, England, advertised for sale an antique Wedgewood china teapot. Medea, a resident of Atlanta, Georgia, emailed Bull and offered to buy the teapot. Bull accepted her offer by email, but he changed his mind and sold it to another purchaser when he learned that Medea is African American. Medea sues Bull in Georgia state court for breach of contract. Are there minimum contacts?

9. Same facts. Bull also sent Medea an email explaining that he was breaching the contract because of her race. Bull used extremely offensive language in the email. Medea received the email at her home in Atlanta. She sues Bull in Georgia state court for intentional infliction of emotional distress. Minimum contacts?

Contacts Contacts

10. Peter, a citizen of California, is injured by wearing a new kind of edible contact lens manufactured by Nutra-Lens, Inc. He purchased the lenses at the local Big Mart store in California. The store bought the lenses as part of its normal commercial activity from distributors who bought the lens from Nutra-Lens.

    Peter sues Nutra-Lens in California state court. Nutra-Lens is a Delaware corporation with its principal place of business in New York. It obtained the components of the product from unknown sources outside the United States. Nutra-Lens has no office, property, or employees in California. Its chief operating officer avers in an affidavit that he was aware of the possibility that Nutra-Lens lenses were sold in California, but he avers that no one at the corporation anticipated that the corporation would be subject to personal jurisdiction in California.

    Does California have constitutionally valid personal jurisdiction over Nutra-Lens?

11. Same facts. But suppose that Peter takes the lenses with him when he goes to college at Colorado College. There his roommate Paul, a Colorado resident, tries the lenses and suffers injuries. Can Paul sue Nutra-Lens in Colorado?

The Wacky Wolverine

12. Bobby Bland, a student at the University of Michigan, bought a Go Blue alarm clock at the campus bookstore. The alarm clock was in the shape of a wolverine — the school mascot — and it played "Hail to the Victors," the school song.

    The clock was manufactured by Acme Novelty Products of Hong Kong, China. The manufacturer packed the clocks in boxes, which it also manufactured. The boxes were printed in English and contained a toll-free number and an email address for the manufacturer's customer service department in China. The boxes were then sold to various intermediary corporations, which sold them to others, which sold them to the campus bookstore.

    Bobby alleges that due to the malfunctioning of the alarm clock, he failed to wake up in time for his final exam. As a result, he claims he failed the class and that his future career as a brain surgeon has been delayed for one full year with a corresponding reduction of life-time earnings of $200,000. He sues Acme Novelty Products in Michigan state court. Should the defendant ignore the lawsuit?

Big Box Slipup Reprise

13. Same facts as Big Box Slipup in Chapter 3. While George from Georgia is vacationing in Florida, he goes to the Big Mart Store to buy some sunscreen. While leaving the store, George slips on a banana peel and is injured. Big Mart is incorporated in Delaware and has its executive offices, training facilities, and other administrative offices in Bentonia, Arkansas. It has at least one large sales facility in every state and maintains warehouse facilities in several states. Big Mart owns and operates ten large retail facilities and a warehouse in Georgia where it employs over 1,000 people and generates millions of dollars in income annually. Where can George get personal jurisdiction over Big Mart?

Explanations

Minimum Contacts

1. Yes. Service under the state long-arm statute does not violate due process because Donson entered the state and committed a tort there. This one minimum contact is the basis of the plaintiff's claim and is sufficient. Since the defendant entered the state and committed a tort there, the courts would find that the exercise of personal jurisdiction was also reasonable or fair. The defendant's traveling to the state indicates the lack of burden in litigating there, and the state has an interest in exercising personal jurisdiction over torts arising in the state. The plaintiff has a strong interest in litigating in the place of injury, which may be both the location of important evidence and a more convenient forum than the defendant's home state. The foggy factors of interstate convenience and the shared interests of the several states probably also support personal jurisdiction by the court where the act and injury occurred.

2. Yes, Bean is subject to the state's personal jurisdiction even though he did not physically enter it. Deliberately causing an intentional tort in the state establishes a minimum contact, and the lawsuit arises out of the contact, so it is constitutionally sufficient. The reasonableness-fairness factors do not prevent personal jurisdiction (see previous answer).

Getting Specific

3. No, the Illinois court does not have valid personal jurisdiction based on long-arm service. Even assuming the state long-arm statute authorizes personal jurisdiction under these facts, such personal jurisdiction would violate due process because Fred does not have minimum contacts in Illinois. Bojangles's claim does not arise out of Fred's activity in Illinois. The fact that the plaintiff is from Illinois and the fact that there

are significant consequences in Illinois are not enough. The defendant's act to establish a minimum contact must be purposefully directed at the forum state. Fred's careless act in Indiana that caused Bojangles's injury was not directed at Illinois.

4. Yes, Ginger's long-arm service on Fred will pass constitutional muster. He physically entered Illinois, entered into a contract there with an Illinois resident, made promises that induced her to extend him credit in the state, and failed to pay in the state. These contacts are also the basis of the plaintiff's claim and thus establish minimum contacts. When a defendant has established minimum contacts in a state by purposely directing acts at forum residents, the Supreme Court has observed that the defendant must make a compelling case that personal jurisdiction would be unreasonable or unfair.

5. No, Ginger's sales activity is in Illinois, and even though she knows that Fred is from Indiana, the facts do not show that she herself engaged in any acts purposefully directed toward the forum state. The case would be different if Ginger was engaged in advertising in Indiana, reaching out to establish a multi-state market for her flowers. But as it stands, knowledge of effects is not enough to establish the purposeful act for a minimum contact in Indiana. When there are no minimum contacts, personal jurisdiction violates due process, no matter how reasonable or fair the exercise of personal jurisdiction may appear to be under the reasonableness-fairness factors.

6. Yes, there is valid personal jurisdiction. Driving in the state is an act purposely directed at the forum, and the cause of action arises out of the act. Fred has minimum contacts in this case, so personal jurisdiction under the long-arm statute is constitutional. This is the same answer we reached when a state authorized service on nonresident motorists by the archaic procedure of serving a person appointed as an agent for purposes of service of process. (See Chapter 3.) The reasonableness-fairness test does not prevent the exercise of personal jurisdiction where the defendant caused injuries in the state. Since the plaintiff and the court have a strong interest in the court exercising personal jurisdiction where the tort occurred, the plaintiff's burden is reduced. In addition, the needs of the interstate system and shared policies of states all weigh in favor of personal jurisdiction, not against it.

Bad Burgers

7. This is the kind of simple example I hate because I am not absolutely sure of the answer but I am sure it should have an easy answer. First, let's not assume facts not in evidence. The case would become messier

if Robert was trying to develop a market in North Dakota by advertising there and trying to lure drivers to his place of business in South Dakota. Such targeting of out-of-state drivers in a particular state would provide a stronger basis for finding purposeful availment even though he did not make the burgers or complete the sales in the state where he tried to reach consumers.

Without sales efforts targeting buyers in North Dakota, the facts establish only that he knew that the products would be purchased by people who would consume them in North Dakota. Under the Court's reasoning in Walden v. Fiore, knowledge of effects is not enough. And under the holding in *World-Wide Volkswagen*, the consumer's foreseeable transportation of the product to the place where it foreseeably causes injury is also not enough.

I should probably leave well enough alone. But I cannot help pointing out that something is missing from this analysis. Unlike the defendant in *Walden* who did not benefit in any way from the plaintiff's activity in their home state, Robert is deriving his profit from the fact that his buyers are eating his burgers after crossing the state line. Obviously, he intended to structure his business to secure this benefit. At the same time, Robert is not purposefully availing himself of the privilege of conducting activities within the forum state so as to invoke the benefits and protections of its laws.

Empty Promise

8. There are no minimum contacts for the contract claim. Looking at the course of the negotiations, the agreement, and the performance, it is unlikely that a court would find that Bull did acts purposely directed at the forum state of such a character that they established minimum contacts. The Supreme Court in *Burger King* found minimum contacts because the contract had a substantial connection to the forum state supported by far more evidence of the Michigan residents' contacts with Florida than are indicated by the defendant's relationship to Georgia in the example. Even if a court found such minimum contacts, it might conclude that the enormous burden on the foreign defendant of being subjected to jurisdiction would make the exercise of personal jurisdiction unreasonable and unfair.

9. The case for personal jurisdiction over the defendant in an intentional tort claim is stronger, but the result is uncertain. The Supreme Court found in Calder v. Jones that a writer and editor in Florida purposefully directed acts toward California when they wrote disparagingly about a California resident and knew the plaintiff resided in California and that her professional career and reputation were centered there. Similarly, Bull may be found to have deliberately made offensive remarks with the

purpose of causing injury to a resident of the forum state in the forum state. This might be enough to establish minimum contacts.

If minimum contacts are present, then, because the defendant directed purposeful acts at a forum resident, the defendant would bear the burden of showing that the exercise of personal jurisdiction was so unreasonable or unfair that it offended traditional notions of fair play and substantial justice. The burden on the defendant of litigating in a distant country with a foreign legal system might lead the court to find personal jurisdiction constitutionally unfair and unreasonable. The Supreme Court in *Asahi* relied heavily on the fact that the defendant was Japanese in finding that the exercise of personal jurisdiction was unreasonable. But the facts in *Asahi* were more extreme, because the plaintiff was also a foreign corporation with no clear need for a California forum, and California had no clear interest in exercising personal jurisdiction in *Asahi* because the indemnification claim did not involve a California resident.

In contrast, in this example at least two factors — the interest of the plaintiff and the forum state — favor jurisdiction. The factors of the interests of the international judicial system and the shared interests of the different countries could point either way. Jurisdiction might be more convenient and fair where the defendant intentionally directed his words and caused injury. But the shared interests of encouraging free flow of international communication over the Internet might favor a finding that jurisdiction was not reasonable.

Contacts Contacts

10. First, there is the question of whether Nutra-Lens has minimum contacts in California. This is uncertain because the Supreme Court remains divided over the circumstances in which a state court has personal jurisdiction over injuries caused in the state by defective products entering the state's market. Four Justices in *J. McIntyre Machinery, Inc.* require that purposeful availment be proved by acts by the defendant targeting the forum state that are not present. Three dissenting Justices in that case would find minimum contacts. The two swing-voters disagreed with the new submission theory of personal jurisdiction but rested their decision on the narrow ground that a single isolated sale does not establish minimum contacts. For the swing-voters a single, isolated sale did not evidence any targeting of the forum. Perhaps, the greater volume of Nutra-Lens sales could help establish such purposeful availment.

Second, even if minimum contacts are present, there is the question of the reasonableness-fairness factors. In *Asahi*, this consideration persuaded the Court that personal jurisdiction violated due process.

But the facts in the example are different, and the factors support a finding that jurisdiction is reasonable and fair. First, the defendant is not severely inconvenienced by being required to answer a lawsuit in a state where its product was delivered and caused injury — not as burdened as the defendant in *Asahi*. Second, the plaintiff has a powerful interest in litigating in a convenient forum and also in the forum where the evidence and witnesses are located. Third, the state of California has a strong interest in exercising personal jurisdiction over claims by persons injured in the state by allegedly defective products. It is hard to see how the foggy factors about the convenience of the interstate judicial system and the shared policies of the states affect the reasonableness or fairness of exercising personal jurisdiction, but they do not seem to weigh against personal jurisdiction in California.

11. Trick question. As my lawyer father used to say, "You can *always* sue." But here there would not be a constitutionally valid basis for long-arm personal jurisdiction over Nutra-Lens, because the product was not brought into the state by the stream of commerce but rather by the unilateral act of the consumer. *World-Wide Volkswagen* held that this is not a minimum contact.

The Wacky Wolverine

12. The defendant should answer this lawsuit and challenge personal jurisdiction. The example makes a number of important points. First, the question of personal jurisdiction is separate from the merits of the lawsuit. Bobby Bland's claim may be weak or even frivolous, but if the court has personal jurisdiction, the defendant must defend and raise defenses on the merits, because defenses to the merits will not provide a ground for avoiding enforcement of the default judgment.

Second, the defendant is a foreign corporation, and enforcing the judgment internationally will be problematic. Nevertheless, because the defendant may be engaged in business in the United States, a judgment may be satisfied against it in a U.S. jurisdiction. For example, the defendant's assets in the United States could be attached, and if U.S. businesses owe the foreign manufacturer money, they could be garnished. Consequently, the foreign defendant should not ignore the lawsuit and risk a default judgment if the court has personal jurisdiction.

Third, it is not absolutely clear whether the court has personal jurisdiction. But in this case, the uncertainty gives the answer: when in doubt, appear and answer, and challenge personal jurisdiction.

Fourth, Michigan probably has personal jurisdiction over a claim based on injury caused to the consumer resident by the allegedly defective product. Minimum contacts are shown by stream of commerce plus additional facts showing targeting, which constitute purposeful availment. For Justice O'Connor and three other Justices in *Asahi*, designing a product for the forum market or establishing means of communicating with forum residents established minimum contacts. Acme had designed the product for the forum market by adding specific design features especially appealing to Michigan fans. The toll-free phone number and email address allow regular communication with Michigan consumers.

Because the defendant purposely directed acts at forum residents, the defendant would bear the burden of making a compelling showing that the exercise of personal jurisdiction is so unreasonable or unfair that it offends traditional notions of fair play and substantial justice. Considering the five fairness factors identified by the Supreme Court, the exercise of personal jurisdiction would not be unconstitutional. The defendant would, of course, be inconvenienced. But the plaintiff forum resident has a strong interest in personal jurisdiction in the state of alleged injury. The forum state has an interest in exercising personal jurisdiction over defective products that cause injury in the state. The factors of the international judicial system and shared interests of the different countries are unclear, but they do not clearly weigh against the exercise of personal jurisdiction.

Big Box Slipup Reprise

13. George cannot get general (all-purpose) jurisdiction over Big Mart in Georgia based on the theory of continuous and systematic business activity, but he can get general personal jurisdiction over the defendant in its place of incorporation (Delaware) and principal place of business (Arkansas). (See Chapter 3.)

George cannot get specific personal jurisdiction over the defendant in Georgia for the Florida slip and fall because the claim does not arise out of or relate to the defendant's contacts in Georgia. Even if Georgia has a long-arm statute, the exercise of personal jurisdiction would be unconstitutional. In contrast, if George brings the action in Florida and arranges for personal service under a Florida long-arm statute, the Florida court's exercise of jurisdiction will be constitutional because George's claim arose out of the defendant's minimum contacts in Florida.

Transfer, Forum Non Conveniens, and Forum Selection Clauses

INTRODUCTION

In many cases plaintiffs can get subject matter jurisdiction, personal jurisdiction, and venue in more than one court. Plaintiffs then have a choice of forums, and smart plaintiffs will pick the court with the most favorable laws and procedures.

This chapter discusses procedures for transferring cases within the same legal system. It also considers the doctrine of forum non conveniens under which a court may dismiss certain cases that are burdensome to the defendant or court. And it explains when and how courts enforce mandatory forum selection clauses.

TRANSFER

Transfers Within Single State Systems Legislatures (and occasionally state constitutions) provide for transferring cases from one court to another within the same state's judicial system. Procedures vary from state to state and are designed to correct filing errors and to promote fairness and administrative convenience. One state cannot transfer a case to a court that is in another state, to a federal court, or to a court in a foreign country.

For example, suppose Sallinger files a copyright infringement claim against Kahn in New Hampshire state court. Federal courts have exclusive subject matter jurisdiction over copyright infringement claims. But the state court cannot transfer the action to federal court. It must dismiss it.

Warning: don't confuse transfer with removal! Removal jurisdiction is a basis of federal court subject matter jurisdiction, and removal occurs automatically when the defendants follow the removal requirements of federal law. Federal courts have removal jurisdiction over Sallinger's copyright action, and Kahn could remove the case to federal court by filing the appropriate pleadings in federal court. (An improperly removed action would be remanded to state court, not transferred.)

Transfers Within the Federal System   Federal statutes authorize one federal district court to transfer a case to another federal court in a different district or division in three situations. Two are designed to cure filing errors and authorize transfer to a proper district or division when the court lacks personal jurisdiction (28 U.S.C. §1631) or when venue is wrong (28 U.S.C. §1406). These two statutes give the trial court the option to transfer rather than dismiss when doing so serves the interest of justice.

Section 1404(a)   The third statute authorizes transfer between federal courts even when the first court has proper jurisdiction and venue. It provides: "For the convenience of parties and witnesses, in the interest of justice, a district court may transfer any civil action to any other district or division where it might have been brought or to any district or division to which all parties have consented." 28 U.S.C. §1404(a).

The Supreme Court has characterized section 1404(a) as a codification of the doctrine of forum non conveniens within the federal system. Atlantic Marine Construction Co. v. U.S. District Court, 134 S. Ct. 568 (2013); Sinochem International Co. v. Malaysia International Shipping Corp., 549 U.S. 422 (2007). The standards for dismissing for forum non conveniens are discussed under forum non conveniens.

Federal statutes do not authorize transfer from federal court to state court or to a foreign country. For example, consider a lawsuit filed in federal court by Franny, a citizen of California, against Angelo, a citizen of California, for breach of contract of marriage in which Franny is seeking damages in the amount of $50,000. The federal court lacks subject matter jurisdiction. It may also lack personal jurisdiction and venue depending on the facts. But it cannot transfer the lawsuit to a California state court to cure the defects. It must dismiss for lack of subject matter jurisdiction.

FORUM NON CONVENIENS

Courts will respect legitimate litigation choices by plaintiffs, but they will sometimes dismiss or transfer a case, even when there is no problem with subject matter jurisdiction, personal jurisdiction, or venue. The doctrine of forum non conveniens recognizes the power of a court to dismiss a lawsuit when there is an alternative forum and when trial in the chosen forum would be undesirable. The standard followed by federal courts requires a showing either of "oppressiveness and vexation to a defendant . . . out of all proportion to plaintiff's convenience" or that the chosen forum would be "inappropriate because of considerations affecting the court's own administrative and legal problems." Piper Aircraft Co. v. Reyno, 454 U.S. 235 (1981). State courts may apply a different standard.

Applying the doctrine of forum non conveniens results in a dismissal. This has the practical result that the lawsuit must be filed and litigated in some other court system.

Judges created the doctrine of forum non conveniens for extreme cases when another better court was available, when there was no good reason to hear a case, and when the plaintiff's reasons for selecting the court were improper or entitled to little respect. The best example of such a case would be a situation where the plaintiff had no reason for selecting a particular court other than burdening the defendant with a seriously inconvenient forum. But the doctrine has evolved. Nowadays courts use it to dismiss cases to enforce forum selection clauses regardless of the convenience of the chosen forum.

Forum non conveniens remains a judge-made doctrine in federal courts and in most states. A few states have enacted statutes that codify the doctrine. It was originally a matter of discretion, but appellate courts have more actively reviewed lower court decisions, and codifications of the doctrine may make dismissal mandatory when the requirements are satisfied.

Alternative Forum Forum non conveniens will not support dismissal when there is no alternative forum. But a defendant can sometimes establish the existence of an alternative forum by agreeing not to raise objections to the alternative court's personal jurisdiction or by agreeing not to raise a statute of limitations defense. A judge may grant a motion to dismiss on grounds of forum non conveniens on the condition that the defendant agree not to raise such defenses in the alternative forum.

Example

Swedish Meatballs

1. Knut, a citizen of Norway, operated a restaurant in Oslo, Norway, that advertised that it offered traditional Norwegian food and used exclusively Norwegian ingredients. Per, a citizen of Norway, ordered meatballs at the restaurant. After the first bite he threw his plate on the floor and shouted (in Norwegian), "These are Swedish meatballs."

   Knut assured Per that the meatballs were Norwegian, not Swedish. But Per did not believe him. The two argued about the meatballs throughout the long Nordic winter.

   Per wanted to make life as unpleasant as possible for Knut. So when Per learned that Knut was traveling to Florida to visit Wonderworld for vacation, Per hired a Florida lawyer to sue Knut in Florida for violating a Norwegian food labeling statute and for breach of contract. The lawyer commences a civil action in a court of general jurisdiction in Florida and serves process on Knut while he is waiting in line to ride the mechanical orca at Wonderworld.

   Knut files motions to dismiss for lack of personal jurisdiction, lack of subject matter jurisdiction, and improper venue. He also moves to transfer the lawsuit to Norway. Alternatively, he moves for dismissal on grounds of forum non conveniens. What should the court do?

Plaintiff's Choice of Forum Rarely Disturbed In applying the doctrine of forum non conveniens, courts will respect a plaintiff's choice of forum even when the plaintiff has chosen a forum to obtain legal or procedural advantages. The Supreme Court has observed that "a plaintiff's choice of forum should rarely be disturbed," that there is a "strong presumption" in favor of the plaintiff's choice, and that the defendant has a "heavy burden in opposing plaintiff's chose forum." Piper Aircraft Co., 454 U.S. at 249, 265; Sinochem International Co. v. Malaysia International Shipping Corp., 549 U.S. 422, 430 (2007).

Example

Bad Blowout

2. Able and Baker, two teenage boys from North Carolina, travel to France on a high school field trip. While they are riding the bus back to the airport in Paris, the bus tire experiences a blowout. As a result the bus turns over and the children are killed.

   The children's parents commence wrongful death and survival actions in North Carolina state court against Big Tire Corp., alleging that Big Tire defectively designed and manufactured the tires. Big Tire is a

Delaware corporation with its principal place of business in New Jersey. It operates a large factory in North Carolina but the tires at issue were not manufactured or designed in the state.

Big Tire moves for dismissal on grounds of forum non conveniens. What result?

Rarely Does Not Mean Never The plaintiff's choice of forum is rarely disturbed, but the doctrine of forum non conveniens will permit dismissal when the choice is improper. And the Supreme Court has concluded that foreign and nonresident plaintiffs choices are entitled to less deference. Piper Aircraft Co. v. Reyno, 454 U.S. 235 (1981); Sinochem, 549 U.S. at 431.

Balancing Private and Public Interest Factors In deciding whether oppressiveness and vexation are out of all proportion to plaintiff's convenience or whether the chosen forum would be inappropriate due to considerations affecting the court's administrative and legal problems, the judge must consider more than the plaintiff's convenience. The judge must also evaluate private interest and public interest factors. Private interest factors relate to the parties' ability to litigate and include the availability of evidence, witnesses, and other practical problems that make the case harder or more expensive. Public interest factors relate to the administrative and legal problems encountered by the courts such as court congestion, interests in trying local controversies at home, avoiding unnecessary problems in conflict of laws or application of foreign law, and avoiding burdening citizens with jury duty in a case involving no local interests. Piper Aircraft Co., 454 U.S. at 241 n.6.

The facts in Piper Aircraft Co. show how courts evaluate private and public interests. In that case Reyno was appointed legal representative for the estate of Scottish citizens who died in an airplane crash in Scotland. Reyno commenced an action against in California state court against the Pennsylvania manufacturer of the airplane and the Ohio manufacturer of the propeller. Reyno chose California because of more favorable law and procedures.

The defendants first removed the action to federal court. Then they transferred it from the federal in California to the federal court for the Middle District of Pennsylvania. Finally, they moved for dismissal on grounds of forum non conveniens. The trial court granted the motion and dismissed. And the Supreme Court agreed. Id. at 255.

First, the court found that an alternative forum existed in Scotland. (Defendants agreed to submit to Scottish jurisdiction and further agreed to waive any statute of limitations defenses.) Second, it found that plaintiff's choice was entitled to little weight because the real parties in interest were foreign citizens seeking a U.S. forum purely for a legal advantage and not for convenience. Third, the court found that private and public interests both favored dismissal.

The private interests pointed strongly toward Scotland. Except for evidence concerning design and testing, all evidence regarding the crash and damages were more accessible in Scotland. The case could be consolidated with other pending claims in Scotland, which would be fairer for defendants. Public interests pointed toward Scotland because the case would be complex and confusing for a jury. Claims against the Pennsylvania manufacturer would be governed by Scottish law, and claims against the Ohio manufacturer would be governed by Pennsylvania law. The case would require the construction of Scottish law with which the court in Pennsylvania was not familiar. Trial in Pennsylvania would be expensive and time-consuming. And it would be unfair to burden Pennsylvania citizens with jury duty in a case with little connection to their state.

Effect of Forum Non Conveniens on Law Applied in Case   A dismissal on grounds of forum non conveniens will have no effect on the law that will be applied when the dispute is litigated in a separate legal system. This means a plaintiff may lose legal advantages available in the chosen forum.

An unfavorable change in law will not by itself prevent dismissal. The Supreme Court emphasized, "The possibility of a change in substantive law should ordinarily not be given conclusive or even substantial weight in the forum non conveniens inquiry." *Piper Aircraft Co.*, 454 U.S. at 247. The Court added some qualifying language that suggested that changes in law that completely defeat plaintiff's rights may prevent dismissal: "[I]f the remedy provided by the alternative forum is so clearly inadequate or unsatisfactory that it is no remedy at all, the unfavorable change in law may be given substantial weight." *Id.* at 254. I am not sure exactly what this means. The important point is that just showing that the law will be "less favorable" in the second court will not prevent dismissal. *Id.* at 247, 254. The fact that the plaintiff will lose under the rules applied in the second court does not mean it is not an alternative forum or that there is no remedy at all.

Order of Decisions   Complex or disputed facts may make it uncertain whether a court has personal jurisdiction, but it may still be clear that forum non conveniens requires dismissal. In such a case, the court may dismiss on grounds of forum non conveniens without first determining whether it has personal jurisdiction. *Sinochem*, 549 U.S. at 435.

MANDATORY FORUM SELECTION CLAUSES

Parties may voluntarily submit to jurisdiction in advance of litigation. (Chapter 3.) They can do so in a permissive forum selection clause. In a mandatory forum selection clause, a party goes one further step and agrees that all litigation must take place only in that court. For example, a party might agree that all litigation must take place in London and no other place.

Once upon a time, courts hated mandatory forum selection clauses and considered them contrary to public policy. Nowadays courts love them. In Carnival Cruise Lines, Inc. v. Shute, 499 U.S. 585 (1991), the Supreme Court announced the rule for admiralty cases that reasonable forum selection clauses are enforceable but are subject to judicial scrutiny for fundamental fairness. That decision has influenced state courts.

When Enforced?   A mandatory forum selection clause is a contract and subject to normal contract law defenses. First, there may be a question as to whether a provision is in fact part of the parties' agreement. Just because something is printed on a form at the bottom of a box or attached to a web page does not automatically make it a contract.

Second, there may be questions about what a provision means. (An agreement that litigation may take place in London probably does not mean that it must take place there.)

Third, mandatory forum selection clauses may be unenforceable because they are unreasonable or because they violate some policy or statute. State laws protecting consumers, workers, or franchisees may limit the effect of such agreements.

How Enforced?   A mandatory forum selection clause is a contract. Courts specifically enforce them by transferring the cases to the chosen court if it is part of the same judicial system or by granting a motion to dismiss (under forum non conveniens or some other ground).

Federal courts will enforce mandatory forum selection clauses by transferring a case under section 1404(a) to another district. In Stewart Organization v. Ricoh, 487 U.S. 22 (1988), the Supreme Court held that federal judges may exercise their discretion under section 1404(a) to enforce forum selection clauses even when the clauses would be unenforceable under state law.

In Atlantic Marine Construction Co. v. U.S. District Court, 134 S. Ct. 568 (2013), the Supreme Court required the enforcement of mandatory forum selection clauses. It reversed a lower court decision not to transfer and announced: "[A] district court should transfer the case unless extraordinary circumstances unrelated to the convenience of the parties clearly disfavor a transfer." While transfer under section 1404(a) is normally a matter of discretion and plaintiff's choice is entitled to some weight, the Supreme Court reasoned that a mandatory forum selection clause eliminates any deference to the plaintiff's choice and removes the need for balancing parties' private interests.

Effect of Transfer on Law Applied After Transfer   Transfer of a case from
one court to another within a state's legal system would have no impact on
the law that applies. The *Erie* doctrine (Chapter 24) often requires federal
courts to apply the state law of the state in which they are sitting. Because of
this, a plaintiff may file suit in a particular federal district in order to get the
benefits of the state law where it sits.

The effect of federal court transfer on the applicable law depends on
how the case was transferred. First, in transfers under sections 1406 and
1631 to cure defects in venue and subject matter jurisdiction, the court to
which the transfer is made (the "transferee" court) must apply the state law
of the state where it sits. Hay et al., Conflict of Laws §11.14 at 521. This
makes sense since the cases should have been filed in those districts to begin
with and the transfer statutes provide a procedure for getting the case to the
correct court without dismissal.

Second, in most transfers under section 1404(a), for the convenience
of parties or witnesses or in the interest of justice, the law of the original
transferring court will apply. Ferens v. John Deere Co., 494 U.S. 516 (1990);
Van Dusen v. Barrack, 376 U.S. 612 (1964). This rule rewards forum shopping. It gives the plaintiff any benefit of the law where the case was properly
filed even though it was subsequently transferred to a more suitable district.

Third, when a case is transferred under section 1404(a) to enforce a
mandatory forum selection clause, the court to which the transfer is made
will apply the law of the state where it sits. Atlantic Marine Construction
Co., 134 S. Ct. 568 (2013). This rule deprives the plaintiff of any benefit of
the law where the case was filed. The Supreme Court reasoned that it is fair
to deprive the plaintiff of the benefit because the plaintiff improperly filed
the lawsuit in the first forum in violation of the forum selection agreement.

Examples

Fun with Forum Selection

3. One evening Samuel Pickwick was doing some shopping over the
   Internet at his home in Uppstate, New York. Always weak on impulse control, Pickwick was unable to resist purchasing a solid gold Chronomaster
   Clamshell Perpetuum watch offered on sale for only $22,000. The seller
   was SuperWatchSuperstore, a website completely owned and operated
   by Job Trotter, a resident of New Jersey.

   Pickwick charged the purchase to his credit card. In completing the transaction over the Internet, Pickwick clicked a message box
   on his screen that stated "Customer Agrees to All Attached Terms and
   Conditions." Pickwick did not actually read the attached terms and conditions. They were accessible at the website and included the following
   clause 8: "It is agreed by and between the customer and the Seller that

all disputes and matters whatsoever arising under or in connection with this Contract shall be litigated if at all in and before a Court located in the country of Barataria to the exclusion of the courts of any other state or country."

The watch arrived the following week. Pickwick wore it proudly while washing the dishes that night because it was supposed to be solid gold and waterproof. Unfortunately, the watch filled with water and its gold finish flaked off.

Pickwick sues Trotter in state court for fraud. Trotter moves to dismiss pursuant to the forum selection clause. A winner?

4. Liz Canter, a lifelong resident of Horse Country, West Carolina, decided to open an equine accessories boutique at the local mall. She entered into a two-year franchise agreement with the retail chain Horselovers Stores, Inc. Horselovers Stores franchises retail stores in ten states. It is incorporated in Delaware and has its home office in Seattle, Washington. The franchise agreement provided that "all litigation under this lease must be commenced in a court located in Seattle, Washington."

Riley Rider bought a defective cinch from Canter, which Canter bought from Horselovers Stores. Rider was badly injured, and Canter settled his personal injury claims against her by paying him $300,000. Then she sued the Horselovers Stores in state court in West Carolina to recover the amount paid. Horselovers Stores asks you whether the forum selection clause is enforceable and whether it matters if the action is removed to federal court for the district of West Carolina. Please explain.

Explanations

Swedish Meatballs

1. Subject matter and personal jurisdiction defenses may be losers. The state court of general jurisdiction has subject matter jurisdiction by definition because such jurisdiction is not taken away by state or federal law. The service of process establishes constitutionally valid personal jurisdiction and probably also establishes valid personal jurisdiction under state law.

Venue defenses would seem more promising but would also require research. The general Florida venue statute limits venue to the place where a defendant resides, an action accrued, or where property in litigation is located, but that statute does not apply to nonresidents. Fla. Stat. §47.011.

There is no way for a court to transfer a lawsuit to another judicial system, so the motion for transfer to Norway must be denied.

This problem demonstrates the need for a doctrine of forum non conveniens. Even though the state court may have jurisdiction and venue, the action should be dismissed. The exact standards applied by state courts vary, but these facts should satisfy any court that recognizes its discretion to dismiss. First, there is an alternative forum. Second, the plaintiff has no legal need for a Florida court. Third, litigation in Florida would be extremely burdensome both to the defendant and to the court itself. Florida cases (I think) require the defendant to show material injustice. That seems easy in this example.

Conflicts scholars and their casebooks focus on the federal standard. Applying the federal standard in this case, (1) there is an alternative forum, (2) the plaintiff's choice is subject to no respect given that the plaintiff is foreign and has chosen the forum simply to harass the defendant, and (3) the chosen forum would result in oppressiveness to the defendant out of all proportion to any conceivable convenience to plaintiff, and it would also result in administrative and legal problems for the court because of the difficulty of construing, interpreting, and enforcing Norwegian law.

Bad Blowout

2. The facts are borrowed from Goodyear Dunlop Tires Operations, S.A. v. Brown, 131 S. Ct. 2846 (2011) (Chapter 4), where the court held there was no general jurisdiction over foreign subsidiaries responsible for manufacturing a tire that caused deaths of North Carolina residents in France. The parent corporation did not contest personal jurisdiction.

   The defendant did not move for dismissal on grounds of forum non conveniens. But if it had, the North Carolina court would not have dismissed on that ground even if another court was available and the chosen court would be seriously inconvenient for the defendant. The plaintiffs' choice of their home state court would be respected both because they have strong reasons of convenience for selecting their home state court and because their state has an interest in providing a forum for its residents. This is consistent with the result in Guidi v. Inter-Continental Hotels Corp., 224 F.3d 142 (2d Cir. 2000), where the Second Circuit reversed a dismissal for forum non conveniens in a case where survivors of people killed in a shooting incident at a hotel in Egypt sued the New York-based hotel operator in New York. The Second Circuit held that the plaintiff's choice should not be disturbed, noting both the inconvenience and emotional burden that plaintiffs would suffer if litigation proceeded in Egypt.

Fun with Forum Selection

3. Trotter will lose. State law governs the enforceability of the forum selection clause. While all states have now followed the lead of the Supreme Court's admiralty decisions and enforce reasonable forum selection

clauses under many circumstances, those clauses remain subject to scrutiny for fundamental fairness. Moreover, states may place additional restrictions on such clauses in consumer sale purchases.

The forum selection clause in *Carnival Cruise* was enforceable because it was reasonable. The Court assumed that the litigation cost savings would be reflected in lower ticket prices. Moreover, the Court found no evidence of bad faith and emphasized that the defendant had good reasons for centralizing litigation at its place of business.

In contrast, Job Trotter has selected a distant, inconvenient forum that does not appear to be reasonable because it has no connection to the transaction or the defendant's business. What is more, the forum selection seems to have been made in bad faith—motivated by the goal of discouraging litigation. Under such circumstances, the forum selection appears to be both unreasonable and void for violating fundamental fairness. Finally, the clause appears to be part of a scheme to defraud.

Note that the fact that Pickwick did not read and was not aware of the forum selection clause does not prevent its enforcement if he had sufficient notice.

4. The enforceability of the forum selection clause in the West Carolina state court will be governed by West Carolina state law. If the state follows the general approach of *Carnival Cruise*, then the agreement appears to be enforceable as a reasonable effort to centralize litigation in a place connected to the parties, and it does not seem to violate fundamental fairness. It is possible, however, that West Carolina courts impose additional restrictions on forum selection clauses.

It may make a difference whether the action is removed to federal court. In federal court, the defendant could make a motion to transfer under section 1404(a) and the motion should be granted under *Atlantic Marine Construction Co.* because there are no extraordinary circumstances unrelated to the convenience of the parties that disfavor a transfer.

PART II

Traditional Choice of Law Rules

6

Torts

THE BIG PICTURE

Until the 1950s most courts followed the traditional choice of law rules. Joseph Story, the famous federalist Supreme Court Justice and Harvard Law School professor, set forth many of the rules in his early, influential treatise on Conflict of Laws (1834). These rules were the basis for the First Restatement of Conflict of Laws (1934).

Traditional, Territorial, Vested Rights   In hindsight scholars have observed an important philosophical shift from Story's emphasis on comity—the policy of respecting laws of other states—to vested rights—the policy of enforcing private parties' legal entitlements. But in fact there were three common features to the traditional rules. First, they were traditional. They claimed to be derived from past judicial practices and succeeded in being widely adopted by courts. Second, they were territorial. They selected the law by reference to some significant event located in a jurisdiction's territory. Torts conflicts, for example, were governed by the law of the place of the accident. Third, they attempted to achieve uniformity of result no matter where the dispute was litigated. The idea of vested rights added a theoretical justification for outcome uniformity: it viewed a legal claim as a property-like right to recover that which is "owned" by the individual that all courts must respect.

     The First Restatement set forth the traditional rules in great detail. The Restatement was supposed to *restate* the laws generally applied by the courts, but the drafters of the Restatement also wanted to rationalize and harmonize legal doctrines, so they also promulgated rules that they thought courts *should* apply, even though there was not always strong legal authority for some of the proposed reforms.

The Incredible Dream The traditional rules were formulated to achieve several goals. First, they were believed to reflect the proper or right result under general principles of law—or standards of good law—that existed outside any particular legal system. The idea that legal standards can exist outside any existing legal system is associated with the idea of natural law. Story believed the common law evolved by discovering the best rules for deciding cases, and he thought Conflicts rules could be similarly derived from objective legal criteria. The vested rights thinking of the drafters of the Restatement likewise dreamed of fashioning rules that would always recognize and enforce the private entitlements individuals had acquired under the law of different states.

Second, the traditional rules sought to achieve uniformity of result. All jurisdictions applying the traditional rules should decide the same case the same way. Uniformity of results would promote the objectively right result and would vindicate individuals' entitlements. It would also discourage forum shopping. Forum shopping was considered to be an evil mostly for the philosophical reason that courts "should" decide cases the same way. Back in the day, courts and scholars were less concerned with the problems of proliferating litigation or the problem that forum-shopping benefits plaintiffs, not defendants.

The Incredible Nightmare Natural law thinking was in steep decline by the early twentieth century. But a kind of neo-liberal attitude prevailed among establishment lawyers—the people who brought us the First Restatement. (Today this attitude would be called neo-conservative.) Courts and lawyers thought individuals owned legal entitlements. These entitlements had an existence distinct from their recognition by particular legal systems. In fact these entitlements even limited the power of states, because states could not legitimately deprive persons of such entitlements.

You probably recall the bad constitutional version of this theory. The pre-New Deal Supreme Court applied vested rights thinking to hold that a state could not outlaw child labor. It reasoned that employers had acquired the legal entitlement to exploit children through formal contracts with the children. By outlawing child labor, the Court reasoned the state was depriving employers of this property-like entitlement without due process.

Such nightmarish consequences led to the near extinction of the vested rights dream. The First Restatement of Conflicts offers one of the most extreme versions of the vested rights dream. But it rolled off the press in 1934, just as the era of vested rights was coming to a timely death.

LAW OF THE PLACE OF THE WRONG

The traditional rule for torts is to apply *lex loci delicti* — Latin for the law of the place of the wrong or tort.[1] The First Restatement refers to this as the law of the place of the wrong.

The First Restatement offers two philosophical rationalizations for this rule. First, it observes that a legal duty to pay arises (or does not arise) at the time of some injury, and all jurisdictions should enforce a plaintiff's entitlement to this payment (or not) by looking to the law of the place where the obligation arises. Second, it observes that each state has power to determine the legal effect of acts done in its territory, and other states should enforce the legal consequences of the acts assigned to them by the state in which they occurred.

Place of the Wrong   The place of the wrong is the place of the accident or injury. The First Restatement defines it more precisely as "the state where the last event necessary to make an actor liable for an alleged tort takes place." First Restatement §377.

The elements of torts vary from tort to tort, and occasionally from jurisdiction to jurisdiction. But the last element will usually be damages. These damages include the present right to recover things that may be lost in the future — such as future pain, medical expenses, or lost wages. Calculating such damages can be a challenge in practice. The important thing for Conflicts is that the place of the wrong will normally be where the first legally recognizable damages occur. The first damages will establish a legal "injury" and fix the place of the wrong. For personal injuries and injuries to land and personal property, the place of the wrong will be "where the harmful force takes effect" upon the body or thing. First Restatement §377 note.

The First Restatement provides a number of special subrules designed to give clear and uniform answers for some torts where jurisdictions are divided over the necessary elements. For poisoning, the place of the wrong is the place where the poison takes effect rather than where the victim ingested the poison.[2] For fraud, the place of the wrong is where the loss

---

1. This applies to substantive issues. Issues of procedure are governed by different rules (usually forum law). The difficulty of distinguishing between substance and procedure is discussed in Chapter 13.
2. This rule actually applies to cases where a person "voluntarily . . . take[s] a deleterious substance." When someone forces the victim to ingest the poison, the tort would presumably be complete at the time of the forced ingestion. Students have repeatedly asked me why the poison does not take effect within the body beginning with its ingestion. I don't know.

is sustained, not where the false statements are made. For defamation, the place of the wrong is where the statement is communicated (where it is heard).

Place of Wrong Applies to Almost Everything The First Restatement contains 20-something rules that apply the law of the place of the wrong to all substantive issues. These issues include the existence of an injury, the standard of care, causation, defenses, vicarious liability, wrongful death actions, and damages. *Id.* §§378-421.

There are two big exceptions. Conduct that is required by the law of one state may not be the basis for liability in another state. Conduct that is engaged in pursuant to a legal privilege of the place of conduct will not be the basis for liability in another state. *Id.* §382.

Other Traditional Rules: Intentional Torts

The Good News The First Restatement applied the law of the place of the wrong to all torts. It did not differentiate between different kinds of claims.

The Not-So-Good News The First Restatement includes some really technical rules that basically apply the law of the place of conduct without saying so. For example, the comment defines or redefines the place of the wrong for defamation cases as the place of communication rather than the place where damages are sustained, and the place of communication is really the same as the place of conduct, not the place of injury.[3]

These inconsistencies in the First Restatement are hints of a broader problem. There was no legal authority for applying the law of the place of the wrong for all torts. The First Restatement was generalizing beyond existing legal authority. In other words, it was making new law. Scholars have argued that its new law was actually at odds with judicial decisions that followed different rules. For example, in Marra v. Bushee, 317 F. Supp. 972 (D. Vt. 1970), *rev'd on other grounds*, 447 F.2d 1282 (2d Cir. 1971), the trial court applied the law of the place of wrongful conduct (adultery) to determine whether there were claims for the intentional torts of alienation of affections and criminal conversation. The court's opinion cited scholarly

---

3. In one especially challenging example, the First Restatement applies the standard of care of the place of the wrong. But it also says that if two jurisdictions have the "same" standard of care, then you apply specific rules of the place of the conduct to determine if the standard has been violated. (Huh?) *See id.* §380(2).

authority that the place of conduct was the traditional rule for intentional torts. Alternatively, the court applied the First Restatement but concluded that the place of conduct was the place of the "wrong" for purposes of the absent spouse's loss of consortium claim.

To the extent traditional jurisdictions applied different choice rules, these jurisdictions could choose different tort rules for the same case. This would frustrate the glorious dream of uniformity of results.

Status

Most Conflicts books devote a lot of attention to problems with the traditional, territorial rules. These problems help explain why so many jurisdictions rejected the rules beginning in the 1950s. But the traditional rules are not all bad. Most courts continued to follow them for decades after the death of the bad vested rights philosophy that the First Restatement adopted to rationalize them.

A few states and numerous foreign countries still follow the traditional, territorial approach. They have often adjusted its application to reach results similar to those reached by courts that reject the traditional, territorial rules.

Although most states moved away from the traditional rules during the Conflicts "revolution" beginning in the 1950s, that revolution has been most influential in the areas of torts and contracts. Courts that follow modern approaches often still apply the traditional rules to property and other issues. Moreover, the traditional rules provide the starting point for some modern approaches. For example, the law of the place of the injury provides the default law under modern New York rules (Chapter 17). Under the Second Restatement of Conflicts, specific rules often select the law of the place of injury unless displaced by other considerations (Chapter 21).

Early Warning — Traditional Dodges

The same courts that worked up traditional, territorial rules designed to achieve uniformity also created a number of doctrines that allows them to avoid applying the law of the place of the wrong in certain situations. Conflicts scholars sometimes call these traditional avoidance doctrines "escape devices" or "wrinkles," though the courts did not call them that. Such devices included the doctrine of applying forum law to procedure, the recharacterization of issues in order to apply a different choice rule, and exceptions for causes of action contrary to the strong public policy of the forum. These topics are covered in Chapters 12 to 16.

Examples

Traditional Targets

1. Duck and Mallard, citizens of the country of Avalon, went hunting in the country of Camelot. Deep in the forest, Duck mistook Mallard for a water fowl and shot him by mistake. Under the law of Camelot, persons are strictly liable for the injuries they cause. Under the law of Avalon, persons are liable for the injuries they cause only if they acted without due care. What standard of care will Avalon apply under the traditional approach?

2. Same facts. What standard of care will Camelot apply under the traditional approach?

3. Same facts. Duck argues that Mallard was partly at fault for his own injury because Mallard was wearing a hat covered with bird feathers and because Mallard was making bird sounds at the time of his injury. Camelot retains the defense of contributory negligence under which a plaintiff cannot recover any damages if he or she was negligent in any degree and the negligence contributed to the injuries. In contrast, Avalon has a form of comparative negligence under which a plaintiff can recover if he or she was negligent but the recovery is reduced by the proportion of the plaintiff's negligence. Assume under these facts that Mallard's negligence is apportioned 60 percent of responsibility for his injuries. If he litigates in Avalon, can he recover anything?

Traditional Guests

4. Gussy and Hoss, citizens and residents of East Carolina, went for a car trip to West Carolina. Hoss drove his car, which was insured in East Carolina to cover liability for accidents wherever they occurred. After entering West Carolina, Hoss carelessly lost control of the car and smashed into a utility pole, causing injuries to Gussy. Under a guest statute in West Carolina, a nonpaying passenger cannot recover for personal injuries caused by the driver unless the driver acted with gross negligence. East Carolina has no similar guest statute. There is evidence of negligence but not gross negligence. What law applies under the traditional approach?

Traditional Property Torts

5. Johnny Rocket launched a toy rocket in the state of Ascent. Its orbit ended in the state of Descent when it penetrated the convertible top of Luke Luckless's car and damaged the upholstery of his back seat. Under the law of Ascent, it is unlawful to launch rockets without a license, and violators are strictly liable for all resulting damages. Under the law of

Descent, rocket launchers are liable only if they are negligent. The orbit was too low to implicate any space treaties. What law applies under the traditional approach?

6. Plutor, in the country of Mordor, operates a belch furnace that emits poisonous gases. The gases travel halfway around the world, where they destroy the flower garden of Fawn in the country of Atlantis. Under the law of Atlantis, polluters are strictly liable for economic damage to land resulting from their acts. Under the law of Mordor, belch furnace operators are liable only if they spent less than $100,000 on pollution control devices in the past 12 months. Plutor spent exactly $100,001 on pollution control devices in the preceding 12 months. What law applies under the traditional approach?

Traditional Manufacturers

7. Acme Manufacturing, Inc., is a manufacturing corporation incorporated under the law of East Dakota, with its principal place of business and manufacturing facilities in East Dakota. The corporation designed and manufactured automatic coffeemakers. It exercised due care at the time it designed and manufactured the product. Unfortunately, after several years of continuous use, its coffeemakers began to explode, causing personal injuries. Polly Plaintiff was injured in West Dakota by one of Acme's products.

   Under the law of East Dakota, a person can recover for personal injuries for a defective product only if he or she can prove the product was designed or manufactured without due care. Under the law of West Dakota, persons can recover in product liability actions by proving the product was defective and that its defects caused injuries. What standard applies under the traditional approach?

8. Same facts. Plaintiff alleges that the manufacturer had actual knowledge of the dangerousness of its product and failed to notify the public. Under such facts, West Dakota permits a plaintiff to recover punitive damages. East Dakota does not permit punitive damages absent additional proof of intent to harm. Under the traditional approach, what law governs the right to recover punitive damages?

Traditional Confusion

9. Don Gunner owned a handgun in the country of Gunopia. He kept it in an unlocked glove compartment in his unlocked car. The gun was stolen by Thief, who took it to the country of Disarmia, where Thief shot and injured Victor. Under the law of Gunopia, all citizens have a constitutional right to own guns. The Gunopia legislature has enacted a Gunowners Freedom Rights Act, which provides that gun owners are

not liable for personal injuries caused by the discharge of their guns unless the gun owner was grossly negligent. Moreover, Gunopia courts have held that a victim of injuries inflicted by a third person using an owner's gun cannot recover from the gun owner because the shooter is the primary and exclusive cause of the injury.

In contrast, Disarmia courts have held that gun owners must take due care to prevent the theft of their guns and have also held that a gun owner whose negligence causes the weapon to fall into the hands of an irresponsible stranger is liable for injuries caused by the stranger to innocent members of the public.

Applying the traditional territorial rules, does Victor have a good claim under Disarmia law, or is his claim barred by Gunopia's defense?

10. Dot Trigger lived in Gunopia. One day she was approached in the parking lot of Megamart by a masked man. She dropped to her knees, pulled a .44 Magnum handgun from her handbag, loaded it, and fired two shots. The first missed her intended target and injured Patterson, who was washing his car in Disarmia.

    Patterson sues Trigger in Disarmia court. Under the law of Disarmia, a person must retreat, if she can do so safely, before using deadly force in self defense. Under the law of Gunopia, a person may use deadly force when she reasonably believes it is necessary to avoid serious bodily harm, and there is no retreat requirement. Under the facts, the parties agree that Trigger could have retreated safely. Does Patterson have a good claim under the traditional approach?

11. Same facts. Patterson's injuries were caused by a bullet coated with Kryptonite. In Disarmia, it is illegal to possess or use ammunition coated with Kryptonite. Violators are strictly liable for injuries caused by such ammunition. In Gunopia, Kryptonite is legal. What law applies under the traditional rules?

Defamation Nation

12. Barry Whiner, a radio talk show host broadcasting from his home country of Libelia, announced one day that Sally Pendergrast, the President of the country of Patagonia was "embarazada" by the ambassador from Libelia. Whiner meant to say that President Pendergrast was embarrassed by some remarks made by the Libelian ambassador. Unfortunately, Whiner's command of Spanish was not very good, and in fact his broadcast statement was heard in Patagonia where it was understood to mean that the President was pregnant as the result of an extramarital affair with the ambassador.

Although the President's public opinion rating soared in Patagonia, her reputation was damaged. The statement was not defamatory under the law of Libelia because the words were not defamatory in that country and because there was no intent to defame, as required by Libelian law. In contrast, under the law of Patagonia, the statement was defamatory and actionable. What is the law of the place of the wrong under the First Restatement?

Explanations

Traditional Targets

1. Applying the traditional territorial approach, Avalon will select the law of the *lex loci delicti* to govern the issue of the standard of care. It will apply Camelot's strict liability rule. Under the First Restatement, you apply the law of the place of the wrong to the issue of the standard of care. The place of the wrong is the place where the last event necessary to give rise to a cause of action for tort occurred. In personal injury claims, this place is the place of the injury, so Camelot's law applies. First Restatement §379.

2. Camelot will apply the same law—the law of the place of the wrong—and apply its own strict liability standard. This question makes the important point that different jurisdictions applying the traditional rules should select the same substantive law to govern the issue. There is no incentive for forum shopping.

3. Defenses, just like standards of care, are governed by the law of the place of the wrong. Here Camelot's form of contributory negligence will provide a complete defense and will be applied by all traditional jurisdictions. *See id.* §385 (specifically providing that contributory negligence is determined by the law of the place of the wrong).

Traditional Guests

4. The law of the place of the wrong, West Carolina's guest statute, applies and bars the claim. *Id.* §384(2) ("[I]f no cause of action is created at the place of wrong, no recovery in tort can be had in any other state.").

    Guest statutes were once common, but they became disfavored by the late twentieth century. Much of the movement away from the traditional torts rules occurred in cases involving guest statutes, where courts questioned the wisdom of the traditional rules. The traditional rules in a case like this were easy to apply and guaranteed uniformity of result, but they selected a law that was unfair and required its application in a case where there was no good reason for applying the law—except, of course, that it was the place of the accident.

Traditional Property Torts

5. An action for damage to personal property is governed by the place of the wrong — the place where the harmful force takes effect on the personal property. Under these facts, the state of Descent's negligence law applies. *Id.* §377 illus. 3 (concluding that stone thrower in state X is liable for injury to property in state Y in accordance with law of state Y).

6. The short answer is that an action for damage to real property is governed by the law of the place where the force damages the real property. Here Atlantis's strict liability should apply. *Id.* §377 illus. 4 (lawsuit stemming from damage to grass by noxious fumes is governed by law where land was damaged).

 But a longer answer is possible. Mordor's law establishes a defense, and if the defense is understood to arise from a legal privilege, then the First Restatement applies the law of the place where the person acted pursuant to the privilege. Unfortunately, the First Restatement does not define what a privilege is (as opposed to a defense). We return to the problem in Examples 9-10.

Traditional Manufacturers

7. The law of the place of the wrong, West Dakota, applies to the standard of care, and the defendant manufacturer is strictly liable for injuries in accordance with the law of the state where the plaintiff was injured. *Id.* §379(c).

8. The First Restatement provides that the law of the place of the wrong selects the measure of damages in general, *id.* §412, and punitive damages in particular, *id.* §421. Accordingly, the plaintiff can recover punitive damages available under the law of West Dakota because that is the place of the injury.

Traditional Confusion

9. This example illustrates the need for careful analysis of issues. It is tempting to see the issue as one of the gun owner's vicarious liability for the acts of the thief. Vicarious liability is *generally* governed by the law of the place of the wrong, but the First Restatement requires that the person held vicariously liable must have authorized the tortfeasor to act in his behalf, and there is no such authorization here. *See id.* §387.

 But the issue is not vicarious liability. Instead of vicarious liability, the plaintiff seeks to hold the defendant primarily liable for his own failure to control the weapon. The case raises two separate issues: the conflicting standards for legal causation and the conflicting standards of care.

Looking at the issue of causation, the First Restatement resolves the conflict between Gunopia's determination that the acts of gun owners are not legal causes and Disarmia's rule that the acts of gun owners are legal causes of resulting injuries by applying the law of the place of the wrong. *Id.* §383 (whether act is legal cause is determined by law of place of wrong). Disarmia's law applies because that is the place of the injury.

Looking at the issue of the standard of care and privilege, it first looks like the negligence standard in Disarmia, the place of the wrong, should apply. *Id.* §379(b). But the First Restatement provides an exception for applying the liability standards of the place of the wrong when a person acts pursuant to a privilege conferred by the law of the place of acting. *Id.* §382(2).

The First Restatement does little to clarify what a privilege is as opposed to other defenses. This should be determined under the standards of the forum (*see id.* §7), and different courts could differ over whether something is a privilege. The Restatement offers only the general suggestion that a privilege is a particularized exception to general principles of liability. *Id.* §382 cmt. c. This is not a useful test because virtually all defenses satisfy it.

Privileges seem to share two ingredients that can be useful in identifying them. First, according to Justice Holmes, privileges are distinguished by the fact that they are designed to encourage behavior in situations where the social benefits of the behavior are more valuable than the harm caused by the behavior. This means the privilege should be advancing some public policy goal. Second, as Richman et al. observe, privilege defenses under the First Restatement arise in situations that support a claim of justifiable reliance upon local law. Richman et al., Conflict of Laws § 65 at 198.

It is not certain whether the defense in this example is a privilege, but both ingredients of privilege may be met in the case of Gunopia's higher standard of care for claims against gun owners. The purpose of Gunopia's law is to encourage gun ownership and use. Gun owners in Gunopia might well rely on their general immunity to negligence claims. Accordingly, there is a strong argument that the Gunopia law establishes a privilege. The argument for privilege would be even stronger if the actor were not liable except in cases of "malice."

Under the First Restatement, a person who acts pursuant to a privilege under the law of the place of acting will not be held liable in any jurisdiction. *Id.* §382(2). If it is not a privilege, then the law of the place of the wrong applies and establishes liability for negligence.

10. The First Restatement thought self-defense was an easy example of privilege. Under these circumstances, the attacked person used force that was privileged in the place where she acted. Accordingly, she is not

liable for the consequences of the act in another jurisdiction. *Id.* §382 illus. 5.

I have given you the "right" answer. But I think this supposedly easy case also illustrates the difficulty of distinguishing privilege under the First Restatement. The general right to self-defense is undoubtedly a privilege. It is designed to encourage protective force. But the particular aspect at issue, the retreat requirement, may be designed to encourage protective force when safe retreat is possible, or it may simply be an accommodation to the reality that persons will not retreat and are not considered blameworthy for failing to do so. The moral considerations justify shifting the losses to the person who is the target of the defendant's protective force (at least when the defendant's reasonable belief in the need to use force is in fact accurate). But it is far from clear to me that the loss should be shifted to the innocent third person.

If you are confused, welcome to the club. The First Restatement makes things even less clear by observing that a method of exercising a privilege that unreasonably endangers interests in another state is not privileged when the same privilege could be exercised in a way that does not endanger interests in another state. *Id.* §382 cmt. b.

11. Disarmia's standard of care applies as the law of the place of the wrong. *Id.* §379(c). This example should remind you that the First Restatement does not incorporate a general exception for the law of the place of conduct when persons may have acted in reliance on that law. Rules are rules.

A minor change in the example produces a different result. If the two states differ not in the standard of care (between strict liability and negligence) but rather between two different constructions of negligence, then the First Restatement applies the law of the place of conduct. For example, suppose the shooter in Gunopia injured someone in Disarmia and both states require due care, but Disarmia cases interpret use of Kryptonite as a violation of due care but Gunopia courts does not. First Restatement courts would apply the legal construction of Gunopia (the place of conduct) that use of Kryptonite does not violate due care. *See id.* §380(2).

This sounds like a potentially huge exception to the rule of the place of the wrong. But the First Restatement indicates that it applies only in the limited situation where both the place of wrong and place of conduct have the same common law standard of care, but the place of conduct has more precisely defined the standard so that it is no longer a question of fact for the jury. This would apply where both jurisdictions require persons crossing train tracks to exercise due care but the place of conduct further defines due care to require a person to stop, look, and listen. All courts should go with the more precise legal construction of the place of the conduct. *See id.* §380 cmt. b.

Defamation Nation

12. The First Restatement applies the law of the place of the wrong to the question of liability, and this is where the last event necessary to make an actor liable for tort occurs. This is usually easy to determine, since damages are usually the last element required. But some intentional torts may not require damages — or jurisdictions may differ over whether damages are required.

    Even if damages are required for defamation claims, it can be difficult to determine where the injury to reputation occurred. It might be where people heard the defamatory statement or where the defamed person was at the time of the statement, or where the defamed person was domiciled.

    To provide some help, the First Restatement offered a more specific rule: harm to reputation occurs "where the defamatory statement is communicated." *Id.* §377 cmt. 5. The First Restatement honestly did not see that the place where "communicated" could mean either where spoken or heard. While your natural inclination (like mine) might be to assume that the rule applies to the place of speaking, the First Restatement illustration indicates that the place of communication is where the broadcast is heard. *Id.* §377 illus. 7. Accordingly, the defamatory character of the words and the standard of care are governed by Patagonia law.

    The First Restatement answer seems reasonable under these facts (derived from its own illustration) where the place of communication is where the defamed person lives and is known. But the place of communication seems less obvious in other common defamation situations. For example, suppose Whiner's statement was broadcast to 20 countries and 19 did not recognize a cause of action. The plaintiff would still have a cause of action (recognized in all 20 countries) if the words were heard in one jurisdiction where her reputation was harmed when that country recognized a cause of action. The gaps in the First Restatement inspired the Second Restatement to design complex rules to deal with multiple publication and multiple jurisdiction tort problems.

    The public policy doctrine under the First Restatement (Chapter 15) provides a device for avoiding the recognition of foreign defamation claims under certain circumstances.

CHAPTER 7

Contracts

INTRODUCTION

Traditional courts never applied the rule of the place of the wrong to contracts. For starters, a place-of-breach rule would be unhelpful for all those contract disputes where parties disagree about who is breaching —and when and where. Plus, a place-of-breach rule would allow the breaching party to decide what law applies. ("Dear Pal, I'm writing this postcard from the beach in Cancun where I just breached our contract. After some research, I decided to take my vacation here because our contract is void and unenforceable under the law of Mexico. Wish you were here.")

Most important, parties hope most contracts won't be breached: they want to honor them. It is important for the parties to know their rights and obligations prior to any breach. In a contract with connections to more than one jurisdiction, the parties need to know in advance what law will govern their contract.

GENERAL RULE: PLACE OF CONTRACTING

Law of the Place of Contracting — Except When It Isn't For most issues, the traditional territorial approach to contracts applied the law of the place of contracting (*lex loci contractus*). This is the place where the contract was made. But traditional jurisdictions differed in how they applied this rule.

And some of them adopted different rules, and selected instead the law of the place of performance or the law of the place that would validate the contract.

The First Restatement of Conflicts applies the law of the place of contracting to most issues, but it applies the law of the place of performance to matters of performance. The First Restatement rules were motivated by the goal of enforcing the vested rights that parties acquired in a contract under the law that applied to the contract when they entered into it. It gave overwhelming preference to the law of the place in which the parties were located at the time they entered into the contract.

In contrast to the First Restatement, some traditional jurisdictions had appreciated the special need in contracts cases to enforce parties' expectations, including expectations about what law would apply. This created tensions when the parties were physically present in one jurisdiction but expected the law of some other jurisdiction to apply. The most obvious example is a contract signed in state X that selects the law of state Y to govern the contract. Under the First Restatement, such a choice of law would be invalid, because the First Restatement rules were not designed to fulfill the parties' intentions but to apply the law that vested in a particular place.

The Big Picture   The big picture shows much confusion in the traditional contracts rules. Back in the days of the First Restatement, Conflicts gurus saw contracts as the biggest area of confusion. In order to understand the traditional approach, you need to understand both the First Restatement rules (and their problems) and the traditional alternative rules. Whenever jurisdictions were applying different rules, the glorious dream of uniformity of result was frustrated.

FIRST RESTATEMENT: PLACE OF CONTRACTING

Place of Contracting Governs Almost Everything   All issues except the manner of performance and damages are governed by the place of contracting. Issues governed by the law of the place of contracting include capacity to make a contract, validity of the contract, need for and sufficiency of consideration, formalities required, extent of obligations, and defenses. First Restatement §§333, 334, 339, 340 & 346.

The place of contracting is a technical term that means the place where the contract became binding on the parties—or would have become binding if it were not invalidated by the law of the place of contracting. Usually, this is where the parties made or executed the contract, but following your heart instead of the picky rules can land you in a heap of trouble. The First Restatement explains that the forum decides what the place of contracting is.

In doing so, the forum should not apply forum contract rules. Rather, the forum should apply general common law rules for contracts to select the place "where the principal event necessary to make a contract occurs." *Id.* §311 cmt. d.

Review of 1L Ks A quick review of first-year Contracts will yield most of the rules you need to determine the place of the contract. At some point negotiations end and an agreement becomes a contract. The place where that occurs is the place of contracting. That point depends on the kind of contract and the form of the offer and acceptance. Minor changes can affect who makes the offer and when and where it is accepted. For example, Nancy may say to Bess, "I'll give you a ride in my blue roadster if you get permission." Bess may accept. Or she may respond, "Gee, I don't know if I can get George to agree, but if I can, will you give me a ride?" And Nancy may say "sure."

Fixing the right place of contracting was so important that even though it was supposedly selected by general common law principles, the First Restatement published 20 specific rules for different kinds of contracts. For an offer that is accepted by an act or that becomes binding upon the occurrence of an event, the place of contracting is the place where the event occurs that makes the promise binding. *Id.* §323. For example, a customer in state X sends an order to Sears for one wagon wheel. Sears ships the wheel from its warehouse in state Y. The law of state Y applies to the customer's obligation to pay.

For offers that invite acceptance by a promise, the place of contracting is where the second promise is made. *Id.* §325. For example, Roy offers to buy Gene's pony for $10 and says the offer is good for a week. The next day, Gene sees Roy at the corral and says, "Agreed." *See id.* §325 illus. 1. When the acceptance is sent by U.S. mail or common carrier (UPS, FedEx), the place of contracting is the jurisdiction from which it is sent. When sent by an agent, the place of contracting is the place where the agent delivers the acceptance. *Id.* §326. For checks and promissory notes, the place of contracting is the place of delivery. *Id.* §312.

Nonevents are hard to localize since they happen—or rather don't happen—everywhere. The First Restatement has a special rule for those unusual situations where offers become accepted by a party's silence or inaction, applying the law of the place of the acceptor's regular place of business, if there is one, or of the acceptor's residence. *Id.* §327.

FIRST RESTATEMENT: PLACE OF PERFORMANCE

The place of contracting governs most things. The big exceptions are the manner of performance and the measure of damages. These are governed by the law of the place of performance. The First Restatement distinguishes between the obligation to perform (governed by the place of contracting) and the sufficiency of performance (governed by place of performance).

The place of performance is sometimes fixed by agreement. For example, Waldo may be obligated to tender payment under a promissory note at the Bunkley office of the Big Bank of Bunkley on April 1, 2013. The place of performance is where the bank is located. But sometimes the place of performance is not known until a party performs. Grandfather offers grandson Waldo $1 million if he marries before the age of 35. The place is not specified. *See id.* §355 cmt. a.

The First Restatement specifies that the law of the place of performance applies to the manner of performance, time and locality of performance, persons who may or must perform, sufficiency of performance, and excuse for nonperformance. *Id.* §358. A party is not obligated to perform an act that is illegal under the law of the place of performance as long as it remains illegal. *Id.* §360. More specifically, the law of the place of performance determines details of manner of performance, when performance is due, the form of payment required, the "exact spot for performance," whether breach has occurred, the right to damages, and the measure of damages, *id.* §§361-372. (Caps on damages are considered in Chapter 13.)

The performance exception can threaten to swallow the place of contracting rule. The First Restatement recognized this problem and insisted that the place of performance applied only to "manner and sufficiency and conditions" of performance, not to the "substantial obligation" of the parties to perform. *Id.* §358 cmt. b. But at the same time it recognized that there was no clear, logical way of distinguishing between matters of substantial obligation and matters of sufficiency of performance. And it is hard to see why the right to and measure of damages is governed by the law of the place of performance while a limitation of liability is governed by the law of the place of contracting. *Id.* §§338 & 372.

There is a special rule for liquidated damages. The validity of a liquidated damages provision is governed by the law of the place of contracting; but even if valid there, its enforcement will be governed by forum law elsewhere. *Id.* §422.

ALTERNATIVE TRADITIONAL RULES IN CONTRACTS

Two cases illustrate the variety of approaches courts traditionally employed in resolving contracts cases. These approaches shared a commitment to applying the law of some territory with a significant connection to the contract, and they sought to elaborate rules. But they arrived at rules that differed from those in the First Restatement, and the differences affected the outcomes of cases.

Place of Law That Validates   In Pritchard v. Norton, 106 U.S. 124 (1882), a Louisiana resident executed a bond in Louisiana in connection with litigation there. A New York resident promised to indemnify the Louisiana resident for any loss. The indemnity agreement was made in New York. Under New York law the agreement was not legally binding because there was no consideration, but under the law of Louisiana it was enforceable.

Under the First Restatement rules, the place of contracting would be New York, and the contract would be unenforceable. But rather than applying the law of the place of contract formation, the Supreme Court announced the general principle that a contract is governed by the law "with a view to which it was made." The Court concluded that the parties must have intended for the contract to be performed under Louisiana law because it would be unreasonable to assume they intended to apply the law of New York, because New York law would invalidate their agreement.

The Supreme Court's approach was motivated not by a theory of vested rights but by the goal of effectuating the intent of the parties. The result was to apply the law that validated the contract — in this case, the law of the place of performance.

Place of Performance (for All Issues)   Justice Story's 1834 treatise directed courts to apply the law of the place where a contract was executed. The place of execution was the place where a contract was formed unless the contract was to be performed in another place, and then that place was the place of execution.

Many courts continued to follow this approach. For example, in Poole v. Perkins, 101 S.E. 240 (Va. 1919), a wife domiciled in Tennessee delivered a promissory note in Tennessee that was payable in Virginia. Under Tennessee law she had a defense of coverture to the note because she was married. Under the law of Virginia, she had capacity and the note was enforceable.

The First Restatement would apply the law of the place of contract formation (Tennessee). But the Virginia court adopted the rule that applies the law of the place where a contract is made unless it is to be performed in another place, in which case it applies the law of that place. (In *Poole* the place of performance was Virginia, where the note was payable.) The rule proposed by Justice Story and followed in Virginia really means that the law of the place of performance governs all issues. When the rules of the place of contracting and performance are the same, the court applies the common rule, which is also the place of performance, and when the laws differ the court always goes with the law of the place of performance. The Virginia court reasoned that this rule was superior because it implements the intention of the parties, which is the "true criterion."

STATUS

As many as ten states still follow the traditional approach to choice of law in contracts. But these rules are modified for contracts governed by the Uniform Commercial Code (UCC) (Chapter 22).

Examples

Sibling Rivalry

1. Joe and Frank are two brothers who are both citizens of Ur. While on an adventure in the country of Mazukaland, Joe offered to buy his older brother Frank's inheritance for some bread and lentils. Frank was starving and quickly agreed. Frank later changed his mind. Joe litigates back home in the country of Ur. Under the law in force in Ur, a promise induced by an offer of food to a starving person is unenforceable as unconscionable. Under the law in force where Frank accepted Joe's offer, the sale is enforceable. What law applies under the First Restatement?

2. Same facts, but assume instead that under the law of Mazukaland, a contract for more than $200 is not valid unless it is sealed with a kiss. The inheritance is worth more than $200. The parties did not seal the agreement with a kiss. What law applies under the First Restatement?

3. Same facts. Under the law of Mazukaland, the total amount of damages recoverable for a breach of contract for the sale of an inheritance is $5,000. Ur permits recovery of damages measured by the value of the inheritance. The inheritance is conservatively valued at $1 million. What law does the First Restatement choose?

Friendly Wager

4. Morphy and Capablanca are playing a chess match in the country of Chekhovia. Two chess fans, Able and Baker, are watching the exciting match on cable television while on vacation in the country of Gambolia. Able turns to Baker and says, "I'll give you $20 if Morphy wins." Baker says, "Agreed." The two shake hands. Morphy wins.

   Able and Baker return to their homes in the state of West Carolina. Able refuses to pay. The promise was enforceable under the contract law of Gambolia and Chekhovia, but it was unenforceable for lack of consideration under the contract law of West Carolina. If West Carolina follows the First Restatement, what law would its courts apply?

5. Same facts. Gambling contracts are illegal under the law of West Carolina, and payment on such contracts is a misdemeanor in that state. What result?

Land Sakes

6. While eating lunch in the state of East Dakota, Ohner and Beier discuss various land deals. Ohner has recently inherited some real estate in the country of Teutonia. Beier offers to buy it for $1,000. Ohner agrees and the two shake hands.

    Under the law of East Dakota, contracts for the sale of land must be in writing and signed by the parties in order to be valid. Under the law of Teutonia, oral land sale agreements are valid and enforceable. What law applies under the First Restatement? What law applies under some of the alternative traditional rules?

7. Same facts. Ohner did not disclose that the property in Teutonia contains an industrial waste site. Under the law of Teutonia a party has an obligation to disclose the presence of industrial waste sites on real estate, and the failure to do so makes the contract unenforceable. East Dakota follows the principle of caveat emptor and imposes no duty to disclose. What law applies under the First Restatement?

Moving Daze

8. Shaker, a citizen of the country of Klingon, accepts a great job offer and decides to move to the country of Upper Vulca. She enters into a written agreement with Glacto Movers to move her property to Upper Vulca. She then travels to Upper Vulca and waits for the delivery of her property.

    Two weeks later, the Glacto Movers ship arrives. The mover's agent refuses to unload Shaker's property until Shaker gives him a certified check. Shaker refuses to deliver a certified check until the property has been delivered.

    Shaker has reached you on your cell phone. You have determined that under the law of Klingon, a party does not need to tender payment until the completion of a contract for services. Under the law of Upper Vulca, payment is due on a moving contract prior to unloading the property. The countries both follow the First Restatement. Please advise Shaker.

Coverture Confusion

9. Mr. and Mrs. Pratt lived in Massachusetts. Mr. Pratt wanted to buy some goods from Milliken in Maine. Milliken insisted that Mrs. Pratt guarantee payment of her husband's debts, so Mrs. Pratt mailed a written promise to pay her husband's debts from Massachusetts to Milliken in Maine.

    After receiving the guarantee, Milliken sent the goods. When Mr. Pratt defaulted, Milliken sued Mrs. Pratt on her guarantee. She raised the defense of coverture. Under this defense a married woman lacked capacity to guarantee her husband's obligations. Massachusetts recognized the defense, but Maine did not. What law would apply under the First Restatement?

Unfair $1 Million Question

10. Sam and Honey lived together as husband and wife in the state of Glitterland. One day when Sam was taking a flight from Zublon, he bought a $1 million accidental death insurance policy from Bigg Insurance Corp. He bought the policy from an agent at the Zublon airport. He filled out the form in Zublon, designating "my wife" as the beneficiary in the event of his death. He paid cash in Zublon.

    Sam died when his plane crashed into the ocean.

    Sam believed he was married when he filled out the form, and he meant to designate Honey as his beneficiary. However, it turns out that Sam and Honey were not validly married, so she was not legally his wife.

    Under the law of Glitterland, the words "my wife" are given their intended effect, and Honey is a beneficiary of the policy. In contrast, under the law of Zublon, Honey is not a beneficiary because she was not legally Sam's wife.

    Under the First Restatement, does Honey get the money?

Explanations

Sibling Rivalry

1. The place of contracting is Mazukaland, where Frank accepted Joe's offer to sell the inheritance and where the sale was completed. The law of the place of contracting governs validity and extent of contractual obligations. Id. §§332 & 346. Accordingly, the contract is enforceable under the law of Mazukaland.

    Under the First Restatement, a forum will not disregard the law of the place of contracting just because the contract would be unenforceable under forum law. But if the cause of action for breach of contract violates a strong public policy of the forum, then the forum may refuse to entertain the action under the public policy escape device (Chapter 15).

2. Sealing with a kiss is a formality required for a valid contract. Formalities are governed by the law of the place of contracting, so the contract is unenforceable.

    The most common formality problem was presented by statutes of frauds, which require certain contracts to be in writing and signed. Some jurisdictions interpreted their statute of frauds requirement as a formal condition for a valid contract. Others interpreted their statute of frauds as a rule of evidence. For example, in a case where a defendant testifies in court that there was an oral contract, the contract will not be enforceable if the statute of frauds is a requirement for a valid contract. But the contract will be enforceable if the statute is only a rule of evidence, since the defendant's testimony provides the necessary evidence.

Under the First Restatement if the statute of frauds at the place of contracting was a formal requirement for a valid contract, then that formal requirement governed. In contrast, a purely evidentiary rule at the place of contracting would not be binding because forums used their own procedural rules of evidence (Chapter 13).

3. The First Restatement applies the place of performance to the measure of damages, id. §§372, 413. The Restatement reasons that because the place of performance governs the manner of performance, its law should determine the consequences for breach. Id. §413 cmt. a. The problem then becomes whether the place of performance is the place of the delivery of the purchased item or the place of payment (surrender of the inheritance). The First Restatement's illustrations indicate that the place of performance is the place of the particular performance that is in issue — the delivery of the inheritance. That was presumably to occur in the country of Ur, where the parties were domiciled, so damages would not be limited. I don't know what would happen under the First Restatement if Frank cleverly maneuvered his brother into visiting Mazukaland and tendered him $5,000 there.

Friendly Wager

4. The First Restatement specifies that whether consideration is required, and, if so, whether it has been given, is governed by the law of the place of contracting. Id. §339. The First Restatement also indicates that the place of contracting for a gratuitous promise is where the promise was made. See id. §339 illus. 1 & 2. Under these rules, Gambolia's law would apply, and Able's promise would be enforceable.

The above answer is correct and gets full points, but the example illustrates some of the areas of uncertainty under the First Restatement. First, applying the no-consideration rule of a jurisdiction is inconsistent with the general definition of the place of contracting, because under the general law of contracts (which requires consideration), the place where gratuitous promises are made is not a place where a contract arises. The specific rule resolves this problem, but it means that common law jurisdictions must enforce gratuitous promises. This would allow residents of a common law jurisdiction to make a gratuitous promise enforceable either by adding sufficient consideration (a peppercorn?) or by traveling to a jurisdiction that enforces gratuitous promises and making the promise there — or maybe even by appointing an agent in such a jurisdiction to make the promise for them there.

Second, there is uncertainty about the place of contracting in the case of a gratuitous promise where payment is contingent on the occurrence of some event. While the First Restatement illustrations pick the place of the promise, such a promise seems also to qualify as an "informal unilateral contract" for which the place of contracting is "where the event takes place which makes the promise binding." Id. §323. For example, where a reward is offered for apprehending a felon, the place of contracting is where the felon is arrested, not where the offer was made. Id. §323 illus. 1. The First Restatement seems to provide conflicting answers: the place of contracting might be either Gambolia or Chekhovia. By a fortuitous circumstance, in this example their laws are the same.

5. Again there is a short right answer—and a longer editorial digression. The short right answer is that the contract (probably) envisaged payment to occur in the parties' home state of West Carolina, thereby making it the place of performance. Under the First Restatement, the place of performance law governs illegality, and there is no obligation to perform so long as the performance is illegal in the place of performance. Id. §360(1).

There is wiggle room, however, for reinterpreting a contract's place of performance to include alternative places where the performance is legal. The First Restatement specifically provides that when the performance is illegal temporarily, there may be a duty to perform as soon as the prohibition is removed. Id. §360(2). It is unclear why there might not also be an obligation to perform at a place where the performance is permitted (but not required).

Land Sakes

6. This example makes the important point that in the First Restatement land sale contracts are governed by the contract rules, not the property rules. Accordingly, the law of the place of contracting (where the offer is accepted) governs the issue of formalities, and the contract must be in writing under East Dakota law. See First Restatement §340 ("law of the place of contracting determines the validity of a promise to transfer or to convey land").

This is the easy and right result under the First Restatement. But it is debatable whether the First Restatement was accurate in its "restatement" of traditional rules for land sale contracts. There was some authority that the law of the place of the land governed the "forms and solemnities" required for a contract to transfer land. See Joseph Story, Conflict of Laws §372e at 630 (3d ed. 1846).

Consider the case where a handshake satisfied the formal requirements for a land sale at the place of the handshake but not where the land was located. In principle, the First Restatement seems to require all jurisdictions, including the law of the place where the land is located, to recognize the handshake. While the handshake did not "convey" land, we all remember from 1L Contracts that the contract is specifically enforceable. The First Restatement rules seem to allow parties to escape the formal requirements imposed by the law of the place where the land is located, and it is questionable how far traditional courts would have followed the logic of the Conflicts contract rule over the logic of territorial sovereignty.[1]

In our example, for both traditional alternatives (the law of the place of performance and the law of the place that validates the party's contract), a court would apply the law of Teutonia. The place of performance would be Teutonia, where the land was located, since that is where the transfer would have to take place. Teutonia law validates the contract, since it does not require that it be written. Of course, traditional jurisdictions applying the law of the place of the land would also apply Teutonia law.

7. The law of the place of contracting governs the extent of party obligations and whether a promise is void or voidable on any grounds. Id. §347. This makes it sound like Beier is stuck with the hazardous waste site. But the right to damages and measure of damages is governed by the law of the place of performance. Id. §372. And if Teutonia law does not provide a recovery for a breach of contracts that do not disclose the defects, then Beier may not be stuck.

Moving Daze

8. Upper Vulca's law applies as the law of the place of performance. The law of the place of performance determines the manner of performance and the time when performance is due. Id. §§361-362. So Shaker must pay first.

Coverture Confusion

9. The facts are borrowed from a famous case, Milliken v. Pratt, 125 Mass. 374 (1878). The case predated the First Restatement but was resolved under similar rule-like logic. The court held that the issue of capacity was governed by the law of the place of contracting, and it determined that the place of contracting was Maine, where the seller received the guaranty and acted on it. Accordingly, the wife had capacity to execute the guaranty.

---

1. Professor Deborah Challener inspired this longer explanation. She was not happy with a short explanation that just gave the First Restatement rule. For good reason.

If you applied the mailbox rule, you get points for remembering that rule but lose points for forgetting that it applies only to those acts that when done in person would have given rise to the contract. If the seller had offered to sell if the buyer promised to pay and provided his wife's guaranty, then the letter accepting and enclosing the guaranty would make the contract binding. And the place of contracting would be the place where it was mailed—Massachusetts. In this case the court reasoned (consistent with most sale situations) that the preliminary negotiations were really a solicitation and that the buyer and his wife made an offer that was accepted by the seller when it shipped the goods.

Unfair $1 Million Question

10. The example is totally unfair. Totally. That is because the rules discussed so far give no clear answer. In fact, the First Restatement offers no formal rules that address conflicts in contract interpretation or construction.

    This gap is surprising because such problems are common. Similar conflicts would arise if the plane was shot down by a hunter and the two jurisdictions differed in whether the resulting death was accidental. The gap is also surprising because the First Restatement provides so many detailed rules for resolving conflicts among rules for construing language in instruments of conveyance (deeds, wills).

    The "right" answer emerges only from passages in the comments in the First Restatement. The drafters thought that problems of interpreting and construing contract language were problems of contract law, not conflicts problems. *See id.* §361 cmt. a. They thought such problems should be resolved by applying the law of the forum. This approach may make sense, but it is not fully explained. It is not consistent with the philosophy of the First Restatement, because the beneficiary's rights that "vested" under the law of the place of contracting are not respected by other courts. And applying forum law is not consistent with some of the other First Restatement rules that govern the construction of language in conveyances.

Property

8

NAME GAME

Under the traditional approach, contracts and torts involving property were governed by the choice of law rules for contracts and torts. Separate rules applied to conflicts involving the existence of interests in property. This meant a contract to sell land would be governed by the contract rules, but a deed of land would be governed by property rules.

Moreover, different rules applied to property conflicts, depending on whether the issue involved land, personal property, trusts, or wills. This chapter covers the basic rules for property transfers during the owner's life. Chapter 9 considers transfers at death and trusts.

Terminology The First Restatement tried to systematize the traditional rules for property. For some reason, it adopted civil law terminology. It calls land or real property "immovable" property.[1] It calls personal property "movable" property. This terminology has been followed by the Second Restatement and by some treatises. These labels can be confusing because personal property includes tangible things that move, but it also includes intangible things (like copyright) that can't move since they don't occupy space. Just remember: land or real property is immovable, and everything else is movable.

---

1. The First Restatement was behind the times in thinking even land was immovable. *See generally* Copernicus and Galileo.

LAND RULES

Almost all issues involving land are governed by the law of the place where the land is. This place is sometimes called the situs. This place's law determines whether the property is real property or personal property. It governs a person's capacity to own and convey, the interests created in land, and the formalities required for conveying title. First Restatement §§215-222.

The First Restatement recognizes only one exception to applying the law of the place where the land is located.[2] When there is ambiguous language in a legal conveyance and the actual intention cannot be determined, then the law of the person's domicile provides the rules for construing the meaning of the language. Id. §214(3).[3] When words have a fixed legal effect regardless of intent under the law of the place where the land is located, then the effect is governed by the law where the land is. For example, if the conveyance "To A and the heirs of A's body" creates a fee tail under the law where the land is, then it is given that effect even if the person meant to convey something else and was domiciled in a place that honored his or her intent.

Examples

Slip Sliding Away

1. Gail Grantor lived in a house she owned in the state of Fixation. She was tired of her microwave oven sliding on her counter top, so she attached it to the wall with one screw. She then went to the state of Konveyanz where she executed a deed to her house to Bob Buyer, a citizen of Konveyanz. Under the law of Fixation, the microwave has become a "fixture," which means it is part of the real estate. Under the law of Konveyanz, the microwave is not a fixture but remains personal property. Does the deed convey the microwave?

---

2. Okay, let's get technical. There is another exception probably no one ever noticed where the First Restatement refers to its own definitions of legitimacy rather than to the law of the place of the land. First Restatement §246.

3. The formal rule looks like it applies to all matters of intent. Commentary clarifies that forum law applies to determine actual intent, when it can be determined. The formal rule is a gap-filler when actual intent is unknown. The idea is to apply the rules of construction of the law of the domicile at the time the conveyance was made. In theory, the time of conveyance could differ significantly from the time of the drafting. Comments explain that the canon of interpretation is based on the probability that a person uses language in accordance with the place of domicile. On this theory, you should look to the law of the person's domicile at the time he or she used the language.

One Good Deed

2. Child Harold inherited his family's estates in the country of Hassam. While visiting Etruria, he became ill and thought he was dying. He wanted to convey all his property to his girlfriend, Mol Flanders, so he grabbed a piece of paper and wrote, "I give all my land to Mol." He signed it and gave it to Ms. Flanders.

   Harold is 14. Under the law of Hassam, a 14-year-old has capacity to convey land. Under the law of Etruria, a 14-year-old lacks capacity to transfer an interest in land. What law applies?

3. The document signed in Etruria satisfies all the formalities required by the law of Etruria for legal transfer of title to land. Under the law of Hassam, where the land is located, the paper is not legally sufficient because it does not employ specific words of conveyance, does not designate the interest conveyed, and does not designate the property with sufficient particularity. Is it a good deed?

Policy Concerns

4. Jenna owned land in the country of New Hibernia. She executed a deed in East Dakota that purported to convey the land to Patrick, and she delivered the deed to Patrick in East Dakota. Under the law of New Hibernia, a deed becomes effective when it has been delivered. Under New Hibernia law, Patrick is not able to own land in New Hibernia because he is of Irish descent. East Dakota's state constitution prohibits restrictions on property ownership based on race, ethnicity, and national origin. Is the conveyance valid under the First Restatement?

Contracts vs. Conveyances

5. Jack and Jill take a vacation in the country of Arugula. There Jill offers to give Jack her estate in the state of South Virginia if he will marry her. Jack agrees and they reduce the agreement to writing and sign it. The agreement fully satisfies all the formal requirements for a valid land sale contract under the law of South Virginia. Under Arugula law, however, promises made in exchange for promises of marriage are void as contrary to public policy. Does Jack get the land if he ties the knot or not?

"The Rule" Rules

6. Crusty Gramps delivered a deed that conveyed "all my property to my grandchildren for life, each grandchild's share to be divided at his or her death among his children then living to hold for life, with each great grandchild's interest to be divided at death among any of his or her children then living named 'Crusty.'"

Crusty owned three pieces of land: Homeacre in Homeland, Blackacre in the country of Blackland, and Whiteacre in the country of Whiteland.

Under the law of Homeland all the future interests conveyed to grandchildren are valid. Both Blackland and Whiteland follow the rule against perpetuities—affectionately known as "the Rule." Under the Rule, an interest must vest or fail to vest within 21 years of a life in being at the creation of the interest. The Rule applies to contingent future interests like the life estates and remainders in Gramps's deed. Under the rule, the conveyance to the children and the grandchildren is valid, because the interests will vest or fail to vest within the lifetime of the grandchildren who are living at the time of the creation of the interests.

Both Blackland and Whiteland recognize a rule violation with respect to the intended conveyance to the great grandchildren. These interests will not necessarily vest within 21 years of any life in being at the time of the conveyance.

Under the law of Blackland, in such a case the grandchild's interest will vest in fee simple. Under the law of Whiteland, the grandchild will take only a life estate. There Gramps has a reversion that follows the life estate.

Who gets what where?

PERSONAL PROPERTY RULES

For personal property (movables), the First Restatement applied the law of the place where the personal property was located for most issues involving transfers during the owner's life.[4]

This rule seemed to respect the rights that "vested" in the thing under the law where the thing was located when the rights were created. The rule looks like it will be easy to apply and seems to promise uniform results. But there are problems. First, movables can be easily moved. Second, some movables (like copyrights) do not have an obvious location. The First Restatement sought to provide greater certainty with specific rules for certain kinds of personal property.

---

4. There was some early authority for applying the law of the place of the party's domicile to personal property. There was an ancient maxim that personal property followed the person (*mobilia sequuntur personam*). Joseph Story approved of the rule in his treatise on Conflicts. Some jurisdictions applied the rule, at least to trusts, and you may see references to it. But under the First Restatement it was displaced by the law of the place where the property was located.

Transfer of Title For property interests bound up in a document (like a car title), whether the title became embodied in the document is governed by the law where the thing was at the time the document was issued. Once the title becomes embodied in a document, the validity of conveyances is governed by the law of the place where the document is. *Id.* §261.

Intangibles, Miscellaneous Other Most personal property is not chattel property. For example, property-like rights to receipt of money (which can be bought and sold), shares of stock, interests in trusts, rights to recovery on a lawsuit, patents, and copyright all fall under the miscellaneous-other category of intangible property.

The First Restatement did a poor job of crafting rules for most of the property in the world. It divided all such property into intangible property that "exists in fact apart from law" and intangible property that arises purely by operation of law. For example, intangible property created in fact is the so-called goodwill of a business. The creation of such property is governed by the law of the place where the property exists. *Id.* §212. (I don't know where that is either.) An example of intangible property created by operation of law would be the property-like rights arising from a contract. Such rights are "governed by the law which created the original intangible thing and interest therein." *Id.* §213.[5]

Once created, intangible property is subject to the general rules governing chattel property. *Id.* §212 cmt. b. There are huge gaps here. Even if it's clear what law originally created property rights in a business's goodwill, it is not clear where that property is, especially if the business moves.

Security Interests Many of the First Restatement rules for movables dealt with different kinds of security interests. In general, the validity and extent of such interests were governed by the law of the place where the thing was when the interests were created, and all jurisdictions were required to recognize the interests. When secured property was moved into another state with the consent of the secured party, the second state's law could apply to alter the rights in the property. *See, e.g., id.* §270. These detailed provisions anticipate some of the rules in the UCC.

Marital Property The rights married persons acquire in each other's individual property are governed by the marital domicile. This means that property held as community property remains community property even if it is moved into a noncommunity property state—and vice versa. *Id.* §§292-293.

---

5. I don't understand this either. I guess it's usually the place of contracting.

Fast Forward: Fate of the First Restatement Property Rules

The First Restatement's land rules are still largely followed today. Personal property rules have been modified. Conflicts concerning liens and other secured interests in personal property are now regulated by specific choice of law rules in the UCC that govern the effect in multiple jurisdictions of the creation and perfection of security interests and the movement of secured property from one state to another.[6] For cases not covered by statute, courts following modern approaches to choice of law will often look to the law of the parties' domicile rather than the place where the personal property was located.

Examples

The Gifted Grifter

7. Flem Snopes agreed to give Bub Varner four ponies. The transaction took place in the state of East Carolina. Snopes signed a written deed to the horses and delivered it to Varner in East Carolina. At the time of the agreement and delivery of the deed, the ponies were located in West Carolina. Before Varner took possession of the ponies, Snopes gave them to Bayard.

    Varner sues Bayard in an action for conversion asserting his ownership of the ponies. Under the law of East Carolina, delivery of a written deed of conveyance passes title to personal property described in it. Under the law of West Carolina, title to personal property passes upon delivery. What law applies under the First Restatement?

Who Gets the Ring?

8. Loveless and Clarissa were domiciled in the country of Brutalica. Loveless took Clarissa to the country of Romanzia, where he gave her a diamond ring and promised to marry her. Clarissa accepted breathlessly. After they returned to Brutalica, Loveless got drunk and assaulted Clarissa. As a result, she refused to marry him. He demands the return of the ring. Under the law of Romanzia, an engagement ring is an unconditional gift. Under the law of Brutalica, an engagement ring is a conditional gift that conveys good title but the legal title returns to the donor upon the donee's refusal to marry. Who is entitled to the ring under the First Restatement?

---

6. The rules are complex, with different provisions for different classes of property and parties. They have also been repeatedly amended. *See* Hay et al., Conflict of Laws §§19.17-19.25 at 1226-1235, Weintraub, Commentary on the Conflict of Laws §§8.27-8.34 at 635-651.

Explanations

Slip Sliding Away

1. The deed conveys the microwave. Whether something is land—immovable property in the language of the First Restatement—is determined by the law of the place where the land is. *See* First Restatement §208 illus. 1.

One Good Deed

2. Capacity to convey is governed by the law of the place where the land is. For land in Hassam, the First Restatement directs all jurisdictions to apply Hassam law to the issue of capacity, and Harold has capacity to convey the land in Hassam. *Id.* §216.

   Note that if this was not a deed but a contract, capacity to contract for land is governed by the law of the place of contracting.

3. It is not a good deed. Formalities are governed by the law of the place where the land is, and the deed fails to satisfy Hassam's formal requirements for a valid deed. *Id.* §217.

Policy Concerns

4. Capacity to take or hold land is governed by the law of the place where the land is, not where the deed is delivered, so the conveyance to Patrick is invalid. First Restatement §219 & cmt. a. This example makes the obvious point that uniformity does not guarantee good results. On the contrary, applying the law of the place where the land is located guarantees uniformly bad results when that law is bad.

Contracts vs. Conveyances

5. The key to this question is distinguishing the question of the land sale contract's validity from property rights. The contract is governed by the law of the place of contracting—Arugula (where Jack accepted Jill's offer). Under the law of the place of contracting, the contract is void. Jack cannot enforce it, and it also will not give rise to any property rights.

"The Rule" Rules

6. This example is easier than it looks. The trick is to apply the rules of the place where each piece of land is located to that piece of land. The rule against perpetuities is a particular favorite of most law students and adds charm, but the solution is no different than if a more obvious legal difference existed with respect to the property rights created.

Under the law of Homeland, the remote future interests of great-great grandchildren named Crusty in Homeacre are valid. Under the law of Blackland and Whiteland, the remote interests of great-great grandchildren are invalid. Under Blackland's rule, the great grandchildren whose interests vest will take in fee simple, while in Whiteland, the great grandchildren whose interests vest will take a life estate.

In each jurisdiction, Crusty retains a reversion that follows all these interests (because they are contingent), and some of his reversionary interests will vest in possession. Of course, Crusty may die before the reversions vest, and the ownership of the reversionary interests will also be governed by the law of the place where the land is located. Absent a will, the reversions will pass according to the local inheritance laws of each jurisdiction. Conceivably, three different persons may inherit.

The Gifted Grifter

7. The validity of the conveyance and the interests created in the chattel are governed by the law of the place where the chattel is. Because the ponies were in West Carolina, that state's law governs, and Bayard is the owner.

    This is intended as an easy example. But it also illustrates the problem of wiggle room under the First Restatement rules. If, for example, a court characterizes the interest created under the conveyance in East Carolina as an intangible right, then that state's law applies. In that case, Bayard gets title to the chattel, but Varner gets a "chose in action" that may be enforced by obtaining the chattel. Similarly, equitable doctrines may be applied by one or more courts to establish an enforceable right to obtain possession from the title holder in possession. This would be the common law doctrine, for example, if Varner paid for the ponies and Bayard was not a bona fide purchaser for value.

Who Gets the Ring?

8. Clarissa gets the ring. The validity of a conveyance and the nature of interests conveyed are determined by the law of the place where the personal property is at the time of the conveyance. The ring was in Romanzia at the time of the gift, and under Romanzia law Clarissa obtained unconditional title. Her property interest is not altered by moving the property to another state. Id. §§258, 260.

Wills, Intestate Succession, and Trusts

ROAD MAP

Chapter 8 covered the traditional rules governing conflicts involving property transfers during the owner's life. This chapter covers the traditional approach to property transfers at death and to trusts.

WILLS AND INTESTATE SUCCESSION

There are two different kinds of property issues that arise at death. The first is: who gets immediate title to property and what are the duties with respect to the property? The second is: who ultimately gets the property when it is distributed?

Land

Under the traditional approach, both the immediate ownership and the ultimate distribution of land are governed by the law of the place where the land is located. The First Restatement added a few more precise rules.

The law of the place where the land is governs the succession of land at death. The validity, formalities, and rights to land devised by will are all governed by the law of the place where the land is. If there is no valid will, the inheritance of land is governed by the law of the place where the land is. The right to take a forced share is also governed by the law of the place where the land is.

The First Restatement recognizes one exception to the law of the place where the land is located. When language has a given legal effect regardless of the testator's intent (like the fee simple created by "to A and A's heirs"), then language is governed by the rules where the land is. But when the language is a question of intent and the person's intent cannot be determined, the First Restatement applies the rules of construction of the person's domicile at the time he or she made the will. First Restatement §251(3).

Personal Property

Administration At common law, the immediate legal ownership of a dead person's personal property passes to an executor (if there is a will) or to an administrator. This person has the duty to manage the estate's assets, is authorized to sell property in order to protect assets and pay creditors, and will eventually distribute the estate property as directed by the will or as required by law.

The First Restatement rules are incomplete but were designed to give legal title to personal property at death to the executor or administrator who gets possession. This would normally be the executor or administrator in the state where the property was located, and the rules sought to facilitate transfer of assets to this person.

Ultimate Ownership The law of the decedent's domicile at death governed most of the issues regarding transfers at death. If there is a will, the validity of a will of personal property is governed by the law of the place where the decedent died domiciled. *Id.* §306. The meaning of ambiguous words in a will or power of appointment is governed by the person's domicile at the time of the execution of the instrument. *Id.* §§285, 308.

The distribution of personal property outside a will, including the rights to a forced share or an allowance to a spouse pending distribution, is governed by the place where the decedent died domiciled. *Id.* §§301-303. When no person is entitled to distribution under the law of the state where the decedent died domiciled, the personal property escheats to the state in which the property is administered. *Id.* §§309-310.

Problems The traditional choice rules can result in different jurisdictions' laws governing different assets. For example, Ted Deadman died domiciled in the state of Propriety leaving personal property scattered around the world, land owned in fee simple in the country of Achufula, and a future interest in land in the country of Broccolia. Deadman executed a will that left all his property to Benny Fischer. The validity of the will for personal property is governed by the law of Propriety (where Deadman died domiciled), while the validity of the will for the land will be governed by the law of Achufula for the land there and by the law of Broccolia for the future interests in land in that country. The will might be valid for some of this property and not for others. If it is not valid, the intestate succession rules will be provided by three different jurisdictions.

Deadman's personal property would be distributed according to the rules of intestate succession of Propriety. His land in Achufula would be inherited according to Achufula law, and the land in Broccolia according to Broccolia law.

Will-Borrowing Statutes

The application of the rules can lead wills to be invalid even when the wills were executed in strict compliance with the law where they were executed, with the law of where the person was domiciled at the time of execution, and even with the law of every place where the person owned property at the time of executing the will.

For example, Tess Trix executed a holographic will that left all her property to her twin sister, Tracy Trix. She was domiciled in the country of Homeland at the time she executed the will, and it was valid under the law of her domicile. She later inherits land in a jurisdiction that does not recognize holographic wills. Her will is not valid with respect to the land. She then moves to another country that requires two witnesses for wills of personal property. Her will is now invalid for personal property.

To avoid invalidating wills in such situations, most U.S. states, England, and Canada have enacted "will-borrowing" statutes.[1] These statutes generally provide that a will is valid when it complies with the legal requirements of the place where executed or of the testator's domicile at the time of execution. Such statutes vary from jurisdiction to jurisdiction and may be strictly construed.

Examples

Landed Gentry

1. Luke and Lorelai got married and lived in Connecticut. One day Lorelai's rich parents gave her a vacation home in the country of El Dorado. Lorelai wanted to make sure Luke got the vacation home if she died.

---

1. *See* Hay et al., Conflict of Laws §20.6 at 1252 n.40.

She executed a will in Connecticut at her lawyer's office. The will specifically devised the vacation home to Luke. The will was properly witnessed and valid under the law of Connecticut. Under the land law of El Dorado, a will of real property must be notarized and filed with the Office of Circumlocution. Lorelai's will does not comply with the El Dorado requirements. Is the will valid with regard to the land in El Dorado?

Fun with Holographic Wills

2. To cut costs, John Dolittle decided to make his own will. He printed out some forms he found on the Internet. The forms contained general language for wills and left blanks that Dolittle filled in directing how he wanted his estate to be distributed. He signed the forms, but there were no witnesses.

In the language Dolittle inserted, he wrote, "I leave my house and property in East Dakota to Flipper and my vacation home in West Dakota to Molly. I give my bank account to Ben and my stamp collection to Sue. I leave all the rest residue and remainder to my best friend Bert." The bank account is in the country of Plutochia and the stamp collection is in East Dakota.

John filled in the blanks and signed the document while he was on vacation in West Dakota. He died domiciled in East Dakota.

Under the law of East Dakota, wills that are partly written by hand and partly printed are valid when the dispositive provisions are written by hand and when the wills are signed. Under the law of West Dakota no will is valid unless it is signed in the presence of two witnesses who also sign. Under the law of Plutochia, a holographic will is not valid unless it is written entirely in the handwriting of the person who signs.

In the absence of a valid will, Betty is the sole heir and next of kin who takes under the law of East Dakota, while Flipper is the sole heir and next of kin who takes under the law of West Dakota. Under the law of Plutochia, any property located in the country that does not pass under a valid will becomes the property of the Plutochia government.

Under the First Restatement, who gets what and why?

More Fun with Undue Influence and Mortmain

3. Mort died domiciled in the country of Marovia. He left a will, formally valid under the law of Marovia, that devised "all my real estate wheresoever situated" to the Church of Marovia and left "all my personal property to Phoebe." He left nothing for his wife Wilma, who lived in the country of Caledonia.

The will was executed four months before Mort died. At death he owned real property in Marovia and in Caledonia. Under the law of Marovia, a devise of real property to a charity or religious organization is void if death occurs within six months of the execution of the will. Caledonia has no restriction on religious and charitable devises or bequests.

Wilma challenges the bequest to Phoebe on the ground that Phoebe was Mort's hairdresser and exerted undue influence on him in persuading him to rewrite his will to include her as a beneficiary. The facts (too sordid to relate at length here) establish grounds for challenging the bequest to Phoebe under the law of Caledonia but not under the law of Marovia.

Under the First Restatement, who gets what and why?

4. Same facts. Mort also owned land in Hibernia that he had inherited prior to his death without knowing it. Under the law of Hibernia, there are no restrictions on religious or charitable devises, but a will in order to validly pass an interest in land must specifically mention and identify the land. The Church of Marovia claims a right to the land under the will, Sonny claims a right to the land as Mort's heir under the law of Hibernia, and Wilma claims a right as heir under the law of Marovia and Caledonia. Who gets the land in Hibernia under the First Restatement?

TRUSTS

Land

The validity of a trust of land and the equitable property interests created by a trust of land are governed by the law of the place where the land is. First Restatement §§239, 241. Administration of a trust of land is also governed by the law of the place where the land is. Id. §243.

Personal Property

The validity of an inter vivos trust in chattels is governed by the law of the place where the chattel is. Id. §294(1). This means that different laws can govern each piece of chattel property, and the trust may be valid with respect to some of the property and invalid with respect to other parts of the property. The validity of trusts in "choses in action"—and presumably all other forms of intangible personal property not covered by the rule for chattels—is governed by the law of the place where the transaction takes place establishing the equitable interest. This is the place where the trust is created or where the trust results from other conduct. Id. §294(2).

The validity of a testamentary trust of personal property is governed by the law of the place where the decedent died domiciled. *Id.* §295.

Issues involving the administration of trusts of personal property are generally governed by the law of the place the settlor (the person who created the trust) intended the trust to be administered. Thus administration of inter vivos trusts of personal property is governed by the law of the place where the settlor located the administration of the trust. *Id.* §297. Administration of testamentary trusts of personal property is normally governed by the law of the place the testator died domiciled, but administration will be governed by another jurisdiction's law when the will shows an intention for the trust to be administered in that place. *Id.* §298.

The meaning of language in a trust of personal property is governed by the law of the place where the settlor was domiciled at the time he or she used the words. *Id.* §296.

Current Status

The traditional rules of the First Restatement for wills still provide the background law that applies in many jurisdictions in the absence of borrowing statutes. But many jurisdictions today will also enforce express choice of law provisions in a will.

The First Restatement trust rules were always incomplete and inadequate. Given that most of the wealth of the country is owned in the form of equitable interests, this was a huge lapse. In theory the First Restatement required a single trust to be governed by multiple laws. But applying all the different laws where land or different items of personal property were located leads to confusion and frustrates the intentions of the settlor.

The First Restatement provides little guidance on common problems. For example, it is not clear where the corpus of a trust in intangibles is located or how to distinguish issues of substance and administration. The First Restatement has little to say about what law governs a trust that results under operation of law rather than from a consensual transaction.

Today few if any courts follow the trust rules in the First Restatement. (They probably never did.) Instead courts defer to law chosen by the settlor when there is a choice of law provision in the trust. Cases also demonstrate a preference for applying law that validates a trust—which may be the law of the location of trust assets, the law of the domicile of the settlor or beneficiaries, or the law of the place of administration.[2]

---

2. *Id.* §20.7 at 1255. For arguments against validating a trust when doing so violates important policies of the home states of the interested parties, *see* Weintraub, Commentary on the Conflict of Laws §825 at 632.

Examples

Land Deal

5. Khan lived in Lalaland. One day before going tiger hunting, Khan executed and delivered a deed to Raj. The deed was for real estate located in the land of Nod. When Khan delivered the deed, he explained that he wanted Raj to hold the deed in trust in case Khan did not return. If he did not return, he instructed Raj to hold the property safely and deliver it to the first of Khan's children who reached the age of 21.

   Lalaland does not have a statute of frauds, and an oral trust for land is valid so long as legal title to the land is effectively transferred by a written instrument. Under the law of Nod, a trust regarding the use and disposition of land must be in writing.

   Khan is never seen again. Is the trust valid under the First Restatement?

Special Delivery

6. During a period of civil war in the country of Dischordia, Felix sent Snoop a valuable coin. Felix sent the coin from Dischordia by special delivery courier service, and Snoop received it in the country of Harmonia. By emails sent after the coin arrived, Felix directed Snoop to hold the coin in his safe deposit box, to sell it at any time when he thought the price was good, and to return the coin or the proceeds of the sale to Felix when Felix asked for its return. If Felix died, Snoop was to hold the property or its proceeds until peace was restored, and then he was to deliver the property or its proceeds to Felix's closest living relatives, who were surviving and living in Dischordia.

   Snoop agreed by email, but neither he nor Felix ever signed a formal writing that set forth the terms of the trust agreement. Under the law of Dischordia, a trust of personal property does not require a signed writing. Under the law of Harmonia, a trust of personal property requires a signed writing. Is the trust valid under the First Restatement?

7. Felix died six months later. He left a signed handwritten note: "The coin Snoop is holding should be sold. The proceeds should be invested for ten years. Then the proceeds should be distributed to my children and grandchildren then alive." Dischordia recognizes the note as a valid holographic will. The note is not a valid will under the law of Harmonia. Does the note establish a valid trust that is good under the First Restatement?

8. Snoop buys the coin from the trust for half its market value and invests the proceeds in mutual funds. The relatives of Felix sue for breach of fiduciary duties and demand that Snoop turn over all assets to them immediately.

Under the law of Dischordia a trustee may not buy assets of the trust, but under the law of Harmonia, a trustee may buy trust assets if the trustee pays a fair price. Under the law of Dischordia, investment in mutual funds is not permitted unless expressly authorized by the settlor. Under the law of Harmonia, investment in mutual funds is permitted. Under the law of Dischordia, a trust must be terminated when all the persons who are presently identifiable as entitled to an interest, even a future interest, join in demanding the termination. Under the law of Harmonia, a trust terminates only when the terms of the trust have been fulfilled. A trustee who terminates prematurely is liable to future beneficiaries. What law governs these issues under the First Restatement?

Explanations

Landed Gentry

1. The will will not be valid with regard to the land in El Dorado even though it will be valid for property in Connecticut. The validity of a will in land and its formal requirements are governed by the law of the place where the land is.

   Note that Connecticut cannot change the result here by adopting a will-borrowing statute. But the outcome would differ if El Dorado's will law included a borrowing statute that validated Lorelai's will.

Fun with Holographic Wills

2. The formal validity of the will of land in East Dakota is governed by East Dakota law and is valid, so Flipper gets that property. The validity of the will of land in West Dakota is governed by the law there where it is invalid, so the property passes to Flipper under the West Dakota laws of intestate succession.

   The personal property items (the stamp collection and bank account) are governed by the law where Dolittle died domiciled, East Dakota, where the will is valid. The executor will ultimately distribute the stamp collection to Sue and the proceeds of the bank account to Ben.

More Fun with Undue Influence and Mortmain

3. The validity of the will of land in Marovia is governed by Marovian law and is invalid. The will of land in Caledonia is governed by Caledonian law and is valid. Accordingly, the Church of Marovia gets the Caledonia land under the will, but the Marovian land passes under the laws of intestate succession in Marovia.

Mort's capacity to make the will of personal property and the validity of the bequests are governed by the law of the place where he died domiciled, Marovia. Accordingly, the personal property will be distributed to Phoebe.

4. This is another formality problem. The formalities necessary for a valid devise of land in Hibernia are governed by the law of Hibernia, where the "rest residue and remainder" clause is ineffective. The land passes to the person—Sonny—who takes under the law of intestate succession of the place where the land is.

   If you are worried about wife Wilma being squeezed out in this hypothetical, there is a lesson: Focus on the question that is *asked*. Maybe Wilma's lawyers committed malpractice by not raising her rights to a forced share. But maybe she already received virtually all her husband's assets in exchange for an agreement not to assert her right to a forced share.

Land Deal

5. The trust is not valid. The validity of a trust of an interest in land is governed by the law of the jurisdiction where the land is. *Id.* §241. This rule applies to inter vivos and testamentary trusts and covers issues like capacity, formalities (including the statute of frauds), and interests created. Here the trust is not valid under the law of Nod.

Special Delivery

6. For chattels, the validity (including formal requirements) of a trust of personal property is governed by the law of the place where chattel property is at the time of the creation of the trust. For choses in action, validity is governed by the law of the place where the transaction takes place. *Id.* §294(2). Snoop received the coin before he became aware of any trust instructions, so the place where the chattel was is Harmonia, and the trust is invalid under its law.

7. Yes, the testamentary trust is valid because it is governed by the law of the place where the testator died domiciled, and holographic wills are valid in Dischordia. *Id.* §295.

8. For inter vivos trusts, matters of administration are governed by the place where the settlor locates the administration of the trust. For testamentary trusts, matters of administration are governed by the law of the testator's domicile at death "unless the will shows an intention that the trust should be administered in another state." *Id.* §298. In this case, the testator obviously located the administration of the trust in Harmonia, where the property had been previously delivered pursuant to a trust

that, it turns out, was invalid. Accordingly, Harmonia law would govern all issues.

Matters of administration include detailed duties regarding the safe-keeping of property. This includes the kind of securities in which the trustee can invest. The First Restatement considers the power of beneficiaries to terminate a trust to be a matter of administration, though this is far from obvious. *See id.* §297 cmt. c. The First Restatement offers little guidance for how to distinguish administrative issues from others, but its broad approach to administration might well lead it to classify the scope of the trustee's fiduciary duties to avoid self-dealing as an administrative issue.

Marriage

INTRODUCTION

Under the traditional approach, the law of the place that a marriage is celebrated (*lex loci celebrationis*) governs the validity of a marriage. But courts would not recognize marriages otherwise valid under foreign law when they were directed not to do so by a statute or when the foreign marriage was contrary to natural law on grounds of incest. Christian countries would refuse to recognize polygamous marriages. More generally, traditional courts would refuse to recognize foreign marriages contrary to a strong public policy of the forum.

LAW OF THE PLACE OF CELEBRATION

The First Restatement provides that a marriage is valid in all jurisdictions "if the requirements of the marriage law of the state where the contract of marriage takes place are complied with." First Restatement §121. This principle of validity is subject to exceptions that are discussed in the next section. The First Restatement also provides that when a marriage is invalid under the law of the place of celebration, it is invalid everywhere. *Id.* §122.

These twin rules flow from the vested rights logic of the First Restatement: rights stemming from a marriage are created and vest under the law of the place where the marriage is celebrated. Hence the law of the place of celebration determines the capacity of parties to marry, necessity for a license, requirements of a formal ceremony, qualifications of the person who officiates, and even the requirements for a blood test or physical examination before marriage. *Id.* §121 cmt. e.

A few special rules address weird situations where both parties are not in the same jurisdiction at the time of the ceremony — marriage by proxy (valid only if the absent party consents), *id.* §124, and marriage by correspondence (governed by the law from which the acceptance is sent), *id.* §125. Marriage on board a ship on the high seas happens a lot in black and white movies. Such marriages are governed by the "law of the flag" of the ship. *Id.* §127.

Subject to important exceptions, a marriage valid under the law where celebrated is valid even if the parties went to the place to get married in order to evade prohibitions of their home state law. *Id.* §129.

EXCEPTIONS

Narrow Scope of Exceptions The First Restatement recognized limited exceptions to otherwise valid foreign marriages. Its goal of uniformity led it to craft exceptions so they too would be binding on all jurisdictions — even those in which the marriages were celebrated. To achieve this result the First Restatement restricted exceptions to marriages that were prohibited under the law of the place of the domicile of at least one of the parties at the time of the marriage.

Validity vs. Incidents The narrow room for exceptions in the First Restatement can have surprising results. A marriage between a mother and son valid under the law of Thebes would be binding on all other jurisdictions if the parties were domiciled in Thebes at the time of the marriage. Polygamous marriages would also be valid, though state statutes may make polygamous marriages void *ab initio*.

To reduce the abrasive effect of its preference for validation, the First Restatement expanded a case law distinction between recognizing the "validity" of a marriage and recognizing its "incidents" or legal consequences. For example, courts in Southern states had vigorously enforced prohibitions against marriages between African Americans and whites. But case law had recognized the right of the (usually white) survivors of such marriages to inherit. These cases reasoned that it did not violate the policies against interracial marriage to permit people to inherit after the death of one of the spouses.

The First Restatement did not invalidate all marriages contrary to public policy. But it provided that a state could refuse to give effect to any "effect" of a marriage contrary to its public policy. Id. §134. The Restatement explained that if a husband and two wives were validly married in one country and moved to another where such a marriage was "void," the second country could refuse to permit them to cohabit. But the second country should recognize the right of the second wife to receive a widow's allowance and of the son by the second wife to inherit as an heir. Id. §134 illus. 1 & 2.

Positive Law Exception — Marriages Contrary to Constitutional or Statutory Prohibitions

Positive Law   Positive law is written law found in a jurisdiction's constitution or statutes. Some traditional authority recognized a general positive law exception to the law of the place of marriage.

The First Restatement limited the positive law exception to marriage of a domiciliary that the party's home state law declared void even when celebrated in another state. Id. §132(d). The First Restatement's commitment to vested rights logic prevented its recognition of a legislature's authority to disregard marital rights validly created under another jurisdiction's laws. See id. §132 illus. 1. The theory was that marital rights vested at the time of the marriage and must be recognized everywhere. The exception was justified on the theory that a party was never validly married when the marriage violated his or her home state law.

Prohibitions on Remarriage After Divorce   It was once common for state law to prohibit divorcing parties from remarrying for a certain period of time. The prohibition served to deter hasty divorces[1] and may also have been designed to delay the legitimation of children born as a result of adulterous affairs.

Divorced persons wanting to avoid the prohibitions sometime got married in other jurisdictions. The First Restatement sought to provide uniformity. It provided that a prohibition against remarriage contained in a divorce decree, as opposed to a statute, did not operate outside the state. For extraterritorial effect to be given to statutory prohibitions on remarriage, the First Restatement required that the state prohibition be imbedded in a statute, that it apply to both parties to the divorce, that it either expressly apply or be interpreted to apply to marriages celebrated in another jurisdiction, and that it apply only so long as the remarrying party remained domiciled in the prohibiting state. Id. §131 & illus. 2 & §132.

---

1. Cf. Johnny Cash, *Jackson* ("We got married in a fever. . . . We've been talking about Jackson ever since the fire went out.").

Natural Law Exception — Marriages Contrary to Strong Public Policy

Natural Law   In addition to the positive law exception, courts traditionally exercised broad authority to declare certain marriages invalid under the natural law. The natural law is a body of unwritten legal principles that embody universal principles of justice. The natural law exception was used to justify the refusal to recognize certain incestuous marriages. Courts also mixed natural law, Christian values, and public policy to invalidate polygamous marriages.

Marriage Contrary to Strong Public Policy   The natural law exception survives in the First Restatement as a residual rule that a marriage is invalid everywhere if it offends the strong public policy of the domicile of any party to the marriage. Id. §132 cmt. b. The First Restatement lists polygamy, incest, and interracial marriages as examples of marriages that might qualify as contrary to the strong public policy of one of the parties' home states. Id. §132(a)-(c). The archaic example of interracial marriages[2] shows how social views about public morality and policy change.

The public policy exception was a concession to the reality of case law in common law jurisdictions, though it violates the First Restatement's commitment to territorial principles. If, for example, Rachel's marriage to Jacob is valid under the law where celebrated, it is unclear on what ground a contrary domiciliary law should apply extraterritorially to invalidate the marriage. The issue is further complicated by the fact that under the First Restatement Rachel's domicile actually depends on the validity of the marriage. Id. §27 (wife has same domicile as husband).

The First Restatement specifically provided that a marriage prohibited by the law of the domicile of either party on the grounds of polygamy was invalid everywhere. Id. §132(a). There was ample authority that common law jurisdictions would refuse to recognize polygamous marriages. But there was scant authority that the parties' domicile was crucial, and there was probably no authority that the land of Polygamy would refuse to recognize its own marriage out of deference to the First Restatement's glorious dream of uniformity.

Incest   The First Restatement provided that a marriage prohibited by the law of the domicile of either party was invalid everywhere when the persons were "so closely related that their marriage is contrary to a strong public policy" of one of the party's home states. Id. §132(b).

---

2. Such prohibitions are unconstitutional. U.S. Const. amend. XIV; Loving v. Virginia, 388 U.S. 1 (1967).

The First Restatement chose its language with care. Some persons might be so closely related that they fell under a home state prohibition against their marrying. Yet they might not be so closely related that the prohibition should be applied extraterritorially as an exception to the general rule validating the law of the place of marriage. For example, Cousin Pons and Cousin Bette, first cousins domiciled in the state of Denial, might travel to the state of Bliss and marry for the express purpose of avoiding Denial's statutory prohibition against marriage between first cousins. Under the First Restatement, all jurisdictions would recognize the marriage unless the relationship was so incestuous that it not only violated Denial's statute but also was contrary to a strong public policy of their home state. (Note that the rule assumes that the statutory prohibition is not enough to show a "strong public policy.")

SAME-SEX MARRIAGE

Why It Matters The legal status of marriage provides important legal rights and benefits. Some of these can be achieved through alternative means under contract and partnership law. But other important rights may be secured only by legal marriage. For example, only a "spouse" may be entitled to adopt children with a spouse, visit a spouse in the intensive care unit, make end-of-life decisions for a spouse, or receive benefits upon his or her death. Moreover, publicly recognizing the legal status of marriage legitimates and encourages certain activity and communicates public values about the worth of certain relationships. Access to the right to marry is a matter of both equal right and human dignity.

Something New Beginning in the 1990s, some states and foreign countries began to recognize same-sex marriages and civil unions. This provoked a wave of state statutes and state constitutional amendments refusing recognition to such marriages. In 1996 Congress enacted the "Defense of Marriage Act," which sought to permit states to refuse recognition of same-sex marriages and to judgments respecting same-sex marriages in other states.

A Fundamental Right Prohibitions against same-sex marriage did not do well in the lower courts. The Supreme Court had long recognized that the right to marry was a fundamental right protected by the Constitution. Loving v. Virginia, 388 U.S. 1, 12 (1967) (invalidating state laws banning interracial marriages). In Lawrence v. Texas, 539 U.S. 558 (2003), the Court had held that states could not criminalize private sexual conduct between same-sex adults. In United States v. Windsor, 133 S. Ct. 2675 (2013), it struck down provisions of the federal law that barred the government from recognizing same-sex marriages that were lawful in the state where they were licensed.

In Obergefell v. Hodges, 135 S. Ct. 2584 (2015), the Supreme Court held that state laws barring same-sex couples from marrying violate fundamental rights protected by both the Due Process and Equal Protection Clauses. Justice Kennedy's opinion for the Court recognized that fundamental liberties "extend to certain personal choices central to individual dignity and autonomy, including intimate choices that define personal identity and beliefs." The individual cases before the Court demonstrated the "grave and continuing harm" caused by anti-same-sex marriage laws. And the Court rejected the policy arguments against same-sex marriage as counterintuitive and illogical.

The Court also held that "there is no lawful basis for a State to refuse to recognize a lawful same-sex marriage performed in another State on the ground of its same-sex character." Given that the decision is grounded on fundamental rights of persons, there is no reason not to apply the holding to valid foreign-country same-sex marriages.

The *Obergefell* decision leaves a few new uncertainties that will delight Conflicts scholars. It is unclear what effect it will have on same-sex couples who get married in foreign countries that do not recognize their marriage. And there are lingering questions about the retroactive application of the decision. For example, what should a court do if Bob and Rob got married ten years ago but were living in a state that did not recognize their marriage? What if they separated, were unable to get a divorce, and then married other people?[3]

FATE OF THE FIRST RESTATEMENT

The First Restatement's detailed rules have been abandoned in favor of more nuanced approaches, including a willingness to concede that jurisdictions can differ in their conclusions about whether a marriage exists. The Second Restatement collapses the rules governing validity into one provision: validity is governed by the law of the state with the most significant relationship to the spouses. The Second Restatement acknowledges an exception

---

3. I don't provide an explanation for this one! If you have a good answer, please let me know. Some state courts contributed to the mess by denying divorces to same-sex couples who had been validly married outside the state. Couples may have relied on such decisions and on state laws declaring same-sex marriages void when they opted not to get a divorce or annulment.

where the law of the place of marriage "violates the strong public policy of another state which had the most significant relationship to the spouses and the marriage at the time of the marriage." Second Restatement §283(1)-(2). Comments observe that most of the more specific rules of the First Restatement still "usually" apply.

There are two notable changes since the First Restatement. First, romantics will be heartened by a general trend to validate marriages. (The wave of anti-same-sex marriage laws wave a marked countertrend.) Marriages that are invalid under the law of the place of celebration have been deemed valid in a majority of cases where one of the parties was domiciled in another state, the parties lived in that state after marriage, and the marriage was celebrated in substantial compliance with the law of their home state. Id. §283 cmt. i, reporter's note.

Second, according to the First Restatement, a jurisdiction could invalidate a marriage offensive to its public policy only when one of the parties was domiciled in the jurisdiction at the time of the marriage. This still had substantial authority in the 1960s. Id. §283 cmt. k. But the anti-same-sex marriage laws showed that many states want to disregard certain marriages they deem offensive regardless of the domicile of the parties at the time of the marriage.

Examples

Honeymoon Hotel

1. Elvis and Stella, unmarried teenagers domiciled in the land of Cottonia, run away from their phony, uptight parents to the country of Pleasure Island. They check into the Honeymoon Hotel, sign the registry as Mr. and Mrs. Smith, and ask for the honeymoon suite. Under the law of Pleasure Island, unmarried couples that spend the night together and hold themselves out as husband and wife are validly married. Under the law of Cottonia, the marriage is not valid. What law applies under the First Restatement?

Friendly Marriage

2. Penn and Sean were members of the Society of the Friends, also known as Quakers. Quakers do not have ordained ministers. Under Quaker practice, members of the Society marry by attending a meeting of members and expressing their commitment to live in marriage. Penn and Sean were citizens of the country of Domestikia. Under Domestikia law, Quakers were prohibited from marrying. Moreover, a valid marriage required a license and the participation of an ordained minister of the Church of Domestikia.

Penn and Sean traveled to the country of Confusion, where they appeared at the weekly meeting of local Quakers and exchanged their promises in accordance with Quaker traditions. Confusion generally recognizes Quaker marriages, but Confusion has enacted a statute that provides that no marriage celebrated in Confusion is valid when such a marriage would be invalid under the law of the domicile of any party to the marriage. Is the marriage valid under the First Restatement?

Pride and Prejudice

3. Wickham persuaded Lydia to run away with him and get married. They were living and domiciled in the country of Albion. Lydia was a minor, and Wickham's conduct constituted felonious abduction under the law of Albion.

   Under the law of Albion, no marriage is valid unless the parties publicly announce their intention to marry for three weeks. So Wickham took Lydia to Caledonia, where he married her secretly without waiting three weeks. Under the law of Caledonia, the marriage was valid.

   Wickham and Lydia return to Albion and live together as husband and wife until Wickham is arrested and charged with the statutory rape of Lydia. It is an element of rape in Albion that the victim be "not the wife" of the defendant. Wickham insists Lydia is his wife.

   What law applies under the First Restatement?

In Bigamy Ignominy

4. Captain John, a U.S. Navy officer stationed in Japan, married Butterfly in accordance with Japanese custom. The marriage was valid under the law of Japan, but its formalities did not comply with the laws of any state of the United States. He then abandoned Butterfly and returned to the United States, where he celebrated a marriage with Lisa. Under the law of the state in which the marriage occurred, a person who is validly married cannot marry a second time. Lisa did not know about John's earlier marriage to Butterfly.

   Butterfly killed herself when she learned of John's betrayal. Many years later, John died of old age. Lisa has found letters documenting John's previous romance and "marriage." She wants to know whether she is John's surviving spouse. Please advise and explain how the First Restatement will resolve this issue.

5. Hubert married both Anne and Betsy, all domiciled in the country of Multitopia, in a ceremony in Multitopia. The ceremony established a

valid polygamous marriage according to the law of Multitopia. Hubert then enrolled in law school at the University of East Dakota and applied for married student housing. He also applied for dependent health insurance for both spouses under the state health care plan.

The UED law school informs Hubert that his marriage to both spouses is not valid in East Dakota and that the school will, accordingly, not provide housing or health care coverage for spouses. Hubert comes to you for legal advice. Apply the First Restatement.

Public Policy

6. Zaara was a citizen and domiciliary of the country of Injustiza. Her family was of South Asian origin. Zaara was forced to flee when the National Patriot Party seized power. She took up temporary residence in the state of West Carolina. There she met and fell in love with Samuel, a domiciliary of West Carolina. They married in accordance with the law of West Carolina, complying with all local requirements.

   The marriage was invalid under the constitution of Injustiza, which was amended prior to the marriage to provide, "Any marriage between a person of South Asian origin and the member of any other racial group shall be void wheresoever celebrated." Marriages between South Asians and other ethnic groups are deemed void in Injustiza because they are considered "abhorrent to the strong social policy of the state."

   Are Zaara and Samuel happily married according to the First Restatement?

All in the Family (In re May's Estate)

7. Sam May, a Jewish man living in New York, decided to marry his half brother's daughter, Fannie, in 1912. A New York statute declared that a marriage between an uncle and niece was "void" and that the persons attempting to solemnize any such marriage were subject to criminal prosecution.

   In an effort to avoid the effect of the New York law, Sam and Fannie traveled to Rhode Island, where they got married. Rhode Island law contained a general prohibition for marriages between uncles and nieces, but it contained a statutory exception to this prohibition for marriages between Jews within degrees of kinship permitted by their religion.

   Sam and Fannie then returned to New York, where they lived together as husband and wife for 32 years and where Fannie gave birth to six children.

Upon Fannie's death in 1951, three of her daughters challenged their father's status as "surviving spouse," and argued that their parents' marriage was invalid. What does the First Restatement provide?

Culture Wars

8. Walt and Peter Ilyich, two men domiciled in Massachusetts, get married in a ceremony that establishes a valid marriage under the law of Massachusetts.

Some time later, while Peter is crossing the street in Massachusetts on his way to a concert, he is struck and seriously injured by a car driven by Tom Tortfeasor, a citizen of West Dakota. Tortfeasor flees the scene of the accident and returns to West Dakota.

Peter settles his personal injury claim with Tortfeasor's insurance carrier. But Walt also presents a claim for loss of consortium, claiming damages for the loss of companionship and support that he has suffered as a result of Peter's disabilities. (Please assume that under Massachusetts law, a spouse has a valid claim for loss of consortium under the facts.) Tortfeasor's insurance carrier refuses to offer anything for Walt's loss of consortium claim.

West Dakota has amended its state constitution to provide:

A marriage is a compact between one man and one woman. A marriage between persons of the same sex is void. No court of this state shall give effect to any right, claim or judgment respecting a relationship between persons of the same sex that is treated as a marriage under the laws of any other state or foreign country.

Walt comes to you for advice. He asks specifically whether he has a good claim for loss of consortium and whether he can enforce it in West Dakota. Please advise.

9. Same facts. Peter Ilyich grows old and dies after inheriting the estate of Blackacre in the country of Theocratia. He leaves no will. Under the law of Theocratia a surviving spouse inherits all land in the absence of a will. If there is no surviving spouse, the land passes to the next of kin. Peter Ilyich's next of kin is Leonard.

Under the law of Theocratia, homosexual conduct is a criminal offense, and persons of the same sex attempting to celebrate marriages in Theocratia have been arrested and fined. Under the First Restatement, does Walt get the land as surviving spouse, or does Leonard get it as the next of kin?

Explanations

Honeymoon Hotel

1. Congratulate the newlyweds! A marriage that results without formal ceremony through the conduct and statements of the parties (a "common law marriage") is governed by the law of the place where the acts occurred. The marriage is valid where celebrated, so it is valid everywhere. Id. §123.

Friendly Marriage

2. The marriage is not valid because it is not valid under the law of the place where celebrated. The local statute that invalidates the marriage sounds like a version of the Uniform Marriage Evasion Act. See Weintraub, Commentary on the Conflict of Laws §5.1A at 334 n.6.

   Quaker marriages posed problems for the common law but are generally valid, sometimes due to special statutes. The Quaker marriage in this case is not valid anywhere solely because it was not valid under the law of the place where it was celebrated.

Pride and Prejudice

3. The marriage is probably valid because it was valid where celebrated. Because Lydia is the defendant's wife, he is not guilty of rape. (He is still guilty of the felonious abduction.)

   If the marriage violated strong public policies of Albion, then it would be invalid everywhere because Lydia was domiciled in Albion at the time of the marriage. Differences in formalities, including the lack of public notice, would not violate a strong public policy. But an age requirement might be found to embody a strong public policy, and the chances of it being so found would increase the younger she was. In the Jane Austen novel, of course, the parties celebrated the marriage in London, and Lydia was young but not too young to celebrate a valid marriage.

In Bigamy Ignominy

4. There is no surviving spouse. Butterfly was the captain's wife, so the second marriage was not valid in the place where it was celebrated.

5. Under the First Restatement Hubert's marriage to both wives is valid everywhere because it was valid where celebrated. The First Restatement polygamy exception does not apply because no party to the marriage was domiciled in a jurisdiction that prohibited polygamy.

Nevertheless, East Dakota may refuse to give effect to any "effect" of the marriage that offends its public policy. Accordingly, it may refuse to allow multiple spouses to live together in married student housing, and it may refuse to extend health care coverage to multiple spouses.

Public Policy

6. The First Restatement requires all jurisdictions to apply the outrageous law of Zaara's domicile to achieve the uniform result that the marriage is void. The First Restatement rules apply logically as follows. A marriage is void everywhere when it is void as contrary to the strong public policy of the law of the domicile of any party. Zaara remains domiciled in Injustiza. Hence her marriage is void everywhere. The example is designed to make the point that uniformity is not always a good thing.

   Note that for the First Restatement to reach this result it does not allow the spouse to acquire a new domicile as a result of the (void) marriage. *See* First Restatement §132 cmt. c & illus. 2 & 3.

   If Zaara had changed her domicile and not just her temporary residence, then the marriage would be valid everywhere under the law of the place of the marriage because the positive law exception would not apply since she would no longer be domiciled in Injustiza.

All in the Family (In re May's Estate)

7. These facts are taken from In re May's Estate, 114 N.E.2d 4 (N.Y. 1953). The New York court construed the New York prohibition to invalidate only marriages celebrated in New York because the prohibition did not expressly apply to marriages outside the state. This construction was guided in part by the general conflicts principle that validity of marriages is governed by the law where they are celebrated. The court then considered a general natural law exception but quickly concluded that the marriage, valid under the law of a sister state (and not expressly prohibited by Leviticus), could not offend the natural law.

   Analysis under the First Restatement would vary only slightly. The general rule that the marriage is valid, because it is valid where celebrated, would apply. It does not matter that the parties went to Rhode Island for the purpose of evading New York law. But if one of the parties was domiciled in New York, then the marriage would be invalid everywhere if it was not only prohibited by New York law but also was between persons so closely related that the marriage violated a strong public policy. The holding in In re May's Estate answers the question — for New York. The marriage would be unlawful in New York, but the parties are not so closely related that it violates "a strong public policy." The marriage is valid everywhere.

Culture Wars

8. Under the First Restatement, the elements of the tort claim would be governed by the place of the wrong (Massachusetts) and the validity of the marriage and Walt's right to loss of consortium as a spouse would be governed by the place of the marriage (Massachusetts). In principle Walt has a good claim. Walt should have no problem litigating in Massachusetts and getting long-arm jurisdiction there over Tortfeasor.

   If Walt recovers a judgment in Massachusetts, there will be no problem enforcing it in Massachusetts against Tortfeasor. Before Obergefell v. Hodges, it was uncertain whether West Dakota could refuse to recognize the same-sex marriage or refuse to enforce the sister-state judgment respecting the same-sex marriage. For that reason, the explanation in earlier editions of this book concluded that Walt should litigate in Massachusetts.

   Now that the Court recognizes a constitutional right to same-sex marriage, the West Dakota constitutional provision is invalid. West Dakota must both recognize the marriage and must give full faith and credit to another state's judgment respecting such a marriage. Walt can litigate in either Massachusetts or West Dakota.

9. The First Restatement requires Theocratia (and all jurisdictions) to recognize the marriage as valid under the law of the place where celebrated. No public policy exception arises since the parties were domiciled in the place of their marriage.

   You may suspect (as I do) that Theocratia would not in fact recognize Walt as the heir. But it would be violating the First Restatement. More consistent with the First Restatement, Theocratia might refuse to give effect to an incident or "effect" of the marriage—the right to inherit—as contrary to its strong public policy. But it is not clear why allowing a homosexual spouse to inherit would offend public policy any more than allowing the homosexual next of kin. (Oh, I forgot to mention that Leonard Dumbledore, the next of kin, is also gay.)

CHAPTER 11

Agency, Partnership, and Corporations

INTRODUCTION

Under traditional choice of law rules, the rights of principals, agents, and partners among themselves are governed by the contract principles of the place of the contract. Whether a corporation exists and its internal affairs are governed by the law of the place of incorporation.

The liability of a principal, partner, or corporation to someone else who is not part of the partnership, agency, or internal corporate relationship is governed by the place of the conduct.

AGENCY AND PARTNERSHIP

Agents and Partners   An agent is a person who acts in behalf of another person (the principal). A partnership exists when there is an association of two or more persons to carry on as co-owners a business for profit. Partners serve as agents for each other and for the partnership.

The First Restatement provides that the rights and obligations of agents and partners among themselves are governed by the law of the place where the agency or partnership agreement was made. First Restatement §342. Conflicts regarding apparent authority are governed by the law of the place where a third person relied upon the apparent authorization. Id. §344.

In contrast, whether an agent's or partner's act is binding on the principal or co-partners is governed by the law of the place where the agent is authorized or apparently authorized to act. Id. §345. Likewise, whether a principal or partner is vicariously liable for an agent's or partner's tort is governed by the law of the place of the wrong when the agent was authorized to act in that jurisdiction. Id. §387.

CORPORATIONS

Corporations are legal "persons." They have the capacity to own property, to sue and be sued, and to authorize others to act in their behalf. Unlike natural persons (individual humans), corporations are purely creatures of law — they are abstractions. This means corporations can act only through people who serve as agents. It is only through human beings that the corporation can act in the world, whether they are serving as its chief financial officer or driving its trucks.

Existence

The existence of a corporation and the consequences of an unsuccessful attempt to form a corporation are governed by the place of incorporation or attempted incorporation. A corporation that comes into existence under the law of one jurisdiction will be recognized by all other jurisdictions. Id. §§154, 155. Dissolution is also governed by the law of the place of incorporation. Id. §§158-161.

Internal Affairs

The rights and duties of the corporation and its shareholders, directors, and officers to each other are generally governed by the law of the place of incorporation. The law of the place of incorporation applies to whether a person is a shareholder; the rights of shareholders to participate in control, to share in profits, and to receive distribution of assets upon dissolution; the right to vote shares held in trust; shareholder liability for contribution for corporate debts; shareholder's right to inspect books, records, and properties; and requirements for calling a shareholders' meeting. Id. §§182, 183, 184, 185, 190, 200 cmt. a, 204.

Partnership Perplexities

3. Anne and Beth, domiciliaries of West Dakota, decided to rehab a house in East Dakota and sell it, hoping to make a profit. They did not discuss how they would share profits and did not consider the possibility of losses. Anne bought the house, and Beth bought most of the supplies and equipment needed to fix the house. Beth also did most but not all of the work on the house.

   They sold the house for $400,000 but now cannot agree how to divide the funds. Under the law of West Dakota, partners in such a situation are deemed to have contributed their property and services to the partnership, and Anne and Beth would share equally in the proceeds of the sale under its law. In contrast, under the law of East Dakota, partners are first entitled to recover the reasonable value of their contributions and services and then share equally any remaining profits. How should the proceeds be divided according to the First Restatement?

4. Same facts. While working on the project, Beth drove to East Dakota to pick up some roofing material for the project. She bought the material on credit from Acme Supplies, which had no reason to think she was buying the material for anyone else.

   Beth refused to pay Acme, and Acme, after learning of the joint project, sues Anne. Under the law of East Dakota, partners are jointly and severally liable for contract debts of their co-partners. Under the law of West Dakota, Anne is not liable. What law applies under the First Restatement?

Corporate Conundrums

5. The Hinterland Trust Corporation was incorporated under the law of the country of Hinterland. It purchased real estate in the state of Piedmont. Under the law of Hinterland, a trust corporation is authorized to own real estate. Under the law of Piedmont, a corporation like the Hinterland Trust Corporation may not lawfully own real estate. An action is brought to force the corporation to sell the land. What is the result under the First Restatement?

6. The Mississippi Bubble Corporation is incorporated under the law of Swindland but has its main offices in the state of Defalkia. For two years Priscilla, president of the Mississippi Bubble Corporation, embezzled corporate funds. Director Dan received anonymous messages accusing the president of stealing. Dan responded by forwarding the letters to the corporation's lawyer, Lawrence. Lawrence was Priscilla's boyfriend and destroyed the letters.

Dan received the letters at his office in the state of Defalkia, and Dan mailed them from Defalkia to Lawrence, who received them in Defalkia. Under the law of Defalkia, Dan's failure to follow up on the anonymous letters constituted a breach of fiduciary duties owed to a corporation. Under the law of Swindland, Dan's mailing of the letters to Lawrence satisfied his fiduciary duties owed to the corporation. Under the First Restatement, will the corporation have a good claim against Dan for breach of his fiduciary duties as director?

7. Donna Donatta graduated from law school and moved to West Carolina. Unable to find suitable legal work, she started a shuttle service that provided transportation services between the University of West Carolina Law School and the airport, which was also located in West Carolina. Donatta formed a corporation, Zoom Transport, Inc., under the law of East Carolina. She selected the law of East Carolina because she was advised that it provided more effective limitation of liability for shareholders.

Donatta bought a van, titled it in the name of the corporation, and began to offer services. Her business succeeded beyond her wildest dreams. She soon expanded, buying additional vans, hiring drivers, and offering shuttle services to shopping malls and other popular destinations.

Zoom Transport, Inc., realized profits of over $1 million during its first two years. Donatta controlled the corporation. She took lavish vacations in Hawaii as part of the corporation's annual meetings, and she diverted all of the profits of the corporation to herself either as a salary or as annual dividends.

Donatta did not maintain the equipment of the corporation, and she hired whatever drivers were willing to work for minimum wage. She did not conduct background checks on the drivers.

At the end of the second year of the corporation's existence, Pat Plinkerton was seriously injured in the state of West Carolina while traveling as a passenger in a corporation van. The accident occurred when Drake Driver, an employee of the corporation, ran into a brick wall. Driver claimed that the steering wheel malfunctioned. He also claimed that he had repeatedly complained to Donatta about the steering wheel, and she had not repaired it. But there was also evidence that Driver was drunk at the time of the accident. And Driver had a long history of criminal convictions for drunk driving when he was hired.

Plinkerton's medical expenses exceed $100,000. The corporation's insurance has lapsed, and because of bank liens on the vans, its total assets are $213.00. Driver is insolvent.

Under these facts, case law in East Carolina permits a plaintiff to pierce the corporate veil and hold a shareholder of an undercapitalized corporation who has controlled the corporation individually liable for the torts of the corporation. Under the law of West Carolina, a victim of a tort cannot pierce the corporate veil under these facts.

Can Plinkerton establish individual liability of Donatta under the First Restatement?

Very Wary, Chary Shareholder

8. Investership is a Delaware limited partnership that owns shares of stock in TechnieCorp., a Delaware corporation. TechnieCorp has entered into an agreement to merge with PubSubCo., a Delaware corporation that is a subsidiary of PubCo., a major international publishing corporation.

   Investership wants to block the merger. It argues that over half the persons who own shares in TechnieCorp reside in California. A California statute provides that California corporate laws apply exclusively to a non-California corporation when more than half the voting securities are held by persons with addresses in California and when the corporation has a certain tax status in California.

   Under Delaware law, a corporate merger by TechnieCorp with another corporation requires a yes vote by the majority of all shareholders of all kinds of stock. But under California law, a merger requires a yes vote by the majority of shareholders of each separate class of stock. Because Investership owns most of the shares of preferred stock, it can block the merger if California law applies.

   PubSubCo. files a complaint for declaratory judgment in Delaware state court. Is Investorship's right to vote governed by California or Delaware law?

Explanations

Agency Agonies

1. The duties owed by the agent to the principal are governed by the law of the place where the agency agreement was made, Neverland. Accordingly, the agent is liable for the additional expenses resulting from the price increases. Id. §342. You get the same result by treating this as a contract governed by the law of the place of contracting. But agency relationships do not require a contract.

2. The vicarious liability of the principal to a third person in torts is governed by the law of the place of the wrong, when the principal authorized the agent to act in his behalf in that jurisdiction. Id. §387. Accordingly, Upahl will be vicariously liable under the law of Lalaland, where Upahl's agent struck Blabbermouth, because Lalaland is the place of the wrong.

Partnership Perplexities

3. This trick question illustrates a big gap in the First Restatement. Under the First Restatement the law of the place of the agency or partnership "agreement" governs the obligations of partners to each other. *Id.* §342. The First Restatement describes this as the place of agreement rather than the place of contract because an agency or partnership relationship can result even if there is no contract. But the First Restatement provides no guidance for deciding what place a partnership arises in when there is no express agreement.

   So the right answer depends on where Anne and Beth first discussed the project and either entered into a contract or where the first one began to act in behalf of both. You get full credit for applying the place of agreement rule—though the facts leave it unclear exactly where that was. The law of the place where the property was located or where the partnership conducted business does not govern unless it was the place of the agreement.

4. The law of the state where Beth was authorized to act for the partners governs the effect of the act and whether it imposes a duty on the other partner. *Id.* §345. Under the law of East Dakota, where Beth was authorized to buy supplies for the partnership, other partners are individually liable for contract debts, so Ann is individually liable to Acme.

Corporate Conundrums

5. The corporation must sell the land and comply with the law where it is located. This is an example of external affairs. Like any other person, a corporation must abide by the law of a state when it comes to visit. The Hinterland Trust Corporation's authority to own land in Piedmont is governed by the law of the place where the land is located.

6. Under the internal affairs doctrine, the Mississippi Bubble Corporation does not have a good claim because the scope of duties owed to the corporation by the director is governed by the law of the place of incorporation. *Id.* §188. The exception that permits (but does not require) imputing liability to a director for acts in which the director participates applies to claims by third persons, not to claims by the corporation. *See id.* §188 illus. 1; Richman et al., Understanding Conflict of Laws §91 at 302-03.

7. Donatta is almost certainly individually liable, but there are several paths to that answer, and the most perilous one is the one that requires a resolution of the conflict of laws regarding piercing the corporate veil.

   First, the corporate rules do not displace other forms of liability. Donatta may have limited liability for the debts of a corporation based on her status as a shareholder. But this limitation in no way provides an immunity for her own torts. Under these facts, Donatta is individually liable for her own negligent acts in failing to maintain property and in negligently hiring and supervising Driver. Indeed, the corporation may have good claims against her, though, because she controls the corporation, it is unlikely it will enforce those claims against her.

Second, under the general rules of the First Restatement, the law of the place of incorporation generally applies to the liability of officers. But where a director or agent—and officers are agents!—participates in the acts of the corporation in a state, that state "can" impose liability on them. Donatta's personal participation in the corporation's business in East Carolina makes it appropriate for that state's law to apply to her in her capacity as officer.

Third, Donatta's individual liability for her own torts and her liability as an officer participant render it unnecessary to pierce the corporate veil to establish her liability as a shareholder. Nevertheless, it is necessary to consider that theory, since the example so clearly raises the issue. Under the First Restatement, the answer is surprisingly unclear. The general rule applies the law of the place of incorporation (where there is no shareholder liability). The exception provides that a state "can" impose liability on a shareholder who is domiciled in the state, participates in the act, or has notice that the corporation was formed to do business in the state. Donatta appears to satisfy each of the three alternative grounds for applying the exception, so the law of the place of the act may apply and impose direct liability on Donatta as shareholder.

Yet it is not crystal clear that the exception applies. First, the exception only permits a state to apply the law of the place of the act; it does not require it. Second, the Comments to the exception in the First Restatement indicate that direct shareholder liability covered by the rule does not include common law liability (like piercing the corporate veil) but is limited to liability imposed by a statute or constitution.

In sum, it is unclear what law applies to the piercing of the corporate veil issue, yet there are alternative theories for establishing Donatta's individual liability.

Very Wary, Chary Shareholder

8. Delaware law applies. The example borrows its facts from Vantagepoint Venture Partners 1996 v. Examen, Inc., 871 A.2d 1108 (Del. 2005). The Delaware court held that the right of shareholders to vote stock as a class was governed by the law of the place of incorporation—Delaware. So the shareholders were unable to block the merger.

   The Delaware court's opinion is notable for its forceful defense of the internal affairs doctrine and for asserting that the internal affairs doctrine is constitutionally binding on other states. The court reasoned that the internal affairs doctrine provides certainty and stability. It observed that without the corporate affairs doctrine the rights and liability of officers, directors, and shareholders were shifting and even unknowable in advance of litigation. It concluded that disregarding the internal affairs doctrine and applying California law, even by California courts, would potentially violate both the Due Process and Commerce Clauses.

Since the parties were properly before the Delaware court and it entered a final judgment that Delaware law applied under its traditional choice of law rules, I am not sure what the discussion of the constitutional "underpinnings" of the internal affairs doctrine added. But it shows how important some courts think the doctrine is.

I'm not convinced the Constitution codifies the internal affairs doctrine. The internal affairs doctrine is well established and is followed by most courts in most situations. But the doctrine arose in an era when all states enforced certain common duties among officers, directors, and shareholders. In some cases there may be good reasons for California to apply its corporate law to the internal affairs or even to the question of the existence of a corporation created under the law of another state or country. For example, suppose some California swindlers create a corporation under the law of Swinlandia and sell shares exclusively to California citizens. The swindlers decide to incorporate in Swinlandia because its law provides no protections for shareholders. No doubt the swindlers relied on Swinlandia law and would want the Constitution to enforce a rule of stability and certainty that makes them immune to California law. But doesn't the Constitution promote legal values in addition to stability? Like justice.

PART III

Traditional Problems and Escape Devices

Manipulation and Characterization

INTRODUCTION

Uniformity of result was the glorious dream of the traditional approach and explains many of the specific rules in the First Restatement. But along with the territorial rules, traditional courts also developed doctrines that provided courts with elbow room in applying the rules. Courts could employ these doctrines to avoid an undesirable outcome. For this reason, the doctrines are sometimes called "escape devices": they allowed courts to escape from the outcome that was dictated by the rigid application of the choice of law rules. Courts sometimes used these escape devices deliberately to reach a desired outcome, and courts sometimes used them without being fully aware of their impact on the predictability and uniformity of outcomes.

Escape devices and some other doctrines frustrated the goal of uniformity of outcome. This is not necessarily a problem, and the modern approaches (Part IV) openly drop uniformity as a supreme value. But such devices existed in tension with the traditional rules, and they can make it impossible to apply the traditional rules with the mathematical precision or certainty envisaged by the First Restatement.

OBSTACLES TO THE DREAM

Two different realities prevented traditional courts from realizing the glorious dream of always applying the same law in a conflicts case. First, courts could adopt different choice rules. Second, they could apply the same rule in different ways.

Different Choice of Law Rules   The First Restatement rules were never really universally followed. Even when particular rules had widespread adherence, there were always a few jurisdictions that would deviate from the rules in some cases. And (horror!) some of the First Restatement rules might never have been adopted by a majority. For example, some traditional courts applied the law of the place of performance for contracts rather than the place of contracting. Some applied the law of the place of conduct for certain intentional torts rather than the place of the wrong. Some applied the law of the place where a trust was administered rather than where it was established. Whenever courts were applying different choice of law rules, they were reaching different outcomes.

The First Restatement drafters hoped their rules would be adopted everywhere and would eliminate non-uniform outcomes resulting from different choice rules. Yet even the First Restatement included some inconsistent rules that permitted courts to apply different laws. For example, a court "can" allow a workers' compensation recovery under its own law rather than apply the law of the place of the wrong. First Restatement §398. A court "can" apply its law and impose direct liability on directors and agents rather than apply the law of the place of incorporation. Id. §188. In such cases, other courts "can" also choose to apply a different law. Possible different laws also apply under the First Restatement to the issue of a child's legitimacy. The First Restatement proclaims that legitimacy is governed by the law of domicile of the parent in question, yet it admits legitimacy might also be governed by the law of the place where the child is domiciled. Id. §137 cmt. d. Different courts, applying different choice rules, could reach different conclusions about whether a child was legitimate.

Different Interpretations of the Same Rules   The First Restatement did not want to admit that courts applied different choice rules. But it could not help seeing that different courts could apply the "same" rule differently. For example, the First Restatement observed that courts might differ about the place where a contract was made. Id. §7 cmt. b. The First Restatement makes clear that courts are to apply their own forum law in interpreting and applying the choice of law rules in the First Restatement. Id. §7(a). Thus a court must decide for itself what the place of contracting is under the First Restatement's rules.

The First Restatement did not think there would be great uncertainty in the application of its rules. For some fields of law it established detailed sub-rules defining. For example, it defines the place of contracting and the place of wrong so as to avoid uncertainty. But in many other areas the First Restatement is a nightmare of uncertainty. For example, it provides virtually no guidance on the location of intangible personal property, trusts of such property, or the location of partnerships that are not formed by an express agreement.

Manipulation In many situations under the First Restatement, courts could apply the same formal rule in different ways in order to reach different outcomes. To the extent courts wanted to avoid a particular outcome, they could also apply the rules in such a way as to avoid the undesired result.

Characterization

The First Restatement formulates different rules for different types of cases and issues. For example, the standard of care in torts is governed by the place of the wrong, while the capacity to contract is governed by the place of contracting. In order to select the right rule, it is necessary to classify the case properly.

Tort claims can sometimes be reconfigured as contract claims — breaches of implied promises — or quasi-contract claims for restitution. Contract claims can sometimes be reconfigured as tort-like breaches of duties of good faith and fair dealing. The same court could characterize the negligent delivery of a telegram as a tort in one case and a breach of contract in another.[1] Flexible principles of equity are often broad enough to permit a party to argue that a trust-like relationship has formed and given rise to fiduciary duties and a constructive trust. If an attempted trust fails under the law of the place of the settlement, then a creative lawyer will argue that the property now in the hands of the designated trustee is held in a "resulting trust" to be governed by law where the property is now located and that effectuates the settlor's intent.

Some legal claims are hard to classify. Product liability claims might be classified as breaches of warranty (contract theory) or strict liability for dangerous products (tort theory). Statutes permitting direct actions against a tortfeasor's insurance company might be conceptualized either as removing privity of contract and extending contract benefits to the plaintiff or as imposing vicarious tort liability on the insurer.

---

1. Hay et al., Conflict of Laws §3.4 at 130 (discussing telegraph cases).

Examples

Troublesome Tortfeasor

1. Vick Visitor, citizen of the country of Susannaland, wins an all-expense paid vacation to the land of Nod. Upon arriving, he takes a taxi from the airport to his hotel. The taxi service is owned and operated by the Yellow Cab Co. of Nod, a corporation. The cab is driven by Hank Hothead.

   Vick and Hank have a discussion about religion en route to the hotel. When they arrive at the hotel, Hank punches Vick in the face and throws his suitcase on the pavement. Vick is embarrassed, requires medical treatment, and suffers property damage.

   Sadly, Hank dies of apoplexy before Vick can sue him. Under the law of Nod, claims for intentional tort do not survive the death of the perpetrator. Moreover, according to Nod case law, under these facts the assault was a frolic and detour and thus not within the scope of the cab driver's authority; consequently, the employer is not liable under the doctrine of respondeat superior. Under the law of Susannaland, the claims against Hank survive, and the cab company would be vicariously liable. Under the First Restatement, what are Vick's best options?

Conniving Contractor

2. Slye, domiciled in the country of Disreputia, was a compulsive gambler. Accordingly, he went to court in Disreputia and had himself declared a spendthrift. Under the law of Disreputia, a person declared a spendthrift by a court has no capacity to enter into valid contracts.

   Slye then communicated by mail with Shirley Goodheart, who was living in the country of Innocenzia. Slye claimed he was hungry and needed money. As a result of their correspondence, Slye mailed a promissory note to Goodheart in the amount of $1,000, and Goodheart mailed a check to Slye in the amount of $1,000. Slye promptly cashed the check and lost it all on the ponies.

   Goodheart has come to you for legal advice. Both jurisdictions follow traditional approaches to choice of law. What to do?

Unhappily Unmarried

3. Daphnis and Chloe, domiciliaries of the country of Romanzia, fell in love and decided to get married. They traveled to the country of Etruria and went to a local church, where they thought they were validly married by a minister. Under the law of Etruria, a minister cannot perform a valid marriage. Under the law of Romanzia, a minister can perform a valid marriage.

The couple returned to Romanzia where they labored as shepherds. They shared joys and concerns, profits and losses. After saving their money for ten years, they bought a comfortable cottage. They invested their savings in a bank account. The house was titled in Daphnis's name, and the bank account was also in Daphnis's name.

Under the law of Romanzia, property acquired during a marriage is marital property owned jointly by the spouses, and title vests in the survivor upon the death of the first spouse. Also under the law of Romanzia, a surviving spouse is sole heir and next of kin in the absence of a valid will.

Daphnis and Chloe lived together for many years in what they thought was marital bliss. One day Daphnis died peacefully in his sleep — without a will. Daphnis's nephew by the half blood claims he is the decedent's only heir and next of kin. Chloe comes to you for legal advice. The First Restatement applies. Please advise.

Dead Wrong

4. Tess Trix was domiciled in the state of East Dakota and opened a bank account at EDB BankCorp. At the time she opened the account she filled out a little blue card and designated her husband, Prince Charming, as the survivor to whom the proceeds of the account should be paid in the event of her death. Tess also executed a will, valid under the law of East Dakota. In the will Tess left all her property to her friend Franzine. She excluded Prince Charming from her will because she believed he would receive the substantial proceeds of the bank account.

   Tess and Prince subsequently moved to West Dakota, where Tess died domiciled. Under the law of East Dakota, the bank account survivor designation would be valid. But under the law of West Dakota, such a survivor form is invalid because it does not satisfy the West Dakota statute of wills. Franzine claims she is entitled to all Tess's property under the will, including the bank account. Prince has come to you for advice. The First Restatement applies.

Explanations

Troublesome Tortfeasor

1. This example is designed to illustrate the need for creative lawyering when you reach a dead end. Tort claims against Hothead are losers. The law of the place of the wrong governs respondeat superior. But Vick may have other options. First, there may be other viable tort theories besides Hothead's assault. For example, there may be a direct claim against the corporation for its own negligence on the theory that it was negligent in hiring or supervising Hothead and that such negligence proximately caused Vick's injuries. Second, if tort theories fail, Vick may still be able

to recover on contract claims. Hothead acted in the scope of authority in agreeing to take Vick to the hotel, and you might argue that the agreement contained the implied obligation to transport Vick safely. The corporation failed to perform as promised.

As it stands, this example is really not a conflicts case. All the traditional rules would select Nod law as the place of the wrongs and the place of contracting. Accordingly, Vick is not in a different position from a local plaintiff. But the example makes the point that when a (local) law frustrates recovery, a good lawyer will often identify viable alternative theories.

By looking for alternative theories, you may also find grounds for a beneficial choice of law argument. For example, if Vick had made reservations over the Internet from his home in Susannaland, you might be able to make a persuasive case that Susannaland law should apply as the law of the place of contract—depending on the circumstances surrounding the making of the contract. (Of course, under the traditional rules, Nod law might still govern matters of performance.)

Conniving Contractor

2. The obvious solution would be to sue on the note. The problem is that the note was executed and mailed from a place where there was a valid defense to liability on the note. The traditional choice rules of the First Restatement will recognize the defense. But don't give up!

First, there may be wiggle room in the traditional contracts rules. Not all courts followed the rigid rules of the First Restatement, and some applied the law of the place of performance. You could argue that the place of performance is the place where the note was payable, and because the note does not prescribe where it was to be paid, you could argue that its place of payment was the payee's home country, where the contract is valid.

Second, you could try to manipulate the First Restatement definition of place of contracting. The First Restatement indicates that the capacity on the note should be governed by the law of the place from which it was mailed. Nevertheless, you might find evidence in correspondence preceding the mailing of the note that the parties had concluded a contract whose performance subsequently involved the reciprocal mailings of the check and note. You would then need to persuade the court that the place of contracting for this prior agreement was Innocenzia.

Third, if there is no valid contract, you still should not give up. If there was no contract, Goodheart still paid money under the mistaken belief that there was such a contract. The payment was not a gift. She may be able to recover the money under a remedial theory of restitution or unjust enrichment.

Fourth, this example presents a strong case for a tort of fraud. The law of the place of the wrong for frauds is where the person sustains loss. That place would be Innocenzia, where Goodheart parted with the check. Id. §377 illus. 4.

Unhappily Unmarried

3. Things look bad. Under the First Restatement the marriage is invalid everywhere because it is invalid where celebrated. Accordingly, Chloe is not Daphnis's "spouse" and has not acquired title to marital property, nor does she have a right to succeed to his property at death as his spouse.

Nevertheless, a court will be sympathetic to Chloe's claims for obvious reasons. Alternative theories that would lead to application of Romanzia law would include trust law and partnership law.

First, even if there was no valid marriage, the parties believed there was one and structured their property relationships with the assumption that they were married. Under these circumstances you could argue that the estate may hold legal title to the property but does so in trust for Chloe, because Daphnis held the property subject to the understanding that he held it for her benefit in the event he died first.

Second, the parties agreed to share profits and losses. This, you could argue, constituted a partnership, and Daphnis held legal title to partnership assets subject to the implied understanding that they would vest in the surviving partner.

Dead Wrong

4. This example offers problems similar to those raised in the last one, but the form of the assets and their location offer additional fun opportunities for creatively manipulating the rules.

In all these cases, start by figuring out which rules apply the law you want. Then flesh out your best argument for applying the rules that achieve your heart's desire.

The validity of a will of personal property is governed by the law of the place where the decedent died domiciled—West Dakota. This is not helpful. But the meaning of a will of personal property may be construed according to the law of the place where the testator was domiciled at the time of the making of the will. Id. §308. You can argue that the meaning of "all my property" in the will does not include the bank account, because the meaning under the law of "all my property" in East Dakota did not include the bank account.

But don't stop with the will. The claim under the will might be a loser. Try the argument that the account established a conveyance of intangible personal property inter vivos whose validity and effect are governed by the law of the place where the transaction occurred (East Dakota) giving rise to the property interests.

Closely related to the personal property argument is a contract argument. The rights and obligations in the account are governed by the law of the place of contracting (East Dakota).

The final characterization may be a winner—as it was in the case that gives us the name "Totten Trusts." You may be able to persuade a court that the bank account was not a legal conveyance or an enforceable contract but rather created a trust during the decedent's life. The validity and interests created in a trust of intangibles are governed by the law of the place where the transaction takes place—East Dakota. Under the Totten Trust analysis, the person designated as the survivor on a bank account is a beneficiary of an inter vivos trust. Prince's interests arguably vested upon Tess's death, so he is now entitled to the proceeds of the trust assets. Under this theory, the bank account does not form part of Tess's property that is distributed under her will.

The outcome of this case—like all the examples in this chapter—is uncertain. But there are a variety of opportunities for creative lawyering, and a court, so inclined, could choose from competing rules to justify an outcome different from that dictated by the rule governing wills.

13

Substance vs. Procedure

THE RULE AND THE PROBLEM

The traditional approach applied choice of law rules only to issues characterized as "substantive." Courts applied their own forum law to matters of procedure. The traditional rule is easily summarized: "All matters of procedure are governed by the law of the forum." First Restatement §585.

But the rule leads to new problems. First, the rule is itself inconsistent with the goal of uniformity since applying forum procedure can and does affect the outcome of cases and provides an incentive for forum shopping. Second, the rule creates a problem of characterization. Labeling an issue as substantive or procedural affects the outcome of the case, providing another arena for creative legal manipulation.

Rationalizations for the Rule

Different reasons have been offered for the traditional doctrine of applying forum law to matters of procedure. On the one hand, the rule has been explained as resting on principles of convenience. It is argued that it is just too hard for courts to follow all the detailed procedures of a foreign court. (This was the rationalization offered by the First Restatement.) On the other hand, the rule has been explained as requiring application of forum law to certain matters that are particularly important to the forum's policy values. The main thing is that there was no coherent theory that explained why forum procedure always applied. In the absence of such a theory, there was also considerable inconsistency in classifying issues as procedural as opposed to substantive.

When "Procedure" Is Not "Procedure"

Courts characterize legal issues as "procedural" for different purposes. And the same issue can be labeled "procedural" for one purpose but "substantive" for another. A famous example is the decision of Guaranty Trust Co. v. York, 326 U.S. 99 (1945). The state itself labeled statutes of limitations as "procedural" for various purposes, including choice of law. This is consistent with the general rule that most statutes of limitations are "procedural" for choice of law purposes (Chapter 14). But the Supreme Court held that the statute of limitations was "substantive" for purposes of the Erie doctrine (Chapter 24).

Matters That Are Procedural

The First Restatement classified many issues as procedural based both on its theory and on case law. In general, procedure includes "access to courts, the conditions of maintaining or barring action, the form of proceedings in court, the method of proving a claim." Id. §585 cmt. a. The First Restatement classifies all the following as procedure, id. §§586-600.

Jurisdiction
Form of action
Service
Proper and necessary parties
Pleading, joinder, and splitting claims
Trial by judge or jury
Competence and credibility of witnesses
Admissibility of evidence
Proof, presumptions, and inferences
Execution of judgments
Appellate process

Some of the procedural rules effectively override other specific rules. For example, defenses to torts are governed by the law of the place of the wrong. Contributory negligence is not available as a (substantive) defense if it is not imposed under the law of the place of the wrong. Nevertheless, where a forum requires a plaintiff to prove freedom from fault, the First

Restatement classifies this requirement as "procedural," and it is binding even if no such requirement exists under the law of the place of the wrong.[1]

Problem Areas

Immunity   Certain parties are immune by statute or common law to civil liability in claims by other parties. For example, in some jurisdictions a spouse may be immune to tort claims brought by the other spouse. The First Restatement does not mention immunities.[2] In general, an immunity sounds substantive, so it should be governed by the law of the place of the wrong. But a defense of immunity might also fall under the literal language of the rule that the "law of the forum decides who may . . . be sued." Id. §588. The First Restatement's comments to this rule do not clarify. It is even possible that a spouse may have a defense of immunity either under the law of the place of the wrong or under forum law.

Limits on Damages   The measure of damages, including limitations on the amounts recoverable, is governed by the law of the place of the wrong. Id. §§414, 417. But the First Restatement also classifies statutory limits on damages as procedural, so courts will apply forum limits on damages even when a greater recovery is the lawful measure of damages under the law of the place of the wrong. Id. §606.[3]

Rules of Evidence as Opposed to Standards of Care   The First Restatement directs the application of the forum court's own law of evidence, including rules that govern what inferences or presumptions can be drawn. But the First Restatement insists on making a big distinction between rules of evidence governing how to prove a breach of a standard of care and rules defining the standard of care.

The First Restatement gives the example of a rule requiring a plaintiff to "stop, look and listen" before crossing a railroad track. Although this may sound like a rule refining the inferences of negligence to be drawn from the plaintiff's conduct, the First Restatement sees this as a refinement of a standard of care, which is governed by the place of the wrong. Id. §595 cmt. b.

---

1. Id. §601. This is a version of the game my older brother Dan taught me as a kid: "Heads I win, tails you lose."

2. Please double check and let me know if I have missed it. It would take a longish footnote to explain why I don't think privileges, governed by the law of the place of conduct, id. §382, apply to things like spousal or charitable immunity.

3. Professor Weintraub says treating limitations on damages as procedure is "monstrous." Weintraub, Commentary on the Conflict of Laws §3.2C4 at 85.

Statutes of Frauds Traditional courts had trouble classifying statutes of frauds as substantive or procedural. These statutes look substantive to the extent they impose a formal requirement of a writing for a valid contract. They look procedural to the extent they establish a rule of evidence for proving the existence of a contract in court.

The First Restatement elevated the level of confusion into a black letter rule. It distinguished between statutes of frauds that were interpreted as requirements for validity and statutes of frauds that were interpreted as excluding oral evidence. When a statute of frauds was a requirement for a valid contract, it was "substantive" and was governed by the law of the place of contracting. Id. §334. When a statute of frauds was a rule excluding oral proof of a contract, it was "procedural" and governed by forum law. Id. §598. Oh, and the classification was not exclusive: a statute of frauds could be both substantive and procedural!

Courts struggled valiantly to classify particular statutes of frauds as substantive or procedural. Sometimes they gave great weight to the technical language of the statute. A statute that speaks of a contract being "void" without a writing might be deemed substantive, whereas one that speaks of a contract being "voidable" or unenforceable without a writing might be found to be procedural. In one case, a judge permitted enforcement of an oral promise, reasoning that the statute of limitations of the place of contracting did not apply because it was procedural, while the statute of the forum did not apply outside the state because it was substantive.[4]

Parol Evidence Rule Under the parol evidence rule parties may agree by contract that their written contract provides exclusive evidence of their agreement. When a contract is so integrated in a writing, the contract can be modified only in writing.

Jurisdictions had difficulty deciding whether the parol evidence rule was a requirement of formal validity (substantive) or a rule of evidence (procedural). The First Restatement classifies the parol evidence rule as substantive. Id. §599. But this is more complicated than it sounds. First, you must look to see if a contract has been integrated under the law of the place of contracting. If so, the law of the state of contracting governs proof of any variation. But if a contract is not integrated under the law of the place of contracting, then the forum may still apply its own parol evidence rule to limit oral proof of alterations to a written agreement. Id. §599 cmt. b.

Testimonial Privilege The First Restatement directs the application of forum law to all matters of evidence and witnesses. There is no exception for

---

4. Richman et al., Understanding Conflict of Laws §58 at 180, discussing Marie v. Garrison, 13 Abb. N. Cas. 210 (N.Y. Sup. Ct. 1883).

testimonial privileges such as the lawyer-client privilege or the spousal privilege. But such privileges are not recognized merely as a matter of forum convenience, which was the First Restatement's rationalization for applying forum law to procedure. On the contrary, privileges exclude otherwise credible evidence in order to promote some more important social good outside the courtroom—such as uninhibited dialog between lawyer and client or between spouses. It may make more sense to apply the law of the place of conduct or of the parties' domicile to claims of privilege, especially when parties relied on the law of the place where they were located at the time of their communication.

Survival and Revival   At common law, a tort claim was personal and did not survive the death of the parties. Over time, this was altered by statute or by judicial decisions that recognized the survival of claims when parties died prior to the commencement of a civil action and the revival of pending claims in situations where a defendant died after a lawsuit was filed. Under the First Restatement, survival was substantive and was governed by the place of the wrong. Id. §390. But revival could be considered a matter of procedure, substituting the personal representative of the decedent as the new proper party, and hence governed by forum law.

Direct Actions   At common law, a victim of a tortfeasor cannot sue the tortfeasor's insurance company. There is no privity of contract, and under contract principles, the plaintiff is not an intended beneficiary of the insurance agreement. A few states have enacted direct action statutes modifying the common law and permitting plaintiffs to sue tortfeasors' insurance companies directly. These statutes came later than the First Restatement, so its drafters obviously did not include them in the lists of things that are substantive or procedural. Courts attempting to apply the traditional rules reached opposite conclusions. Some held that the right to sue the insurance company is substantive and governed by the law of the place of the wrong. Others held that the issue is procedural and governed by forum law.

Examples

The Maligned Mule

1. Mule claims Donkey slandered him by calling him a "half-breed" in the country of Jungalia. Under the law of Jungalia, the expression "half-breed" is defamatory when spoken about a Mule under certain circumstances. Donkey contends his words were a "joke," which can be a defense under Jungalia law.

Mule sues Donkey in the country of Forumia. Forumia law permits service of process by first-class mail with a signed receipt. Jungalia requires personal service of process by a process server. Mule arranges for service by first-class mail with a signed receipt. Donkey moves to dismiss for insufficiency of service. What is the right ruling under the First Restatement?

2. Same facts. Under Jungalia law, a defendant has a right to trial by jury in a libel case. Under Forumia law, all tort cases are tried to the court without a jury. Mule demands trial by jury. Under the First Restatement, does Mule get a trial by jury?

3. Same facts. Under the law of Forumia a plaintiff must plead and prove the lack of truth as an element of a defamation claim. No such requirement exists under Jungalia law, and truth is not necessarily available as a defense. Mule did not allege the lack of truth in the complaint. Donkey moves to dismiss. Apply the First Restatement.

4. Same facts. Under the law of Forumia, defenses must be raised in the answer or they are waived. Under Jungalia law defenses can be raised any time prior to trial. Donkey did not raise the defense that the statement was a "joke" in the answer. Donkey later raises the defense. What is the result under the First Restatement?

The Regrettable Apology

5. Pinky, a citizen of Fredonia, visited the country of Excludonia on business. He was injured leaving the Excludonia airport when Cubby, a cab driver, ran over Pinky's left foot, crushing his small toe. Cubby immediately stopped the cab, got out, and apologized to Pinky, saying, "I am so sorry I ran over your foot. It was all my fault. Is there anything I can do to help?"

At the time of the injury, Cubby was driving a taxicab owned and operated by Airport Services International Corp., a business incorporated in the country of Fredonia. Pinky sues the corporation in Fredonia for the personal injury, alleging negligence. The corporation denies that Cubby was negligent and contends that Pinky stupidly and unlawfully stepped in front of the cab's tire at a time when he was not visible to the cab driver and did not have the right of way.

Pinky wants to testify about Cubby's statement at the scene of the accident. The defendant moves to exclude the evidence. Admissions of liability are admissible evidence in Fredonia. But under an Excludonian statute designed to encourage apologies, a statement of apology, acceptance of liability, and offer to help are inadmissible evidence. Under the First Restatement, is the evidence admissible?

The Case of the Baleful Bailee

6. Eliot wanted to take a vacation so he took his cat Jennyenny to Dr. Darth, a licensed veterinarian. He left Jennyenny with Dr. Darth, who agreed to provide room and board for the cat for one week.

   When Eliot returned from his vacation and went to pick up Jennyenny, Dr. Darth could not find Jennyenny anywhere.

   Eliot commences a civil action against Dr. Darth in the state of West Dakota. The plaintiff and defendant are both domiciled in the state of West Dakota. But the veterinary clinic where Eliot left Jennyenny was located in the state of East Dakota.

   Under the law of West Dakota, the bailee of personal property is absolutely liable for the value of lost property regardless of fault. Under the law of East Dakota, a bailee is liable only for the negligent damage or loss of personal property. Under the law of West Dakota, unexplained loss of property gives rise to the presumption that the person in control of the property acted negligently, and the defendant must rebut this presumption. Under the law of East Dakota, a person who bears the burden of proving negligence must provide affirmative evidence of negligence, and the unexplained disappearance of property does not give rise to any presumption of negligence.

   Discovery has been completed, and there is still no explanation for Jennyenny's disappearance. Eliot moves for partial summary judgment on the issue of liability. He argues that Dr. Darth is absolutely liable. Alternatively, he argues that Dr. Darth is liable for negligently losing the cat. Rule on the motion applying the First Restatement.

7. Same facts. East Dakota permits recovery of damages for emotional distress resulting from injury to or loss of a companion animal. West Dakota measures damages for injury to or loss of a companion animal by the fair market value of the companion animal. East Dakota does not limit the amount of compensatory damages. But a West Dakota statute limits the amount of damages recoverable for emotional distress to no more than three times the value of pecuniary loss. Jennyenny's fair market value was $3.00.

   Under the First Restatement, does Eliot have the right to recover damages for emotional distress in the lawsuit filed in West Dakota, and are such damages limited?

A Question of Survival

8. Two cars with passengers from the sovereign territory of Tralfamadore collided in the country of Magrathea. Drake Driver, the driver of one of the cars, died in the collision. Three passengers in the other car allege

that Driver negligently caused the accident and seek to recover damages for their personal injuries.

After the death of Driver, the passengers commence a civil action against the estate of Driver in Tralfamadore, the home state of all the parties. Under the law of Tralfamadore, tort claims survive the death of a tortfeasor. But under the law of Magrathea, tort claims do not survive the death of the defendant. The estate of Driver moves to dismiss under Magrathea law. Rule on the motion applying the First Restatement.

Explanations

The Maligned Mule

1. The service is good because it conforms to the requirements of the law of the forum. Service is a matter of procedure, so its validity is governed by forum law.

2. Mule does not get a trial by jury. The matter of the mode of trial—judge or jury—is a matter of procedure and governed by forum law. Here forum law does not provide for trial by jury.

3. It is necessary to distinguish elements of claims and burdens of proof. The elements of a tort claim are governed by the law of the place of the wrong—Jungalia. Under Jungalia law, the elements of a plaintiff's defamation claim do not include lack of truth. Donkey's motion to dismiss should be denied.

4. Pleading requirements that regulate the sequence and time for raising issues, and the consequences for failing to raise them, are procedural. Forumia law applies, and the defenses have been waived.

The Regrettable Apology

5. The testimony about the apology is admissible because evidence is a matter of procedure and governed by forum law. Under forum law the evidence is admissible.

Getting the right answer is easy under the First Restatement rule. But this example serves to illustrate the difficulties of explaining the logic behind the First Restatement rules. The general justification of convenience does not adequately explain the result, because excluding the evidence might be more convenient. Nor does the "unimportance" of procedure explain the result, because the foreign jurisdiction has some strong policies for its exclusionary rule.

The example also illustrates how applying forum law decisively affects outcomes. The driver's statement may be crucial to the plaintiff's case. If the plaintiff litigates in the place of the wrong, the crucial evidence is excluded, and plaintiff loses. If plaintiff sues in a forum that will admit the evidence, then the plaintiff may win. The traditional rule that forum law governs procedure frustrates the glorious dream of outcome uniformity and encourages forum shopping.

The Case of the Baleful Bailee

6. It is necessary to distinguish the claims or causes of action from the law regulating proof. The standard of care is a matter of substance and is governed by the law of the place of the wrong. If the claim were brought under a contract theory, it would be governed by the law of the place of contracting. The law of East Dakota applies to the issue of the standard of liability, and the plaintiff must establish negligence. The forum's strict liability rule does not apply.

   But inferences and presumptions that regulate how negligence is proven are matters of procedure and are governed by forum law.

   Accordingly, Eliot is entitled to judgment on the issue of liability when there is no evidence to explain the disappearance, because Dr. Darth is liable for negligently losing the cat under the law of the place of the wrong. Such negligence is inferred when the cat disappeared from the doctor's custody without explanation under the law of the forum. The plaintiff is probably entitled to judgment on this issue at the summary judgment stage, but jurisdictions may vary, and the standards for summary judgment are procedural and governed by forum law.

   The language of presumptions can be confusing. Most presumptions are rules that regulate matters of proof. They are called "rebuttable." In contrast, an "irrebuttable presumption" is really a substantive legal rule. Such a rule is governed by the law of the place of the wrong. For example, if a jurisdiction had an irrebuttable presumption that a bailee was negligent for damage to bailed property, this would be the same as a rule that a bailee was strictly liable — a matter of substance governed by the place of the wrong.

7. This is another example of the confusing way the First Restatement classifies certain issues as substantive and procedural. The type of damages that are recoverable is substantive, so Eliot can recover damages for emotional distress under the law of East Dakota. But caps on damages are procedural, id. §606, and West Dakota will apply its forum rule and limit damages to three times the value of the pecuniary loss ($9.00).

A Question of Survival

8. The right answer under the First Restatement is that the question of survival is substantive and is governed by the law of the place of the wrong (Magrathea), so the claims should be dismissed. First Restatement §390.

But survival and revival were problem areas where courts did not always agree on how to characterize the issue. This provided room for manipulating the rules. The facts in the example are taken from Grant v. McAuliffe, 264 P.2d 944 (Cal. 1953), where California domiciliaries were injured in an accident in Arizona. The California court decided that the matter of survival was procedural and governed by forum law. The court rejected the First Restatement's authority, noting that older cases had characterized survival as procedural. The court also observed the close connection between survival and revival, which the parties conceded was procedural. Finally, the court reasoned that survival did not form "an essential part of the cause of action" but instead related to the procedures for enforcing the claim.

14

Statutes of Limitations

INTRODUCTION

Problems involving conflicting statutes of limitations arise frequently in practice—and on Conflicts finals. Traditional courts characterized most statutes of limitations as procedural and thus applied forum law. But they labeled some kinds of statutes of limitations as substantive and applied the limitations selected by choice of law rules. The traditional rules created strong incentives for forum shopping. And this led many legislatures to enact borrowing statutes.

THE MAIN RULE: MOST STATUTES OF LIMITATIONS ARE PROCEDURAL

The traditional theory for most statutes of limitations was that they cut off the time period for litigating a right but did not extinguish the right. In cases with multi-jurisdictional ingredients, more than one court might have jurisdiction; more than one court could apply forum procedure; and more than one court might apply its own statute of limitations.

The First Restatement was clear: statutes of limitations were governed by forum law. First Restatement §§603, 604. A forum would apply its own shorter statute of limitations to bar claims even when they were not time-barred by the law of the place where the claim arose. The First Restatement explained that applying a shorter time period under forum law would promote the forum jurisdiction's policy of confining claims to a time period during which the forum "believed substantial justice" could be achieved. Id. §603 cmt. a. The First Restatement also explained that applying a longer forum statute of limitations promoted the forum's policy of permitting claims that were not time-barred under the forum statute.

The rationalizations for the traditional rule are weak. It would certainly be more convenient to dismiss claims barred by foreign statutes of limitations. Barring such claims would also achieve uniformity of results. Nevertheless, the First Restatement rules were well established and widely followed.

THE EXCEPTIONS: STATUTES OF LIMITATIONS EXTINGUISHING RIGHTS

About 87.6[1] percent of statutes of limitations were procedural and governed by forum law. But traditional courts recognized a few situations where the lapse of time had the effect of extinguishing substantive rights. Such time bars were governed by the law selected by normal choice of law rules.

Adverse Possession Under substantive property law, parties can acquire good title to real property when they satisfy the requirements of the doctrine of adverse possession. A similar doctrine, sometimes called title by prescription, shifts ownership of personal property. The legal source for these property rights may be located in statutes of limitations that require claims for the recovery of property to be brought within a certain period of time. But the lapse of time does not merely cut off the procedural opportunity to recover the property; it also confers superior title on the new owner. Statutes of limitations resulting in title by adverse possession are substantive and are governed by the law of the place where the property is located. Id. §§224 & 259.

Time Limit as Condition of Right The First Restatement recognized another exception when a claim was based on a foreign statute that imposed a time limit on bringing the claim as a condition for bringing the claim. The Restatement reasoned that a right that expired after a certain period of time under the law creating the right could not be enforced in any jurisdiction after the expiration of the right. Id. §603.

The First Restatement gave the example of a statute that created a new cause of action for wrongful death and at the same time provided that the

---

1. I am making up the number, but you get the idea.

claim must be brought within one year of the death. Other courts with longer general limitations periods must dismiss such a wrongful death claim when brought after one year. *Id.* §605 illus. 1.

The challenge is determining when a statute of limitation falls under the condition-of-right exception. Traditional jurisdictions sometimes used a specificity or built-in test: a statute of limitations that was enacted as part of a new cause of action and that applied specifically to the new cause of action would be substantive. The most common example of such built-in limitations is the same as the example offered by the First Restatement — wrongful death statutes that specifically require litigation within a certain period of time.

Statutes of Repose Statutes of repose are super-statutes of limitation, designed to avoid the problem of the lagging enforcement of statutes of limitations that may result from the delayed manifestation of injuries, from rules tolling the running of the statutes, and from the willingness of other courts to apply their own longer limitations periods. An example of a statute of repose is a statute that bars absolutely all medical malpractice claims after a certain number of years from the date the medical services were rendered. The lapse of the time period in a statute of repose cuts off even unknown claims, so the time period will often be longer than for a statute of limitations. Statutes of repose extinguish the right as well as the remedy — and are thus substantive.

Whether a time period prescribed in a statute is a procedural statute of limitation or a substantive statute of repose cannot always be determined by the language of the statute. The legislative purpose and the structure of the statute may provide guidance. Suppose a statute requires medical malpractice claims to be brought within two years of the discovery of the claim or 15 years from the date of the incident that gave rise to the claim. The purpose of the 15-year cutoff was probably to extinguish all claims by that outside date. If so, the statute is a statute of repose, is substantive, and bars litigation of the claims in all other courts.

BORROWING STATUTES

The traditional characterization of most statutes of limitations as procedural created a huge incentive to forum shop. A claim time-barred under the law of the place of the wrong could still be litigated in all jurisdictions with longer statutes of limitations. Of course, the plaintiff would also need to find a court with personal jurisdiction, but that task became easier as jurisdictional limits were relaxed over the course of the twentieth century.

Shopping for forums where claims were not time-barred under forum limitations became widespread. In response most states enacted borrowing statutes. Borrowing statutes vary from jurisdiction to jurisdiction. They typically provide that a cause of action is time-barred when it is time-barred under the law of the place where the cause of action arose or accrued. Some also borrow the law of the defendant's domicile to bar a claim. Some provide exceptions that permit forum residents to sue under the longer forum limitations periods. When borrowing statutes direct courts to apply the limitations law of some other jurisdiction, they are often interpreted as borrowing the foreign jurisdiction's law on when an action commences and is tolled, in addition to borrowing the specific time period in the borrowed statute.

Warning: when a claim is *not* time-barred under the law of the place where the action arose, a borrowing statute does not automatically permit litigation. Instead the borrowing statute does not apply. In that case, another forum statute of limitations that bars the claim will apply.

Examples

Classical Rules

1. Aristotle punches Plato in the country of Sparta. Under Spartan law, the statute of limitations for assault and battery claims is two years. Fourteen months later, Plato sues Aristotle in the country of Athens, where the statute of limitations for all intentional torts is one year. Aristotle moves to dismiss under the forum country's one-year statute of limitations. What is the result under the traditional rules?

2. Ludwig punches Wolfgang in the country of Dischordia. Two years later Wolfgang sues Ludwig in the country of Sonatia. The statute of limitations for assault claims in Dischordia is one year, while in Sonatia it is three years. Is the claim time-barred in Sonatia?

3. While Ella is visiting Bessie at her home in the country of Blueland, Ella offers to buy a 78 rpm record from Bessie for $2.00. Bessie accepts the offer, and the two shake hands. They do not reduce their contract to writing.

   Eight years later, Bessie moves to the country of Redland and takes the record with her.

   Nine years later, Ella sues Bessie for breach of contract in the country of Pinkland. The statute of limitations for breaches of oral contracts is ten years in Pinkland, eight years in Redland, and four years in Blueland.

   Is the contract claim time-barred under traditional rules?

Consumer Confusion

4. The country of Camelot enacts a new Consumer Credit Refund Act. The Act provides:

> A consumer may rescind a sales contract and recover the purchase price plus interest when the seller did not disclose the consumer's rights at the time of the purchase as required by this Act, provided that the action to enforce rights under this Act is commenced within one year of the alleged violation of the Act.

Cathy Consumer sues Sid Seller for violating the Act in the country of Narnia. She commences the action 16 months after the alleged violation of the Act. The Narnia statute of limitations for actions for breaches of sales contracts is three years. Is Cathy's action barred under the traditional rules?

Adverse Possession

5. In East Dakota, there was a big rain storm 12 years ago. When the flood waters receded, the creek that formed the border of Farmer Jones's property changed course. Farmer Jones began to plough new land that appeared on his side of the creek. He continually ploughed the land and treated it as an extension of his farm property for 11 years.

   Under the law of East Dakota, all actions for the recovery of real property must be brought within ten years. Under East Dakota property law, where a person publicly and continually occupies land for ten years, that person acquires title to the property under the doctrine of adverse possession.

   After 11 years, City Slicker became the heir to the person who died holding the title of record to property adjacent to Farmer Jones's farm. The decedent's title extended to the former location of the creek. This includes land that Farmer Jones has been farming for 11 years. Under the property law of East Dakota, the former location of the creek remains the border of property when the creek changes location suddenly.

   Within one year of inheriting the land, City Slicker, a domiciliary of Forumia, commences an action to recover the land. The Forumia statute of limitations on actions to recover land is 14 years.

   What law applies under the traditional rules?

Horsey Set

6. The country of Equestria enacted the Horselovers Protection Act, which provides that "all claims against owners of horses for injuries inflicted by horses must be brought no later than four years after the date that the

cause of action arose or accrued." Peggy was injured in Equestria when a horse she was riding rolled over on her. Five years later, Peggy sues the horse's owner in the country of Longeria. Longeria's general statute of limitations for personal injury claims is six years. Is Peggy's claim time-barred under the traditional rules?

7. Same facts. But Longeria also has enacted a borrowing statute that provides, "No cause of action shall be maintained when such cause of action is barred by the law of the place where it accrued." What is the result?

Explanations

Classical Rules

1. The forum will dismiss, applying its own, shorter statute of limitations. *See* First Restatement §603 illus. 1.

2. The claim is not time-barred in Sonatia. Courts will apply the longer forum statute of limitations and permit the claim to go forward even though it would be dismissed by a court in the country where the claim arose. *Id.* §604 illus. 1.

3. The forum will apply the forum statute of limitations under which the claim is not time-barred. This example does not really add anything new, but it reinforces the rule: apply forum law to most statutes of limitations. The more complicated facts may suggest one strong reason in favor of applying forum law. If forum law did not apply, it would not be easy to decide what other law should apply. For torts, the obvious choice would be the law of the place of the wrong. But for contracts, the place of contracting and performance might not make sense or might be hard to find.

Consumer Confusion

4. The one-year statute of limitations embedded in the Camelot Consumer Credit Refund Act falls into the "condition of right" exception and is substantive. The forum must apply the shorter statute of limitations of the law creating the right rather than its own, longer procedural statute of limitations. Evidence that the right is conditioned upon it being brought within the time period consists of the following: (1) the cause of action is a new claim created by statute rather than an existing common law right; (2) the statute of limitation was enacted at the same time as the statute creating the claim; and (3) the statute uses language of condition ("provided that"). The statute thus satisfies the "specificity" or "built-in" tests sometimes employed to identify substantive statutes of limitation.

Even though I have made up the law in the example so it meets all the criteria for a substantive statute of limitations, it is possible that courts would still construe it as procedural. If so, then Narnia would follow the normal rule and apply its own three-year statute of limitations.

Adverse Possession

5. The law where the real property is located governs substantive issues of property law, including the effect of a change in the course of the stream and the requirements for acquiring title by adverse possession. Under the law of East Dakota, the shift of the creek by avulsion has not changed the property lines. Farmer Jones did not become the owner of the land between his property and the new location of the creek. But by occupying and farming the land for ten years, Farmer Jones acquired the land.

The effect of the East Dakota statute of limitations is to extinguish and transfer substantive rights. Accordingly, Forumia will apply the statute of limitations of the place where the land is and not its own longer statute of limitations.

Adverse possession claims raising conflicts problems were rare back in the day, partly for jurisdictional reasons. Traditionally, courts refused to exercise jurisdiction over actions for recovery of land or for trespass to land when the land was located in another state. The First Restatement sought to resolve many real property conflicts through this jurisdictional rule. Id. §§613-616. But ownership claims involving the application of statutes of limitations could arise in other ways. For example, Farmer Jones might use force to expel City Slicker from the disputed land. In an action for assault and battery, a privilege to use limited force might be lawful only if the defendant was in fact the owner. This in turn would require a consideration of the applicable law of adverse possession.

Horsey Set

6. This example illustrates the problem of telling whether a statute of limitations is a statute of repose. There is nothing in the language of the statute that provides a clear answer, so the general rule that statutes of limitations are procedural might come into operation. If so, then the forum will apply its longer forum limitations period and permit Peggy's claim to go forward.

But perhaps the horse owners' lobby persuaded the legislature to adopt this specific statute in order to cut off claims that were pending for too long under the general statute of limitations. If so, the statute might act to extinguish rights as a statute of repose and would bar litigation in other courts.

One important thing to note: just because a statute of limitations is new, speaks in prohibitory terms, and addresses a specific kind of claim does not mean the statute meets the "specificity" test some courts use for finding that a statute is a condition of right. The specificity test links a specific statute of limitations to specific legislation creating the claim. The Horselovers Protection Act does not create any new cause of action, so it does not fall under the specificity or condition-of-right forms of "substantive" statutes of limitation.

7. Ah, finally another easy one! Regardless of whether Equestria's statute is substantive or procedural, Longeria's borrowing statute borrows it and applies it to claims like Peggy's that arose in Equestria and that are time-barred under Equestria law.

15 Public Policy

INTRODUCTION

One super-escape device permitted traditional courts to refuse to enforce rights created by foreign law when the foreign law was offensive to the forum's public policy. This chapter considers the doctrine, its restrictions, and problems in its application.

ACTIONS CONTRARY TO PUBLIC POLICY

The Rule The First Restatement formulated the traditional public policy doctrine: "No action can be maintained upon a cause of action created in another state the enforcement of which is contrary to the strong public policy of the forum." First Restatement §612.

The rule does not apply to defenses. The language of the First Restatement restricts the public policy doctrine to causes of action. It does not permit a forum to disregard defenses that arise under foreign law, no matter how offensive. In a case where a German employer fired a Jew in Germany pursuant to Nazi laws requiring the firing of Jews, a New York court refused to strike the defense. It was offensive to public policy, but it was a defense, not a cause of action. See Holzer v. Deutsche Reichsbahn-Gesellschaft, 14 N.E.2d 798 (N.Y. 1938).

Effect   The public policy doctrine permits a court to refuse to recognize a cause of action created by law sufficiently offensive to its own policies. For example, a court could apply the doctrine to refuse to enforce a contract for prostitution even if the contract was valid under the law of the place of contracting. But it is ambiguous about what exactly should happen in such a situation. The First Restatement suggested that the offending claim should simply be dismissed. *Id.* §612 cmt. a. This would permit the plaintiff to refile elsewhere. Some traditional courts applied the public policy doctrine more aggressively to decide the case, displacing the offensive foreign law — sometimes including even defenses — and substituting their own law. This would result in a judgment on the merits that could bar litigation in another court.

"Strong Public Policy"

The Need to Define Restrictively   In every case involving a conflict between the law of the forum and another state, the policies of the other state are different from and contrary to the policies of the forum state. Mere legal differences cannot justify disregarding foreign law — otherwise courts would never apply the law from other jurisdictions.

The public policy doctrine provides an exception to the normal choice of law rules. The First Restatement even says there is a "strong public policy" in favor of applying the normal rules to enforce claims created by foreign law. To prevent the public policy exception from swallowing the rules, it must be restricted. The First Restatement emphasizes that its application is "extremely limited." *Id.* §612 cmt. c.

The classic, restrictive definition of public policy is: courts "do not close their doors" to causes of action that arise under foreign law that just seem unfair unless enforcing the foreign law "would violate some fundamental principle of justice, some prevalent conception of good morals, some deep-rooted tradition of the common weal." Loucks v. Standard Oil Co. of New York, 120 N.E. 198, 202 (N.Y. 1918).

PENAL CLAIMS

The Rules   Traditionally, courts refused to recognize some penal claims arising under the law of other jurisdictions. The First Restatement provides that "no action can be maintained" by a private person "to recover a penalty" granted by foreign law. It has a similar provision that no action can be maintained by a foreign government entity to enforce its government interests. *Id.* §§610-611 & cmts.

The penal claim rule does not prohibit the enforcement of punitive damages. The availability of punitive damages is normally determined by the law of the place of the wrong. Most punitive damages serve overlapping purposes, including fully compensating the plaintiff, that are not purely penal. If, however, punitive damages are available in addition to full compensation, the First Restatement says they may satisfy the definition of a penal claim, id. §611 cmt. b(3). Nevertheless, courts have enforced punitive damages and even statutory provisions for double damages on the theory that a private right of recovery granted to an individual is not penal.

Factors to Consider   The reasons for the penal claim exception are unclear, and there is no uniform test for determining whether a claim is penal. In dictum the Supreme Court defined a penal law as one whose purpose is "to punish an offense against the public justice of the state" as opposed to providing private parties a remedy for wrongful injuries. Huntington v. Attrill, 146 U.S. 657, 674 (1892).

One court considered a variety of factors from earlier decisions: (1) whether the purpose of the law is to punish a violation of individual rights rather than duties owed to the public; (2) whether the penalty is recoverable by an individual or public entity; and (3) whether the law's main purpose is to punish for past injuries to an individual or coerce future compliance and achieve public retribution. See Republic of the Philippines v. Westinghouse Electric Corp., 821 F. Supp. 292 (D.N.J. 1993). In that case, a foreign government sought punitive damages under foreign law for a corporation's bribery of its former president. The court concluded that the factors indicated that the claim was penal. Accordingly, it did not permit the claim. The decision did not rely on the First Restatement rules, but the same conclusion could be reached even more quickly under the First Restatement's prohibition of government actions for foreign public rights.

Examples

Bad Old Days

1. Thomas owned Douglass as slave property in the country of Bondland. Sojourner secretly helped Douglass to escape from slavery and to flee from Bondland by providing Douglass with a map and false identification papers. Sojourner's activity was illegal under the law of Bondland and supported claims there for conspiracy, conversion, and trespass to chattels. Thomas sues Sojourner in Soujourner's home country of Fredonia, where slavery is illegal. His claims are based on Bondland law. Will Fredonia recognize the claims?

2. Same facts. Prior to Douglass's escape, Thomas entered into a lease with Hugh in Bondland. Under the terms of the agreement, Thomas agreed

to deliver Douglass to Hugh and granted Hugh permission to employ Douglass. Hugh was entitled to retain any income generated by Douglass. In return Hugh agreed to pay Thomas $1,000 per month. Hugh refused to pay Thomas, and Thomas sues Hugh in the country of Fredonia. Does the public policy doctrine prevent recognition of the claims?

Good Intentions

3. Reverend Sunday, a citizen of the state of Rektitudia, went on a church mission to the country of Shameland. While driving a truck in Shameland, Sunday accidentally struck and injured Terry Vickers. Reverend Sunday returned to his home state, and Vickers died.

   The administrator of Vickers's estate has filed a wrongful death action against Sunday in Rektitudia. The lawsuit asserts claims under the Shameland death statute that entitles the estate of a person wrongfully killed to recover damages, including damages measured by the expected income that the decedent would have earned if he or she had lived.

   Vickers was a prostitute. The administrator of Vickers's estate demands damages in the amount of $50,000, which is the present value of the amount of income that Vickers would have earned as a prostitute.

   Prostitution is criminal in Rektitudia. Sunday moves to dismiss the cause of action as violating Rektitudia's public policy. Rule on the motion and explain.

4. Same facts. Vickers's estate also presents an alternative claim under the Shameland death statute that entitles the victim's estate to recover $25,000 for each person whose careless conduct caused the decedent's death. The amount of the recovery is fixed and bears no relationship to the economic loss sustained by the estate.

   Sunday moves to dismiss the claim as penal. Rule on the motion and explain.

Foreign Libel

5. Meena, a citizen of the country of Harmonia, went on an exchange program and lived for six months in the country of Swindland. There she became very angry when she learned about the amount of bribery and political corruption. One day she submitted a letter to the editor of the *Swindland Times*. In it she wrote, "Swindland Hospital is so dirty, dangerous and corrupt that the most obvious explanation for the fact that it has not been closed down is that someone has been bribed."

   After Meena returned home, she was served with a lawsuit commenced in Harmonia by Swindland Hospital Corporation and its president. The complaint alleges that Meena violated Swindland libel law by accusing the hospital of committing or benefiting from criminal acts.

Under the law of Swindland, suggesting that someone committed crimes is libel. Truth is not a defense.

In contrast, the Harmonia constitution is based on the U.S. Constitution. Under Harmonia law, Meena's letter to the editor would be protected as political speech, as opinion, and possibly as true.

Meena moves to dismiss the foreign cause of action as offensive to the public policy of Harmonia. What is the result under the First Restatement?

Hot Tamales

6. Tammy lives in Memphis, Tennessee and sells hot tamales at Little League games in Mississippi. Tammy has not paid the privilege tax required of hot tamale vendors.[1] Mississippi sues her in Tennessee to collect the fee. What is the result if Tennessee applies the First Restatement rules to this claim?

Spitting Image

7. Bill Spatz spit in public in the country of Spitzland. A Spitzland anti-spitting statute specifies that any spectator spying another person spitting in public may bring a lawsuit against that person and recover $50 for each spitting incident. No more than one claimant can recover under the statute for each spitting incident.

Sam Witness records an image on his cell phone of Spatz spitting in Spitzland. He sues Spatz in East Dakota under the Spitzland anti-spitting statute. Spatz moves to dismiss the claim as a penalty. Will Spatz win this spitting spat?

Direct Action

8. Plaintiff, a resident of West Dakota, was injured in West Dakota by a car driven by Driver. West Dakota has joined three other U.S. jurisdictions in enacting a direct action statute that permits the victim of a tort to sue the tortfeasor's insurance company.

At the time of the accident, Driver was insured by Everystate Insurance Corp., an insurance company incorporated under the law of East Dakota. Plaintiff sues Everystate in East Dakota court under the West Dakota direct action statute.

East Dakota has not enacted a direct action statute. Under its local law, an insurance company is not liable directly to the plaintiff in a tort

---

1. Sadly, the state repealed its special tax for tamale vendors, but the sellers are still subject to general privilege taxes.

action. Moreover, East Dakota rules of evidence prohibit the introduction of any evidence that a defendant is insured, because such evidence is considered likely to prejudice factfinders against the defendant and encourage them to award excessive damages.

The insurance company moves to dismiss the direct action as offensive to East Dakota's strong public policy. How should the court rule according to the First Restatement?

Shareholder Sanctions

9. Anne, Beth, and Cathy decided to open a lawn service in East Carolina. They agreed to form the business as a corporation under the law of East Carolina in order to limit their individual liability in the event the business sustained losses. Cathy obtained all the necessary licenses, completed all the paperwork, and filed almost all the forms required to complete the process of incorporation. Unfortunately, she forgot to file a copy of the corporate charter in the county where the lawn service maintained its principal place of business.

   Two years later, the business became insolvent. Under East Carolina Code section 223, the failure to complete all filings required to incorporate makes each shareholder jointly and severally liable for all debts of the corporation. Bankco, a creditor of the corporation, has discovered that Anne is one of the shareholders. It sues Anne in her home state of West Carolina seeking to hold her individually liable for the full amount of the corporate debt to Bankco. Under West Carolina law Bankco could not hold Anne individually liable based on the failure to file the form.

   Anne moves to dismiss the cause of action, arguing that East Carolina Code section 223, imposing individual liability on her for such a technical violation, is a penalty. Rule on her motion applying the First Restatement.

Explanations

Bad Old Days

1. This is an obvious example of an action contrary to strong public policy. But the legal institutionalization of immoral practices raises all sorts of potential problems that are not so easy. If Sojourner commits other unlawful acts motivated by her desire to free Douglass, the narrow public policy doctrine would not be available. For example, if she steals a horse or threatens someone with violence, the causes of action stemming from the theft of the horse or the assault would not themselves be offensive to public policy.

2. The answer is not so clear, and the example serves to make two points. First, the legal consequences of widespread immoral but legal acts are not so easily resolved by denying all claims. In the United States, even after the abolition of slavery, there were lingering cases involving breaches of contract for the delivery of slaves prior to abolition.

   Second, the determination of whether the cause of action offends strong public policy is a value judgment of the forum, and different jurisdictions may resolve this differently. If this result seems counter-intuitive, then consider the problem that arises when the proceeds of a slave sale are invested in Big Bank Corp, and the bank refuses to return the funds to a depositor and raises public policy as its defense.

Good Intentions

3. This example illustrates a dilemma for the First Restatement. The First Restatement explicitly prohibits enforcing an action when the enforcement would be contrary to the strong public policy of the forum. Even though the Shameland law is not offensive in general, the forum could refuse to enforce rights under it in this case because the award would be offensive to its strong public policy. The dilemma, however, is that the First Restatement limits the forum to refusing to enforce the foreign claim. If the forum dismisses in this case, the wrongdoer may have no liability at all since Shameland may not have long-arm jurisdiction. Even if it does, the defendant could resist enforcement of a foreign country judgment in his home country based on its repugnance to public policy (Chapter 30).

   Traditional courts were sometimes more flexible in applying the public policy exception than the First Restatement. A more reasonable response to the policy issues raised by the example (though not authorized by the First Restatement) would be for the forum to disregard the offensive foreign damages and substitute an alternative measure of damages available under forum law.

4. The sum fixed automatically for wrongdoers regardless of pecuniary loss looks like a penalty. But it is in part an effort to fix by statute the value of private loss suffered by the estate. The First Restatement does not classify statutory death damages as a penalty even when the amount is fixed arbitrarily. Id. §611 cmt. d(4). So Sunday's motion is denied.

Foreign Libel

5. Swindland is the place of the wrong, so its law applies to create a cause of action. But under the First Restatement, the forum will dismiss the defamation claim because enforcing it would offend its strong public policy.

Hot Tamales

6. This is an example of a claim by a foreign government or state to enforce its own government interest. Under the First Restatement, the action cannot be maintained.

    This is as good an example as any for pointing out that the rule may not make any sense. It does not seem unfair for Tennessee to enforce Mississippi's claim if it wants to, and the state might benefit if Mississippi reciprocated. The result differs when the state has reduced a tax claim to judgment. Such a judgment must be given full faith and credit by other states (see Chapter 31).

Spitting Image

7. Spatz should win. The statute is a penalty. It seeks to punish bad conduct. It provides for a fine that is unrelated to any economic loss or injury suffered by the plaintiff. Under the First Restatement, the action cannot be maintained.

Direct Action

8. Most traditional courts knew they did not want to enforce direct actions but were not sure why. Some avoided enforcing them by classifying them as procedural. But under facts similar to those in this example, Illinois determined that Wisconsin's direct action was not procedural yet refused to enforce it on the ground that it violated Illinois public policy. Marchlik v. Coronet Insurance Co., 239 N.E.2d 799 (Ill. 1968).

    The result is hard to square with the classical, restrictive definition of strong public policy. It is hard to accept that a sister state's different method for resolving tort claims really offends the public morality of Illinois. And the Illinois court did not even try to explain why its legitimate concerns with preventing the factfinder from knowing about the existence of insurance could not be accommodated in other ways—for example, by substituting the names of tortfeasors. The court acknowledged that a difference between laws is not sufficient to deny enforcement, yet it relied heavily on the "complex problems" resulting from litigating under the unfamiliar law.

    In sum, a restrictive application, in keeping with both the letter and spirit of the First Restatement, would not refuse to enforce rights under the direct action statute on the ground that doing so was offensive to strong public policy. But *Marchlik* provides a good example of the wiggle room that the public policy doctrine provided courts for avoiding undesirable results.

Shareholder Sanctions

9. A statute imposing joint and several liability on an individual shareholder for a technical failure to file incorporation papers looks at first
like a penalty. This is especially true if the plaintiff had no reason to
know about the existence of the shareholder and did not rely on his or
her assets in extending credit to what looked like a corporation. For this
reason, some courts have refused to recognize claims under such statutes
as penal claims.

But other courts do not classify this as a penalty. They emphasize that
the statute creates a private claim and that the amount of recovery is not
arbitrary; it is measured by the plaintiff's economic loss. Moreover, while
the statute might appear to impose a punishment, it effectively preserves
the background liability of the parties as partners that would exist in the
absence of effective incorporation. Under the First Restatement, this is
probably not a penalty. Id. §611 cmt. d(3).

16 Renvoi

INTRODUCTION

The problem of renvoi does not arise in every case. It arises when a court applies its choice of law rules to select another jurisdiction's law, and instead of stopping with the foreign substantive law (for example, its torts law), it applies the foreign choice of law rule. Renvoi arises when the foreign choice rule would select a law other than its own to govern the case.

With few exceptions, traditional courts did not engage in renvoi, and the First Restatement rejected it, too. But rejecting renvoi meant that courts did not always decide cases the same way. Illinois might apply Florida law in a case where Florida would apply Illinois law. This obviously frustrated the glorious dream of uniformity of result. Moreover, rejecting renvoi produced the paradoxical consequence that courts would apply the law of another jurisdiction in cases where the other jurisdiction would not apply its own law.

Although the First Restatement outlawed renvoi in most situations, courts sometimes balked at the resulting inconsistency. Selective use of renvoi provided yet another escape device for avoiding outcomes dictated by the mechanical application of the First Restatement rules.

THE TRADITIONAL RULE

Just Say No! The First Restatement rule is easy: do not apply renvoi. When the First Restatement selects the law of some foreign jurisdiction—the place of the wrong, the place of contracting, or the place of marriage—it selects only the local law of that jurisdiction, not its choice of law rules. When the conflicts rules of states differ, "the foreign law to be applied is the law applicable to the matter in hand and not the Conflict of Laws of the foreign state." First Restatement §7(b).

Land and Divorce Exceptions The First Restatement acknowledged that rejecting the foreign conflicts rule "may result in a decision contrary to that which would be reached in a court in that state." Id. §7 cmt. d. In two kinds of cases, the First Restatement deemed outcome uniformity so important that it requires application of the foreign court's choice of laws rule (possibly resulting in renvoi) in cases involving title to land and the validity of divorce decrees. Id. §8.

Embarrassment of Renvoi

Renvoi is a skeleton in the closet of the First Restatement. First, renvoi should not even exist. In the ideal world, all jurisdictions should apply the same (First Restatement) choice rules to select the same law to govern no matter where the case is filed. Renvoi only exists because jurisdictions do not always have the same choice rules. Second, the traditional solution for renvoi that is adopted by the First Restatement (except for land title and divorce decrees) is incompatible with its goal of outcome uniformity. Rejecting renvoi also frustrates the philosophical goal of enforcing vested rights because rejecting renvoi potentially leads to the disregard of rights that have vested under the law of another jurisdiction.

Terminology

The First Restatement avoids some of the weird jargon associated with renvoi. Unfortunately, Conflicts professors are fascinated by renvoi, and most casebooks—and some cases—will require you to know some or all of the following.

Renvoi The term renvoi is French for "send back" or "cross-reference."[1] A forum court is said to "accept" renvoi when it engages in renvoi and follows the whole law of the foreign court to some other jurisdiction's law.

---

1. It is also French for "belch." Although this may be the key to unlocking the secrets of renvoi, this fact is not included in the casebooks or treatises and will probably not be on your final exam.

Whole Law and Local Law "Whole law" means the whole law that a jurisdiction will apply in a particular case, including any foreign law selected by its choice of law rules. "Local law" means the jurisdiction's local, internal, or substantive law—its own local torts, contracts, or property rules. Renvoi problems arise when a court looks to a foreign jurisdiction's "whole law." The First Restatement avoids renvoi problems by directing application only of the foreign jurisdiction's local or internal law—except for land title and divorce decrees.

Remission and Transmission When a court looks to the whole law of the foreign jurisdiction, there are three possibilities. First, the foreign court's whole law could direct the application of its own local law, in which case there is no renvoi problem. This is the ideal state of things under the First Restatement, where both jurisdictions' conflicts rules select the same place's law to apply. Second, the foreign court's whole law could select the law of the court that is looking to its law. For example, New York's choice rule might select California's law, where in the same case California's choice rule selects New York's law. "Remission" is the term that describes this sort of reciprocal or circular renvoi situation. Third, a foreign court's whole law could select yet a third jurisdiction's law. For example, New York's choice rule might select California's law, where in the same case California's choice rule selects the law of Delaware. "Transmission" describes this renvoi situation where New York would apply California law but California would apply Delaware's.

SO WHAT'S THE PROBLEM?

The First Restatement followed the consensus of American case law in rejecting renvoi in most situations. Renvoi is permitted more widely in Europe. Several justifications have been offered for the traditional American rejection of renvoi. First, there is no better way to end renvoi than at the beginning. Second, rejecting renvoi avoids the practical difficulty of determining the content of foreign choice of law laws. These justifications probably do not fully explain the traditional judicial hostility to renvoi.[2]

Inconsistent Application Rejecting renvoi will produce different outcomes when New York's choice of law rule selects California tort law and California's choice rule selects New York tort law. Yet another problem with renvoi is that courts have not always approached it consistently. If New York

---

2. Some prominent scholars encourage greater resort to renvoi to achieve outcome uniformity. Hay et al., Conflict of Laws §3.13 at 144-45.

sometimes applies California tort law but sometimes applies California whole law to select some other state's tort law, then New York can manipulate the outcome of cases by picking and choosing when to apply California tort law and when to look at California's conflicts rules.

Outlaw Courts

It is not hard to find examples of outlaw courts that refuse to follow the First Restatement and get into renvoi trouble. In University of Chicago v. Dater, 270 N.W. 175 (Mich. 1936), a wife sent a joint promissory note from Michigan to Illinois, where it was accepted. She later raised a defense of coverture, arguing lack of capacity under the law of Michigan.

The court thought renvoi provided an easy solution. It reasoned that either Michigan or Illinois law applied. If Michigan law applied, then the wife lacked capacity. But if Illinois law applied, then Illinois law would apply Michigan law, and again the wife lacked capacity. The court did not see that it was using the word "law" in two different ways. For Michigan "law," it meant Michigan local contract law. For Illinois "law," it meant the whole law of Illinois, including Illinois's conflicts rules. The court's logic failed to explain why Illinois choice rules should apply—or why, if they did, Michigan's choice rules should not apply and select the law of Illinois.

It applied Michigan law, a result inconsistent with the First Restatement. If Illinois was the place of contracting, then Michigan should have applied only Illinois contract law.

Examples

One-Way Drivers

1. John Limon and Lucy Passenger, domiciliaries of the country of Pepperland, went for a day trip to the country of Nowhereland. While John was driving, the tire blew out, and the car crashed into a brick wall. The country of Nowhereland has a guest statute that bars all claims for personal injuries by nonpaying passengers against their drivers. Pepperland has no guest statute. Moreover, in litigation involving guest statutes, Pepperland applies the law of the parties' common domicile. Accordingly, in claims stemming from car accidents in Nowhereland between Pepperland parties, the Pepperland courts apply the law of Pepperland.

   Passenger sues Limon in Nowhereland, and Limon moves for summary judgment under the Nowhereland guest statute. Passenger argues that Nowhereland should apply Pepperland law. Nowhereland follows the First Restatement. Rule on the motion and explain.

2. Dereck Trucker stopped for lunch at Mom's Chili restaurant in the state of West Dakota, where he consumed a large bowl of chili. He got back on the highway. After crossing into the state of East Dakota, Trucker became violently ill from the chili. He suffered injuries when he lost control of the truck and collided with a brick wall.

   Trucker seeks to recover damages from the restaurant. The restaurant insists that it took all possible precautions with its food and is not responsible for any defects in ingredients that it was not possible to detect. Under the law of West Dakota restaurants are liable only for injuries caused by their negligence. Under West Dakota's choice of law rules, the place of the wrong in food poisoning cases is the place where the harmful food takes effect upon the body. Under the law of East Dakota, restaurants are strictly liable for injuries caused by defective food. But under East Dakota's choice of law rules, food poisoning cases are governed by the law of the place where the allegedly defective food was served and consumed.

   What law would East Dakota and West Dakota courts apply to the issue of the restaurant's standard of care under the First Restatement?

Contractual Confusion

3. Bob Bayard ordered a custom suit over the Internet from Snafuco Importers. Bayard viewed the seller's Internet site from a desktop computer in his home in the country of Recovery. The seller received the authorization and shipped the merchandise from its place of business in the country of Denial. The form contract on the Internet excluded liability for consequential damages.

   The first day that Bayard wore the suit, he was caught in a light rainstorm. The rain washed the color out of the suit fabric. The bleeding dye also ruined the shirt and tie that Bayard was wearing.

   Bayard seeks to recover the cost of the suit and also the consequential damages caused to his other clothing. Under the contract law of Denial, exclusions of consequential damages are valid, but under the law of Recovery, exclusions of consequential damages are not valid in sales to consumers.

   Under Recovery's choice of law, the place of contracting that governs damages is the place where the order was accepted and from which the goods were shipped. Under Denial's choice of law, questions of damages are governed by the law of the place of performance.

   What law will Recovery apply to the issue of consequential damages according to the First Restatement?

Intriguing Intestacy

4. Gulliver, a citizen of the country of Albion, died domiciled in the country of Lilliput, leaving personal property located in Albion. According to

A promise to make a will is within the Avalon statute of frauds and must be in writing. But Avalon cases recognize an exception where a party has relied upon an oral promise. In such cases, an oral promise is enforceable even if there is no writing. Moreover, Avalon cases recognize that a promise to leave a person property by will creates an equitable property interest in the land that can be enforced against the estate or against third persons who claim an interest but who are not bona fide purchasers for value.

In contrast, in East Dakota, a promise to make a will must be in writing. Moreover, even a valid promise to make a will does not convey an interest in land; it creates only a cause of action for damages against the estate. Does Lance acquire an interest in Blackacre?

Explanations

One-Way Drivers

1. Summary judgment is granted to the defendant Limon. This is an easy case. Nowhereland will apply its own guest statute. Nowhereland is the place of the wrong, so its law will govern liability and defenses. It will grant judgment for the defendant. There is no choice of law rule that authorizes Nowhereland to apply the law of Pepperland, and the fact that Pepperland would decide the case differently will not prevent Nowhereland from applying its normal choice of law rule. Applying that rule does not give rise to renvoi because Nowhereland's law does not include a choice rule that selects some other jurisdiction's law in this case.

   In other words, different outcomes do not necessarily mean there is a renvoi problem. Applying Nowhereland's guest statute obviously produces a different result than would be obtained in the other jurisdiction's courts. Given the outcome, you can see why competent counsel for the plaintiff would never have brought the case in Nowhereland.

2. This case sets up renvoi problems because the conflicts rules differ and because the law of the place of the wrong selected by each court will be the law of the other state. According to the First Restatement, the courts should avoid renvoi and apply only the local internal law of the place whose law governs under their choice of laws rule.

   If the case is litigated in East Dakota, East Dakota courts should apply the forum's conflicts rule, which selects the law of the place where the food was served and consumed. It should apply only the local internal tort rules of that place (West Dakota). Under West Dakota tort law, the restaurant is liable only for negligence.

If the case is litigated in West Dakota, West Dakota courts should apply their forum conflicts rule, which is the place where the food poisoning took effect on the driver (East Dakota). The court should apply only the East Dakota tort law of strict liability, not its conflicts rules. Under East Dakota's torts rule, the restaurant is strictly liable.

This case demonstrates the right way to resolve renvoi problems under the First Restatement. It also demonstrates the paradoxical consequence of the First Restatement's solution. In this case, East Dakota will apply West Dakota's negligence law, while West Dakota will apply East Dakota's strict liability law.

Contractual Confusion

3. Recovery will apply its choice of law rule—the place of shipping—to select the local contract law of Denial. It will avoid renvoi by disregarding Denial's conflicts rules. Under the contract law of the place of shipping, the exclusion of consequential damages is valid.

    The trick to solving renvoi problems is to treat each jurisdiction separately. Do not get thrown by the fact that one court may decide the case differently from another. In this case, for example, Denial might well decide that Recovery is the place of performance and apply Recovery's contract law to reach a different result.

    This explanation illustrates the operation of the First Restatement rules. Given the outcome, it would not be surprising to find that states have adopted consumer protection laws that limit the enforcement of contractual exclusions of liability in consumer sales.

Intriguing Intestacy

4. Albion will apply its own conflicts rule under which the distribution is governed by the law of Lilliput, where the decedent died domiciled. It will apply only Lilliput's law of intestate succession, not the conflicts rules that Lilliput would employ in this case. Accordingly, under Albion law, Gaston is entitled to the personal property under the law of succession of the place where decedent died domiciled. See First Restatement §7 illus. 1. This outcome differs from the outcome that would have resulted if the issue were litigated in Lilliput's courts. Courts have occasionally balked at applying foreign rules of succession in cases where the foreign courts would not have applied them. See Weintraub, Commentary on the Conflict of Laws §3.3 at 106, discussing the English case of In re Annesley [1926] Ch. 692.

5. The facts are taken from In re Estate of Domato, 206 A.2d 171 (N.J. 1965). The New Jersey court decided the case like a good First Restatement court. It applied its choice of law rules to hold that the validity of the

trust was governed by the law of situs of the trust corpus, Florida. It applied only Florida trust law, not Florida conflicts rules, and found that the accounts established an inter vivos trust that vested upon the decedent's death. Accordingly, the son was entitled to the proceeds of the trust. Litigation in Florida would have produced a different result.

Exceptional Land

6. Mordor courts will apply Mordor law because that is the law that applies under the statute where the land is located. The deed is valid because it is valid under the whole law (including the conflicts rules) of the place where the land is located. The purpose of the exception, which requires consideration of the whole law of the place of the land, is to make sure that all courts decide disputes involving land titles the same way as would the courts where the land is located.

7. Lance has an equitable interest in Blackacre that gives him good title against all but bona fide purchasers for value. The key is recognizing that the issue involves title to land. Once you properly identify the issue, the rest is simple: all courts should apply the same law (including the conflict of laws rules) as the place where the land is located. The goal of uniformity of result for land title cases requires "accepting" the renvoi.

   Uniformity of result is a helpful guide for resolving renvoi problems involving land. But complete uniformity is not an absolute rule. For example, forums still normally apply forum rules of procedure and evidence.

PART IV

Modern Choice of Law Approaches

CHAPTER 17

The New York Approach

INTRODUCTION

Beginning in the 1950s, New York courts moved away from the traditional choice of law rules in a series of famous[1] cases. The New York decisions played a major role in the evolution of modern choice of law theories. Casebooks, courts, and Conflicts gurus still give much attention to them.

The New York courts offered different and changing reasons for selecting law in ways that differed from the traditional choice rules. There was a shift from early decisions that grouped territorial *contacts* to later decisions that rely on state *interests*. The New York courts were influenced by theories like interest analysis (Chapter 18), and their decisions in turn influenced other modern approaches.

Most of the torts cases involved guest statutes. By the 1970s, the New York courts felt confident enough to formulate new general rules for guest statute conflicts. By the 1980s New York applied these rules to all sorts of "loss-shifting" torts laws.

This chapter has two goals. First, it surveys the evolution of New York decisions. Second, it presents the formal rules that New York adopted to resolve choice of law problems. This chapter will also consider some of the problems with New York's solution, which helps explain why the rest of the world has not adopted its rules.

---

1. Famous to people who teach Conflict of Laws.

EARLY RUMBLINGS IN CONTRACT CASES

Auten v. Auten The New York Court of Appeals (the state's supreme court) rejected the traditional "rigid general rules" for contracts in Auten v. Auten, 124 N.E.2d 99 (N.Y. 1954). The court held that a separation agreement should be governed by English law even though the agreement was made in New York. The court emphasized that all the other factual contacts were in England—the wife and children lived there, the husband was domiciled there at the time of the agreement, and performance was to occur there. The court announced a new "center of gravity" or "grouping of contacts" theory for choice of law. The goal was to determine what place has "the most significant contacts" with the dispute and thus to apply the policy of the jurisdiction most concerned with the outcome.

Haag v. Barnes The court applied its new approach to more difficult facts in Haag v. Barnes, 175 N.E.2d 441 (N.Y. 1961). In that case a married Illinois lawyer had sexual intercourse in New York with a legal secretary. She became pregnant and alleged he made false promises of marriage.

The woman followed the lawyer to Illinois. He refused to see her but arranged for her to give birth at an Illinois hospital. She returned to New York, but the lawyer's lawyers persuaded her to return to Illinois for the purpose of entering a support agreement. The agreement did not admit paternity, terminated when the child reached age 16, and expressly provided that it would be governed by the laws of Illinois.

The mother later sued in New York for additional support, and the lawyer moved to dismiss under the Illinois support agreement. Under New York law, a support agreement was not valid without judicial approval. In contrast, under Illinois law a support agreement was valid without judicial approval if it provided for a total amount of $800 or more, which the support agreement in the case did.

Applying New York's new-fangled approach, the court applied Illinois law and upheld the agreement because Illinois had the greater number and more significant contacts. First, the court gave great weight to a choice of law provision selecting Illinois law. Party choice of law would have been decisive under New York's traditional approach, and the court observed party choice would also be given "heavy weight" under its new approach. Second, the court found that the intent of the parties and the other Illinois contacts were more numerous and substantial than the presence of the mother and child in New York—decisive factors in leading to the opposite result in *Auten*—and the fact that the sexual intercourse and allegedly false statements occurred in New York.

Much Ado About Nothing? The first striking fact about the contracts cases is that the newer, more flexible contacts approach was unnecessary. The older New York choice rules would have produced the same outcomes. Both cases thus reveal the spirit of the times — the judicial eagerness to reach out for new choice of law theories.

The second striking fact about the two cases is that the court did not see the lack of coherence in its talk of contacts, state policies, and party expectations. The court did not provide guidance for evaluating contacts and did not even explain why contacts were relevant. This led the court itself to manipulate and multiply contacts in *Haag*, perhaps without realizing what it was doing. For example, the court listed the fact that the parties' attorneys in drafting the contract were Illinois residents without explaining the relevance of that contact. It listed the defendant's payments from Illinois as a contact with Illinois but did not list the fact that they were paid to a mother in New York as a contact in New York.

The third striking fact is that the cases are not easily reconciled with each other — except by reference to the choice of law provision in *Haag*. The court was oblivious to the possibility that such an agreement, including its choice provisions, could be a contract of adhesion. Though Illinois law would require the recognition of support agreements that were inadequate in some cases, the New York court concluded that the support in the case before it was adequate. It did not explain why the appellate consideration of adequacy in deciding whether to recognize the Illinois agreement was preferable to the ordinary New York requirement of trial court approval for all support agreements.

THE GUEST STATUTE REVOLUTION

Babcock v. Jackson The single most influential choice of law decision ever is Babcock v. Jackson, 191 N.E.2d 279 (N.Y. 1963). Three friends, all residents of Rochester, New York, went for a weekend car trip to Ontario. After crossing into Canada, the driver lost control and smashed into a stone wall.

Babcock sued the driver for negligence in New York. The defendant raised the defense of the Ontario guest statute. Under the statute, a driver was not liable for personal injuries caused negligently to persons he was transporting without compensation.

According to traditional rules, the guest statute would apply as the law of the place of the wrong. Even if the statute was repugnant to forum public policy, the traditional public policy exception would not permit a court to disregard a defense.

The court in *Babcock* rejected the traditional rules, applied New York tort law, and permitted the plaintiff to recover. Comparing the "contacts" and "interests" of New York and Ontario, the court concluded that New York had the greater and more direct concern in the case while Ontario had either no concern or a minimal interest in the case.

First, New York was the place of residence of the injured guest and the negligent driver. The car was garaged, licensed, and insured in New York. The trip was planned to begin and end in New York. In contrast, Ontario's only relationship was the "purely adventitious circumstance" that it was the place of the accident.

Second, New York had a state policy of requiring negligent drivers to compensate guests for personal injuries. Despite the Ontario statute, the court found that Ontario had "no conceivable interest" in applying its guest statute to prevent a New York plaintiff from recovering from a New York tortfeasor. The court determined that the purpose of the Ontario guest statute was to prevent collusive claims against insurance companies, and the Ontario statute was designed to prevent claims only against Ontario defendants and their insurance companies.

The opinion distinguished Ontario's lack of interest in applying its guest statute to nonresidents from Ontario's strong interest in applying its law governing rules of the road, rules affecting behavior in Ontario such as the requirement that drivers must exercise due care. The opinion suggested that the place of the conduct would usually have such a strong interest in applying its own conduct-regulating rule that applying some other state's rule to such issues would be "almost unthinkable."

College Crash Cases   In hindsight, *Babcock* was an easy case. Guest statutes were in rapid decline, and all jurisdictions were beginning to seek ways to limit their application in multi-state accidents. Moreover, everything in the case — all contacts and interests — pointed to New York, except for the fact that Ontario was the place of the accident.

The court's reasoning in *Babcock* was what Freud would call overdetermined. In other words, there were multiple and possibly inconsistent arguments in favor of applying New York law. One argument was that almost all the territorial contacts were in New York. Another argument was that parties expected New York law to apply. Another was that New York law should apply to a relationship that began in New York and was between New Yorkers. Still another argument was that New York law should apply because Ontario had no interest in applying its law because the purpose of its law was to prevent fraud only in cases between Ontario residents.

Two later cases illustrate the difficulty New York courts experienced in deciding exactly which factors were most important in *Babcock*. Both cases involved New York students who were living in another state and attending college there. In both cases the students went for a car trip and had an accident in a state with a guest statute. In Dym v. Gordon, 209 N.E.2d 792 (N.Y. 1965), the court applied the Colorado guest statute to New York domiciliaries who met while taking courses at the University of Colorado. The court distinguished *Babcock* because *Dym* stemmed from a collision with another car and because one of the purposes of the Colorado guest statute was to bar claims by passengers in order to preserve defendants' assets for other claimants. The court also found that the parties' prolonged stay in Colorado gave that state an interest in applying its law. For all these reasons, the court concluded that the Colorado guest statute applied.

The court effectively overruled *Dym* in Tooker v. Lopez, 249 N.E.2d 394 (N.Y. 1969). There the court refused to apply the Michigan guest statute to a fatal accident involving New York domiciliaries attending Michigan State University. The *Tooker* court explained that the only issue was whether New York and Michigan had state interests in applying their conflicting laws in the case. It concluded that "the instant case is one of the simplest" because New York had an interest in applying its tort law to compensate persons domiciled in New York while Michigan had absolutely no interest in applying its guest statute to prevent recovery. In determining state interests for a loss-shifting rule like a guest statute, the court made clear that the only relevant fact was the parties' domicile. Their physical presence in Michigan for an extended period was "plainly irrelevant."

Time for Rules   In a concurring opinion in *Tooker*, Chief Judge Fuld suggested the time had come to formulate black letter rules for guest statute cases. The full court adopted his proposed rules in Neumeier v. Kuehner, 286 N.E.2d 454 (N.Y. 1972).[2] In that case, a man domiciled in Ontario was killed in Ontario while riding as a guest in a car owned and driven by a New York defendant. To try to avoid the application of the guest statute by Ontario courts, the decedent's widow brought a wrongful death action in New York.

The lower court was confused. (It's not just you!) It concluded that *Tooker* supported the application of New York law. The high court reversed. It emphasized that New York had a deep interest in protecting its residents injured in a foreign state from anachronistic defenses of that state. But New York had no legitimate interest in ignoring the interest of the foreign jurisdiction in applying its unfair law to parties domiciled in that state. Accordingly, Ontario's guest statute applied.

The opinion announced the following rules for deciding guest statute conflicts:

---

2. The case was decided two years after Graham Nash argued, "For you who are on the road must have a code that you can live by." *Teach Your Children*, 1 Crosby, Stills, Nash & Young, Déjà Vu 2 (1970). Pure coincidence? You be the judge.

1. Apply the law of the parties' common domicile when they are domiciled in the same state and the car is registered there.
2. Apply the law of defendant's domicile when the defendant acted in his or her home state and is not liable under its law. Apply the law of the plaintiff's domicile when the plaintiff is injured in his or her home state and can recover under its law.
3. In other cases, apply the law of the place where the accident occurred unless displacing that normal rule will advance the relevant substantive law purposes without impairing the smooth working of the multi-state system or produce great uncertainty.

The court applied rule number three in *Neumeier*. In applying the law of the place of the accident, it emphasized that displacing the Ontario guest statute would not have advanced any substantive tort law purposes of New York because New York had no interest in compensating Ontario plaintiffs. It also reasoned that displacing Ontario law would have impaired the smooth working of the multi-state system by producing uncertainty and encouraging forum shopping. Accordingly, it applied Ontario's guest statute.

Everyone's a Critic The court's black letter rules should have pleased Conflicts gurus who thought the wishy-washy modern decisions should lead to specific rules of general applicability. But critics raised a number of objections.

First, some people thought judges should decide individual cases only and not announce general rules for future decisions when the legislature has not done so.

Second, some people thought the rules were bad. Judge Bergan dissented from the holding of *Neumeier*—and questioned its rules. He contended that the exclusive focus on state domicile as the key to state interests produced outcomes that were indefensibly discriminatory. One plaintiff wins because she is a citizen of New York, while another loses because she is a citizen of another jurisdiction.

Third, critics objected that cases actually decided by the New York courts did not provide authority for the rules. Most notably, there was no authority for applying the law of common domicile to the "reverse *Babcock*" situation where Ontario parties were injured in New York. And it is not so obvious why that rule should apply, especially if Ontario would apply New York law and there is no incentive for forum shopping.

Fourth, the rules included extraneous considerations. While decisions since *Babcock* had referred to the place of the car's registration as a guide to the expectations of insurance coverage, they never really explained its significance. The car-registration requirement looks weird, and its importance is uncertain.

APPLYING THE RULES TO OTHER LOSS-SHIFTING CASES

By the time New York formulated its choice of law rules for guest statutes, such statutes were becoming as scarce as ivory-billed woodpeckers. There were reasons to question the wisdom of expanding these choice rules into other areas of torts. First, guest statutes were not typical, so conflicts rules generalized from decisions about them might not be good for other kinds of cases. Second, guest statute rules did not differentiate the place of wrongful act and resulting harm. The place of negligence and damages would (almost) always be the same in cases involving guest statutes. But the place of the accident—or tort—could become far more complicated in other areas. *See* Hay et al., Conflict of Laws §17.5 at 718.

Schultz v. Boy Scouts of America In the 1980s the New York Court of Appeals applied the guest statute rules to other kinds of torts but limited them to loss-distributing or loss-shifting as opposed to conduct-regulating rules. Loss-distributing rules reflect a policy about who should bear the financial consequences of an accident or loss. Conduct-regulating rules are designed to change the conduct that causes the accident or loss.

In Schultz v. Boy Scouts of America, Inc., 480 N.E.2d 679 (N.Y. 1985), two children were sexually assaulted by a man who was both their teacher and Boy Scout leader. The assaults took place in New York and New Jersey. The younger boy subsequently died from a drug overdose, an apparent suicide provoked by his trauma. The teacher was a member of the Franciscan order, which provided teachers to the boys' school, and the assaults occurred during Boy Scout camping trips.

The children's parents sued the Franciscan Order and the Boy Scouts. They claimed the defendant organizations either knew or should have known the teacher had been dismissed from other Scout camps for similar assaults. Their lawsuit sought to recover damages suffered by the children and also damages suffered by the parents for the death of their child.

New Jersey recognized a defense of charitable immunity that barred all claims. In fact, New Jersey courts had dismissed a related claim brought against the archdiocese that operated the school. In contrast, New York tort law did not recognize a defense of charitable immunity.

The New York court ultimately held that the claims were barred by New Jersey law. Its opinion separately analyzed the claims for injuries to the children and the parents. It found that the locus of torts affecting parental rights was in New Jersey, where the parents suffered damages. It concluded that New York had absolutely no interest in applying its law to these claims involving torts in another jurisdiction affecting entirely foreign parties. But it found that the locus of torts affecting the children's personal injuries was New York, where most but not all of the assaults occurred.

The court reviewed the recent history of New York conflicts rules. It emphasized that the interests of states depend on the type of tort issue in conflict. "[W]hen the conflicting rules involve the appropriate standards of conduct, rules of the road, for example, the law of the place of the tort 'will usually have a predominant, if not exclusive, concern.'" In contrast, when tort rules relate to allocating costs, then the parties' home states have greater interest.

The court announced that the *Neumeier* rules should apply to all loss-distribution conflicts. It then determined that charitable immunity is a loss-distribution rule because its purpose is to shift loss and encourage the growth of charitable activity in New Jersey. The court also observed that New Jersey citizens benefited from this activity, so it was fair to saddle them with the corresponding burdens of New Jersey's law.

Because the two defendants were incorporated in different states, the claims against them were governed by different *Neumeier* rules. Defendant Boy Scouts had its national headquarters in New Jersey at the time of the torts, so the claim against it was governed by rule number one: the court applied the law of the parties' common domicile and recognized the defense of charitable immunity.[3]

Defendant Franciscan Brothers was incorporated in Ohio, a state that did not recognize charitable immunity as a defense under the facts. Accordingly, the claim against it was governed by rule number three, which called for applying the law of the place of the tort unless displacing that law would advance substantive policies without impairing the smooth working of the multi-state system or producing great uncertainty.

In applying rule number three, the court concluded the law of the place of the tort (New York) was displaced by New Jersey's interest in binding New Jersey domiciliaries to the burdens as well as benefits of its loss-distribution rule and by New Jersey's interest in promoting the expansion of charitable activity in that state. It found no significant New York interest in applying its law. And it found that applying the defense would enhance the

---

3. The majority looked to the corporation's national headquarters at the time of the tort and disregarded its later move to Texas, a state that rejected charitable immunity. A dissenting opinion observed that defendant's move deprived New Jersey of any interest in applying its defense. The majority responded by asserting that the change of domicile did not establish any New York interests in applying its own law. The problem of post-occurrence change in domicile is discussed in Chapter 23.

smooth working of the multi-state system by preventing forum shopping and increasing certainty.

Conduct-Regulating Rules

From the beginning of the guest statute revolution, the New York court emphasized it was announcing new choice of law rules only for loss-shifting rules. It recognized that the law of the place of the conduct or harm would normally apply to tort rules whose purpose was to influence conduct. Properly classifying a rule as either loss-shifting or conduct-regulating can decisively affect the outcome of the case. The problem of making this classification is discussed more fully in Chapter 18. But, for now, you can probably see that many torts rules are both loss-shifting and conduct-regulating.

The New York courts considered this problem in Padula v. Lilarn Properties Corp., 644 N.E.2d 1001 (N.Y. 1994), where a New York resident was injured in Massachusetts while working at a construction site on property owned by a New York corporation. The plaintiff brought a claim under New York labor laws imposing strict and vicarious liability on the owners for injuries sustained at unsafe workplaces.

The court restated the rule that conduct-regulating rules are generally governed by the law of the place where the tort occurred. It reasoned that the law of the place of the tort has the greatest interest in regulating behavior within its borders. While strict vicarious liability had both conduct-regulating and loss-shifting functions, the court concluded that workplace safety liability is "primarily conduct-regulating." For this reason it held that Massachusetts law applied.

Sorting Cases

Padula shows how properly classifying an issue affects the outcome. The court applied the place of the tort because the rule was primarily conduct-regulating, but if it had been primarily loss-shifting, the court would have applied the law of common domicile. Cases provide important guidance.

Loss shifting	Conduct regulating
guest statutes	standards of care
charitable immunity	rules of the road
wrongful death statutes	workplace safety standards
vicarious liability statutes	hotel safety standards
contribution and indemnification among defendants	

Examples

Bad Apples

1. Jonathan and MacIntosh, husband and wife, are domiciled in New York. They take a vacation in Pommerania, where Jonathan bakes an apple pie and serves it to MacIntosh. Unfortunately, the pie included a rotten apple, and MacIntosh becomes ill. Under Pommeranian law, all servers of food are strictly liable for injuries caused by serving bad food. Assume that New York requires negligence. What law would New York courts apply?

2. A New York domiciliary inflicts personal injuries on another New York domiciliary in Pommerania. Pommerania limits damages to the equivalent of $1,420.00 in all personal injury actions. Will New York recognize the limit?

3. Pommerania has enacted the Sanctity of Marriage Freedom Act, which provides: "Spouses are absolutely immune to all claims for civil liability for personal injury." New York does not have spousal immunity. If a New York spouse injures her spouse in Pommerania, will New York courts bar his claim under the act?

Contributing to Confusion

4. Franny's brakes failed and she collided with Zooey. Both lived in East Carolina where the accident occurred. Franny's insurance company settled with Zooey. The insurance company, a New York corporation, now seeks to recover its payments from Sloe Brake, Inc., another New York corporation and the source of the bad brakes. New York law permits contribution among tortfeasors. The law of East Carolina prohibits such recoveries as contrary to public policy. What law applies?

Empire State Imperialism

5. Defendant, a citizen of the country of Autokria, visited New York City. Defendant gave an interview where she stated that General Stinker, a citizen of Autokria, was ruthless and violated the law. The statement was reported in the Autokria media and seriously injured the general's reputation in Autokria.

    Under the law of Autokria, it is unlawful to accuse military officers of legal violations without first submitting the claim to the National Board of Military Inquiry, and an officer may bring a civil action for damages against his or her accuser.

    Under the law of New York and the United States, Defendant's statement is absolutely privileged because it is true. The purpose of the New York law is to protect freedom of speech.

    General Stinker sues Defendant in New York for the statement arguing that Autokria law should apply. What law applies?

Unbuckled Guests

6. Winesap, a citizen of New York, was driving through Lilliput on the way to Mordor. He stopped and picked up Baldwin, a hitchhiker, who was domiciled in Ohio. Winesap fell asleep at the wheel, collided with a tree, and injured Baldwin. The accident occurred in Mordor. Under the Mordor guest statute, a guest cannot recover from a driver in the absence of malice. Mordor cases have held that falling asleep is not malice.

   Baldwin sues Winesap in New York. New York, Lilliput, and Ohio do not have guest statutes. What law does New York apply?

7. Same facts. Baldwin was not wearing a seatbelt at the time of the accident and was thrown from the car. Under the law of Mordor, it is negligent not to wear a seatbelt. Mordor has a form of comparative negligence that bars recovery when a plaintiff is more than 10 percent responsible for his or her own damages. Winesap argues that Baldwin's claim should be barred under Mordor's version of comparative negligence. The claim would not be barred (though recovery might ultimately be reduced) under the law of New York or Ohio. What law would New York apply?

Forest and Trees

8. Killer, a domiciliary of the country of Murdrum, kidnapped Victim, a domiciliary of Murdrum, transported him to New York, and killed him in New York. Killer suffers from severe mental illness and believed his actions were compelled by Thule, a deity. Under the law of Murdrum, persons who cause injuries as a result of their serious mental illness are immune to civil liability for the injuries. Victim's estate sues Killer in New York. Killer raises the defense of immunity under Murdrum law. New York recognizes no defense of insanity for intentional torts or negligence claims. What law applies?

Explanations

Bad Apples

1. The issue is a standard of care, which is primarily conduct-regulating. New York courts will normally apply the law of the place of the tort, and there does not seem to be any reason it would not apply Pommerania's theory of strict liability.

   The same result would obtain if the parties or law were reversed: New York would apply the law of the place of the tort to the issue of the standard of care because it is primarily conduct-regulating.

2. The cap on damages is loss-shifting, so New York courts will apply the Neumeier rules. This case falls under rule number one and is governed by

the law of the parties' common domicile. The courts will apply New York law and disregard the limit on damages.

3. Spousal immunity is loss-shifting, so New York will apply the *Neumeier* rules and, under the first, apply its own law as the law of the parties' common domicile. This example emphasizes the point that the fervor of a state's motives for enacting a law does not alter the characterization of that law as loss-shifting or conduct-regulating.

Contributing to Confusion

4. The New York court has already decided that contribution is loss-shifting. *Cooney v. Osgood Machinery, Inc.*, 612 N.E.2d 277 (N.Y. 1993). Accordingly, the law of the parties' common domicile should apply under the first *Neumeier* rule, and New York will permit contribution.

Empire State Imperialism

5. New York law applies. The law protecting freedom of speech is conduct-regulating. It is designed to promote and encourage public discussion of potentially offensive ideas. Even though the injury may have occurred in Autokria, New York will apply the law of the place of conduct to this conduct-regulating rule.

Unbuckled Guests

6. Guest statutes are loss-shifting, so the court will apply the *Neumeier* rules. Since the parties do not share a common domicile and neither party is acting in his or her home state, the court will look to rule number three. This directs the court to apply the law of the place of the tort (which has a guest statute) unless applying some other law will advance the substantive purposes of the law and not impair the smooth working of the multi-state system or produce great uncertainty.

The right answer is to apply Ohio law (which is the same as New York law). In this case, applying the pro-recovery law of the plaintiff's domicile (which is the same as the law of the defendant's domicile) will advance the substantive loss-shifting tort policies of the plaintiff's domicile. It will not impair any interests of New York (because New York's law is the same). This case differs from *Schultz* where applying the law of the place of the wrong would have frustrated the substantive law purposes of the place of the parties' domicile.

Professor Weintraub even says the case where the parties have different domiciles and both of their home states impose liability is the best possible example for an exception to applying the law of the place of the tort under rule number three. Weintraub, Commentary on the Conflict of Laws §6.23 at 455. In Chila v. Owens, 348 F. Supp. 1207 (S.D.N.Y.

1972), the court reasoned that such a case was more analogous to the situation where parties shared a common domicile and applied rule one rather than rule three.

The only conceivable argument for applying the law of the place of the tort would be to discourage forum shopping. The New York court advanced this as a reason against applying New York law in *Schultz*. But in this case the anti-forum-shopping argument is either weak or illegitimate. Forum shopping might possibly be a good reason for adopting a rule of general application. It should never be a good reason for deviating from such a general rule because avoiding forum shopping is a factor that invariably favors one group of parties (defendants). Elsewhere in *Schultz*, the court rightly rejected pro-recovery policies for exactly the same reason — they invariably favor plaintiffs.

7. This could be a tough one in theory because you could argue that different forms of comparative negligence are primarily conduct regulating — designed to heighten care by passengers. But New York cases have decided that comparative negligence is primarily loss-allocating. *See* Cain v. Greater N.Y. Council of Boy Scouts, 519 N.Y.S.2d 43 (N.Y. App. Div. 1987) (applying New York's form of comparative negligence in lawsuit between two New Yorkers rather than law of place of tort).

Once we know the issue is loss-allocating, the longer answer would look exactly like the answer to the preceding question. The right result would be to apply Ohio law (which is the same as New York's).

Forest and Trees

8. New York law applies. If you started to analyze this case under *Schultz*, you have gotten lost in the forest. This is an easy case. New York's tort rule permitting a recovery is conduct-regulating. It is designed to prevent killings in New York. Of course, it is also designed to shift losses from victims to tortfeasors. (In contrast, the immunity law of Murdrum is purely loss-shifting.)

New York has an interest in preventing killings in the state of New York. Applying its law advances that interest.

Schultz differs from this case in two crucial ways. First, the plaintiffs in *Schultz* were not seeking to recover from the criminal for intentional torts he committed in New York. Instead, they were seeking to recover on negligence theories from entities that allegedly failed to supervise the criminal. Second, the issue in *Schultz* was charitable immunity, and the court concluded (possibly wrongly) that applying the defense would not significantly impair a New York interest. In this case, New York's interest in deterring intentional torts in the state would be significantly impaired by applying Murdrum's defense.

211

18

Interest Analysis

INTRODUCTION

The term "interest analysis" is confusing. The modern approaches followed by most states examine or analyze state interests, and it is tempting to call all of them interest analysis jurisdictions. But Conflicts scholars reserve the name "interest analysis" or "governmental interest analysis" for one very specific choice of law theory. The theory has been extremely influential. For example, it influenced the development of the New York approach. But interest analysis in its pure form has been adopted by only about three states.

This chapter will discuss how to apply interest analysis. It will also identify some of the problem areas, which may help to explain why interest analysis has not been adopted everywhere.

PARENTAGE AND BIRTH

Interest analysis is a theory proposed by law professor Brainerd Currie. Currie shared the legal realists' skepticism of the traditional territorial approach and welcomed the emerging modern conflicts decisions in the 1950s. He published a complete form of his theory in the early 1960s, and his writings influenced courts that were moving away from the old approach.

The Theory and Rules

Professor Currie was a legal positivist. He believed law was nothing other than what courts said it was. He took a functional view of courts. For Currie courts were organs of sovereign states or countries, and their purpose was to advance the policies of the states that created them.

Currie's approach reflects his underlying assumptions. First, he thought courts should normally apply the law of the states that created them, and the default rule should be to apply forum law. Second, in conflicts cases where some party argues that another jurisdiction's law should apply, courts should determine the governmental policy expressed by the law of the forum and apply forum law if doing so would promote the governmental purpose behind the law. Third, if the policy behind the forum law is not advanced by applying forum law to the dispute before the court, then the forum court should apply the law of the other jurisdiction if that jurisdiction's policy would be advanced by the application of its law.

In other words, Currie proposed that courts should look behind the laws that are in conflict in a particular case and ask what the purposes of the laws are by looking at the policies of the states with different laws. This requires asking what interest each state has in the application of its law to the factual dispute. This is the interest analysis part of interest analysis. (Well, duh.)

If only one state has an interest in the application of its law, then interest analysis says the court should apply that state's law. But if more than one state has an interest, then the forum should apply forum law. There is no weighing or balancing of interests or policies. A forum should apply forum law even if the forum interest is slight or trivial as compared with the interest of another state.

Types of Cases

Interest analysis established the following classifications of cases, and it created new labels for them. In each classification, the laws of two jurisdictions differ. If the laws were the same, there wouldn't be a conflict, and it wouldn't matter which law applies.

True Conflicts True conflicts are cases in which each jurisdiction has an interest in the application of its law to the dispute. In such cases each jurisdiction has a policy that would be promoted by applying its law.

Currie thought forum law should always govern true conflicts. His reason for applying forum law depends on the kind of true conflict. Some true conflicts involve a clash between forum law and some other state's law.

Other true conflicts involve a clash between two other state laws but do not involve any forum state interest. Currie's belief that courts are organs of state policy explains why forum law should apply in true conflicts when the forum has an interest. Forum law also applies as the default rule to true conflicts involving other states when the forum state itself has no interest.

False Conflicts   False conflicts are cases in which only one jurisdiction has an interest in the application of its law. In such cases the laws of states conflict, but the governmental policy behind one of the laws will not be advanced by the application of that law. In such cases all jurisdictions apply the law of the only state that has an interest in the application of its law.

Remember: false conflicts are still conflicts in that the laws of different jurisdictions would give different results. They are classified as false conflicts only after interest analysis analyzes the interests behind the laws that are in conflict.

Unprovided-for Cases   It is possible for there to be disputes where, after analyzing the policies of the laws in conflict, a court determines that no state has an interest in applying its law.[1] In such a case, the default rule, forum law, would apply.

Currie recognized this was not a perfect solution. He thought unprovided-for cases would be rare and might be dismissed on grounds of forum non conveniens. He suggested applying forum law until someone came up with a better idea.

WHAT'S NOT TO LIKE?

Most Conflicts gurus like Currie's proposal that courts should examine the policies behind laws that are in conflict. Many scholars and courts share his belief that it is possible for a state not to have an interest in the application of its law in a particular case. They accept his solution for false conflicts that courts should apply the law of the only state that has an interest in having its law applied to the facts.

But interest analysis has its critics. Some Conflicts gurus challenge Currie's underlying functional view of courts as too narrow. The approach's preference for forum law is both celebrated (as honest) and vilified (as parochial).

---

1. The cases are called "unprovided for" not because Professor Currie forgot them but because in such cases no state policy is advanced, so Currie's goal of implementing state policies does not provide an obvious answer. See Larry Kramer, The Myth of the "Unprovided-For" Case, 75 Va. L. Rev. 1045 (1989).

Other critics accept the basic premises of interest analysis but question the application of forum law in all cases of true conflicts. They don't think forum law should apply automatically when some other state has a far greater interest in the application of its law. They have proposed a variety of modifications of interest analysis that are discussed in the next chapter.

One of Currie's proposals is even unconstitutional—the application of forum law to certain cases where there is no forum interest. As we will see (in Chapter 26), both due process and full faith and credit prohibit the application of forum law unless the forum has a significant contact or significant aggregation of contacts creating state interests.

LOSS-SHIFTING vs. CONDUCT-REGULATING LAWS

One of the challenges in applying interest analysis is figuring out what the policies are of the different states or countries whose laws are in conflict. Currie thought this would not be difficult in most cases and was not different from the kind of policy analysis that courts regularly conduct.

Currie's own application of interest analysis provides important guidance that has shaped the understanding of the theory by scholars and courts. He elaborated his theory by discussing old state laws that prevented married women from entering into contracts. The policy behind such laws was to protect married women from imprudent contracts. But states with such laws, according to Currie, did not seek to protect all the married women in the world from bad contracts. Instead, he thought the policy of those states was to protect married women domiciled in them.

By narrowing the state policies to protecting wives domiciled in the state, Currie concluded that the state's interest was not advanced by voiding contracts entered into by women domiciled in other states that did not provide such defenses.

In tort cases, interest analysis distinguishes between loss-shifting and conduct-regulating rules. The classic example of a pure loss-shifting rule is a guest statute. Guest statutes were once common but now exist in only two states. Guest statutes bar passengers from recovering from negligent drivers and thus prevent injured passengers from shifting the cost of their injuries to the persons who caused the injuries.

Interest analysis classifies guest statutes as loss-shifting not just because they provide a defense. They are loss-shifting because the policy behind the defense is to allocate the loss, not to regulate conduct. It is important for the classification that the purpose of guest statutes is not to affect driver behavior. The reason guest statutes don't influence driver conduct is because drivers are already deterred from negligent acts because they are subject to the same risks as their passengers. It is implausible that a driver would be willing to risk injuring himself or herself but would be deterred from negligent conduct because of the additional risk of a money judgment recoverable by a guest passenger. In addition, drivers are unlikely to be aware of the existence of guest statutes in most cases.

According to interest analysis, the policies behind loss-shifting rules are designed to protect only persons domiciled in the state with such rules. These policies are not advanced by applying them to parties domiciled in other states. This means a state should apply pro-recovery loss-shifting rules in favor of plaintiffs domiciled in the state and should apply loss-shifting defenses that deny recovery in favor of defendants domiciled in the state. According to interest analysis a state has no interest in applying its own loss-shifting rules to benefit parties domiciled in other states.

In contrast, interest analysis recognizes that states always have an interest in regulating conduct within their territory. Examples of conduct-regulating rules would be standards of care or remedies designed to affect behavior. The state's interest in regulating conduct does not depend on whether the parties are residents or nonresidents.

It becomes all-important to distinguish loss-shifting and conduct-regulating rules. The distinction produces important subrules:

1. The law of common domicile applies to loss-shifting rules. When the plaintiff and defendant are from the same state, only their home state has an interest in applying its law to the facts when the purpose of the law is to shift loss and not regulate conduct. This rule is appealing in theory and has been adopted in practice by the vast majority of states that no longer follow lex loci, even those that do not follow interest analysis. *See* Hay et al., Conflict of Laws §17.39D at 798.
2. Forum law governs conduct in the forum state when the rule is conduct-regulating, because the policy of regulating conduct is advanced by applying it regardless of where the parties are domiciled.

The Good News — and the Bad

First the good news. Interest analysis has great appeal. It promises to replace the old mechanical rules with the sort of judicial policy analysis familiar to modern legal thinking. It allows courts to resolve choice of law disputes by openly applying the law that advances the social goals of the law. This is something a lot of scholars thought courts were already doing (but not openly) by manipulating, bending, and occasionally breaking the old territorial rules.

Interest analysis seems to do away with the need for any special public policy exceptions, since the policy of the laws is directly considered in making the initial choice. By focusing on the policy goals of the laws in conflict, Currie thought interest analysis would abolish recurring problems like renvoi and the judicial search for the hidden territorial limits of specific laws.

Now the bad news. Interest analysis can become a justification for applying forum law in any case where a court is resourceful enough to identify some state policy advanced by the application of forum law. Currie recognized the danger of over-applying forum law. In later formulations of his theory he urged courts to consider whether a more limited construction of the forum's interest in applying its own law could avoid a true conflict. But interest analysis doesn't give clear guidance on how to construe states' interests.

The dilemma of whether—and how—to construe forum interests is illustrated by Bernkrant v. Fowler, 360 P.2d 906 (Cal. 1961). The case stemmed from an oral promise to forgive a debt in a will. The man making the promise died without fulfilling it. The promise was made in Nevada for the purpose of refinancing property located in Nevada. The alleged promise-breaker died a resident of California, where his estate was admitted to probate. The California statute of frauds required such a promise to be in writing, but the Nevada statute did not.

The California court applied interest analysis. This had the immediate payoff of avoiding the traditional sticky problem of needing to decide whether statutes of frauds were substantive or procedural. Interest analysis directed the court to consider the more relevant issue of the policies behind the rules in conflict. Obvious policies of statutes of frauds would seem to be advanced by the application of the California statute. For example, one purpose of the statute might be to require written records of agreements so people wouldn't wait until other people died and then lie about what the dead people promised before they died.

But instead of finding such an interest, the California court transformed the dispute into a false conflict by resorting to the supposition that the legislature ordinarily intends for a statute to govern purely local transactions. The trouble with this solution is that if we really knew the legislature meant to legislate locally, then there would be no conflict to begin with. The whole problem is that we do not know what the scope of the legislation was—because the legislature didn't tell us. One of the benefits of interest analysis was supposed to be the elimination of just this kind of search for fictitious legislative intentions regarding the territorial reach of rules.

Of course, you might argue that Bernkrant was just a badly reasoned interest analysis opinion. But its author, Justice Traynor, was one of the legal wizards of his day. If he had trouble properly classifying a true conflict, what hope is there for us muggles?

More bad news. *Bernkrant* illustrates other possible problems with interest analysis. Through the years more than one student has suspected that what really happened was that Justice Traynor did not want to apply California law and creatively manipulated his analysis to achieve a different result. There were lots of reasons why applying California law to invalidate a promise made in Nevada would have stunk. But if the opinion is result-oriented, then that illustrates two additional points about interest analysis. First, courts aren't always happy with interest analysis's solution to true conflicts even when it means applying forum law! Second, interest analysis, just like the traditional rules, can be subject to result-oriented manipulation.

The final good news. Many interest analysis cases, including those that regularly appear on final exams, can be solved pretty easily. Even when they are hard (or impossible), you should get full points for effort, provided you look hard for the state policies behind the laws, discuss the difficulty of making the proper classification, employ the right jargon, and remember which rules apply to each classification.

Examples

Seeing Red

1. Why does the following faux final exam answer make your Conflicts professor see red?

Nancy is a citizen of the state of East Carolina. She took riding lessons in the state of West Carolina from Ned, a citizen of West Carolina. One day Nancy fell off a horse during her lesson because Ned forgot to tighten the saddle. She was badly injured. The East Carolina legislature has enacted a statute that bars negligence claims for injuries caused during horse riding lessons. West Carolina has no such bar, and riding instructors are liable for actual damages caused by their negligence. Nancy has filed her lawsuit in East Carolina, which has adopted Professor Currie's theory of interest analysis. In this case, East Carolina has an interest in applying West Carolina's law because West Carolina law favors the party domiciled in East Carolina.

Singing the Blues

2. Why does this passage from a student's final exam have your Conflicts professor singing the blues?

In conclusion, in this true conflict we evaluate the relative strength of each state's interest in having its law applied, and since everything happened in state A and all the parties are from state A, state B has very little interest in this case, so we apply state A's law.

Trick Question

3. Wilma, a resident of the country of Avalon and the wife of Hubbard, signed a contract with Friendly Bank Corp. in which she guaranteed a loan the bank made to Hubbard. The bank was located in the country of Camelot, and Wilma signed the contract in the bank's office in Camelot. According to the law of Avalon, a wife lacks capacity to enter into a contract to guarantee the debts of her husband, and all such contracts are voidable. The purpose of the law is to protect wives from imprudent contracts and protect their assets. There is no similar defense under the law of Camelot, and wives have full freedom of contract and such contracts are enforceable. Hubbard later defaulted on the note. Friendly Bank Corp. has retained you as its lawyer and wants to know whether a court that applies interest analysis will recognize Wilma's defense to the contract. Please advise.

Easy Interest Analysis (Sort of)

4. Betty is a resident of the country of Narnia. She and her husband Barney visit the country of Oz, where they decide to buy a house. Barney signs a purchase agreement, and Betty signs a contract guaranteeing Barney's payment. Seller lives in Oz. Under the law of Oz a wife lacks capacity to enter into a contract to guarantee her husband's obligations, and her contracts are voidable. The purpose of Oz's law is to protect wives from being coerced by their husbands into entering bad contracts. Under the law of Narnia, however, all parties, including wives, have full freedom of contract. Barney defaults, and Betty is sued on her contract in Narnia. Narnia follows interest analysis. Will Narnia courts apply Oz law and permit Betty to void the contract?

Old Chestnut

5. Babs goes for a car ride with Jack. Babs and Jack are both residents of state A. The car trip takes them to country B. After entering country B, Jack negligently drives off the road, injuring Babs. Babs sues Jack in state A court. Jack raises the defense that country B has enacted a guest statute that provides a defense to all claims for negligence brought by nonpaying guests against their drivers. Country B cases explain that the purpose of the statute is to protect drivers' insurance companies from fraudulent claims. Jack's car is licensed in state A, and that is where he bought his car insurance. State A has no guest statute and follows interest analysis. Will state A apply country B's guest statute?

College Crush Crash

6. Sam and Dave were born and raised in the state of Homestate. They went away to college and enrolled at the state university in the state of Awaystate. They met in college, fell in love, and lived together for three years in Awaystate but never changed their legal domicile in Homestate. One evening, they went for a moonlight drive in the countryside of Awaystate. Dave was driving when he veered off the road and hit a utility pole. Seriously injured, Sam commences a civil action against Dave in Homestate. Homestate has no guest statute, but Awaystate does. According to Awaystate courts, the purpose of the state's guest statute is to protect drivers from lawsuits. Homestate courts follow interest analysis. Do they recognize the guest statute? Why or why not?

Seeing Green

7. Brittney and Paris went for a road trip from their home state of East Dakota to the state of West Dakota. While Brittney was driving in West Dakota, she negligently drove off a bridge, injuring Paris. Paris sues Brittney in East Dakota. East Dakota has no guest statute, but West Dakota has recently enacted the Green Rider Act of 2009. The purpose of the Act is to remove legal disincentives that may discourage people from sharing rides. One section of the Act provides: "Any driver who furnishes transportation to a passenger without monetary compensation shall be immune to all civil liability arising from the negligent operation of the vehicle that causes injury to such passenger during transportation." Brittney raises the defense of the Green Rider Act. Both states follow interest analysis. Will East Dakota recognize the defense? What about West Dakota?

When Worlds Collide

8. Avril, a tourist from Vogon, visited Julie at Julie's office in Tralfamadore, where she cruelly punched Julie in the nose and called her a lying liar. Fifteen months later, Julie commences a slander action in the courts in Vogon. Vogon has a one-year statute of limitations for slander actions, but Tralfamadore has a two-year statute for such lawsuits. Vogon has adopted interest analysis. Will Vogon dismiss the action as time-barred? What if the action is commenced in Tralfamadore, and it too has adopted interest analysis?

More Interesting Interest Analysis

9. Prima Donna drove from the state of Glitterdom, where she resided, to the country of Genovia. In Genovia, she picked up Vickie, a hitch-hiker who was a citizen of Genovia. Donna negligently drove into a train

in Genovia, killing herself and Vickie. Vickie's estate has commenced a wrongful death action in the Glitterdom state court against Donna's estate. The estate raises the defense of the Genovia guest statute. The Genovia statute bars negligence claims by nonpaying passengers. The purpose of the statute, according to Genovia courts, is to protect owners and drivers from ungrateful guests. Glitterdom follows interest analysis. Does Glitterdom apply the Genovia guest statute? Why or why not?

10. Clint, a citizen of the state of West Texas, was driving in West Texas when he negligently hit Pedro, a pedestrian, in a crosswalk. Pedro, a citizen of the country of Patagonia, was visiting West Texas. Pedro dies as a result of the accident, and Pedro's personal representative brings a wrongful death action against Clint in West Texas. Clint's lawyers argue that the case should be governed by a Patagonian law under which damages in actions for wrongful death are limited to $500 or ten days' wages, whichever is higher. West Texas does not limit damages in tort cases. The general purpose of compensatory damages in torts is both to compensate victims for losses and to deter tortious acts. West Texas follows interest analysis. Will the West Texas court apply the Patagonian limit on damages?

Consortium Confusion

11. George and Martha were married and living in the state of W. One day George drove to state O, where Dobby, a resident of state O, negligently caused George serious personal injuries. George settled his claims against Dobby. But Martha filed a separate lawsuit in state O against Dobby. Martha seeks to recover for loss of consortium (her loss of companionship and support from her husband that was the result of his injuries). The law of state O recognizes a wife's claim for such loss of consortium, but state W courts reject such claims in order to protect defendants from excessive claims and multiple litigation. Dobby moves to dismiss, arguing that the court should apply W's law. O courts follow interest analysis. Rule on Dobby's motion and explain.

Big Spender

12. The state of Confusion has a legal procedure by which certain people can be adjudicated incompetent to enter into binding contracts. The purpose of the procedure is to prevent financially irresponsible people from wasting their families' resources. Under Confusion's law, any person so adjudicated has a complete defense to an action for breach of contract. Slickster, a resident of Confusion, is adjudicated incompetent. Then he goes to Florida, where he checks into an expensive hotel. He stays for two weeks, dines daily at the hotel's pricey bistro, and sips

mixed drinks by the hotel's pool. Slickster charges all his expenses and leaves without paying. He returns to Confusion rested and tanned. The hotel, a Florida corporation, sues Slickster in the state of Confusion. Slickster moves for summary judgment, attaching a certified copy of his adjudication of incompetence. Confusion adopts interest analysis. Rule on the motion and explain.

Double Trouble

13. Pat Pato was a citizen of the state of Harmony. One day he drove to the state of Recovery to go to a mall. While entering the mall parking lot, he was struck by a truck driven by Gus Gans. Pato was badly injured in the collision.

    Gans was also a citizen of Harmony. At the time of the collision, Gans was employed by Harmony Church Corporation, a religious organization incorporated under the laws of Harmony. Gans was making a delivery to the mall when he struck Pato's car. The accident was caused by Gans's operation of the truck at an unsafe high speed.

    Gans had been first hired by Harmony Church one week prior to the collision with Pato. In hiring Gans, Harmony Church asked to see his driver's license and proof of citizenship. It did not ask about his driving history, nor did it obtain a copy of Gans's driving record from a public authority. A reasonable investigation would have disclosed that Gans had been cited 14 times for traffic violations in the two years before Harmony Church hired him. Gans had been named as a defendant in civil actions six times in the prior four years. Over half the incidents resulted from Gans's operation of trucks at unsafe speeds.

    The state of Harmony has adopted a statute that bars all tort claims against charities. Harmony Church qualifies as a charity under the statute. Recovery permits recovery against defendants, including charities, for personal injuries resulting from their negligence.

    Pato's lawyer commences a civil action against Harmony Church in the state of Recovery. The complaint contains two separate causes of action. The first states a claim for damages based on a theory of derivative liability stemming from the employee driver's negligence under the doctrine of respondeat superior. The second states a claim based on the theory that Harmony Church was itself negligent in hiring Gans because it failed to act reasonably in investigating his driving record, and its negligent hiring proximately caused Pato's injuries.

    The state of Harmony still follows the traditional territorial rules, but Recovery has adopted Professor Currie's interest analysis. Harmony Church moves to dismiss both claims, arguing they are barred by the Harmony charitable immunity defense. Rule on the motion and explain.

Explanations

Seeing Red

1. Besides the fact that most instructors hate it when the answer wastes time by repeating all the facts, this answer gets red marks for failing to analyze the policies behind the state laws. Probably the most common final exam error on interest analysis questions is the statement that a state has an interest because a party domiciled in the state would win. Interest analysis does not prescribe always applying the law that favors persons domiciled in the forum state. (Wouldn't such a rule be unfair—and maybe a tad unconstitutional?) But it is easy to see the source of this error. Interest analysis does favor the application of a forum state rule that advances a purely loss-shifting compensatory policy when a forum plaintiff is involved, and it favors applying a forum defense where a forum defendant is involved when the purpose of the defense is loss-shifting.

   A good answer needs to analyze the interests behind the state laws in conflict—and then classify the case. Under these facts, the purpose of East Carolina's statutory defense is unclear. It is loss-shifting in part, but the legislative goal of shifting the loss of injuries to student riders may also be motivated by the desire to encourage certain behavior that was deterred by the fear of liability for negligent acts. These policies would be advanced by applying the defense to cases involving defendants domiciled in East Carolina and cases involving lessons in the state. But the policies would not be advanced by applying them to this case, where the defendant is domiciled in another state, the conduct occurred there, and that other state does not recognize the defense.

   In contrast, West Carolina's pro-recovery rule incorporates the general goals of common law negligence. Some of these goals are to shift the costs of injuries after the accidents, and some of them are to deter acts that cause injuries in West Carolina. West Carolina has an interest in the application of its conduct-regulating rule to reduce the risk of injuries to persons (including nonresidents) in its state. So West Carolina has an interest in applying its law, while East Carolina does not. This is a false conflict, and West Carolina law applies.

Singing the Blues

2. Never weigh state interests in interest analysis! If both states really have an interest, then there is a true conflict. Interest analysis applies forum law to true conflicts. (If the forum has no significant interest—for example, if the dispute has no connection with the state except for the fact that it is being litigated there, and two other jurisdictions each have some governmental interest that would be advanced by applying their

laws—then the interest analysis solution raises constitutional problems. See Chapter 26.)

Trick Question

3. The trick is that the answer depends on where the case is litigated. This example illustrates the important point that interest analysis encourages forum shopping. The case is a true conflict, so every court that follows interest analysis will apply its own law.

   If this dispute is litigated in Avalon's courts and they apply interest analysis, Avalon courts will determine that the purpose of Avalon's law is to protect wives domiciled in Avalon. Wilma is domiciled in Avalon, and applying Avalon's law promotes Avalon's government policy. Avalon's courts will allow the defense.

   If the case is litigated in Camelot and Camelot's courts apply interest analysis, Camelot's courts will conclude that the purpose of Camelot's law is to protect freedom of contract and enforce the bargains parties have entered into—especially where a bank doing business in Camelot is concerned! Camelot courts will reject the defense.

   Other countries applying interest analysis would be disinterested forums in this case. So the default rule would be to apply forum law.

   Did I say interest analysis "encourages" forum shopping? Wouldn't it be malpractice not to forum shop?

Easy Interest Analysis (Sort of)

4. Betty loses. Currie would analyze this as a false conflict. While Oz's law provides a defense, and (depending on its choice of law approach) Oz might apply its law to the case, Oz's interest in protecting wives from contracts extends only to wives domiciled in Oz. Betty is domiciled in Narnia, and Narnian law provides no defense. On the contrary, Narnia's policy is to promote freedom of contract. This policy will be advanced by applying its law.

   This example makes the important point that, while interest analysis definitely favors application of forum law, doing so does not necessarily benefit forum residents. States have important economic policies for recognizing and enforcing contracts involving nonresidents, and they also have interests in enforcing residents' contracts entered into outside the state—even when they are losers!

Old Chestnut

5. This example obviously steals its facts and names from Babcock v. Jackson, 191 N.E.2d 279 (N.Y. 1963). Under interest analysis, state A courts will reject the guest statute and apply forum law. This is a classic false conflict. Country B's policy is to protect insurance companies from

the law of Albion, personal property is distributed according to the law of the decedent's domicile at death. But according to the law of Lilliput, personal property is distributed according to the law of the decedent's national citizenship. Alfred is the next of kin entitled to the personal property under Albion's law of intestate succession. Gaston is the next of kin entitled to the personal property under Lilliput's law of succession.

The estate is being administered in part in Albion, and the administrator appointed in Albion asks you who is entitled to the personal property. What is the right answer under the First Restatement?

5. Damato died domiciled in New Jersey. At the time of his death he owned two bank accounts in Florida for which he designated his son as the owner upon his death. Under the law of New Jersey at the time, the attempt to pass property at death required a valid will. The forms designating the son as the survivor, signed by the decedent when he opened the accounts, did not satisfy the requirements for a valid will. Under the law of Florida, where the accounts were located, the survivor forms were effective and conveyed a property-like interest in the proceeds of the account on the theory that they created a valid inter vivos trust that vested on the death of the settlor.

New Jersey cases held that the validity of a trust was governed by the law of the place where the trust was established (Florida). But Florida cases held that the validity of a trust was governed by the law of the settlor's domicile (New Jersey). Does the son get the bank accounts?

Exceptional Land

6. Oona Ohner, the owner of land in the country of Gondor, executes a deed transferring the land to Grant Grantee. Ohner signed and delivered the deed to Grantee while the two were at dinner in the country of Mordor. The deed did not satisfy the formal requirements of the local law of Gondor because it did not use the required language of conveyancing and did not properly describe the land to be conveyed. However, Gondor has a statute that provides that a deed of real property is valid if it satisfies either the law of Gondor or the law of the place where the deed was executed. In contrast, the deed satisfied the requirements for formal validity of the law of Mordor. What law will Mordor courts apply if the deed is challenged there?

7. Tess promised Lance that she would execute a will devising to him the estate of Blackacre, located in the country of Avalon, if he married her. Lance married Tess, and the couple moved to the state of East Dakota, where Tess died domiciled. She left a holographic will that was not valid under the laws of either Avalon or East Dakota.

fraudulent claims, and its interest is limited to preventing such fraud against insurance companies in (or perhaps doing business in) B. B also has an interest in protecting the courts of B from adjudicating fraudulent claims. Country B has no interest in applying its guest statute defense to this dispute litigated in state A involving a car licensed and insured in state A. State A, however, has an interest in applying its negligence law to compensate the injured person who is domiciled in the state.

Note the important point that country B does not have an interest in applying its law here, even though B courts might in fact have applied B's law to the case.

If you reached the right result by classifying this as a true conflict and applying forum law, you get no points. Hint for the final exam: even the experts can have trouble properly classifying cases under interest analysis. When in doubt, cover your bases. Show how a case may be a true conflict (governed by forum law) or might also be analyzed as a false conflict (governed by the law of the only jurisdiction with an interest in the application of its law).

College Crush Crash

6. Interest analysis treats this as a false conflict and does not apply the guest statute. Awaystate has no interest in protecting driver-defendants domiciled in other states, while Homestate has an interest in compensating the plaintiff who is domiciled in Homestate. See Tooker v. Lopez, 301 N.E.2d 394 (N.Y. 1969).

This example shows how rigidly interest analysis treats party-state affiliation. You might think Awaystate has a strong interest in applying its law to students who are living in the state for an extended period of time and from whom the state derives substantial revenues. But interest analysis tends to treat domicile as all or nothing for purposes of determining a state's interest.

Seeing Green

7. What differs in this example from the earlier guest statute examples is the different state policy for the defense. The different policy can change the outcome.

The old-fashioned guest statutes were designed to shift an economic loss but not to influence conduct. Interest analysis concluded that the states with such statutes had no interest in preventing the shifting of loss in cases involving parties domiciled out of state because the loss-shifting did not affect the state's policy goals. But in this example, West Dakota's policy goal is to encourage ride-sharing in West Dakota. Applying the defense encourages ride-sharing even if it is applied to drivers domiciled in other states. This gives West Dakota an interest in the application of its law to this dispute. On the other hand, East Dakota has an interest in compensating plaintiffs domiciled in the state who are injured negligently.

In other words, changing the state policy transforms the guest statute case, the classic false conflict, into a true conflict. The answer should now be easy: each state will apply its own law. Brittney wins in West Dakota (which applies the statutory defense) and loses in East Dakota (which does not apply the statutory defense).

When Worlds Collide

8. Interest analysis requires a consideration of the state policy behind rules and does not have formally different rules for matters that are procedural or remedial. The solution thus requires you to identify whether Vogon has an interest in applying its statute of limitations.

Policies served by statutes of limitations are to bar older claims, to encourage prompt litigation of disputes, and to preserve judicial resources for claims that are presented in a more timely fashion. Applying the shorter forum statute (regardless of where the parties are domiciled) would advance these policies, so forum law applies.

The flip side of this problem would require similar analysis of Tralfamadore's government policies. Tralfamadore's two-year statute of limitations is designed to give litigants (at the very least those domiciled in Tralfamadore!) ample time to investigate disputes, prepare cases, and seek access to courts. These policies would be frustrated by applying the shorter foreign statute of limitations.

In other words, the case is a true conflict, so Tralfamadore would apply its statute, while Vogon would apply its statute.

More Interesting Interest Analysis

9. These facts are inspired by Neumeier v. Kuehner, 286 N.E. 2d 454 (N.Y. 1972). My favorite casebook classifies *Neumeier* as an unprovided-for case, because the policy of Genovia's guest statute is to protect defendants domiciled in Genovia, and the defendant is domiciled in Glitterdom. The state of Glitterdom has a pro-recovery loss-shifting rule, but that rule is designed to compensate plaintiffs affiliated with Glitterdom, and Glitterdom has no state policy that requires the compensation of the plaintiff domiciled in Genovia when the plaintiff's home law bars recovery.

The question is hard because of the problem presented by unprovided-for cases. The short answer (which gets full points from me) is that the default rule (forum law) should apply. Currie was uneasy enough with this answer that he suggested other possibilities and challenged the world to come up with a better answer. If you have a better answer (within the confines of interest analysis), you get bonus points and are sentenced to life as a tenured professor of Conflicts.

I am almost afraid to bring up another reason why this case is hard, because I don't know the answer. The problem illustrates some of the underlying frustrations with interest analysis. Genovia courts said that Genovia's policy was to protect owners and drivers against ungrateful guests. Interest analysis tends to assume laws serve either a loss-shifting or conduct-regulating function. It concludes that a loss-shifting bar on recovery is properly limited to persons affiliated with the state who bear the loss. But what if Genovia's policy is more moralistic in purpose — to deter or punish ingratitude? This may be a bad or stupid purpose, but is it legitimate? And how does interest analysis know whether to extend such a purpose to foreign passengers? If there is any such interest, then Genovia's law should apply because it would become a false conflict — because Genovia would have some interest in applying its law, while Glitterdom still has no compensatory interest implicated under the facts.

10. The facts borrow from Hurtado v. Superior Court, 522 P.2d 666 (Cal. 1974). The California court and some of the brightest Conflicts gurus see this as an obvious example of a false conflict. *See* Richman et al., Understanding Conflict of Laws §78 at 256. West Texas's pro-recovery rule is designed not only to shift losses (an interest that would not be implicated in a case with a foreign plaintiff) but *also* to regulate conduct in the state by discouraging negligence on state roads. In contrast, Patagonia's limitation on damages is purely loss-shifting: its goal is to protect Patagonia defendants but not to encourage negligence in other states. Under this reasoning West Texas is the only state with an interest in applying its law, so every court applying interest analysis should ignore Patagonia's cap on damages.

So what's so hard about the case? Some Conflicts gurus see this as an unprovided-for case because the limits on damages — which admittedly amount to a denial of any recovery — are no more likely to affect driver conduct than the presence of a guest statute. Weintraub, Commentary on the Conflict of Laws §6.25 at 457. These scholars reason that drivers will not drive less carefully because a potential tort victim might end up being from a state that limits liability. If neither compensatory damages nor the defense affects behavior, then the case should be seen as involving a conflict between pure loss-shifting rules. According to this analysis, neither jurisdiction has a real interest in applying its loss-shifting rule, because the pro-recovery rule applies in favor of a plaintiff from the country that provides the defense, while the country whose law limits recovery would be applied to the benefit of a defendant from another country. If this analysis is correct, then the dispute is an unprovided-for case, and forum law would apply under the default rule.

To add to the confusion, a nontrivial argument might even be made that this case is a false conflict if Patagonia has a national policy for limiting damages in death actions that is not purely loss-shifting — for example, if Patagonia has a policy of discouraging wrongful death actions on the moral ground that such actions cheapen life or encourage greed. If only Patagonia has an interest in applying its law, then this is a false conflict and Patagonian law applies.

Consortium Confusion

11. This example borrows from Erwin v. Thomas, 506 P.2d 494 (Or. 1973), which the court classified as an unprovided-for case because the rules are purely loss-shifting. It reasoned that O's (Oregon's) interest in compensating wives was limited to wives domiciled in O while W's (Washington's) interest in protecting defendants was limited to protecting defendants domiciled in W. In this case neither state had an interest requiring application of its law. The Oregon court applied Currie's default rule, forum law.

Big Spender

12. This example is inspired by one of my favorite cases, Lilienthal v. Kaufman, 395 P.2d 543 (Or. 1964). Under interest analysis the forum court classified this as a true conflict and applied forum law. Even though the court observed that the extraterritorial extension of the defense to a contract entered into out of state permitted the defendant to perpetrate "a species of fraud," the court concluded that the purpose of the defense would be promoted by applying it. The "right" answer is thus to grant the motion for summary judgment because this is a true conflict. Confusion has an interest in applying its defense to protect incompetents domiciled in state, but Florida has an interest in enforcing contracts performed in Florida.

    Give yourself bonus points if you see that this might also be treated as a false conflict if Confusion could narrow its construction of the defense so as not to apply to these facts. Do forum interests really require the application of the defense to situations that constitute "a species of fraud"?

    Give yourself double bonus points if you see that the forum state's interest is doubly doubtful because, if it's a true conflict, this will be the last case of its kind ever litigated in Confusion courts. After Confusion applies the defense, won't it be malpractice for a lawyer representing an out-of-state plaintiff to litigate another case like it in Confusion? Other Confusion defendants may be the real losers. There will always be long-arm jurisdiction and minimum contacts in those states where the contracts were made.

Double Trouble

13. The key to answering a question like this is to analyze the claims separately and to do a careful job identifying the state policies behind the laws that are in conflict in each.

    The first claim is based on the common law doctrine of respondeat superior. This doctrine makes an employer automatically liable for the personal injuries committed by its "servant" employees when they are committed in the scope of employment. The policy behind the doctrine is to shift losses from injured persons to the businesses employing the tortfeasors because the businesses are better able to bear the costs or get insurance. The purpose of the doctrine is probably not to reduce negligence, because the doctrine does not add to the deterrent effect of the personal liability that already should be inducing the driver to take due care. Accordingly, the doctrine of respondeat superior is a loss-shifting rule. This analysis is consistent with New York opinions characterizing vicarious liability rules as primarily loss-shifting. (See Chapter 17.)

    Harmony's charitable immunity statute also appears to be a loss-shifting rule. Its goal is to lower costs of charities in order to encourage charitable activity. Even though Harmony would not apply its own charitable immunity in this case (because it follows the traditional territorial rules), Harmony's goal of reducing the costs of charities would be furthered by applying the defense. In contrast, Recovery has no interest in applying its pro-recovery loss-shifting rule of respondeat superior because no Recovery plaintiff would benefit from the application of the rule. Consequently, the first cause of action gives rise to a false conflict and should be resolved by applying the law of Harmony, the only state with an interest in having its law applied.

    It is also arguable, however, that Recovery's doctrine of respondeat superior is also conduct-regulating. This would be the case if the policy behind the rule is to deter employers from hiring careless drivers. Even though the rule makes employers strictly liable for their employees' negligence, it is possible that the goal of this transferred liability is to make employers act more carefully in hiring and supervising employees. If that is a policy behind the rule, then Recovery has an interest in applying its doctrine of respondeat superior because it affects conduct in the state when employers delegate driving to employees who drive trucks and cause injuries in Recovery. This analysis is consistent with California decisions construing California's permissive-owner statute that makes car owner's vicariously liable for torts committed by persons who drive their cars with the owner's permission. The California courts see a "primary" conduct-regulating purpose in encouraging owners to exercise care in permitting others to use their cars and in protecting persons on California roads. This conduct-regulating purpose is limited to California. In addition, the California courts see a loss-shifting purpose in protecting California residents, which extends to out-of-state torts. *See* Terry McCann v. Foster Wheeler, LLC, 225 P.3d 516, 533 (Cal. 2010), discussing Castro v. Budget Rent-A-Car System, Inc., 154 Cal. App. 4th 1162 (2007).

If Recovery has a conduct-regulating policy served by respondeat superior, then the case becomes a true conflict, and Recovery would apply its law. But the argument that respondeat superior serves conduct-regulating goals is inconsistent with the fact that Recovery has a separate theory of liability that is directly based on negligent hiring.

The second claim is based on the charity's own negligent hiring, not on its derivative liability for the driver's acts. Recovery's tort law that allows recovery for negligent hiring serves the general purposes of tort law. These are both loss-shifting and conduct-regulating. Holding employers liable for negligent hiring will encourage employers (including those in other states) to hire better drivers, and this will reduce injuries and deaths in the state of Recovery. This gives Recovery an interest in applying its negligent hiring rule to the facts of the case. Harmony still has a loss-shifting interest in applying its charitable immunity defense to reduce the costs of charities. Consequently, the second cause of action gives rise to a true conflict, and Recovery will apply forum law.

Under interest analysis, Recovery should grant the motion to dismiss the first cause of action if it finds that respondeat superior is loss-shifting and deny it if it finds that respondeat superior is conduct-regulating. It should deny the motion to dismiss the second cause of action (negligent hiring).

Comparative Impairment and Modified Interest Analysis

CONSUMER WARNING

Do not read this chapter if you have not read the chapter on Interest Analysis. Comparative impairment and other forms of modified interest analysis build on interest analysis. They adopt the analytical framework, classifications, and terminology invented by interest analysis. And they resolve many cases exactly the same way pure interest analysis does.

WHAT NEEDS MODIFYING IN PURE INTEREST ANALYSIS?

Currie insisted that a state court should apply its own state's law if doing so would promote the state's policy. One consequence of interest analysis is that a jurisdiction will apply its own law to cases where the forum has only a slight interest in the application of its law, yet another state has an overwhelming and powerful interest in application of its law.

Responding to criticism, Currie in later formulations of his theory urged courts before finding a true conflict to reconsider whether a more careful analysis of state interests might disclose that one state lacked an interest in applying its law to the facts. But Currie never revoked his conclusion that where a true conflict was found, the forum should apply forum law.

Currie's theoretical analysis of governmental interests and his classification of cases influenced many scholars and courts. In contrast, his proposed treatment of true conflicts was always controversial. His proposal seemed to reach hard or unfair results in extreme cases where the forum's governmental interest was trivial compared to another state's. (Many students instinctively understand this problem and try to balance state interests when applying interest analysis. Don't be one of them!)

Currie's treatment of true conflicts was controversial because it directly rejected some of the traditional goals of choice of law. His rejection of the idea of superlaw above and beyond local state law was not controversial, nor was his abandonment of the goals of uniformity and predictability of results. These theories had been largely discredited in practice, and most modern decisions and theories reject them. But Currie went still further in adopting a local perspective of the policymaking role of courts. He tended to repudiate the goals of trying to accommodate the conflicting policies of other jurisdictions and of effectuating the expectations of private parties based on other jurisdictions' laws.

For functional reasons, Currie remained skeptical about the political and institutional competence of courts to elaborate rules designed to accommodate conflicting laws from other jurisdictions. But he did not always advance the strongest argument for applying forum law in true conflicts. Instead, he claimed he did not know what else to do. He challenged others to come up with a better theory. This was like waving a red flag in front of law professors, who were eager to offer a better answer.

ANOTHER PROFESSOR, ANOTHER THEORY

Professor William Baxter invented the theory of comparative impairment as a response to dissatisfaction with Currie's treatment of true conflicts. He agreed with pure interest analysis's treatment of false conflicts. Hence the first rule of comparative impairment is: apply the law of the only state with an interest in the application of its law in false conflicts.

Professor Baxter shared Professor Currie's functional view of courts as institutions designed to promote state policies. But Baxter argued that all states would be winners in the long run if they followed a sort of golden rule. The professor put it this way: "if the process is to have a normative basis, the criterion must be maximum attainment of underlying purpose by all government entities."[1] Baxter's proposed solution for true conflicts is:

---

1. William F. Baxter, *Choice of Law and the Federal System*, 16 Stan. L. Rev. 1, 12 (1963).

apply the law of the state whose interest would be more severely impaired if its law were not applied in the particular context presented by the case.

Note that comparative impairment's rule is formulated as a double negative. The formulation selects the law of the jurisdiction whose governmental policies would be most *impaired* if that jurisdiction's law is *not* selected. It is tempting to untangle this into a rule that calls for the application of the law of the state that has the greatest interest in the case. Resist the temptation! Comparative impairment should be kept in its double negative form. First, accurately stating the rule will get full points on the final exam. Second, jurisdictions like California and Louisiana that have adopted comparative impairment have done so in the double negative form. Professor Baxter, like Currie, rejected the possibility or desirability of directly comparing or weighing different state interests. But Baxter believed it was possible to identify the consequences that would result from refusing to implement a state's law in a particular case and to evaluate the extent to which such consequences would frustrate the policy goals of the state's law.

All states applying comparative impairment should select the same state's law. In false conflicts they will apply the law of the only state with an interest. In true conflicts they will apply the law of the state whose interest is more seriously impaired. Baxter argued that uniformity of result was another advantage over pure interest analysis because it promoted predictability. In contrast, under pure interest analysis parties do not know in advance the place of litigation and so do not know which forum's law will apply.

Pros and Cons of Comparative Impairment

Comparative impairment offers an elegant solution to Currie's challenge of finding a better answer for true conflicts. It restores the courts to the business of accommodating different states' laws in conflicts cases. And it offers a rule that in practice promises to make all jurisdictions better off in the long run.

So what's not to like? First, if you don't like interest analysis for reasons other than its treatment of true conflicts, then you won't like comparative impairment. Second, if you agree with Currie that courts should implement forum law where it serves the governmental interests of the forum state, regardless of the interests of other jurisdictions, then you will not like comparative impairment.

Comparative impairment also presents new problems. To begin with, it is often hard to tell which jurisdiction's governmental interests will be more impaired by the nonapplication of that jurisdiction's law.[2] Moreover,

---

2. Baxter acknowledged that comparative impairment was vulnerable to attack on grounds of uncertainty and vagueness but maintained it was superior to the alternatives. *Id.* at 20.

the benefits of comparative impairment are conditional. In any given true conflict, applying another jurisdiction's law will sacrifice some government objective of the forum state. The benefits the forum is supposed to receive depend entirely on other states adopting comparative impairment. In fact very few states have adopted comparative impairment. It is unclear to me why the largest states would ever benefit from applying comparative impairment. Because so many cases are litigated in those states, they might be better off not to follow the golden rule. They might be better off instead applying their home state law to all true conflicts even if all other states likewise applied their own home state laws.

Jurisdictions

California and Louisiana have adopted comparative impairment.[3]

COMPARATIVE IMPAIRMENT IN PRACTICE

The leading comparative impairment case in the casebooks is Bernhard v. Harrah's Club, 546 P.2d 719 (Cal. 1976). The defendant operated a casino in Nevada and advertised in California "knowing and expecting" that California residents would drive to the casino. A California couple drove to the casino, where they were served drinks until they became intoxicated. Driving back home in California, the drunk driver veered into oncoming traffic and hit and severely injured the plaintiff, a California resident.

The plaintiff sued the Nevada casino in California state court. Under Nevada law, tavern keepers were not liable for injuries proximately caused by serving alcoholic beverages to intoxicated patrons who inflicted injuries on other persons. The trial court applied Nevada law and dismissed the lawsuit.

The California Supreme Court reversed. First, it found a true conflict. Nevada had an interest in denying recovery in order to avoid imposing ruinous liability on Nevada tavern owners. California had an interest in protecting the public from injuries resulting from intoxicated drivers.

Second, the California court applied Baxter's principle of comparative impairment. It observed that California's goal of reducing injuries extended to California residents injured on California roads by drunk drivers returning to California after having been induced to leave the state by

---

3. Louisiana is unusual in that its legislature enacted choice of law rules. Professor Symeonides, a moving force behind the state's codification, is a fan of comparative impairment for true conflicts.

advertisements targeting California consumers. The court reasoned that Nevada tavern keepers targeting California residents placed themselves at the heart of California's regulatory interest. Moreover, the court determined that California could not effectuate its injury-avoiding policy if it did not extend the regulation to such tavern keepers. In sum, California's interest would be "very significantly impaired" by its nonapplication under the facts.

In contrast, the court found that imposing liability under California law would not impose inconsistent duties on Nevada tavern keepers because a Nevada statute already made it a misdemeanor to provide drinks to drunk customers.[4] The court observed that increased liability is a foreseeable and insurable business expense. And it found that applying California law would not greatly frustrate Nevada's goal of limiting liability because such liability would only be imposed on Nevada businesses that targeted California drivers. The California court concluded that California's interest would be more severely impaired if California's law extending liability to tavern keepers was not applied. Accordingly, it applied California law.

The Hard Part: Wrong and Right Factors to Consider

The hard part of comparative impairment is figuring out which state's interest is more impaired. Courts and Conflicts gurus have trouble with this, too, so don't despair. The key is to avoid considering the wrong factors—and to consider the right ones.

Wrong Factors   As a modified form of interest analysis, comparative impairment seeks to replace territorial analysis by a consideration of the policy objectives of the laws in conflict. The first edition of this book emphasized that you should avoid sneaking territorial values back into your analysis. It cautioned against the tempting error of assuming that one state's interest is less seriously impaired just because the consequences are felt outside that state or because some event occurs outside the state.

But the Supreme Court of California was not reading the first edition. It was busy writing the opinion in McCann v. Foster Wheeler LLC, 225 P.3d 516 (2010), where it did exactly what I said it shouldn't. It concluded that California had less interest in applying its longer statute of limitations in favor of a California resident when the resident was injured as the result of conduct outside the state. The case involved claims for cancer resulting from exposure to asbestos many years earlier. Where the defendant had manufactured a product in New York that was installed at a factory in Oklahoma, the

---

4. The Nevada statute was repealed after the accident but before the California opinion analyzing Nevada's governmental interests. The court was apparently unaware of the repeal.

court held that Oklahoma's statute of repose governed the case and barred the claims: "[W]hen the law of the other state limits or denies liability for the conduct engaged in by the defendant in its territory . . . [then] California's legitimate interest in providing a remedy for, or in facilitating a recovery by, a current California resident properly must be subordinated because of this state's diminished authority over activity that occurs in another state." *McCann* shows how a court can look to territorial considerations—the policies at the place of conduct aimed at shielding businesses from liability for the purpose of encouraging them to do business in the state.[5] But the case also shows how territorial events should be considered in light of the government interests behind the laws in conflict.

A common mistake to avoid is weighing state interests. The comparative impairment rule is specifically formulated to avoid comparing the relative value or weight of competing state interests. This means you should avoid comparing the importance of the state interests directly. Don't conclude that a safety or regulatory interest is more important than a loss-shifting interest. Don't conclude that a right to privacy is more valuable than freedom of speech. Instead, consider the consequences of not applying the state laws at issue. For example, conclude that not recognizing a defense of right to privacy under one state's law will more significantly impair that state's interests by describing how not recognizing the defense will encourage intrusive publicity in a way that frustrates core values of individual autonomy promoted by state law. Then consider the effect that not applying the other jurisdiction's law will have on the policies of the other jurisdiction.

Example of How Comparative Impairment Modifies Interest Analysis

In the last chapter we considered the case of Lilienthal v. Kaufman, 395 P.2d 543 (Or. 1964). Under Oregon law a person adjudicated a "spendthrift" had a complete defense to all contracts. One such spendthrift traveled to another state and entered into contracts with unwitting parties. When one of the victims sued the spendthrift in Oregon, the Oregon state supreme court found that the purpose of the spendthrift defense was to protect the

---

5. The case is discussed more in Chapter 23. I try hard not to say it was wrongly decided, but it is not clear how applying Oklahoma's statute of repose encourages businesses to do business in that state. The court of appeals unanimously concluded that the defendant did not rely on Oklahoma's statute and that Oklahoma either had no interest or that its interest was minimally impaired by not applying the statute of repose. McCann v. Foster Wheeler, 73 Cal. Rptr. 3d 96, 103 (Cal. App. 2008). The defendant did not renew its reliance argument before the state supreme court, and the court mentioned in a footnote that Oklahoma did not enact its statute of repose until 21 years after the defendant's activity. McCann v. Foster Wheeler LLC, 225 P.3d at 528 n.6.

assets of spendthrifts. It acknowledged that Oregon shared with other states' common interests in enforcing contractual expectations. The court also recognized that applying the spendthrift defense to out-of-state contracts with out-of-state defendants permitted a defendant to perpetuate a "species of fraud." Nevertheless, the Oregon court concluded that because there was a true conflict, it must apply the Oregon spendthrift defense under pure interest analysis.

In contrast, comparative impairment would offer the forum an opportunity to apply the law of another state by finding that the other state's interest would be more seriously impaired by not applying its law. In *Lilienthal*, the impairment of foreign state interest would also coincide with some important local interests: not applying the other state's contract laws would frustrate expectations, disrupt the agreement of private parties, and even allow a person to obtain an unfair advantage by relying on his or her home state defense to avoid financial responsibility for promises. In contrast, the goals of forum law would be minimally affected by not applying forum law.

While forum law provides a defense for spendthrifts, that protection is largely illusory in disputes arising from out-of-state contracts, because such disputes can be brought in other state courts, which will refuse to recognize the defense. Because the interests of the other state (many shared by the forum) will be significantly impaired if the contract is unenforceable but the forum's interest in protecting spendthrifts will not be significantly eroded by disregarding the defense in out-of-state contracts, then the forum under comparative impairment will recognize the contract claim and disregard its peculiar spendthrift defense.[6]

MISCELLANEOUS OTHER MODIFICATIONS OF INTEREST ANALYSIS

Law professors have peddled a variety of other theoretical solutions for true conflicts. So far jurisdictions are not buying. Casebooks cover these approaches in notes (if at all).

Professor Weintraub suggests applying the law of the state that advances the shared underlying policies of the states whose laws are in conflict. In a wills case, this might mean applying a law that validates a will and disregarding a peculiar invalidating rule. *See* Weintraub, Commentary on the Conflict of Laws §6.25 at 458-459.

---

6. This is not the only solution under comparative impairment! Professor Kramer argues that Oregon's interest would be more seriously impaired, so Oregon law should still apply. Larry Kramer, *Rethinking Choice of Law*, 90 Colum. L. Rev. 277, 323-324 (1990).

Professors Richman, Reynolds, and Whytock propose the great heresy of balancing competing state policy interests. Richman et al., Understanding Civil Procedure §79[d] at 267. They argue that courts engage in such balancing routinely in domestic cases. California seems to have engaged in such balancing of interests in some of its comparative impairment decisions. For example, in Offshore Rental Co. v. Continental Oil Co., 583 P.2d 721 (Cal. 1978), the California Supreme Court refused to apply a California statute that seemed to permit a corporation to recover for losses of services from key employees who were injured. In doing so, the court emphasized that the California statute was archaic, while the foreign law, denying such derivative claims, was mainstream. The court's analysis displayed the sort of weighing of interests that both interest analysis and its comparative impairment modification prohibit.

Examples

You Were Warned

1. Homer and Madge, citizens of the country of Patagonia, were married in Patagonia in accordance with Patagonian law. They traveled to the country of El Dorado for their honeymoon. While swimming in the hotel's pool in El Dorado, Homer jumped off the diving board and struck and injured Madge.

   Upon returning to Patagonia Madge commenced a tort action against Homer. Homer moved to dismiss under the law of El Dorado. El Dorado law recognizes a defense of spousal immunity for all tort claims. El Dorado courts have explained that the purpose of the immunity is to promote family harmony and to prevent married persons from colluding in presenting fraudulent claims against insurance companies. Patagonia does not recognize spousal immunity.

   Both Patagonia and El Dorado follow Professor Baxter's comparative impairment theory. What law do they apply?

Close but No Cigar

2. What's wrong with this final exam answer?

   > Alban, citizen of Albion, traveled to Caledonia, where he accused Clyde, a citizen of Caledonia, of being a "lying liar." The accusation took place in a spirited public political debate. Clyde has commenced a slander action against Alban in Albion court. The words are defamatory, and Clyde has a good claim under the law of Caledonia. Although Albion decisions have squarely held that the words "lying liar" are protected under principles of free speech in political debate, Albion follows comparative impairment in choice of law cases. This case is a true conflict because Albion has an interest in applying its defense to promote

free speech by its citizen while Caledonia has an interest in applying its slander law to compensate its citizen. But in applying comparative impairment, Albion has less of an interest in applying its speech-encouraging rule to conduct that occurred in Caledonia, whereas Caledonia has a much stronger interest in protecting its citizens from harm to their reputation caused by words spoken in Caledonia. For this reason, the Albion court will apply the law of Caledonia and permit a claim.

Lucky Loser

3. Drunk Driver, a citizen of the state of Inebriation, went to the Lucky Dog Casino, Inc., a business incorporated under the laws of the state of Inebriation. At the casino Drunk played poker for 12 hours. As long as he was playing poker, the casino continued to serve free alcoholic drinks. As a result, Drunk became extremely intoxicated.

   After winning a total of $1,000, Drunk decided to drive to visit his girlfriend, Gal, who lived in the neighboring state of Sobriety. After crossing into Sobriety, Drunk lost consciousness, ran off the road, and struck and killed a pedestrian, Pete Pederson, a citizen of Inebriation.

   Pederson's estate brings a civil action against the casino in Sobriety state court. Under the law of Sobriety, a tavern keeper is liable to third persons who are injured by intoxicated persons whom the tavern keeper served to the point of intoxication knowing that they would drive in an intoxicated condition. The casino is in a secluded location that requires customers to drive to and from the casino. Accordingly, the casino employees knew that Drunk would be required to drive after becoming intoxicated. The employees also knew that serving drinks continuously for a 12-hour period would cause Drunk to become too intoxicated to drive safely.

   The casino has moved to dismiss the lawsuit under the state of Inebriation's Casino Freedom Responsibility Act. The Act, sponsored by casinos and insurance companies, recites in a preamble that its purpose is to "restore personal responsibility and prevent ruinous litigation." The Act provides that individual customers are responsible for the consequences of their own conduct and that "casinos are immune to civil liability for injuries caused to third persons in lawsuits alleging that the casinos served casino customers to the point of intoxication."

   Sobriety follows comparative impairment. Rule on the casino's motion and explain fully.

Charity Begins at Home

4. Big Church Co. is a nonprofit religious organization that distributes church supplies, with its principal place of business and place of

incorporation in the state of East Dakota. Big Church Co. hired Deadeye Dick as a truck driver after he filled out an application form and provided evidence of a valid truck driver's license. The corporation did not contact any of Dick's references, nor did it conduct a search of Dick's driving records. Although Dick's responses to his job application indicated that he had been involved in no driving accidents, in fact Dick had been convicted once of vehicular manslaughter and four times of driving while intoxicated in East Dakota.

While Dick was making a delivery for Big Church Co. in the neighboring state of West Dakota, Dick got drunk and collided with a car, seriously injuring Mabel and Freddie. Mabel is a citizen of East Dakota while Freddie is a citizen of West Dakota.

Mabel and Freddie have sued Big Church Co. in West Dakota state court asserting two causes of action. First, they allege that Dick caused the accident negligently and that Big Church Co. is liable under the doctrine of respondeat superior. Second, they allege that Big Church Co. negligently hired and supervised the driver and that the negligent hiring and supervision proximately caused their personal injury damages.

East Dakota recognizes a defense of charitable immunity under which a charitable organization like Big Church Co. is immune to all civil liability for personal injury tort claims based on negligence. The purpose of the defense is to encourage charitable activity by reducing economic disincentives to such activity. West Dakota recognizes no defense of charitable immunity.

East Dakota does not recognize a cause of action for negligent hiring and supervision. When faced with such a claim, the East Dakota courts opined that "such novel theories are best left to the legislature." In contrast, West Dakota courts have recognized a cause of action for negligent hiring and supervision. The West Dakota decision recognizing a cause of action for negligent hiring and supervision opined that

> it is only fair to shift the cost of the loss caused by such negligence to the person or entity in the best position to avoid creating the risk of the loss, and doing so will cause employers to be more careful in hiring dangerous employees, thus reducing the risk of harm created by their business activity.

West Dakota follows comparative impairment. What law will it apply to Mabel's claims?

5. Same facts and laws. What law will West Dakota apply to Freddie's claims?

Tricky Charity

6. Same facts and laws. What law will East Dakota apply to all claims if it too follows comparative impairment?

And Now for an Easy Statute of Frauds Case. Not.

7. Ron, citizen of the country of Romulus, traveled to the country of Camazotz and entered into an oral contract with Cammy, a citizen of Camazotz. According to the contract, Ron agreed to remove four galvanized widgets from Cammy's warehouse in Camazotz within 14 months from the date of the agreement. In return Cammy promised to give Ron four peppercorns upon timely removal of the widgets.

    Ron refused to perform, and Cammy sues Ron in a Romulan court for breach of contract. Ron raises as a defense Romulus's statute of frauds that requires all contracts that cannot be performed in 12 months to be in writing. Cammy argues, however, that the court should apply Camazotz's statute of frauds, which provides that all contracts that cannot be performed within 15 months must be evidenced by a writing. The courts in both states explain that the purposes of their respective statutes of frauds are to ensure that some writing exists to prevent plaintiffs from presenting fraudulent claims for nonexistent contracts.

Telephone Tort

8. Plaintiffs, California residents, made and received numerous long distance telephone calls with a firm in Georgia. Without their knowledge or consent, the firm recorded the phone conversations in Georgia. Under California law, recording telephone communications without consent is a criminal offense and gives rise to a cause of action for invasion of privacy. In contrast, under Georgia law, recording telephone conversations is lawful if either party to the conversation consents. Plaintiffs litigate in California, which follows comparative impairment. Hello, what's the right answer?

Explanations

You Were Warned

1. In this case, both countries would apply Patagonian law and permit recovery. The answer does not require reference to any special principles of comparative impairment; instead, it requires you to remember that comparative impairment adopts the analytic framework of interest analysis and resolves false conflicts the same way pure interest analysis does.

    The case is a false conflict because Patagonia has an interest in applying its loss-shifting rule to provide a recovery for its resident. In contrast, El Dorado's interest in promoting family harmony extends only to El Dorado marriages, and its interest in discouraging collusive claims does not extend to claims by nonresidents in foreign courts in disputes where any insurance is likely to be with a foreign insurance company.

Patagonia's law should be applied by all interest analysis (and modified interest analysis) jurisdictions because Patagonia is the only state with an interest in its law applying. For loss-shifting rules, apply the law of common domicile.

Close but No Cigar

2. The spirit of the answer is right, but the answer loses major points for failing to state the comparative impairment rule and failing to employ the right terminology. In theory, comparative impairment rejects weighing state interests just as interest analysis does. In practice, comparative impairment sometimes seems to weigh interests.

To avoid confusion (and get full points), a good answer would stick to comparative impairment's terminology: the comparative impairment court will first determine if this is a true conflict. The case appears to be a true conflict unless the forum interest in promoting free speech can be limited. As a true conflict, the court must apply the law of the country whose interests would be most impaired if its law were not applied. This can be difficult to determine but involves a consideration of the effect of not applying a jurisdiction's law. In this case, not applying Caledonia's defamation law would leave a person whose reputation was injured without compensation. This would appear to completely frustrate the underlying remedial goals of defamation law. In contrast, not applying Albion's defense would deter free speech, but it would do so under limited circumstances involving conduct in another country that caused injuries to citizens of that country. Albion's policies would not be as significantly impaired as Caledonia's, so its law should apply.

This is not the only possible solution but it gets full points for stating the rule, employing the right terminology, and making a good faith effort to determine which state's governmental policies would be most seriously impaired.

Lucky Loser

3. The facts, obviously stolen from *Bernhard*, describe a true conflict. Sobriety has an interest in imposing liability on tavern keepers in order to reduce drunk driving accidents on Sobriety's roads. This is a conduct-regulating policy that will be advanced by applying its law to out-of-state casinos. Note that if the social policy behind Sobriety's third-party liability rule was solely to provide adequate compensation for persons injured by drunk drivers, then this case would be a false conflict. Sobriety would have no interest in applying its loss-shifting rule in favor of a noncitizen plaintiff whose home state law provided no compensation.

Inebriation's interest is less obvious. Despite the colorful language in the preamble of the Act, Inebriation's policy goal is probably to reduce the liability of tavern keepers in order to lower their costs of business and increase their profitability. Its goal is not to encourage drunk driving (which is presumably illegal even in Inebriation, though the facts don't say so). The stated goal of encouraging individual responsibility is already served by the existing tort liability of drunk drivers for their own negligent acts. The state obviously has an interest in applying this loss-shifting rule in a case involving a business incorporated in the state. *McCann* suggests that a state might have a broader interest in encouraging businesses to do business in the state, and such an interest would be advanced by applying its law to all defendants.

Because both Sobriety and Inebriation have an interest in applying their law to the facts of this case, it is a true conflict. Under comparative impairment, the court must then determine which state's law would be most impaired by its nonapplication. In contrast to the facts in *Bernhard*, the driver here was a citizen of Inebriation. Moreover, the casino did not advertise in Sobriety or especially encourage Sobriety customers to drive to Inebriation. Accordingly, the defendant had less reason to anticipate the consequences of its conduct in Sobriety and would have less reason to be deterred from engaging in conduct that might establish liability under Sobriety's tort law. Under these facts, Sobriety's interest in regulating conduct in Sobriety would not be significantly impaired by not imposing liability on the innkeeper.

In contrast, under the reasoning in *Bernhard*, Inebriation's policy of reducing third-party claims against casinos is directly frustrated if another state recognizes a claim by an Inebriation plaintiff that would be barred under Inebriation law. And to the extent the Sobriety rule might also advance a loss-shifting policy, such a policy is not advanced in a claim by an Inebriation plaintiff against an Inebriation defendant.

This is not the only possible good answer—though it's the "right" one indicated by dictum in *Bernhard*. You could certainly argue that casinos in certain geographical areas benefit from continuous traffic from adjacent nongaming states. And you could elaborate an argument that, regardless of advertising, such businesses benefit from the laws of such states prohibiting gaming and also knowingly cause many effects in such states, including increased drunk driving accidents and deaths. You could conclude that Sobriety's goal of reducing drunk driving required its application to casinos that served persons who subsequently drive in Sobriety.

Pitfalls to avoid are concluding that Sobriety's safety goal is more important or weightier than Inebriation's economic (or moral responsibility) goal. Likewise, subtract points if you concluded that Inebriation's goal is less impaired just because the case involved an accident in another state.

Charity Begins at Home

4. This hypothetical is reminiscent of the issues raised in Schultz v. Boy Scouts of America, 480 N.E.2d 679 (N.Y. 1985) (see Chapter 17). The problem illustrates the importance of separately analyzing different claims and different parties in applying comparative impairment.

Plaintiff Mabel and the charitable defendant share a common domicile. This makes it easy to resolve her tort claim based on respondeat superior as a false conflict. Both East and West Dakota share the common goals of tort law to the extent they provide recoveries for losses. Such goals are both loss-shifting and regulatory. But East Dakota's denial of recovery for the tort is the result of a loss-shifting rule. The goal of the immunity is to shift the loss with the attendant benefit of removing disincentives to charitable activity. The goal is not primarily to regulate conduct because its goal is not to increase careless driving—though that is a possible side effect. Because the rule is loss-shifting and plaintiff Mabel and the defendant charity are both from the same state, then comparative impairment, like interest analysis, will classify the claim as stating a false conflict and apply the defense of charitable immunity of the place of common domicile.

Analyzing Mabel's second claim based on West Dakota's law of negligent hiring and supervision is more challenging. This cause of action advances goals that are both loss-shifting and conduct-regulating. To the extent the goals are loss-shifting, West Dakota does not have an interest in applying its law to the claim by a plaintiff from East Dakota. To the extent the goal is to reduce accident-creating conduct, West Dakota has an interest in applying its law.

East Dakota's policies are hard to evaluate. Its refusal to recognize the cause of action of negligent hiring and supervision expresses a deference to the constitutional role of the East Dakota legislature in adopting new tort theories. In fact this results in a policy against shifting losses until authorized by the legislature, but it is unclear whether this expresses an affirmative social policy or is simply the default rule based on stare decisis. East Dakota also recognizes a defense of charitable immunity to all claims, including the claim of negligent hiring and supervision. The goal of the defense is loss-shifting. East Dakota thus clearly has an interest in applying its loss-shifting rule to the facts of this case involving an East Dakota charitable corporation.

Because there is a true conflict, comparative impairment requires the application of the law of the state whose interests will be most impaired by the nonapplication of the state's law. The result is uncertain but requires comparing the impairment of West Dakota's conduct-regulating goals with the impairment of East Dakota's loss-shifting goals. On the one hand, you could argue that West Dakota's conduct-regulating goals would not be greatly sacrificed by applying East Dakota law to a claim by an East Dakota plaintiff. The general deterrent effect of the state's law would be preserved because most accidents in West Dakota would involve injuries to West Dakota plaintiffs. On the other hand, you could argue that East Dakota's loss-shifting goals would not be seriously impaired because liability could be limited to injuries foreseeably caused by hiring dangerous drivers who are engaged to make deliveries in other states. In such circumstances, charities might reasonably anticipate limits on charitable immunity and get insurance against resulting losses.

The "right" answer probably depends on how much additional deterrent effect you think imposing negligent hiring and supervision liability in favor of East Dakota plaintiffs will achieve over and above imposing such liability in favor of West Dakota plaintiffs. I suspect it will achieve little to no additional deterrent effect, in which case the issue in conflict begins to look more like a loss-shifting issue, and I would lean toward applying East Dakota law either because it is a false conflict or because applying East Dakota's nonliability rule would interfere minimally with West Dakota's state interests in this case, whereas permitting Mabel to recover under West Dakota law would significantly interfere with the loss-shifting goals of East Dakota.

5. Changing the plaintiff's domicile changes the claim based on respondeat superior from a false conflict into a true conflict. West Dakota has a state interest in compensating its citizen (Freddie) that will be advanced by applying its law and disregarding the East Dakota defense. East Dakota has an interest in applying its loss-shifting charitable immunity defense in favor of its home state charity.

Pure interest analysis would dictate the application of forum law. But under comparative impairment, we must apply the law of the state whose interests would be most seriously impaired by the nonapplication of the state's law. This is one of the simplest possible scenarios for comparative impairment. But if you are not sure of the result, you are in good company. Even seasoned conflicts scholars have argued that this could go either way.

You could argue that West Dakota's interest in providing compensation for injured West Dakotans would be completely frustrated by refusing to apply its law to permit recovery under the facts. In contrast, East Dakota's loss-shifting goals behind charitable immunity would still be achieved in most cases, and East Dakota charities could limit their exposure to such liability either by restricting their activities in West Dakota or by obtaining insurance for losses in that state.

It is also possible to argue that West Dakota's interest in obtaining relief for state victims of torts would not be completely frustrated if the plaintiff was able to recover directly from Drunk Driver. The plaintiff could also recover for some of his losses under his own insurance policy. In such a scenario, West Dakota's recognition of East Dakota's defense would not prevent compensation for some or all losses; it would only prevent additional recovery from the charity. In contrast, you could emphasize that disregarding the charity's defense would completely frustrate East Dakota's loss-shifting goal and expose charities to the fear of uncertain economic risks that the defense was designed to eliminate. Even remote possibilities of liability might frustrate East Dakota's goal of removing disincentives to charitable activity.

Freddie's negligent hiring and supervision claim will also be analyzed differently from Mabel's. As we saw, the negligent hiring and supervision claim advances both loss-shifting and conduct-regulating goals of West Dakota. In Freddie's case West Dakota has an interest in applying its cause of action to achieve both the loss-shifting and conduct-regulating goals. East Dakota's goals behind not recognizing a cause of action for negligent hiring and supervision either express judicial inertia or are loss-shifting. West Dakota's application of West Dakota law will not interfere with East Dakota's desire to leave the recognition of new causes of action to the East Dakota legislature. But applying West Dakota's cause of action will interfere with an East Dakota loss-shifting goal of reducing employer costs for negligent hiring.

West Dakota's interest in compensating West Dakota plaintiffs would arguably be significantly impaired by not applying the cause of action for negligent hiring and supervision. In contrast, East Dakota's interest in limiting costs to its state employers could be reduced by narrowly tailoring the holding so that it applied only to hiring of drivers with records of drunk driving who will be employed to drive in other states. Employers should already anticipate being subject to other states' laws in such cases and could obtain insurance.

While the comparative impairment determination of loss-shifting interests might possibly go either way, West Dakota's law also advances a conduct-regulating purpose of deterring hiring dangerous drivers. This deterrent effect would be substantially eroded if the cause of action were not applied to cases involving out-of-state defendant employers. In fact, refusing to hold the nonresident defendant liable would create an incentive for resident employers to move out of state. In contrast, East Dakota's loss-shifting goals can be accommodated by other means. In conclusion, the West Dakota court applying comparative impairment should apply West Dakota law to the claim by the West Dakota plaintiff based on negligent hiring and supervision. On the one hand, not applying West Dakota law would decisively impair the accident-avoidance and loss-shifting goals of West Dakota's law. On the other hand, not applying East Dakota's law would not decisively frustrate East Dakota's goal of leaving the issue to the state legislature. Limiting recovery to claims against employers who hire drivers with records of drunk driving who will be employed to drive in other states will not completely frustrate the state's interest in avoiding shifting losses to employers.

Tricky Charity

6. This question is only tricky if you missed an obvious point. East Dakota will apply its own defense of charitable immunity to the claim by the East Dakota plaintiff against the East Dakota charity — just like West Dakota. This is a false conflict, and only East Dakota has an interest in applying its law.

   The other claims present true conflicts. For true conflicts, comparative impairment directs a jurisdiction to apply the law of the state whose interest would be more impaired if its law is not applied. All jurisdictions applying the comparative impairment rule for true conflicts should come up with the same answer. Unlike pure interest analysis, comparative impairment promotes uniformity of results for true conflicts. This means East Dakota's resolution of the choice of law analysis for true conflicts should be exactly the same as West Dakota's if they both follow comparative impairment.

And Now for an Easy Statute of Frauds Case. Not.

7. This is a true conflict. The statutes of frauds in this case are procedural or evidentiary in purpose. Romulus has an interest in applying its statute of frauds to prevent a possible dishonest claim. Camazotz has an interest under its law of contracts in enforcing an otherwise valid obligation between the parties because the contract is not within its statute of frauds.

   As a true conflict, comparative impairment requires application of the law of the state whose interest would be most impaired by not applying its law. In this case Camazotz's normal principles of contract law would be seriously impaired if its law is not applied because the private agreement between the parties and their justified expectations would be disregarded. In contrast, applying Camazotz's law would not so seriously interfere with Romulus's interests. First, Camazotz concurs with Romulus in enforcing oral contracts for obligations performable within 12 months. Camazotz also shares Romulus's goal of requiring contracts to be in writing when they cannot be performed within a limited period of time. Camazotz differs only in allowing oral contracts to be enforced when performance can be achieved in 15 months. In other words, Camazotz's law will not completely frustrate Romulus's goals but will allow enforcement of a limited class of contracts (those performable between 12 and 15 months).

Moreover, to the extent the purpose of both jurisdictions' statutes of fraud is evidentiary, the goals of avoiding fraud based on claims of oral promises may be achievable by other methods (such as the evidence of parties). Accordingly, Romulus should apply Camazotz's statute of frauds.

Telephone Tort

8. I have borrowed the facts without knowledge or consent from Kearney v. Salomon Smith Barney, Inc., 137 P.3d 914 (Cal. 2006). This one is harder than it sounds. The real challenge is in identifying the policy (if any) served by Georgia's policy of nonliability for persons who secretly record others.

First, you need to determine if there is a true conflict. California's prohibition of such recordings is designed to protect the privacy of people who speak in California. This interest would be served by applying the prohibition to confidential communications that take place in part in California and in part in another state. The hard part is figuring out what Georgia's interest is in its policy of nonliability — and whether that interest is served by applying its law in this case. For example, if Georgia's policy is to permit investigative journalists to tape their sources, then the policy would not be served by applying Georgia law in a case involving retail banking transactions.

The California court concluded that Georgia had an interest in applying its law permitting recordings. It reasoned that the Georgia law of nonliability expressed a Georgia interest in providing "general ground rules" to regulate such recordings. This is a little unclear. Maybe what the court meant was that Georgia's nonliability expressed an affirmative policy of nonregulation of recording behavior that served to remove administrative inconveniences. In any event, this is not the only solution. If Georgia's law does not advance some governmental interest in the case at hand, then the case should properly be classified as a false conflict. (I suspect that the California court's reluctance to do so was clouded by its conviction that Georgia businesses had relied on Georgia law.)

Having concluded that the different laws expressed a true conflict, the California court then applied comparative impairment analysis. On a final exam, I would award full credit for accurately defining the comparative impairment test and making a reasonable effort to apply it to the state interests you have identified.

The California court observed that many businesses engage in telephone conversations with California residents. From this it was an easy call that permitting secret recordings pursuant to Georgia law would substantially undermine the privacy protections afforded by California law.

In contrast, the court concluded that applying California law would not seriously impair the interests of Georgia or other states in permitting recording. First, the decision did not impair Georgia's interest in protecting privacy because California provided greater protections to privacy interests. Second, the decision did not seriously impair Georgia's interest in permitting businesses to record calls because the decision would affect only those calls to and from California. Moreover, a Georgia business with a need to record a call could satisfy California law and lawfully record a conversation simply by notifying a party the call was being recorded.

Perhaps the court was not entirely persuaded by its own reasoning. Although it decided that comparative impairment required application of California law, it refused to apply its holding to claims for monetary relief for past violations. The court expressed concern that Georgia businesses had relied reasonably on their expectation that Georgia law would apply to their recording activity in Georgia. In contrast, it observed that the compensatory value of money damages for invasions of privacy was uncertain and that awarding money damages could not deter past behavior.

20

The Better Law
Approach

INTRODUCTION

In the 1960s Conflicts professors were spinning new choice of law theories faster than Diana Ross and the Supremes were spinning number-one hits. The Legal Academy should have awarded a prize for coining the best new name. The winner would have been Professor Robert Leflar, who proposed the "better rule of law" or "better law" approach. Anyone opposed to the better law has some serious explaining to do.

MORE THAN IT SOUNDS LIKE

Leflar's approach was unique among modern choice theories. First, he shunned general theories and did not try to formulate a series of rules. Instead he emphasized a flexible approach that was consistent with actual judicial practice. Second, he paid serious attention to the impact of the content of the laws in conflict on the outcome of judicial choice of law analysis. While other modern theories emphasized the importance of state policies or interests, they did not recognize that courts exhibit a preference for some laws over others. To the extent other scholars noticed such a preference, they tended to regard it as improper in the same way that a preference for certain parties would be improper.

Leflar proposed five considerations that did and should influence courts in making choice of law determinations.[1]

1. Predictability of Results

Leflar believed outcome uniformity was desirable both for avoiding forum shopping and for enforcing the justifiable expectations of parties created in consensual transactions. Predictability is especially important for contracts, property transfers, and other planning situations where parties need to know what law would govern.

2. Maintenance of Interstate and International Order

To promote harmony among different jurisdictions, Leflar argued that a forum should not apply its law to a dispute when its concern was "negligible" and another jurisdiction had a "clearly superior concern." While avoiding the terminology of interest analysis and comparative impairment, his second consideration embraces their spirit of avoiding the mechanical application of some law to a case where application of the law does not advance a real state interest.

3. Simplification of the Judicial Task

Leflar believed courts prefer simple, easy-to-apply rules. He endorsed simple "mechanical" choice rules when such rules do not frustrate other goals (like the goals of implementing state policies, achieving predictability, or selecting the better law). As an example, he observed that a forum's adoption of forum procedural law was grounded on simplicity or ease of use.

4. Advancement of the Forum State's Governmental Interests

Forums should promote local forum interests in resolving conflicts cases. But before applying forum law in a conflicts case, the forum should make sure the forum has a genuine interest in applying its law. Unlike interest analysis, Leflar insisted that a forum's interests are not necessarily expressed by the local law of the forum. In some cases, local interests might be advanced by applying some other law. This is especially possible when the local rule is "old or out of tune with the times."

5. Application of the Better Rule of Law

Leflar's most controversial consideration is his claim that courts in conflicts cases are influenced by their preference for laws they consider better.

---

1. Robert A. Leflar, *Choice Influencing Considerations in Conflicts Law*, 41 N.Y.U. L. Rev. 267 (1966), Robert A. Leflar, *Conflicts Law: More on Choice-Influencing Considerations*, 54 Cal. L. Rev. 1584 (1966).

Jurisdictions

Three states apply some version of the "better law" approach.

Better — Says Who?

It did not trouble Leflar that a judge might prefer his or her forum's law. For him such preference explained many decisions. It also justified more directly the application of forum law that modern theories supported indirectly based on state interests.

Leflar also thought judges can appreciate that their forum law is not always better. He identified a few criteria for deciding what law is better. He remarked that reasonable courts will "prefer rules of law which make good socioeconomic sense for the time when the court speaks." Courts, he believed, will sometimes apply non-forum law to achieve individual justice in a case. For example, courts may prefer law that validates a contract in order to protect the expectations of parties despite a local law that frustrates such expectations.

Leflar argued that preference for the better law should be objective, not subjective. By this he meant preference can be explained by rational criteria such as socioeconomic benefits or avoidance of unfair surprise. The clearest examples of laws that are not better are rules that are anachronistic or disfavored.

THE WORST RULE?

The better law has its share of critics. Many law professors hate it. The problems begin with exactly what Leflar means by preference for the better law. He might mean two things: (1) courts *do* in fact prefer some laws, or (2) courts *should* prefer some laws. Many of us may agree that courts prefer certain laws. Guest statutes were highly disfavored by the 1950s. Surely it is no "adventitious circumstance" (Babcock v. Jackson) that courts adopted new conflicts rules to avoid applying guest statutes. But just because courts *do* something does not make it right or good. Philosophers refer to this as the "is-ought" dichotomy.

Leflar sparks controversy when he is interpreted as encouraging courts to follow their hearts and apply the better law as part of good choice of law analysis. There are two aspects to applying the better law that make modernist theorists crazy. First is the problem of determining what law is "better." Critics dismiss Leflar's hopes for objective criteria as a naïve version of bad old super law. Maybe some laws "are neither better nor worse in an objective way, just different." Jepson v. General Cas. Co. of Wisconsin, 513 N.W.2d 467, 473 (Minn. 1994).

Second, critics question the appropriateness of applying a law even if it is objectively better. There are two possibilities if a court applies a law because it is better. On the one hand, a court may find that forum law is better. (If a judge does not find that his or her law is better in most cases, he or she should probably retire and run for the legislature.) But the problem with applying better forum law is that choice of law rules are designed to prevent wholesale application of forum law, so a consideration that favors forum law because it is "better" is not necessarily desirable.

On the other hand, in weird cases, courts may find that some other jurisdiction's law is objectively better. The problem with applying better foreign law is that if a court can say that the other jurisdiction's law is objectively better, then the court should adopt that as the law for all cases, not just conflicts cases. In other words, the court should change bad local law so there is no conflict. The only reason for not changing worse local law must be that the forum court's authority not to apply the local law is limited under its state constitution. But if the state legislature has adopted bad law and its law advances a state policy, then (as critics point out) state courts should apply the bad law in conflicts cases just as they are required to do in local disputes.

More Problems: Which Considerations Count Most?

Leflar knew his five considerations could yield inconsistent outcomes in the same case. Yet he neither assigned relative value to the five considerations nor provided helpful guidance as to how to reconcile conflicts among them.

There are a variety of possibilities. Some authorities emphasize better law should guide a court only in a true conflict.[2] Their version of the better law approach is thus a form of modified interest analysis. Other courts have applied the better law despite lack of a demonstrable state interest.

Moderate Better Law

In Clark v. Clark, 222 A.2d 205 (N.H. 1966), a New Hampshire driver injured a New Hampshire passenger in Vermont where there was a guest

---

2. Fuerste v. Bemis, 156 N.W.2d 831 (Iowa 1968); Weintraub, Commentary on the Conflict of Laws §6.29 at 469. Everyone seems to have forgotten that Leflar himself originally limited his proposal to true conflicts. Leflar, *Choice-Influencing Considerations in Conflicts Law*, 41 N.Y.U. L. Rev. at 282 n.55.

statute. The court applied the better law approach. It found that the first consideration (predictability) did not apply to torts. It found that the second consideration (maintenance of interstate and international order) did not apply, because that consideration was designed to prevent the application of the law of a jurisdiction that had no interest in applying its law. The forum obviously had an interest in applying its loss-shifting rule to residents of the forum state. It found that the third factor (simplification of the judicial task) would never prevent a forum from applying forum law.

The court relied on considerations four (advancement of forum's governmental interest) and five (better rule of law). It concluded that the forum had a governmental interest in permitting a forum resident to recover under forum common law. And it concluded that the forum law was better than the foreign guest statute. It reached this conclusion by determining that guest statutes were anachronistic, no longer served their original purposes, and had been narrowly construed by courts.

The decision provides an example of a moderate better law approach because the better law consideration was not the only factor that supported application of forum law. On the contrary, the forum had a strong interest in application of its law, and the foreign state had little or no interest in the application of its guest statute to a case involving parties and an insurance company who were not nonresidents of the foreign state. Although incompatible with the traditional territorial rule, the *Clark* decision reached the same outcome as all other modern approaches.

Extreme Better Law

In Milkovich v. Saari, 203 N.W.2d 408 (Minn. 1973), an Ontario driver injured an Ontario passenger in Minnesota. The Minnesota court rejected Ontario's guest statute, relying heavily on the better law.[3]

Milkovich exemplifies an extreme version of the better law approach because it reaches a result that differs from that of other modern approaches. The decision drives interest analysis scholars crazy. They see it as the classic false conflict—one in which the forum has no interest in applying its loss-distribution rule, but the home state of the parties has an interest in applying its law to prevent recovery. Critics see the decision as displaying parochial preference for local law.

The *Milkovich* court concluded that none of the first three considerations applied to a tort for the same reasons given by the New Hampshire court in Clark v. Clark. Applying the fourth consideration, the court found that Minnesota had neither a conduct-regulating nor a loss-distributing interest

---

3. Minnesota has since switched from the better law to the most significant contacts approach.

in applying its law to permit a recovery. But the court concluded that the forum nevertheless had an interest "as a justice-administering state" in applying forum law to the dispute between residents of another state. The court then applied the fifth consideration and concluded that common law liability was clearly superior to the guest statute. Consequently, the court applied forum law.

Milkovich's treatment of the fourth consideration is what makes the decision extreme. All forums (we hope!) have an interest in achieving justice. Read broadly, Milkovich guarantees a forum will always have an interest in applying forum law and should apply its own law whenever it is better.

The decision can also be read more narrowly and offers additional grounds for finding a forum interest in the outcome. First, the court suggested that there might be a slightly greater deterrent effect in applying the forum's pro-recovery rule. Second, the court observed that the forum has an interest in compensating tort victims injured in the forum because such parties often incur debts to forum residents as a result of their injuries. (In fact, the plaintiff in Milkovich was hospitalized in Minnesota for over one month.) The forum has an interest in applying its law so that injured debtors are able to reimburse local resident creditors. Third, the court's discussion of justice may be limited to the context of guest statutes. Such statutes may be motivated in part by the goal of protecting a foreign court system from collusive claims that do not concern the forum court. Moreover, such statutes may be bad law because they do not advance the purposes ascribed to the defense. If no Ontario state interest is advanced by Ontario's law, there may be no good reason to apply it.

Examples

Best of All Possible Worlds

1. Pangloss, a citizen of the country of Besserland, stopped his car to avoid hitting a dog while driving in Besserland. Pangloss did not look in his rear view mirror before stopping, and his brake lights were not working. Candide, a citizen of the country of Leibnitzia, was driving behind Pangloss. Candide collided with Pangloss's car, causing injuries to Pangloss. Pangloss was partly at fault, and Candide was partly at fault.

   Pangloss brings a civil action in Besserland court against Candide. Leibnitzia retains the doctrine of contributory negligence. The Besserland high court recently adopted comparative negligence in a lawsuit between two residents of Besserland, opining that "comparative negligence achieves greater distributive justice by allocating losses in proportion to fault without significantly eroding parties' incentives to take care to avoid injury to themselves."

The Besserland courts follow Leflar's better law approach. Candide moves to dismiss under the Leibnitzian law of contributory negligence. Explain whether Besserland will apply comparative or contributory negligence.

2. Same facts. The Leibnitzia courts have repeatedly refused to adopt comparative negligence, opining that "judicial adoption of such a radical change in the law would exceed the constitutional authority of Leibnitzia courts." Leibnitzia courts follow the better law. Explain whether they will apply comparative or contributory negligence.

Better Dramshop Rules

3. State X has a dramshop law that imposes civil liability on persons who sell liquor to obviously drunk buyers when the sale proximately causes damages to a third person. State Y has no such law.

   Seller in state X sells liquor to Drunk, who drinks the liquor, drives into state Y, and seriously injures Vick. Vick, resident of state Y, brings a civil action in state X court against Seller, a resident of state X. Seller moves to dismiss under state Y law. State X courts follow the better law approach. What happens?

4. Same facts but the case is litigated in state Y, which has steadfastly refused to impose liability on dramshops in actions brought by third persons. State Y courts follow the better law approach. What law applies?

Dishonorable Checks

5. Cheater, a citizen of the state of West Texas, traveled to Lalaland. There he visited the Hotclub Casino, a Lalaland corporation. An employee of the casino engaged in sexual conduct with Cheater for money, and Cheater paid the casino with a check drawn on his bank account in West Texas.

   When Cheater returned to West Texas, he stopped payment on the check. Prostitution is illegal in West Texas, and contracts for payment of prostitutes are void. The supreme court of West Texas has specifically held that a check for prostitution services is invalid and may be dishonored with impunity. Under the law of Lalaland, prostitution is not illegal, and the check is valid.

   West Texas follows the better law. Is the check valid?

She Said He Said She Said by the Seashore

6. Maybelle heard Freddie say "She said, 'By the Seashore.'" The statement was made and heard in Marovia, a civil law jurisdiction, which does not have the hearsay rule of evidence.

In civil litigation in Gondor between Andrew and Beth, citizens of Gondor, Andrew calls Maybelle as a witness and asks what Freddie said. She said, "He said, 'she said, "By the seashore." ' " Gondor is a common law jurisdiction. Beth moves to strike Maybelle's answer under Gondor's hearsay rule.

Andrew argues the statement is admissible under Marovia's law of evidence. Gondor follows the better law approach. Rule on the motion to strike and explain.

More Fun with Statutes of Frauds

7. Walker, resident of the state of East Louisiana, agreed orally with Doglover, resident of the state of West Wyoming, to walk Doglover's dog every day for two years for the price of $2.00 per day. The conversation took place in East Louisiana. After meeting Fido, Walker refused to perform.

   Doglover sued Walker in West Wyoming. West Wyoming's statute of frauds provides "no action shall be brought on any contract not to be performed within one year unless it be in writing, signed." East Louisiana has no applicable statute of frauds.

   Walker moved to dismiss under West Wyoming's statute of frauds. West Wyoming follows the better law approach. Rule on the motion and explain.

Kissin' Cousins

8. Elvis and Dolores were cousins, both domiciled in the state of Disapproval. Under the law of Disapproval, cousins as closely related as Elvis and Dolores are prohibited from marrying. Disapproval statutes provide that an attempt to celebrate such a marriage in Disapproval is a misdemeanor, and that any such marriage is void.

   Elvis and Dolores traveled to the state of Approval, whose law permitted such marriages, and were married after complying with all local requirements for a valid marriage. After returning to Disapproval, Dolores woke up, smelled the roses, and commenced a suit to annul the marriage on the ground that it is void. Elvis responded, "Don't be cruel."

   Disapproval follows the better law approach. Is the marriage void?

Surprising Damages

9. Goodman, a citizen of Besserland, took a vacation in Patagonia. He bought a bus ticket for a trip between two Patagonian cities from Patagonia Bus Lines, a Patagonian corporation. Goodman was seriously injured when the bus driver negligently drove off a cliff.

   Goodman sues the bus company in Besserland court. Besserland, a common law jurisdiction, permits recovery of actual compensatory damages in torts. Patagonian law limits recovery to 100,000 cruzeritos, the equivalent of 97 dollars.

Besserland follows the better law approach. Will it limit Goodman's damages under Patagonian law?

Racial Injustice

10. Plaintiff, a citizen of the country of Krankreich, was employed as a pilot by Devian Airways, a firm incorporated under the laws of Krankreich. Plaintiff flew airplanes from Krankreich to a number of locations, including, on two occasions, the state of Equality.

    During a period of political turbulence, Krankreich adopted a Racial Freedom Fairness Act that imposed racial quotas on all employment contracts. The purpose of the act was to reduce the employment of certain disfavored minority races and ethnic groups. The Act specifically provided, "Any private employer who discharges an employee due to the employee's race or ethnicity shall have an absolute immunity to claims for breaches of contract."

    Devian Airways fired Plaintiff because of his race in violation of the terms of the employment contract. Plaintiff commenced a civil action for breach of contract in the state of Equality. Under Equality law, the contract would be enforceable, and the race-based defense offends basic civil rights guaranteed in the federal and state constitutions.

    The parties file cross-motions for summary judgment, raising the issue of the applicability of the defense provided by Krankreich's law. Equality follows the better law approach. Rule on the motions and explain.

Explanations

Best of All Possible Worlds

1. You can easily guess the outcome: the forum will apply its comparative negligence standard as the better law. But to get full points you should first consider the possible application of all five choice-influencing considerations. Then you should argue how comparative negligence is objectively better.

    (1) Predictability has no relevance for unplanned events like torts. (2) Maintenance of the interstate and international order also provides no guidance. That consideration prevents application of a state's rule when the state has a negligible concern in the application of its rule. In this case both states have an interest in applying their loss-shifting rules. (3) Simplification of the judicial task also provides little guidance. This consideration never prevents a forum from applying forum law.

(4) Advancement of the forum's governmental interests clearly favors application of forum law. The forum has a governmental interest in applying a forum loss-shifting rule that permits partial recovery by a forum citizen. (5) Application of the better rule of law also clearly favors forum comparative negligence over Leibnitzia's contributory negligence.

Arguments that comparative negligence is objectively better include the fact that most states have adopted the rule, and contributory negligence has become anachronistic or disfavored. Comparative negligence achieves superior distributive justice (according to Besserland decisions). And contributory negligence does not achieve a significantly greater deterrence of injuries.

2. This one could go either way. Again you get full points for making a creditable effort to apply the five considerations and for attempting to make a persuasive "objective" argument for the better law.

    The first three considerations provide little guidance. (See last answer.) The fourth (advancement of the forum's governmental interest) seems to favor applying the forum loss-shifting defense in a case involving a forum defendant. While this would get full marks from me, you could also point out that Leflar emphasized that a forum's governmental interests need not coincide in conflicts cases with the policies advanced by local laws. This leaves room for accommodating other states' interests. And it leaves room for applying the better law. The fifth consideration (better law) could also possibly go either way. Leflar encourages states to apply newer rules that promote state policies over anachronistic, disfavored rules. You could argue that comparative negligence is better on objective grounds. (See last answer.) If Leibnitzia courts find that comparative negligence is a better law, they should apply it in a conflicts case even though they have not adopted it as the law in local litigation. But if Leibnitzia courts retain a conservative vision that contributory negligence is better, not just because it is older, but because it deters more injuries, then they should apply contributory negligence as the better law.

Better Dramshop Rules

3. This hypothetical comes from the Man himself—Professor Leflar. Leflar observes that none of the first three considerations guide the court. He argues that consideration four (advancement of forum's governmental interest) favors applying the dramshop rule. He reasons that the forum's goal is to reduce the risk of drunk driving accidents, and this conduct-regulating goal applies to all potential plaintiffs, not just residents of the forum state. He argues that consideration five (better law) will also favor forum law, unless for some reason the forum courts have had negative experiences with dramshop liability or the law is becoming antiquated

or disfavored by state X courts. He concludes that state X courts will apply the forum dramshop rule.

4. Leflar invented the better law approach. He made up the hypothetical, and he concluded that Y would probably apply state X's dramshop law. His argument duplicated the argument for applying the dramshop law in state X. The first three considerations do not guide the court. He argued that consideration four (advancement of forum's governmental interest) does not favor applying Y's law because Y has no interest in applying its law so as to deny recovery. Under consideration five (better law), Leflar believed Y courts would probably prefer the dramshop law unless there was some reason to think such a law was becoming outmoded or disfavored.

Leflar assumed courts would prefer the dramshop law. His assumption reflected the legal ethos of the mid-1960s, when courts were optimistic about regulating conduct through civil liability and were eager to expand enterprise liability. A generation later, however, legislatures and courts have severely restricted third-party civil liability. For example, the California legislature repealed the tavern keeper liability imposed by Bernhard v. Harrah's Club (see Chapter 19). Few experienced plaintiffs' lawyers today would assume a court would prefer a foreign dramshop law even in a case against a foreign dramshop.

Dishonorable Checks

5. The check will probably not be enforceable if presented by the casino (against whom there are underlying defenses to the contract). There is a far stronger argument in favor of the validity of the check if it has been negotiated to third persons. Predictability favors enforcement of contracts that parties expected in good faith to be valid. Predictability and maintenance of the international order are of paramount importance with respect to negotiable instruments and strongly favor enforcement of the check if it has been negotiated to third persons. But as between the original parties to the transaction, maintenance of the international order does not require deference to Lalaland law. On the contrary, growing international concerns with sex tourism may favor disregarding Lalaland law.

Simplification favors neither law. The forum's governmental policies against prostitution are strong and are probably grounded in moral, economic, and public health objectives. These objectives would be advanced by applying its law to discourage its residents from patronizing prostitutes in other jurisdictions.

Finally, the forum would probably prefer its own law as the better law. However, the forum might also recognize the peculiar injustice of allowing its resident both to engage in antisocial conduct and to benefit financially from application of the forum law to avoid payment. Considerations of individual justice might favor applying foreign law as the better law under the facts.

She Said He Said She Said by the Seashore

6. Strike the hearsay under forum law pursuant to consideration three (simplicity and ease of application). Factors one and two do not seem to have any application. Under consideration four, applying forum law would advance the governmental interest behind the hearsay rule of excluding unreliable testimony and providing an incentive for calling witnesses alleged to be the source of out-of-court statements. Under consideration five (better law), a common law court would probably prefer the hearsay rule as objectively better, but the outcome is not certain.

    Probably more important, the forum has a strong interest in the routine operation of trial procedures according to its own procedural rules and rules of evidence. Leflar suggested that such forum rules would normally apply. In fact, he may have invented consideration three in order to explain why such rules normally apply! These rules should be distinguished from evidence rules such as privilege that promote important policies other than factfinding and are designed to affect behavior outside the courtroom.

More Fun with Statutes of Frauds

7. This hypothetical is also taken from Leflar. The first thing to note is that the statute of frauds, regardless of its wording, affects the validity and enforceability of the contract. So forum law does not necessarily apply as "procedure," as it did in the last example.

    Since validity of the contract is at issue, Leflar gives great weight to consideration one (predictability). Predictability or certainty favors applying East Louisiana's law — either because that was where the contract was made, because parties expected East Louisiana law to apply, or because East Louisiana law has the effect of validating the contract. Considerations two (maintenance of the interstate and international order) and three (simplicity) have little relevance. Under consideration four (advancement of forum governmental interests), Leflar acknowledged that West Wyoming has some interest in applying its statute of frauds in order to prevent fraudulent claims. But he observed that West Wyoming's interest might not be very strong because statutes of frauds are somewhat disfavored, construed narrowly, and subject to many exceptions. He predicted that an "enlightened" court in West Wyoming would enforce the contract under East Louisiana's better law. He predicted with still greater confidence that East Louisiana's courts would refuse to apply the foreign statute of frauds.

Kissin' Cousins

8. This is modified from Leflar's hypothetical about a state law declaring the marriage of a 14-year-old "void." Don't know the answer? Neither did Leflar. Once again, setting up the analysis and considering all relevant factors is as good as it gets.

   The main point of this hypothetical is that predictability (consideration one) is of overriding importance with respect to the validity of marriages. Spouses, third parties, and state governments all need to know whether a marriage is valid. The traditional rule that the validity of a marriage is governed by the place of celebration provides certainty. The needs of the interstate and international system are also important, and those needs also strongly favor predictability and uniformity so that the same marriage is not valid in one state and criminal misconduct in another.

   Simplicity (consideration three) probably does not help. It is equally simple for the forum to apply the law of the place of celebration or its own prohibition.

   The interests in predictability run counter to consideration four (advancement of forum state interests). So the outcome depends on the strength of the forum's policy interests against incestuous marriage or, more narrowly, against cousins marrying.

   Note that the traditional rule already included a sort of better law exception. The general rule recognized the validity of marriages that were lawful under the law of the place of celebration. The First Restatement provided that marriages prohibited by the domicile of a party were invalid everywhere when they were both incestuous and between persons so closely related that the marriage was contrary to a *strong* public policy of the domicile. First Restatement §132.

   Leflar did not hazard a guess about whether a state's interest against 14-year-olds marrying would overcome the contrary interest in predictability. I would predict that courts in states with statutory rape laws that protect 14-year-old victims and that do not include a marriage exception would find the marriage void. In less offensive relationships, courts would probably be more inclined to give greater weight to predictability and recognize the marriage despite the forum's policy against courtin' kissin' cousins. *See generally* Jane Austin, Mansfield Park (holding cousins could marry and live happily ever after but without kissing).

Surprising Damages

9. Another hypo from Leflar — but one where the Master's solution is less helpful. While predictability has little relevance to the accident, it probably favors application of local limits, where the local company plans its business and gets insurance (or not) based on local law. Maintenance

of the international order may also favor application of Patagonia's limits. This would be especially true if the limits resulted from a deliberate Patagonia policy of encouraging new business by reducing costs. (This is what Leflar thought.) Patagonia's limits might be entitled to less international respect if they originally provided for a meaningful recovery but have plummeted over time due to inflation.

Simplification of the judicial task does not strongly favor either law. Normally a forum applies its own procedure, but there would be no difficulty in applying Patagonia's cap on damages.

The outcome of the choice of law determination depends on the strength of the forum's interest in applying its law. Besserland's governmental interest in providing full, adequate compensation for its injured citizens is obviously advanced by applying its own loss-shifting rule. Yet Leflar concluded that the forum's concern was minor under these facts. He, accordingly, concluded that the forum preference for its own better law would be "near to zero" in importance compared to other considerations and it should apply the cap on damages. I am not sure why he thought this, and a good answer using his theory could reach the opposite conclusion by finding that the forum state had a powerful interest in applying its loss-shifting rule and that it would also prefer to apply its own better law.

Racial Injustice

10. Apply Equality law as the better law. But don't forget the other considerations. Predictability favors validity of contracts. Maintaining the international order would normally require a consideration of the adverse impact of applying Equality law on the governmental interests of Krankreich. But Krankreich's governmental interest in racial discrimination is entitled to no respect. On the contrary, the shared values of countries other than Krankreich would be furthered by refusing to give extraterritorial application to Krankreich's policies. Simplicity probably does not favor application of either law.

Applying Equality law advances important governmental objectives. First, Equality has an interest in applying its contract law to employee contracts performed in part in Equality. Second, Equality may also have an interest as a "justice-administering state" in avoiding participating in racial discrimination and in refraining from applying law to claims in its courts that violate public policy and deeply offend the public values of Equality. (This second governmental interest is more controversial and is employed by the extreme version of the better law. It would encourage application of Equality law even to contracts with no relationship to the state.) Finally, Equality law is clearly better.

Second Restatement Approach to Torts

INTRODUCTION

The official version of the Second Restatement of Conflicts was adopted in 1969. The Second Restatement was influenced by modern decisions and theories. Its adoption in turn spurred more courts to abandon traditional thinking on conflicts.

For torts the Second Restatement selects the law of the state with the most significant relationship to the occurrence and parties. It requires an evaluation of various contacts and interests. In addition it provides a series of specific rules that apply to different kinds of torts.

HISTORY OF HODGEPODGE

The basic assumptions of the glorious First Restatement of Conflicts were already dated when it was published in 1934. By the 1950s the territorial rules it codified no longer accurately described the way courts actually decided many cases.

Drafting of the Second Restatement began just at the time when courts were boldly going where no court had gone before and when Conflicts professors were inventing new theories—including interest analysis, comparative impairment, and the better law approach.

The Second Restatement's drafters tried to accomplish three things. First, they wanted the new Restatement to describe the rules employed by courts. Second, they wanted to provide rules to guide courts in resolving conflicts cases. Third, they wanted to incorporate the best new theoretical understanding.

The Second Restatement has been popular with the courts. But most Conflicts professors hate it, and most Conflicts casebooks devote surprisingly little coverage to it.

Some problems with the Second Restatement's goals are clear in hindsight. The cutting-edge judicial decisions were uniform in their distaste for the First Restatement, but they did not share a common vision and reached results incompatible with each other. The new theories, too, were diverging rather than converging. Finally, the Second Restatement's twin goals of guidance and flexibility were in tension with each other.

Jurisdictions

Twenty-two states have adopted the Second Restatement's approach to torts. The federal government follows it (or something similar to it) in areas of special federal jurisdiction like admiralty.

Nevertheless, the apparent dominance of the Second Restatement can be misleading. Its widespread adoption is due in part to the fact that the Second Restatement can be read to support different approaches. Different jurisdictions can and do apply the Second Restatement to reach different results in similar cases.

THE BIG PICTURE

The drafters of the Second Restatement formulated a more flexible choice of law rule for torts than the law of the place of the wrong. Its general rule (section 145) requires application of the law of the state with the most significant relationship with the occurrence and parties.

The early draft formulated a rule that required a consideration of multiple territorial "contacts." The first contact in order of importance was the place where the injury occurred.[1]

Professor Brainerd ("Interest Analysis") Currie and others protested against the territorial bias of the early draft and the omission of consideration of governmental interests or policies. In response, the drafters eliminated

---

1. *See* Second Restatement §379 cmt. b (tentative draft 8 1963).

the priority of territorial contacts and added a new provision — section 6 (general principles applicable to all conflicts), which authorizes consideration of interests and policies.

The general rule (section 145) was reformulated. It has four "contacts" and cross-refers to section 6, which has seven "factors." The rule provides no priority among the factors or contacts when they point toward different states.

How the Restatement Evolved — and Why It Matters

The early version of the Second Restatement contained more mechanical rules that resulted in more predictable outcomes. For example, it stated that when conduct and injury occur in the same state, that state's law would "almost invariably" apply. It provided an illustration where parties domiciled in one state were involved in an accident in another state. In an action for damages, it concluded (in the absence of other facts) that the law of the place of the accident and injury would apply.

The final version of the Second Restatement modified the rule and cut the illustration. Instead it requires all choice of law to consider governmental interests and policies. This change means courts must look closely at the legal issue in conflict. They should not just count territorial contacts; they must determine which contacts are relevant to the choice of law issue before them.

Differing Answers to the Same Question

Changes to the Second Restatement affected the analysis and outcome in many situations. For example, suppose Plaintiff and Defendant are domiciled in one state and have a car accident in another state. Defendant raises a defense of contributory negligence that is available under the law where the accident occurred but not under the law where the parties are domiciled. The early draft of the Second Restatement would apply the defense because it was the law of the place of the conduct and injury.

The final version of the Second Restatement requires consideration of policies of the laws in issue. If contributory negligence does not really provide a greater deterrent effect than comparative negligence, then the effect of the law is loss-shifting. For a loss-shifting rule, the only contacts relevant in determining what law to apply would be the parties' domicile. The state of common domicile has a powerful interest in applying its comparative negligence to permit partial recovery while the law of the place of injury has little to no interest in applying its law. Thus, under the final version of the Second Restatement, the law of the parties' domicile would apply.

GENERAL "PRINCIPLES": INTERESTS AND CONSIDERATIONS THAT ALWAYS APPLY

The general section on "choice-of-law principles" (section 6) recognizes the power of the legislature to enact valid choice of law rules:

> 1. A court, subject to constitutional restrictions, will follow a statutory directive of its own state on choice of law.

Most cases are not governed by statutory choice rules. For such cases, the Second Restatement lists factors to be considered by the courts in making their own choice of law.

> 2. [F]actors relevant to the choice of the applicable rule of law include:
>   a. the needs of the interstate and international systems,
>   b. the relevant policies of the forum,
>   c. the relevant policies of other interested states and the respective interest of those states in the determination of the particular issue,
>   d. the protection of justified expectations,
>   e. the basic policies underlying the particular field of law,
>   f. certainty, predictability and uniformity of result, and
>   g. ease in the determination and application of the law to be applied.

Section 6 applies to all areas of conflicts, not just torts. The section does not explain how the listed relevant "factors" are to be applied.

Comments explain the purpose of the factors. Factor (a) (needs of the interstate and international systems) expresses the goal of avoiding conflicts rules that impede commerce between different jurisdictions. It rarely applies in torts cases. Factor (d) (justified expectations) and factor (f) (certainty, predictability, and uniformity) apply to planned transactions or situations where parties rely on law in advance. Those factors have no relevance for negligent torts.

The General Rule for Torts

The broad, general "factors" of section 6 apply to all choice of law situations. Torts are governed in addition by the rule in section 145:

> 1. The rights and liabilities of the parties with respect to an issue in tort are determined by the local law of that state which, with respect to that issue, has the most significant relationship to the occurrence and the parties under the principles stated in §6.

2. Contacts to be taken into account in applying the principles of §6 to determine the law applicable to an issue include:
   a. the place where the injury occurred,
   b. the place where the conduct causing the injury occurred,
   c. the domicil, residence, nationality, place of incorporation and place of business of the parties, and
   d. the place where the relationship, if any, between the parties is centered.

Note that section 145 provides a general rule (of sorts) in contrast to section 6's principles and factors.

Section 145 offers important clarifications. First, it makes clear that only one jurisdiction's law should properly apply to a given issue because only one state will have "the most significant relationship" to the occurrence and parties with respect to that issue. Second, it requires an issue-by-issue analysis—what older cases called dépeçage. This means the Second Restatement may select different states' laws to apply to different issues in the same case. Third, section 145 selects the *local* law of the state with the most significant relationship. The Second Restatement should avoid renvoi problems that arise when choice rules select another state's "whole law."[2]

Section 145 lists factual contacts that bear on the determination of which state has the most significant relationship. These are not exclusive, and the Second Restatement offers no clue about the priority or weight of different contacts other than stating they "are to be evaluated according to their relative importance with respect to the particular issue."

Specific Rules

In addition to the general rule, the Second Restatement offers specific rules that follow a common pattern. For personal injuries, wrongful death, and injuries to land and tangible personal property, it applies the local law of the place of injury—unless with respect to a particular issue some other state has a more significant relationship to the occurrence and parties.[3]

More than 30 specific rules apply either to particular types of torts (like malicious prosecution) or issues (like contributory negligence). The rules for specific torts select the law of some jurisdiction unless another jurisdiction has a more significant relationship under section 6's principles. The rules for specific issues typically state that the issue is governed by the law

---

2. Examples in the commentary, however, repeatedly scrutinize the whole law of other states for evidence of the governmental interest of those states. This is discussed in Chapter 23.
3. Second Restatement §§146, 147 & 175. For wrongful death, the place of injury is the place of the initial injury that causes death, not the place of death.

selected by the general rule (section 145) but add that the issue is "usually" governed by the law of some specific jurisdiction. Professor Symeonides calls the specific rules with "unless" language presumptions and rules with "usually" language pointers. The difference is unclear.

Courts take three approaches to the specific rules. First, some courts mention specific rules but then give those rules no additional weight in deciding what state has the most significant relationship under the general rules and principles in sections 6 and 145. Second, some courts do not even mention specific rules; they go straight to the general rules. Third, a few courts apply specific rules mechanically without considering whether another jurisdiction has a more significant relationship to the occurrence and parties.

There may be good reason to disregard the specific rules. Such rules tend to restate the territorial preference that was deliberately eliminated from the final version of the general rule of the Second Restatement. For example, section 164 (on contributory negligence) says both that section 145 applies and that the applicable defense will "usually" be where the injury occurred. The problem is that sections 6 and 145 do not select the place of injury when its law does not further that state's own interest. It is not clear that the place of injury has an interest in applying its contributory negligence rules to a dispute between nonresidents.

The Lesson   Never stop with a specific rule on point. Consider also the application of the general principles and general rule (sections 6 and 145). If these general rules indicate that some other state has the most significant relationship to the occurrence and parties on the issue, then apply the law of the state with the most significant relationship.

Whatever You Want It to Be?

The interplay between section 6 (policies and interests) and section 145 (contacts) allows the Second Restatement to be applied in different ways. Some courts emphasize factual contacts and the specific rules. This converts the Second Restatement into a form of modified territorialism that departs from the traditional lex loci rules only when other factual contacts establish a stronger connection with another jurisdiction. Other courts (those approved by most law professors!) emphasize policies and interests. This converts the Second Restatement into modified interest analysis.

False Conflicts

The Second Restatement indicates clearly (but in commentary rather than in the specific rule) that interest analysis should be applied to determine if there is a true or false conflict. If only one state has an interest in the application of its law, then its law should apply. In such a case, the contacts of other states are not relevant contacts. This leads to an unstated rule generally supported by case law: Apply the law of common domicile to a loss-shifting issue.

Revenge of the Ungrateful Dead

Babs and Jacks are domiciled in the state of X. They go for a car ride in an adjacent foreign country, where Babs is killed by Jack's negligent driving. The foreign country has a guest statute that bars a wrongful death claim based on negligence. The purpose of the guest statute is to protect foreign insurance companies and to lower the rates of insurance for drivers who live in the foreign country.

Under these facts borrowed from Babcock v. Jackson, the Second Restatement applies the law of common domicile as the law of the only state with an interest in the application of its law. The parties' domicile is the only factual contact relevant to the determination of which state has the most significant relationship to the occurrence and parties. Note that this result not only disregards most of the contacts listed in Restatement section 145; it also displaces the specific result indicated by section 146.

True Conflicts — Balancing

The Second Restatement does not offer a clear resolution for conflicts in which multiple jurisdictions have an interest advanced by the application of their law. The black letter rules of the Second Restatement indicate that you should apply the law of the state with the most significant relationship. Comments suggest you should consider whether conflicting state policies and interests can be accommodated. This means you should evaluate the importance of state interests and policies and balance or weigh the importance of the different state interests against each other.

SECOND RESTATEMENT IN REAL LIFE

Cases Emphasizing Contacts   The Tennessee case of Hataway v. McKinley, 830 S.W.2d 53 (Tenn. 1992), announced the state's adoption of the Second Restatement. The case arose from the death of a Tennessee college student during a field trip in Arkansas. The parties were all Tennessee residents. Arkansas provided a potentially more generous measure of damages for wrongful death and had also adopted a comparative negligence rule, while Tennessee still retained contributory negligence. The Tennessee court cited provisions in the Second Restatement but then summarily concluded that Tennessee law applied because all the contacts were in Tennessee except for the "fortuitous circumstance" of the place of the injury. It did not consider the policies of the law or state interests.

Courts emphasizing contacts do not necessarily disregard the place of injury. Bates v. Superior Court, 749 P.2d 1367 (Ariz. 1988), considered the problem of what state's law applies to a tort claim of bad faith against an insurance company. The plaintiff was originally insured as a Michigan resident, and the defendant was a national insurance company with its place of incorporation and principal place of business in Ohio.

The insurance company continued to make payments for a number of years, during which time the plaintiff relocated to Arizona. The insurance company eventually denied coverage, and the plaintiff brought a bad faith claim in Arizona court. The insurance company argued that the bad faith claim should be dismissed because the issue should be governed by Michigan law, and Michigan had not recognized such a claim.

The court applied Arizona law, relying heavily on the contacts and especially on section 146 providing that in personal injury actions the law of the place of the injury applies unless some other state has a more significant relationship. The court classified the relationship claim as a personal injury because the plaintiff sought damages for personal injury, mental suffering, and physical harm.

The court counted contacts under section 145, finding they were almost equally divided between Arizona and Ohio — with none in Michigan. It briefly considered section 6, observing that no state interests or legal policies were involved (!) except possibly the goal of protecting justifiable expectations. It then concluded that a national insurance company had no legitimate expectation that the law of a party's original place of residence would govern bad faith claims.

Finally, the court concluded that the contacts were not co-equal in value because of the specific rule in section 146. It applied the specific rule and held that Arizona law governed the issue of bad faith.

Case Emphasizing Interests and Policies From the very same jurisdiction comes a good example of a decision that relies more on section 6 interests than contact counting. In Gordon v. Kramer, 604 P.2d 1153 (Ariz. 1979), two Arizona residents drove to Utah. The passenger was injured in an accident in Utah and sued the driver in Arizona. The driver raised the defense of the Utah guest statute.

The court began by noting that under the specific rule in section 146 the law of the place of the injury governed unless another state had a more significant relationship to the occurrence and parties. It then applied sections 6 and 145. Reviewing the section 6 interests and policies, it eliminated the factors like predictability and ease of application and concluded that the basic policies of tort law were deterrence and compensation. With respect to the specific issue of guest statutes, it found that applying a guest statute advanced neither deterrence nor compensation for loss.

As for the factual contacts, the ones most relevant to the determination of state interests were the residences of the parties. The court found that Utah, the place of the injury and negligence, had no interest in applying its guest statute in the case. In contrast, Arizona had strong interests in applying its loss-shifting rule to residents of Arizona.

IT'S NOT AS BAD AS IT SOUNDS

The Second Restatement's torts provisions can be used to reach different results in the same case by emphasizing different contacts, interests, and policies. But the Second Restatement is probably no more uncertain than other modern approaches.

The key to applying the Second Restatement is to take seriously the interplay between identifying the interests and policies raised by the issues in conflict (section 6) and the evaluation of relevant contacts in searching for the state with the most significant relationship (section 145 and any specific rule sections). The following steps are recommended — though they are not the only possible combination or sequence.

Separately discuss each issue on which the jurisdictions provide conflicting laws.

Identify any applicable specific rule (like the place of injury for personal injury claims).

Consider whether another place has the most significant relationship to the occurrence and parties with respect to the issue.

Identify applicable interests and policies (section 6).

If there is a false conflict, apply the law of the only state with an interest.

If there is a true conflict, evaluate the relative strengths of the states' interests in applying their law.

Discuss contacts that relate to those interests and policies (section 145).

Examples

Crash and Burn

1. Why did the author of the following final exam answer "crash and burn"?

   Most of the parties were domiciled in the state where the negligence and resulting train wreck occurred, so this is an easy case. The Second Restatement applies that place's law to the issue of contributory negligence, the issue of limits on damages for burn victims, and the question of whether use of marijuana while driving a train establishes negligence per se.

Lazy Teacher

2. What's the right answer—and why is this a bad question?

   Sketchie approached Dirty Harry in a threatening way in the state of Injuria. Dirty Harry shot and injured Sketchie without attempting to retreat. Sketchie has sued Dirty Harry for personal injury in the state of Forumia. Under Injuria law a person may protect himself or herself with deadly force when he or she reasonably fears death or serious bodily injury. Injuria imposes no duty to retreat before using deadly force. Under the law of Forumia, a person must retreat before using deadly force. Harry claims he was in reasonable fear of death or serious bodily injury but concedes he could have retreated. What law applies under the Second Restatement?

Rough Riders

3. Edna ("EZ") Rider and her husband Teddy ("TR") are domiciled in the state of East Carolina. They went for a motorcycle ride to West Carolina. There, while EZ was driving, she lost control and collided with a tree. TR, riding as a passenger, suffered head injuries.

   West Carolina has a helmet law that requires motorcycle drivers to make helmets available to passengers. West Carolina courts explain that the purpose of the law is to avoid injuries, and they hold drivers strictly liable for head injuries suffered by passengers who do not wear helmets. East Carolina has no helmet law. According to the Second Restatement, what law applies?

4. Same facts. West Carolina courts hold that spouses are immune to tort claims by spouses. The West Carolina courts state that the purpose of the immunity is to promote family harmony and discourage collusive claims. East Carolina has no spousal immunity. What law applies under the Second Restatement?

Counting Contact Contacts in Context

5. Mason, a citizen of the state of Myopia, ordered some contacts over the Internet from Drake, a citizen of the country of Stanistan. Drake obtained

the contacts from PanOpticon, a corporation incorporated under the laws of the country of Stanistan. The contacts were manufactured at PanOpticon's factory in Stanistan. Drake mailed them to Mason from Stanistan.

After using the contacts for six months, Mason began to experience pain and redness in his left eye. Mason has learned that his eye has been injured by the contacts. As a result he will never be able to use contacts again. The cause of the injury was phlogiston, a substance legally used in optical products in Stanistan but banned under the law of Myopia because of its risk of causing the sort of injuries Mason has suffered.

Mason sues PanOpticon, alleging that he was injured by its defective product. The use of phlogiston satisfies Myopia's legal definition of a defective product. The defendant moves to dismiss, arguing that the product was legal under the law of the place of manufacture. The forum applies the Second Restatement. What law applies?

Bad Tan

6. Sue, a citizen of the state of Sunshine, died from skin cancer. For many years she used a tanning bed manufactured and distributed by Eurosalons, Inc., a business located in and incorporated under the laws of the state of Penumbria.

Sue's estate sues Eurosalons in the state of Penumbria, claiming the tanning bed was a defective product. Sunshine law has a $50,000 limitation on damages for wrongful death. Penumbria has no limitation. What law applies under the Second Restatement?

Tricky Truck Problem

7. Trish Driver, domiciliary of the state of Denial, drove trucks for Truckco, a business located in and incorporated under the laws of the state of Denial. Driver drove a Truckco truck to the state of Recovery, where she made a delivery. She then drove the truck to visit her boyfriend in Recovery. While pulling into her boyfriend's driveway, Driver negligently injured Vance Victim, a domiciliary of Recovery.

Victim sued Truckco under a theory of respondeat superior. Under case law in Denial, respondeat superior does not apply because the driver was not acting in the scope of her employment while driving to meet her boyfriend. Under case law in Recovery, respondeat superior applies because the driver was acting in the scope of her employment. What law applies under the Second Restatement?

The Wronged Woman

8. Flip Flipper, citizen of the country of Fredonia, traveled to the country of Honoria to close a business deal for his employer. At a party in Honoria celebrating the deal, Flipper was photographed with Hub

Hubbard. In the photograph Flipper, for a joke, held his hand behind Hubbard's head and extended two fingers visible above his head.

The photograph was published in Honoria papers. Flipper's gesture is widely understood in Honoria to mean that Hubbard's wife has committed adultery. As a result, Hubbard and his wife have suffered great humiliation and injury to their reputations. What law applies to the issue of whether Flipper's flippant gesture was defamatory?

9. Truth is a defense in defamation cases under the law of Fredonia, but not Honoraria. According to the Second Restatement, what law applies to a claim arising from a defamatory statement communicated in Honoraria?

10. The law of Honoria allows recovery of punitive damages for defamatory statements without proof of actual damages. Fredonia requires proof of actual damages and limits punitive damages to the amount of actual damages recovered. What law applies under the Second Restatement?

Explanations

Crash and Burn

1. The answer goes down in flames for two reasons. First, it fails to state and apply the Second Restatement rule directing the application of the local law of the state that has the most significant relationship to the parties and occurrence for each issue (under sections 6 and 145). Second, it fails to consider the policies or interests of states in applying their law to the different issues and fails to identify which contacts are relevant to such an analysis. For example, if a state's purpose behind a rule was to prevent accidents, then that rule would apply regardless of where the injured people were domiciled.

Lazy Teacher

2. Injuria law is the only answer possible given these facts, but the question—like the Second Restatement's own illustrations to section 163 (on privilege)—gets low marks because it does not provide additional facts, notably the domicile of the parties. This prevents a complete evaluation of interests and policies under section 6 that might indicate a contrary result.

    A good answer would begin by observing that under the Second Restatement the specific rule in section 146 (personal injury actions) applies the law of the place of injury unless some other state has a more significant relationship to the occurrence and parties. This specific rule directs an application of the general rules in sections 6 and 145.

The state with the most significant relationship to the occurrence and parties appears to be the place where the defendant acted and caused injury. Indeed, under the facts, Injuria is the only place that has a relationship to the occurrence and parties with respect to the issue of self-defense.

Injuria probably has a strong governmental interest in applying its version of self-defense. Its lack of a duty to retreat advances the purpose of removing disincentives to the use of deadly force in self-defense. Injuria may have refused to require retreat out of tradition, notions of personal autonomy, or a consideration that discouraging protective force might increase the risk of injury to innocent persons. In any case, Injuria's rejection of the defense is designed to regulate conduct in Injuria, not just shift economic losses. This conduct-regulating governmental interest would be advanced by applying Injuria law regardless of where the parties are domiciled.

Other section 6 considerations like predictability and justified expectations also indicate application of the law of the place of defensive conduct. Although these considerations have little relevance in tort claims based on negligence where parties do not plan their conduct in reliance on any particular law, the factors have special relevance here. The use of the gun was intentional, and persons making intentional decisions about using guns may well inform themselves about the law where they are acting and rely on rights provided under local law.

Rough Riders

3. The specific rule (section 146) selects the place of the injury, West Carolina, unless East Carolina has a more significant relationship under the analysis required by sections 6 and 145.

West Carolina's helmet law is at least in part a conduct-regulating rule, and the state has a governmental interest in applying its rule of the road to nonresidents who drive in the state. East Carolina, by not requiring helmets and imposing liability only for negligence, asserts a loss-shifting policy of not shifting loss under the circumstances and a conduct-regulating policy of holding passengers accountable for their own choices and permitting motorcyclists to engage in certain risky conduct without fear of liability. Considering the needs of the interstate and international systems, East Carolina's conduct-regulating policy does not extend to conduct in West Carolina because East Carolina has no legitimate interest in regulating conduct in a sister state so as to influence the risk of injuries suffered in that state. Relevant contacts favoring application of West Carolina law are the place of the injury and place of the conduct.

East Carolina may still have some loss-shifting policy interest against application of strict liability for violation of the helmet law. Contacts relevant to this interest are the residence of each party and the place where their relationship was centered.

This conflict can be resolved in three ways consistent with the Second Restatement. First, you could apply the specific rule under section 146 since no other state clearly has a more significant relationship. Second, you could argue that the place of the injury contact is more important for personal injury torts, and thus section 145 selects West Carolina as the place with the most significant relationship. See Second Restatement §145 cmt. f. Third, you could balance the relative interests and conclude that West Carolina's interest in reducing head injuries is more important than East Carolina's interest in permitting helmetless driving—at least for accidents in West Carolina. See id. §145 illus. 2.

4. This question demonstrates the need for analyzing issues separately because the case is strong for applying the law of common domicile, East Carolina's law, rather than the law of the place of injury, to the issue of spousal immunity.

Spousal immunity is a loss-shifting rule. Whatever its purposes, spousal immunity is not designed to encourage conduct that increases risks of injury between spouses. No governmental interest of the place of injury is advanced by barring recovery between foreign parties whose home state law permits recovery. In contrast, the state of common domicile has a strong interest in applying its policy to permit recovery by the injured spouse. The only contacts relevant to the determination of the place with the most significant relationship with respect to the issue of spousal immunity are the parties' places of domicile. Despite the preference indicated in section 146 for the place of injury, a consideration of interests and policies under sections 6 and 145 demonstrates that the place of injury has no real interest and that East Dakota law should apply. This result is consistent with one of the Second Restatement's specific rules (not covered in most Conflicts casebooks). See Second Restatement §169 and cmt. b.

Counting Contact Contacts in Context

5. After noting the preference of the specific rule (section 146) for the place of the injury, the first thing to consider (under section 6) is whether governmental interests of both jurisdictions are advanced by applying their law. The state of Myopia has a powerful interest in applying its law to regulate the sale of dangerous products in the state, to compensate a person injured in the state, and to protect citizens of the state from dangerous products. The contacts relevant to these interests are the location of the place of injury and the domicile of the plaintiff.

The country of Stanistan has an interest in applying its loss-shifting law to reduce costs and encourage the growth of business in Stanistan. The contacts relevant to this are the place of manufacture and the place of incorporation and place of business of the defendant.

The Second Restatement suggests that the law of the place of injury should govern because no other state has a more significant interest in the application of its law. (This treats section 146 like a tie-breaker. See Second Restatement §157 illus. 1 & §159 illus. 1.) The Second Restatement also observes that it would be unfair to allow a defendant to escape liability under the law of the place where the person's act caused injury. Id.

More cogent reasons have been offered by some opinions. The needs of the international system favor application of local laws providing recovery. The contrary rule — applying the law of the place of manufacturing — would lead to the rapid decline of safety standards internationally by encouraging all manufacturing to relocate to jurisdictions with low standards. Predictability and enforcement of justified expectations paradoxically also support applying variable local standards. To the extent manufacturers consider potential liability, they do not reasonably expect all claims to be governed by favorable home state law. Accordingly, manufacturers are in the best position to evaluate their compliance with variable safety standards and to obtain adequate insurance for losses in multiple jurisdictions. See Phillips v. General Motors Corp., 995 P.2d 1002 (Mont. 2000) (rejecting the law of the place of manufacture in a defective product case and permitting recovery under the local law of the plaintiff's domicile where the place of domicile had a strong interest in reducing injury to state residents from unsafe products and a strong interest in compensating residents for injuries).

Bad Tan

6. This problem is similar to that faced by the court in Johnson v. Spider Staging Corp., 555 P.2d 997 (Wash. 1976), where the forum state was the home state of the defendants and the place of the manufacture of the allegedly defective scaffolding, while the injury and death occurred in Kansas. Washington law did not limit death damages, but Kansas law imposed a $50,000 limit.

   The Second Restatement indicates that the law of the place of injury applies in wrongful death actions unless some other state has a more significant relationship. Second Restatement §175. A separate rule applies this place's law to the measure of damages. Id. §178. The Washington court did not rely on such specific rules as tie-breakers. Instead, examining state policies and interests (section 6), the court determined that the purpose of limitations of damages was loss-shifting — the protection of

Kansas defendants from excessive losses. Consequently, it found that no Kansas interest would be advanced by applying the Kansas law to a case against foreign corporations.

In contrast, the court determined that the forum law that permitted full recovery for defective products causing death was both loss-shifting and conduct-regulating. It found that applying Washington law would advance the forum interest of deterring dangerous products. Accordingly, it held that Washington law applied as the law of the place with the most significant relationship. By similar reasoning, the Penumbria courts might conclude that a Penumbrian interest in reducing deaths is advanced by applying Penumbrian law against Penumbrian manufacturers.

Tricky Truck Problem

7. Applying sections 6 and 145 probably leads to application of the law of the place of accident and injury—though I don't think this is as easy as the Second Restatement commentator does. *See* Second Restatement §174 cmt. b.

   State interests are divided under section 6. The place of injury has a strong interest in applying its broader form of respondeat superior as a loss-shifting rule that benefits a domiciliary of the state. The place of employment also has an interest in applying its loss-shifting rule to prevent excess liability. Other section 6 considerations probably have little application except for the needs of the interstate system. This consideration may favor applying the pro-recovery law of the place of the accident to the issue of derivative liability. (The alternative—denying recovery under foreign law—would disadvantage local claimants and result in hostility toward interstate commerce.) Such an underlying rationale may explain why the Second Restatement concludes summarily that the pro-recovery law of the place of injury should apply when the local law is not aberrational.

   Section 145 contacts also favor applying the law of Recovery. While the parties' domicile is divided, the place of injury and place of conduct causing injury are all in the state of Recovery. Section 146's specific rule also favors the law of Recovery.

The Wronged Woman

8. The Second Restatement provides a specific rule (section 149) for defamation that occurs in one jurisdiction. The rule selects the law of the place of publication unless with respect to that issue another state has a more significant relationship. This then requires a consideration of sections 6 and 145.

Interests under section 6 lean toward applying the law of the place of conduct. The place of conduct has a powerful interest in defining what conduct is actionable as defamatory. This is a conduct-regulating rule. Other jurisdictions may have no interest in applying a different standard of defamation or may have a contrary interest in encouraging freedom of expression. Predictability and uniformity have some application to intentional torts, unlike negligence claims, and they favor applying local law. The needs of the international system also (probably) favor applying local law to the extent there may be competing interests. All the contacts relevant to these considerations are in Honoria, the place of conduct, except for the defendant's domicile. Accordingly, the law of Honoraria should apply.

9. The defense of truth in libel is conduct-regulating, so it should probably be resolved the same way as the definition of defamatory statements—by applying the law of the place of publication unless displaced by the law of a state with a more significant relationship.

   You might argue, however, that the defense of truth is a privilege designed to advance the public good (dissemination of accurate factual information) in which Fredonia has an interest. If this is a policy objective of Fredonia's law, then it would be implicated even more in a claim against a Fredonia citizen. If Fredonia has a "more significant relationship" with respect to this issue, then all jurisdictions following the Second Restatement should apply its law. But you might not be surprised to find different jurisdictions reaching different conclusions and applying their own law. This example illustrates the survival of true conflicts—and inconsistent results—under the Second Restatement.

10. The issue of punitive damages is conduct-regulating. It provides greater deterrence against defamatory communications regardless of the economic impact of the communications. Accordingly, this issue should probably be resolved the same way as the choice of law of standards defining what is defamatory. However, the prospect of punishing persons for unintended consequences of their behavior and for making true statements raises serious issues of public policy. Chapter 23 discusses the question of whether the Second Restatement contains a separate public policy exception.

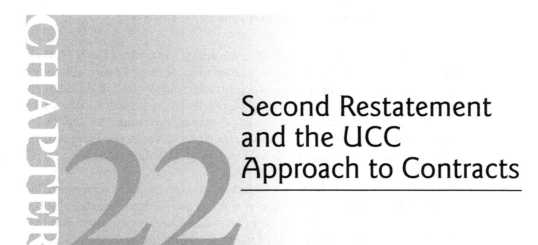

Second Restatement and the UCC Approach to Contracts

INTRODUCTION

This chapter deals with contracts conflicts under the Second Restatement of Conflicts and the Uniform Commercial Code (UCC).

History and Overview

Modern approaches to contracts (including the Second Restatement and UCC) reject rigid territorial rules. Instead, modern approaches honor most agreements by parties that a particular jurisdiction's law should govern their contract. In the absence of such an agreement, modern approaches generally apply law that validates contracts.

The modern preference for upholding contracts can be explained as the result of an evolving consensus that all jurisdictions benefit from the enforcement of private obligations with multi-state contacts. It can also be explained as a preference for predictability, respect for party autonomy, and the enforcement of justified expectations.

Jurisdictions

Some version of the UCC and its choice of law rules are adopted by every state. The UCC applies to many contracts, including contracts for the sale of goods. It does not apply to contracts for the sale of land or services.

Where the UCC choice rule does not apply, a majority of states follow the *general* approach of the Second Restatement. Some 23 states adhere to the Second Restatement approach to contracts. Some follow all the detailed provisions of the Second Restatement, but in practice most of them follow the approach stated in the broad provisions (sections 187 and 188). Other modern-approach states apply similar rules (with the exception of pure interest analysis jurisdictions). Hay et al., Conflict of Laws §18.21 at 1148.

The case law leads Professor Weintraub to conclude that courts usually enforce parties' designated choice of law. For cases without such a choice, "the emerging consensus . . . appears to be that questions of validity should be controlled by the law of the state having the most significant or closest relationship with the parties and with the transaction." Weintraub, Commentary on the Conflict of Laws §7.3D at 529. Because this consensus is consistent with the general approach of the Second Restatement, it is fair to say that the Second Restatement has been more successful in "restating" the modern conflicts rules for contracts than it has been in the area of torts.

THE UCC

The purpose of the UCC was to make commercial laws uniform. Since all states adopt some version of the UCC, their commercial laws are often the same, and there will not be conflicts. But there can still be conflicts issues in a UCC jurisdiction when there are different versions of the UCC on some issue, when the issue is governed by one state's UCC but not covered by another state's UCC, or where the UCC rule conflicts with applicable law from a non-UCC country.

The UCC is full of specific choice of law rules that apply to specific problems like the perfection of security interests. In addition, the UCC provides general gap-filling choice of law rules. There are currently two different versions of the UCC general choice rules.

Honoring Party Choice When Transaction Has Reasonable Relationship to Chosen Law The original version of the UCC contained a general choice of law rule that honored the parties' choice of law of either the forum UCC or some other jurisdiction's law "when a transaction bears a reasonable relation to this state and also to another state or nation." UCC §1–105(1). When there is no choice of law or when the choice is invalid because of the absence of a reasonable relationship to the jurisdiction, then the older version applies the forum UCC law "to transactions bearing an appropriate relation to this state." UCC §1–105(2). This section was renumbered 1–301.[1]

Some states construe "appropriate relation" broadly and apply forum UCC law in the absence of a valid choice when the forum has a minimal basis for applying its law. This results in a clear preference for applying the forum UCC. Other states construe "appropriate relation" to mean the *most significant* relationship to the transaction. This converts the older version of the general choice rule into a Second Restatement-type rule.

The older version UCC choice rules do not select a governing law when there is neither a valid choice nor an appropriate relationship to the state. Such cases will fall under the forum's general choice rule, which will probably be some version of the Second Restatement for contracts.

SECOND RESTATEMENT ROAD MAP

The Second Restatement validates a contractual choice of law provision whenever the issue is one of the parties' intent. Their chosen law applies automatically to issues that they could have resolved in advance by private agreement. For example, chosen law will provide definitions of terms and fill gaps regarding details that the parties could have inserted on the theory that contract law should normally enforce the intentions of the contracting parties, and the choice of law indicates their intentions.

The Second Restatement also validates the parties' choice despite an intent-frustrating rule except in two situations. One of these situations will require consideration of the general choice rule that would apply in the absence of an effective choice by the parties.

When the parties choose some law to apply, the Second Restatement assumes the parties mean to apply only that jurisdiction's local law in the absence of an indication of intent to the contrary.

In contracts without a valid choice of law provision, the Second Restatement's section 187 requires an issue-by-issue analysis and applies the local law of the state with the most significant relationship to the transaction and parties. Section 187 requires a consideration of section 6 principles (most of which favor validating multi-state agreements), and section 187 lists factual contacts relating to contracts. Other sections in the Second

---

1. The number change resulted when a 2001 revision radically altered the section to eliminate the reasonable relationship requirement. The revision proved unpopular. As of 2007 only the Virgin Islands adopted it. Oops. The revision was withdrawn, and a "new" section 1-301 was proposed that basically restated section 1-105, which the states had all kept. *See* Hay et al., Conflict of Laws §18.12A at 1124.

Restatement provide specific rules for different kinds of contracts and contract issues.

Contracts with Choice of Law Provisions

Gap-Filling Rules to Which the Parties Could Have Agreed   The Second Restatement applies the law chosen by the parties "if the particular issue is one which the parties could have resolved by an explicit provision in their agreement directed to that issue." Second Restatement §187(1).

The purpose of this rule is to maximize the enforcement of private agreements by parties on matters they may control under the general law of contracts.[2] This leads to one important exception: when the law chosen by the parties invalidates a contract they expected to be valid or that conflicts with a specific provision of the contract, then their chosen law will not be applied; it will be considered a mistake. *See* Second Restatement §187 cmt. e.

Rules to Which Parties Could Not Have Agreed in the Contract   For issues that the parties could not have decided in advance by agreement, the Second Restatement still expresses a preference for applying chosen law when it makes sense to do so. Section 187(2) expresses this preference by a rule that directs the application of the chosen law except in two situations.

> The law of the state chosen by the parties . . . will be applied, even if the particular issue is one which the parties could not have resolved by an explicit provision in their agreement directed to that issue, unless either
> (a) the chosen state has no substantial relationship to the parties or the transaction and there is no other reasonable basis for the parties' choice or
> (b) application of the law of the chosen state would be contrary to a fundamental policy of a state which has a materially greater interest than the chosen state in the determination of the particular issue and which, under the rule of §188, would be the state of the applicable law in the absence of an effective choice of law by the parties.

This means a choice of law by the parties will be ineffective in only two situations. First, on a matter the parties could not have resolved in advance by agreement, the parties' choice is ineffective when the chosen jurisdiction has no substantial relationship to the transaction and there is no reasonable

---

2. The Second Restatement rules for property and wills generally follow the First Restatement. But consistent with its preference for applying rules chosen by the parties to matters of intent, the Second Restatement directs the application of the law designated by the parties to issues of construction. Second Restatement §§224, 240, 244(2) & 264.

basis for selecting that place's law. The Second Restatement observes that irrational or arbitrary choices of law are rare. Examples of contacts that establish a reasonable basis for choice of law include the place of performance by any party and the place of domicile or principal place of business of any party.

Second, the parties' choice on a matter they could not have resolved by agreement is ineffective when the chosen law is contrary to a *fundamental policy* of the jurisdiction with the most significant relationship and that state has a *materially greater* interest in applying its law than the chosen state.

Contracts Without (Valid) Choice of Law Provisions

The Second Restatement's general choice-influencing considerations come into play in those cases where parties have made no choice or where the choice is invalid. You must also consider them in deciding whether a choice is valid.

Section 188 directs the application with respect to each issue of the local law of the state that has the most significant relationship to the transaction and parties under the principles stated in section 6.

The principles in section 6 relate to all conflicts cases:

a. needs of the interstate and international system
b. relevant policies of the forum
c. relevant policies of other interested states
d. protection of justified expectations
e. basic policies underlying the particular field of law
f. certainty, predictability, and uniformity of result
g. ease in determination and application of the law

Four of these considerations (a, d, e, and f) have special relevance for contract disputes and favor validating contractual obligations that the parties expected to apply.

In applying the fall-back rule under section 188, the Second Restatement identifies the following contacts to be taken into account in determining what law applies:

a. the place of contracting
b. the place of negotiation
c. the place of performance
d. the location of the subject matter of the contract
e. the domicile, residence, nationality, place of incorporation, and place of business of the parties

The Second Restatement does not indicate the priority or weight of these contacts.

Performance

Illegality Questions of illegality are governed by the general rules governing contracts — the chosen law and law of the place with the most significant relationship. In addition, a performance illegal in the place of performance will usually not be enforceable.

Details of Performance The Second Restatement applies the law of the place of performance to details of performance (§206). The law of the place of performance applies even when the parties have selected another place's law unless the parties clearly intended the chosen law to govern details of performance. The Second Restatement assumes parties did not intend chosen law to apply to such details in the absence of clear intent.

Specific Rules

The Second Restatement provides specific rules for many particular kinds of contracts (like land sale contracts) and issues (like the measure of damages). Some of the rules select a particular place's law to apply to an issue *unless* another jurisdiction has a more significant relationship. Others say that some place's law *usually* applies.

The most useful of the specific rules states that the local law of the place of negotiating and performance "usually" applies when negotiating and performance are in the same state. Second Restatement §188(3).

The Second Restatement provides additional special rules for validity — for land sales, the law of the place of land; for chattels, the place of delivery; for repayment of money lent, the place of repayment; for contracts for services, the place of the major portion of services. The special rules incorporate a number of validating preferences. Capacity under a party's domicile will *usually* be upheld everywhere. Satisfying the statute of frauds or other formalities of the place of execution will *usually* be accepted everywhere. All of these specific rules are displaced by an effective choice by the parties or by the law of the state with a more significant relationship selected under section 188.

In practice, for contracts with no valid choice of law provision, you can make the correct determination by starting with section 188 and determining the law of the state with the most significant relationship. The law of that state will often be the law selected by the more specific rules, and when it is not, you should still apply it.

Examples

Fun in the Sun

1. Davis Miles, citizen of Illinois, meets Darrow Clarence, also a citizen of Illinois, while the two are vacationing in the country of Suntopia in the Caribbean. Clarence is a lawyer, and Miles describes his legal problem back home. Clarence agrees to investigate and to file a lawsuit if necessary. The two sign a detailed written contract in Suntopia that provides that if Clarence files a lawsuit, Clarence will be entitled to compensation in the amount of one-third of the amount of any judgment or settlement recovered for Miles.

   Under the law of Illinois, the contingent fee agreement is valid. Under the law of Suntopia, such agreements are void. Suntopia courts refuse to enforce such agreements because they believe contingent fee agreements encourage frivolous litigation. The fee agreement does not contain a choice of law provision.

   Is the contract valid?

Uniform Commercial Confusion

2. Adam Smith Co., a business incorporated under the laws of the state of Northern Virginia, entered into a contract for the sale of 20,000 widgets to Ricardo Corp., a local business in the country of Xanadu. Adam Smith Co. manufactured the widgets in Mexico. The contract was negotiated in Xanadu, where the widgets were to be delivered.

   An issue arises concerning the validity of the contract. Northern Virginia follows the UCC. It also follows the Second Restatement. What law applies?

3. Same facts. But suppose the contract includes a choice of law provision that states, "All issues under this contract will be governed by the law of Saudi Arabia." None of the parties had any connection with Saudi Arabia, and nothing in the contract had any possible connection to that country except for the choice of law clause.

   Northern Virginia has retained the older version of the UCC choice of law rule. What law will its courts apply?

Choices, Choices

4. Fred promised Barney to reduce one stack of rocks to rubble. Barney agreed to give Fred two clams upon completion. The parties agreed that the law of the country of Paleolithia would apply. The parties shook hands and agreed to the contract in the country of Neolithia. Under the contract law of Paleolithia the contract is valid. But Paleolithia follows the First Restatement and would apply the law of the place of the contracting, Neolithia. Under the Second Restatement, what law have the parties selected?

Details, Details

5. In a written contract Bullwinkle, a citizen of Canada, agrees to sell Rocky 20,000 acorns and to deliver them to Rocky's home in the state of North Minnesota "for the amount of $1,000." The contract provides "this agreement shall be governed by the law of Canada." At the time of delivery, the Canadian dollar is worth more than the U.S. dollar. Does the "$1,000" refer to Canadian or U.S. dollars? Apply the Second Restatement.

6. At the time of delivery, Bullwinkle insists on payment before delivering the acorns. Rocky insists that Bullwinkle must complete delivery before he makes payment. What law governs who goes first? Apply the Second Restatement.

7. Rocky is prepared to pay the appropriate amount in either U.S. dollars or by a certified check drawn on a North Minnesota bank payable in the appropriate amount of U.S. dollars. Bullwinkle insists on payment in Canadian cash. What law governs the form of payment? Apply the Second Restatement.

Statute of Frauds

8. Paganini, a citizen of the country of Uppland, visited Stradivarius, a citizen of the country of Downland, and agreed orally to buy a violin from Stradivarius for 10 million lira. Stradivarius promised to finish the fiddle and have it available for Paganini to pick up at his shop one year from the date of the agreement. The parties agreed that the contract would be governed by the law of Uppland. Downland has a statute of frauds that requires all contracts for the sale of goods valued over 5 million lira to be evidenced by a signed writing. Uppland has no statute of frauds, and the oral promise is enforceable under Uppland contract law. What law applies under the Second Restatement?

Smoking Peppercorn

9. Hadley promised to give Baxendale a peppercorn if Baxendale would stop smoking. Baxendale agreed and promised to give Hadley $1,000 if he was unable to stop smoking. The parties reduced their agreement to writing. The parties were domiciled in the country of Avalon, where the agreement was negotiated and signed.

The contract selected the law of Fumaria to govern all issues. Fumaria had no connection to the parties or to the transaction. The parties selected it because Fumarian law enforces written promises regardless of consideration. Fumarian law also enforces promises to pay specified or liquidated damages.

Hadley caught Baxendale smoking in the stairwell. Avalon requires consideration for contracts and does not consider the offer of a pepper-corn to be consideration. Avalon also does not enforce liquidated damages that bear no relationship to economic loss. Accordingly, Hadley cannot recover under Avalon law but can recover under Fumarian law. What says the Second Restatement?

Refrigerator Litigator

10. Husband and Wife, domiciled in the state of East Dakota, drove to the state of West Dakota, where they bought a refrigerator from Sal Seller, a domiciliary of West Dakota. Seller delivered the refrigerator to the buyers' home.

     After six months, the refrigerator stopped working suddenly while the buyers were on vacation. They returned to find the contents of the refrigerator spoiled. Buyers seek to recover both the repair costs for the refrigerator and the costs of the food spoiled by the refrigerator's malfunction. East Dakota permits recovery of consequential damages for the costs of spoiled food. West Dakota does not permit recovery of consequential damages for the spoiled food. What law applies under the Second Restatement?

11. Same facts but the contract specifies that "all claims are to be governed by the law of West Dakota."

     When Wife opened the door of the refrigerator, the top shelf fell out and jabbed her with a jagged plastic edge, causing serious injuries. Wife commences a product liability action against Seller, alleging that the refrigerator was defectively designed. The product design was defective according to East Dakota's standards but not according to West Dakota's. What law applies under the Second Restatement?

Explanations

Fun in the Sun

1. The contract is valid. The First Restatement had problems with a situation like this because its general rule directed the application of the law of the place of contracting. Under the Second Restatement, Illinois law applies. The contract is for services, is not covered by the Uniform Commercial Code,[3] and contains no choice of law provision. So the Second Restatement applies in most jurisdictions.

---

3. Since we are in a real jurisdiction now, it would be the Illinois version of the UCC, not the model "uniform" code.

As is often the case, the Second Restatement provides some specific rules, but they do not completely answer the question. For example, section 196 provides that the validity of a services contract without a choice of law provision is governed by the local law of the state where most of the services are to be performed unless some other state has a more significant relationship. Many courts — and many Conflicts courses — overlook the more specific rules and turn to the general rule (section 188) that governs contracts when there is no choice of law. Other specific provisions state that validity is determined by section 188. Second Restatement §§200-203.

Under section 188, a contract with no choice of law provision is governed with respect to each issue by the local law of the state with the most significant relationship to the transaction and parties. Section 188 directs a consideration of various contacts, but these must be considered in light of the section 6 principles, and some are more important in this case than others. In this case the place of contracting and negotiation do not establish any governmental interest in Suntopia in applying its law because the contract is to be performed elsewhere. Suntopia's policy is directed against frivolous litigation in its own courts (or possibly frivolous litigation involving its citizens in other courts). In this case the law of the place of contracting would not protect party expectations. The parties thought they had entered a valid contract, and applying Suntopia law would frustrate their expectations.

In contrast, the place of performance and the parties' citizenship implicate important principles for applying Illinois law. Illinois has strong policies, both in regulating attorney-client relationships and in protecting the expectations of parties that are served by applying Illinois law. The additional section 6 principles are: policies underlying the particular field of law (contracts); certainty, predictability, and uniformity of result; and ease in determination and application. These would be served by applying the law of the parties' common domicile and place of performance to validate an agreement.

Note that a good Second Restatement analysis requires more than counting contacts. It requires a consideration of the contacts that are relevant to the principles in section 6. The most important principles for contracts cases will be party expectations and state interests. In the Suntopia example, applying this analysis results in applying a law that would also be selected by interest analysis (which would characterize the conflict as a false conflict), and it illustrates the tendency of courts to apply law that validates contracts.

Nevertheless, the Second Restatement will sometimes apply intent-frustrating law when it serves identifiable state policies. For example, suppose two citizens in the country of Mortalia enter into a contract in Mortalia. They agree that they will go to the country of Vivacity, where one party will help the other to commit suicide. Assisted suicide agreements are valid in Mortalia, but assisted suicide is a crime in Vivacity, and agreements there to assist another in committing suicide are void as illegal. Vivacity's powerful interest in controlling criminal conduct in its territory would make the place of performance more important than the more numerous contacts relating to the citizenship of the parties and the places of negotiation and contracting. While applying Vivacity law might not protect party expectations, it would promote the needs of the international system by assuring sovereign control over criminal conduct within the country's territory. The Second Restatement also provides a specific rule that when a contract's performance is illegal where it is to take place, then the contract will "usually" be denied enforcement. Second Restatement §202.

Applying section 188 should get you to the right result even if you don't know the specific rules. When section 188 selects some law that differs from the specific rules, it normally trumps them.

Uniform Commercial Confusion

2. If Northern Virginia construes "appropriate relation" broadly, it will apply Northern Virginia's version of the UCC under section 1-301 (old §1-105(1)) because it will find an "appropriate relation" satisfied by the fact that one of the contracting parties is incorporated in that jurisdiction.

    If Northern Virginia construes "appropriate relation" narrowly, it will make a choice of law determination by applying the Second Restatement. The Second Restatement directs the application of the local law of the jurisdiction with the most significant relationship to the transaction and parties with respect to the issue of validity. This would "usually" be Xanadu, the place where the contract was negotiated and is to be performed.

3. Under the UCC, the choice of Saudi Arabian law is not valid because it bears no reasonable relation to the transaction. (Note: there must be some reason for selecting the law other than mere convenience or else all choices would be reasonable and enforceable.) Accordingly, the forum will apply its own version of the UCC if there is an appropriate relationship to the forum or the Second Restatement if there is no such appropriate relation. (See Explanation 2.)

    Under the Second Restatement, the choice of Saudi Arabian law is not automatically valid because the issue (validity) is not one that the parties could have resolved by agreement. Parties cannot make an invalid contract valid by agreement! Nevertheless, the chosen law might still apply unless there is no substantial relationship or other reasonable basis for the choice or unless it violates fundamental policy of another state with a materially greater interest. Here there is no substantial relationship or reasonable basis for the choice of Saudi Arabian law. Accordingly, the Second Restatement does not enforce the chosen law.

Choices, Choices

4. In the absence of an indication of contrary intent, the parties have selected the local contract law of Paleolithia, not its choice of law rules, to govern their contract.

Details, Details

5. Interpretation is tricky. The Second Restatement tries to effectuate the intent of contracting parties when their intent can be determined. In other words, when their intent can be determined under forum law, a forum court will not find a conflict and will not employ the Second Restatement's choice of law rules.

But when the parties' meaning is unknown and the contract's language is given a different legal construction under different laws, then there is a conflict. In such a situation the Second Restatement rules apply the gap-filling rules of construction.

In this case, the choice of local Canadian law on this issue of the meaning of "$" is effective because this is a matter that the parties could have resolved by private agreement. Bullwinkle and Rocky could have designated that payment be measured by Canadian dollars. A good guess is that under Canadian local law, the meaning of "$1,000" is "1,000 Canadian dollars."

6. Not sure? Join the club. The example is designed to illustrate the problem of deciding what is a detail of performance as opposed to an obligation. The exact time and place of performance are details of performance governed by the law of the place of performance, but the order of performance, fixing the legal conditions for an enforceable obligation, should be governed by the law chosen by the parties or by the law of the place with the most significant relationship in the absence of an effective choice. You could also argue under the rationale of the Second Restatement that parties would not normally intend the chosen law to apply to trivial matters of sequence of performance and that such issues should be governed by the place of performance.

7. The form of payment is a detail of performance, so payment (of the appropriate amount) in the form of an equivalent amount in U.S. dollars or a certified check in U.S. dollars will be satisfactory if the payment is in compliance with the law of North Minnesota.

Statute of Frauds

8. Issues of formality are governed by an effective choice of law by the parties and, in the absence of an effective choice, by the law of the place with the most significant relationship. Here the parties' choice is not automatically valid because the issue of formalities is not something the parties could have resolved by private agreement. Statutes of frauds are designed to frustrate intent, and parties cannot dispense with a statute of frauds by agreeing that it will not apply.

    Nevertheless, their choice is still valid unless there was no reason for selecting Uppland law or the Uppland law is contrary to a *fundamental* policy of Downland and Downland is both the jurisdiction with the most significant relationship and has a *materially greater* interest in applying its law than Uppland.

    The buyer's citizenship in Uppland establishes a reasonable basis for applying Uppland law. However, Downland appears to be the state with the most significant relationship because it is the place of negotiation and performance and has a strong interest in protecting Downland citizens from false claims of oral promises.

    The question is whether the Downland statute of frauds advances a fundamental policy. The Second Restatement indicates that the forum determines what a fundamental policy is. Commentary observes that issues of formalities will rarely advance a fundamental policy and offers an example where the chosen law validates a contract that is within a statute of frauds. Second Restatement §187 illus. 6 and cmt. g.

    If the statute of frauds does not advance a fundamental policy, then the chosen law should apply. But, you could argue, contrary to the Second Restatement's commentary, that some evidence of writing, required by most jurisdictions for high-price sales, advances fundamental policies of documenting significant obligations and alerting the contracting parties to the legal consequences of their conduct.

    If the statute of frauds serves a fundamental policy, then the next question is whether Downland has a materially greater interest in applying its statute of frauds. This could go either way, depending on the relative strength of Uppland's interest in enforcing expectations arising from oral promises as compared with Downland's interest in requiring contracts of this type to be in writing. One reasonable answer might recognize the great interest in enforcing justifiable expectations, but it would also note that such expectations have less weight regarding formalities, where parties may expect some matters to be governed by the law of the place of execution. Uppland's and the international commercial interests generally favor validation.

But, if Downland's policy advances a strong interest, it would not be unreasonable to find that competing interests should yield to a strong local policy requiring a writing. The facts that the formality is easily complied with and that similar formalities are required in most jurisdictions further support the application of Downland law by reducing the risk of surprise.

Smoking Peppercorn

9. Both issues are resolved the same way. The attempted choice of Fumaria law is ineffective. Requirements of consideration and limits on liquidated damages are intent-frustrating, and parties could not have resolved the conflict by privately agreeing that no consideration was required or that liquidated damages would be valid. Chosen law will still be applied to such issues in some cases, but not in this one, where there is no substantial relationship to the parties or transaction or other reasonable basis for selecting the law.

   Accordingly, the issues of consideration and damages are governed by Avalon law. Avalon is the place of negotiating and performance, so its law usually would apply. It is the state with the most significant relationship with respect to those issues. Indeed, it is the state with all contacts and the only state with any interest in applying its law.

Refrigerator Litigator

10. The example is inspired by the Second Restatement (§207 illus. 1). The law of the state with the most significant relationship with respect to the issue of the measure of damages is probably East Dakota, but the result is not certain. The case is not easily decided under the preference for applying the law of negotiation and performance, because the sale took place in one state, and the seller's breach of performance occurred in another state.

    The contacts are pretty evenly divided, but the point of the Second Restatement is not to count contacts but to evaluate relevant contacts in determining what state has the most significant relationship to the contract with respect to the particular issue (measure of damages).

    The Second Restatement asserts that the buyers' home state law should apply, reasoning that the domicile of the parties and place of delivery are contacts that establish their home state's "dominant interest" in the measure of damages. Yet the Second Restatement does not explain the purposes of the state rule. Obviously, a consumer-protecting policy would establish a strong interest.

    I give the Second Restatement's own explanation low marks for failing to explain which section 6 considerations apply and for rushing to the conclusion that a forum has an interest in applying a pro-recovery rule to favor its own parties. A better answer would try to explain the state interests and consider other section 6 factors. Certainty, predictability, and enforcing justified expectations, often of great importance in upholding contracts, have little to no force regarding the measure of damages. However, the needs of the interstate system may encourage application of local laws favoring recovery, since to apply the foreign seller's law would disadvantage local sellers by holding them (and their insurers) to a higher standard.

11. This is a trick question. Product liability claims are torts, not contracts, so the choice of law has no impact. The Second Restatement tort rules would apply the law of the place of the injury. See "Counting Contacts in Context" example in Chapter 21. The problem of characterizing or classifying issues under modern approaches is considered in Chapter 23.

Modern Answers to Traditional Problems

CHAPTER 23

INTRODUCTION

This chapter considers how modern approaches handle problem areas for traditional choice of law rules — characterization, procedure, statutes of limitations, public policy, and renvoi. It also examines how domicile emerges as a new problem area for modern approaches.

CHARACTERIZATION

Under traditional choice of law rules, the law that was selected depended on the characterization or classification of the legal issue. For example, a personal injury characterized or classified as a tort would be governed by the law of the place of injury. The same injury characterized as a breach of an implied contract would be governed by the law of the place of contracting.

Characterization permitted parties and courts to manipulate the traditional rules. This led to even more rules to govern characterization issues. One casebook confesses, "Conflicts casebooks are replete with examples of cases in which courts applying the traditional theory characterized identical issues in irreconcilable ways."[1]

---

1. Symeon C. Symeonides et al., Conflict of Laws: American, Comparative, International: Cases and Materials 54 (2d ed. 2003).

The widespread manipulation of characterization prevented the traditional rules from achieving uniformity of result. This was one source of the dissatisfaction with the traditional approach that eventually led most states to adopt various modern approaches.

Persistent Problem   Modern approaches do not do away with the need for characterization. To the extent modern jurisdictions adopt different choice of law rules for different types of issues, those jurisdictions still must characterize the issue in order to determine what rule applies. For example, the Second Restatement has different rules for torts and contracts. Similarly, jurisdictions employing interest analysis must also characterize the laws in conflict. For example, if a law is conduct-regulating, then according to interest analysis a government has an interest in applying its law to conduct in the government's territory even to people from other states.

Dépeçage   Modern American approaches employ what older authorities called dépeçage.[2] This is the practice of treating different legal issues separately. This multiplies opportunities for creative characterization because one state's law can apply to one issue and another's to a different issue.

Contractual Choice of Law   Modern approaches display a strong preference for respecting parties' private choice of law. This is reflected in the basic rules of the Second Restatement and the UCC. Enforcing such party choices promotes party autonomy and judicial convenience.

Many courts give broad effect to choice of law agreements. They avoid narrow constructions of choice of law language. And they apply the contractual choice of law language not only to contract claims but to related tort claims. For example, in Nedlloyd Lines B.V. v. Superior Court, 834 P.2d 1148 (Cal. 1992), the parties signed a contract that provided the agreement was to be "governed by and construed in accordance with Hong Kong law." The plaintiff sued for violation of an implied duty of good faith and fair dealing (a contract claim) and for breach of fiduciary duties (a tort claim). Both claims were valid under California law. Neither was valid under Hong Kong law.

Applying the Second Restatement, the California court concluded that the parties had validly selected Hong Kong law to govern the contract claim. The court also concluded that the tort claim was barred under Hong Kong law. Even though the contract's language did not mention torts, the court construed the contract to effectuate the presumed intent of the parties for

---

2. European courts avoid dépeçage and tend to find that an entire case is governed by a single jurisdiction's law.

Hong Kong law to govern all claims "arising from or related to their contract." The court emphasized the policies of respecting party autonomy and found that applying Hong Kong law to the tort offended no fundamental California policy.

Examples

Bad Faith

1. Pam, a citizen of East Carolina, has an insurance policy with Defensco, an East Carolina corporation licensed to sell insurance in East Carolina. The policy covers reasonable and necessary medical expenses.

   Pam is hospitalized in East Carolina where she incurs medical expenses. She then relocates to West Carolina and submits a claim to Defensco. For one year, Defensco refuses to respond to Pam's written communications. Then Defensco demands that Pam submit written proof from a third party that her medical expenses were reasonable and necessary. When she submits the proof and seeks further reimbursement for the cost of providing that proof, Defensco denies her claim because she did not use claim forms, which it did not provide.

   When Pam threatened to sue, Defensco insisted on submitting the dispute to nonbinding arbitration. When the arbitrator found for Pam, Defensco refused to pay. Only when Pam filed her lawsuit did Defensco offer to settle.

   Pam has learned that Defensco's response to her claims was the result of a company policy to deny all claims. She alleges that the company's denial aggravated a preexisting anxiety disorder, caused pain and suffering, and interfered with her emotional relationship with her husband.

   West Carolina recognizes causes of action for bad faith against insurance companies for failing to settle claims in good faith. East Carolina does not recognize such causes of action. Under the Second Restatement, what law applies?

In a Jam

2. Dundee and Chivers are citizens of the country of Marmaland. Dundee operates Outdoor Adventures and takes customers on hunting expeditions. One day Dundee takes Chivers on a hunting trip to the country of Jungalia, where Dundee negligently shoots and injures Chivers.

   Marmaland follows the common law of negligence. Jungalia has enacted a statute that provides a defense against personal injury negligence claims brought against persons who provide hunting services. Why is this so interesting for interest analysis?

PROCEDURE VS. SUBSTANCE

Traditional courts applied forum law to procedure even when their choice of law rules selected another jurisdiction's law for matters of substance. For example, in a personal injury tort case, a traditional court would apply its own forum law to admissibility of evidence even though it would apply the law of the place of injury to the issue of the standard of care.

Modern approaches treat the substance-procedure problem differently but have not solved it.

Second Restatement The Second Restatement says, "A court usually applies its own local law rules prescribing how litigation shall be conducted even when it applies the local law rules of another state to resolve other issues in the case." Second Restatement §122. Specific rules direct the application of forum law to many issues that were characterized traditionally as procedural. The Second Restatement also reclassifies a number of issues as substantive, including statutes of frauds and damages.[3] The Second Restatement reasons that the forum has the strongest interest in applying its own procedural rules to such issues. The Second Restatement classifies the following as procedural and substantive.[4]

Procedural	Substantive
capacity of parties	survival of tort claims
competence of witnesses	contribution
pleadings and motions	measure of damages
mode of trial and burdens of proof	interest on damages
enforcement of judgments	statutes of frauds
how litigation is conducted	parol evidence rule
	evidentiary privilege

---

3. The Second Restatement provides that the measure of damages is controlled by the general tort and contract rules. Second Restatement §§171 & 207. This was a change from the First Restatement where the law of the place of performance governed damages in contracts. The Second Restatement does not include the First Restatement rule that forum courts will apply local legislative caps on damages. This seems like another big change. But the Second Restatement casually mentions in commentary that a "forum will follow its own local practices in determining whether the damages awarded by a jury are excessive." Id. §171 cmt. f. Weintraub reads this as retaining the "monstrous" rule that caps are governed by forum law (Chapter 13). It is possible to read the comment more narrowly as directing the application of forum law on the judge-jury division of labor and on judicial standards governing reasonableness of jury awards.
4. Second Restatement §§133, 139, 140, 141, 167, 171 & 173.

While forum law governs the capacity of parties, it is not applied so as to substantially affect the liability of parties. For example, direct liability of an insurer under a local action statute is not procedural, nor is the issue of whether defendants are jointly and severally liable. *Id.* §125 cmt. a.

Claims of testimonial privilege are not automatically governed by forum law. Instead, the Second Restatement adopts rules that lean toward admitting privileged evidence. Evidence that is privileged under the law of the forum but not under the law of the state with the most significant relationship with the communication will be admitted "unless the admission of such evidence would be contrary to the strong public policy of the forum." Evidence that is not privileged under forum law will also be admitted even when privileged by the law of the state with the most significant relationship unless there is "some special reason" for not doing so. *Id.* §139(1)-(2).

The Second Restatement applies forum law to presumptions and inferences, except where the purpose of the foreign presumption is to "affect decision of the issue rather than to regulate the conduct of the trial." *Id.* §134. An example of an evidentiary presumption treated as procedural is an inference that a railroad is aware of its defective equipment. It is procedural because it is based on notions of administrative convenience, imposing a burden of rebutting an inference on a party who is in a better position to have access to evidence.

An example of a substantive presumption is an inference that people die simultaneously when they die in the same accident. It is substantive because its purpose is to regulate the order of succession at death in the absence of additional information.

Interest Analysis Interest analysis resolves conflicts by evaluating the government policies behind the rules at issue. It does not separately characterize issues as substantive or procedural and apply a different rule to matters of procedure. Nevertheless, an interest analysis court is likely to find that an issue characterized by other courts as "procedure" is governed by forum law. Even in cases where a court has no other interest in applying forum law, it will likely find an administrative interest in applying forum law to many issues characterized as procedural. This is because "the forum state has an interest in its own administration of justice," because applying its own rules is more efficient, and because parties do not normally rely on the rules governing judicial administration. Equitable Life Assurance Society v. McKay, 760 P.2d 871 (Or. 1988) (holding that forum law applied rather than foreign dead man rule of evidence).

Based on such governmental purposes, interest analysis is likely to find that forum law applies in most of the situations where the Second Restatement applies forum law. Yet by examining the governmental policies behind rules, including procedural rules, interest analysis may reach a result that differs both from the traditional rules and from the Second Restatement.

Examples

Promises, Promises

3. Plaintiffs bought real estate from Ganrud in Nevada and were making payments to him. Ganrud needed cash for other investments, so he persuaded Plaintiffs to refinance. Plaintiffs agreed to alter the terms of payment, and advanced more money than required by their old note. In return, Ganrud promised orally to write a will forgiving any debt that remained at the time of his death.

   Two years later Ganrud died domiciled in California. His will did not forgive Plaintiffs' debt. Plaintiffs, residents of Nevada, sued Ganrud's estate to enforce the oral promise. The California statute of frauds provided that a contract to forgive a debt in a will is invalid unless in writing. Plaintiffs argued the issue should be governed by Nevada law, under which it appeared that the oral promise was enforceable. What law should apply under interest analysis and the Second Restatement?

STATUTES OF LIMITATIONS

The traditional approach treated most statutes of limitations as procedural and applied forum law. This had the result that claims that were time-barred in a jurisdiction where they arose could be successfully litigated in other courts with longer statutes of limitations. There was an exception for statutes of limitations considered substantive. Many jurisdictions responded to traditional problems by enacting borrowing statutes (see Chapter 14).

Second Restatement Original Version   The original version of the Second Restatement adopted the traditional rule. It directed courts to apply the forum's statute of limitations, whether longer or shorter. Second Restatement §142. It provided the traditional exception: a shorter foreign statute of limitations in the state of the otherwise applicable law would bar a claim if the purpose of the foreign statute was to bar the "right and not merely the remedy." Id. §143.

Second Restatement Revised Version   By the late twentieth century, the traditional treatment of limitations was eroding as the result of two developments. First, many state legislatures enacted borrowing statutes that barred claims that were time-barred under the law of the place where the cause of action occurred or accrued. Second, a growing number of courts employing modern approaches began to re-characterize limitations issues as substantive.

The Second Restatement rule on statutes of limitations was revised in 1988. The revised rule states that limitations issues will be determined under the general principles in section 6. It does *not* apply the law of the state with the most significant relationship; instead, it formalizes the preference for applying forum law. Except for unusual circumstances where the result is "unreasonable," the revised rule directs a state to apply a shorter forum statute of limitations to bar a claim. It also generally applies a longer forum statute of limitations except when the forum has no substantial interest *and* the claim would be barred by a state with a more significant relationship to the parties and occurrence. Second Restatement §142 (1988 revision).

Interest Analysis   Interest analysis and modified interest analysis will evaluate the purposes of conflicting statutes of limitations in order to determine whether there is a true conflict. Purposes served by statutes include protecting a jurisdiction's residents from stale claims and conserving judicial resources.

Examples

How Long, How Long?

4. Cal, a resident of California, negligently injured Tex, a resident of Texas, in Alaska. Tex commenced a civil action in California more than one year after the cause of action arose. The claim is time-barred under the statute of limitations in California but not under the statutes of limitations of Texas or Alaska. What statute applies?

5. Cal, a resident of California, was injured in Arizona by a truck operated in behalf of Acme Trucking Inc., an Oklahoma corporation with its principal place of business in Oklahoma. For some reason, Cal sues in California, where his tort claim is time-barred under the short California statute of limitations. It is not time-barred under the statutes of limitations of other states. What statute applies?

6. McCann resided in Oklahoma in 1957 and worked at an oil refinery in the state where he was exposed to asbestos. The asbestos was part of a large boiler that was designed and manufactured in New York by Foster Wheeler LLC, a corporation headquartered in New York. Foster Wheeler manufactured the boiler in New York and shipped it to Oklahoma for installation at the refinery.

   McCann later left Oklahoma and settled in California, where he lived from 1975 until his death. In 2005 McCann was diagnosed with a rare form of cancer caused by exposure to asbestos. He sued Foster Wheeler in California alleging that defendant's asbestos caused the cancer.

Meanwhile in 1979 Oklahoma had enacted a statute of repose that bars all claims arising from improvements to real property after ten years. Oklahoma applies the statute retroactively. Since 1851 California has had a borrowing statute that borrows the shorter statute of limitations of the place where a cause of action has arisen. But the California borrowing statute does not apply to a citizen of California who has held the cause of action from the time it accrued.

California follows comparative impairment. Should the California court dismiss McCann's lawsuit under the Oklahoma statute of repose?

RENVOI

Renvoi was a special embarrassment to proponents of the traditional approach, where uniformity of result was a high priority. By selecting a foreign jurisdiction's local law in a case where the foreign jurisdiction would itself apply some other jurisdiction's law, a court was obviously reaching a different outcome. Yet the effort to decide the case under a foreign court's choice of law rules could produce a never-ending circle where those rules selected some other court. The traditional solution to renvoi was, with few exceptions, to apply only local law. Law professors and courts who formulated modern choice of law approaches attempted to avoid the renvoi problem. They get a B for effort.

Interest Analysis Professor Currie believed interest analysis would eliminate renvoi problems by focusing attention on the governmental interests behind the particular rules in conflict. In general, he thought these interests were expressed by local laws. He did not think choice of law rules normally identified the interest a state would have in the application of its law to a particular issue.

Nevertheless, interest analysis aficionados have pointed out that a state's conflicts rules can help in identifying a state's interest in applying its law. This is especially true when the foreign jurisdiction's choice of law rules employ some form of interest analysis. It seems reasonable that a state's restrained conclusion that its own governmental policy need not be applied in a particular kind of case should be respected by other courts. The same court's conclusion that its governmental policy requires application of its law provides evidence of a state interest.

Interest analysis does not adopt renvoi. It does not apply the foreign state's conflict rules to apply yet another state's law. But interest analysis can look to how a foreign state would decide the case — and whether the foreign state would apply its own or some other jurisdiction's law — as evidence of

23. Modern Answers to Traditional Problems

whether the case is a true conflict for purposes of interest analysis. Voilà, if this isn't renvoi, it's déjà vu.

Second Restatement   The Second Restatement rules avoid renvoi in torts and contracts by directing the application of the local law of the state with the most significant relationship or the local law of the jurisdiction whose law is selected by an effective choice of law.

Although this seems to eliminate renvoi for torts and contracts, the Second Restatement, like interest analysis, permits a consideration of foreign conflicts law. The Second Restatement emphasizes in its comments that a limited construction of the territorial scope of a law may avoid conflict. In addition, the Second Restatement officially requires renvoi in cases involving interests in real property. In order to achieve the same result as the courts of the place where the land is located, it directs courts to apply "the law that would be applied by the courts" of the place where the land is located.[5] This requires application of those courts' whole law, including choice of law rules. While the Second Restatement observes that courts "usually" apply local law to land in their state, the Second Restatement leads to renvoi whenever a court where the land is located would apply another state's law.

Modern Courts   A number of courts applying modern approaches in torts and contracts have examined the conflicts rules of other jurisdictions as a way of deciding whether the other jurisdictions have an interest, or a strong interest, in applying their own law.

Examples

Going Around in Circles

7. Tinkerbelle, hunting in the country of Neverland, shoots at a bird and hits Wendy while Wendy is located in the sovereign territory of Indian Country. Wendy is a citizen of Indian Country. Neverland courts hold hunters liable for negligently causing personal injuries. Indian Country courts hold hunters liable only for gross negligence. Neverland applies the law of the place of the injury, and Indian Country courts apply the law of the country of the wrongful act to torts issues. What law will a third forum apply under the Second Restatement or interest analysis?

---

5. Second Restatement §§222 cmt. e & 223. The Second Restatement more generally prescribes applying whole law when the objective of the forum choice rule is to reach the same result as another state's courts. Id. §8(2). It directs application of the whole law of other states when the state has no substantial relationship to the dispute and all other states reach the same result. Id. §8(3). The meaning of and authority for these last two is questionable.

8. Pierre and Michelle, citizens of the country of Walloonia, go for a vacation to the country of Leberwurst, where Michelle injures Pierre. Leberwurst has enacted a form of strict liability under which an injured person can recover his or her economic damages from the person that caused the damages without needing to prove negligence or other fault. Walloonia requires a party to show fault in order to recover. But Walloonia's decisions do not apply Walloonia's fault requirement to injuries that occur outside of Walloonia. What law will apply under the Second Restatement and interest analysis?

PUBLIC POLICY

The traditional territorial rules provided an important public policy exception: a court would not recognize a cause of action contrary to the strong public policy of the forum. This offered a useful escape device that permitted jurisdictions to avoid enforcing causes of action selected by a territorial rule when the causes of action were deeply offensive to local public morals. The Second Restatement preserves the traditional exception. "No action will be entertained on a foreign cause of action the enforcement of which is contrary to the strong public policy of the forum." Second Restatement §90.

The public policy exception provided an important limitation to the mechanical results of the traditional rules. Yet you could argue that such a limitation is not needed for modern approaches. Modern approaches can avoid the application of offensive foreign law in their initial choice of law selection because they can consider the policies behind the laws in conflict. For example, in a true conflict, pure interest analysis will apply forum law and avoid offensive foreign laws.

Modified forms of interest analysis will give consideration to the strong policy interest of the forum in determining whether to apply offensive foreign law in true conflicts. Second Restatement courts will also consider the strong policy of the forum in determining what law has the most significant relationship. The better law approach obviously considers the forum preference in making its choice of law. Nevertheless, cases still arise where modern approaches can select a foreign law that offends the public policy of the forum. The most obvious example will be false conflict cases in which the forum has no interest in applying its law and the otherwise applicable law offends forum public policy.

Modern approaches that retain a separate public policy exception face the same old problems the traditional jurisdictions did. The Second Restatement provides little guidance about what laws are not only different from forum law but offend forum public policy. The language of its rule emphasizes that the law must offend a strong public policy, and its comments observe that the rule is to be applied sparingly.

The Second Restatement rule is placed with the rules on jurisdiction, not choice of law. This indicates that the rule permits a court to dismiss a claim that strongly offends public policy; the rule does not in theory support the application of another jurisdiction's law.

In fact, courts applying a modern approach are split over how to treat public policy. In extreme cases, all jurisdictions would no doubt follow the letter of the Second Restatement and dismiss claims (if not defenses) that violate public policy when the foreign law is sufficiently repugnant. But it is less clear whether such dismissals would operate as judgments on the merits. Professor Weintraub insists that under the functional analysis of modern approaches, a forum should never use public policy by itself as the reason for applying its own law. Weintraub, Commentary on the Conflict of Laws §3.6 at 122. Nevertheless, some courts have applied their own law and even disregarded defenses considered offensive to the forum's public policy. Kilberg v. Northeast Airlines, Inc., 172 N.E.2d 526 (N.Y. 1961) (recognizing foreign wrongful death cause of action but refusing to recognize limits on damages under the foreign statute on grounds that the limits offended public policy); McDaniel v. Ritter, 556 So. 2d 303 (Miss. 1989) (applying forum's comparative negligence statute and rejecting Tennessee contributory negligence defense on grounds of public policy in a case where Tennessee law governed all other issues as the place with the most significant relationship). Several courts retaining the traditional rules have likewise expanded the public policy exception and applied it to defenses—notably guest statutes. E.g., Owen v. Owen, 444 N.W.2d 710 (S.D. 1989); Paul v. National Life, 352 S.E.2d 550 (W. Va. 1986). Other courts have expanded the idea of public policy as a ground for not enforcing novel claims such as direct action statutes. Marchlik v. Coronet Insurance Co., 239 N.E.2d 799 (Ill. 1968).

Still other courts, applying some form of interest analysis, have narrowly applied public policy. They have concluded that public policy does not survive as a separate consideration. As a result, an otherwise offensive foreign law will not be disregarded when the forum has no other interest in applying its law. Schultz v. Boy Scouts of America, Inc., 480 N.E.2d 679 (N.Y. 1985) (recognizing foreign defense of charitable immunity even though arguably counter to public policy when contacts between forum, parties, and occurrence were insufficient to apply forum law). Courts have also been reluctant to find a foreign law offensive to public policy in the absence of a strong forum interest. For example, the California court did not find a Mexican prohibition against non-Mexicans owning land to offend California public policy even though California's constitution guaranteed the right of noncitizens to own land in California. Wong v. Tenneco, Inc., 702 P.2d 570 (Cal. 1985).

Despite some confusion, the big picture seems clear. First, modern approaches can and do consider the strong public policy of the forum in deciding what law applies in a conflicts case, but (except under the better law approach) public policy should never be the only reason for selecting some jurisdiction's law. Second, where the forum has no connection with a case that justifies application of its own law, then it should either apply some other jurisdiction's law under modern choice rules or dismiss an action that is offensive to a strong public policy of the forum.

Examples

Policy Odysseys

9. Kev and Bev get married and live in the state of Northern California. Kev travels to East Carolina for a meeting. There he has sexual intercourse with Dev.

   Bev sues Dev in Northern California for the torts of criminal conversation and alienation of affections. These common law torts have been eliminated in Northern California because the courts concluded that they frustrated sound public policy by encouraging contentious litigation, aggravating domestic conflicts, and wasting social and judicial resources. In contrast, East Carolina courts have retained these tort causes of action and have opined that "deterring and punishing wrongful acts interfering with the institution of marriage are essential for promoting the value of marriage and for deterring acts of private retribution."

   Will Northern California recognize Bev's claims against Dev?

10. Shylock agrees to lend Bassanio 3,000 gallactic currency units. Antonio promises to guarantee repayment and agrees that if he fails to repay the loan in three months, Shylock may cut him open and take one pound of flesh and other body parts. The contract specifically provides that blood will be included as part of the flesh. Contra William Shakespeare, The Merchant of Venice. The parties are from Venus, and the contract specifies that all disputes will be governed by the law of Venus.

    The day before the due date, Antonio hops the space shuttle to the sovereign jurisdiction formerly known as the planet Pluto. The contract is enforceable under the law of Venus but deeply offensive to the public policy of Pluto. Shylock sues Antonio in Pluto for the pound of flesh, etc. Will the public policy of the puny planetoid prevail?

DOMICILE

Law professors long thought domicile was declining in importance. They noted the increasing mobility of parties with ties to multiple jurisdictions, and they noted that the tests for domicile were applied differently in different legal contexts.

Don't be fooled! A party's domicile plays a crucial role in modern choice of law. According to interest analysis, domicile controls whether a state has an interest in applying its loss-shifting rules. For example, a state has an interest in applying its pro-recovery loss-shifting rule in favor of a plaintiff domiciled in the state but not in favor of a plaintiff domiciled elsewhere. The Second Restatement also requires a consideration of domicile under section 6's consideration of state interests. It lists as one of the contacts to be taken into account for both torts and contracts: domicile, residence, nationality, place of incorporation, and place of business in the state.

Domicile raises two new problems for modern choice of law approaches. Both problems reveal a tension between the functional motives behind modern approaches (which require courts to consider the concrete impact of their decisions in real life) and the trend of modern approaches to achieve formal rules (that can be applied at times without regard to their practical effect).

Technical Domicile The formal definitions of domicile assign a person one and only one legal domicile. That domicile remains the person's domicile until he or she has established a new domicile. A person may leave a jurisdiction for decades and plan never to return, but that jurisdiction will remain the person's domicile unless a new one is established. Professor Weintraub calls this "technical domicile" and argues it should not be sufficient for personal jurisdiction. Weintraub, Commentary on the Conflict of Laws §2.15A at 46. Nevertheless, the black letter rules announced by most courts seem to leave little room for a technical domicile exception, though scholars want one.[6]

A strong argument could be made that technical domicile should never be enough to establish a state's interest in applying its law to a case. However,

---

6. The Second Restatement originally accepted even technical domicile as a basis for personal jurisdiction. Second Restatement §29. This was later revised to provide an exception for "the highly unusual case where the individual's relationship to the state is so attenuated as to make the exercise of such [personal] jurisdiction unreasonable." Id. 1988 revision.

interest analysis and the Second Restatement do not always encourage a consideration of the real circumstances of a party's relationship to a jurisdiction. This is especially evident in cases where parties are domiciled in one state but have been living for extended periods in another state.

Courts employing interest analysis tend to consider only the interests of the state of legal domicile, even though the state of residence may have a more immediate interest in the well-being of the parties. For example, guest statute cases involving college students have applied the law of common legal domicile even when both students are adults, living for extended periods — indeed their entire adult lives in some cases — in another state. MacDonald v. General Motors Corp., 110 F.3d 337 (6th Cir. 1997) (applying legal domicile of college student rather than state where she attended a state university in an accident occurring during a school-sponsored trip); Tooker v. Lopez, 249 N.E.2d 394 (N.Y. 1969) (finding New York had "only real interest" in case involving 20-year-old student living most of the year in Michigan, attending Michigan State University, and killed in Michigan). It is unclear why the state of legal domicile has an interest in applying its law under such circumstances, or why, if it has some interest, its interest is greater than that of the place where the parties were living. Reliance on domicile seems motivated more by formalism, the desire to adhere to black letter rules, than by any functional analysis of policy consequences.

Changing Domicile   A special problem for modern approaches arises in cases where parties have changed their domicile after the occurrence or transaction that is the subject of litigation. Most of the cases involve post-accident changes of domicile in torts, and the problem is also referred to as the problem of after-acquired domicile. The Second Restatement recognized the problem. Without formulating a rule, it observed, "Presumably, this change of domicil should have no effect upon the law governing most of the issues involving the accident. But is this necessarily true of all issues? The problem is not dealt with in the Restatement . . . because existing authority is too sparse to warrant doing so."[7]

Courts are divided but show a strong preference for applying parties' domicile at the time of the occurrence. When plaintiffs change domicile, courts have refused to consider the post-accident move. The opinions explain this by pointing out that recognizing a beneficial change of domicile would encourage forum shopping. They do so even in cases where forum shopping can be excluded as a motive. Reich v. Purcell, 432 P.2d

---

7. Second Restatement topic 1 (torts), introductory note at 414.

727 (Cal. 1967); Hall v. General Motors Corp., 582 N.W.2d 866 (Mich. App. 1998). When plaintiffs move to a new jurisdiction whose law denies recovery, courts have also disregarded the change of domicile. Phillips v. General Motors Corp., 995 P.2d 1002 (Mont. 2000); Gore v. Northeast Airlines, 373 F.2d 717 (2d Cir. 1967). In such cases, courts reason that conduct-regulating interests are advanced even if the plaintiff has moved. They also observe that such moves are never motivated by forum-shopping goals and that it would be unfair to punish parties for changing residence for other valid reasons.

Courts have been less uniform in their treatment of cases where defendants have changed domicile. In Miller v. Miller, 237 N.E.2d 877 (N.Y. 1968), a New York resident was killed in Maine, which limited wrongful death damages. The defendant moved from Maine to New York before the lawsuit was filed. In applying New York law and rejecting Maine's limits on damages, the New York court observed that the post-accident move was not motivated by forum shopping, and it reasoned that Maine no longer had an interest in applying its law. In contrast, in Schultz v. Boy Scouts of America, Inc., 480 N.E.2d 679 (N.Y. 1985), the court disregarded a defendant's move of its national headquarters from a foreign state whose law provided a defense of charitable immunity to another foreign state whose law did not provide a defense. Rather than reasoning that the original state no longer had an interest in applying its law, the court distinguished Miller and emphasized that the change did not affect New York's interests as a forum.

Example

Moving Home

11. Mr. and Ms. Pendergast, citizens of the state of South Jersey, decided to move to West Dakota. They paid off all their debts, loaded all their earthly goods into a trailer, hitched the trailer to Mr. Pendergast's pickup, and set off for West Dakota. All along the way, they sang, "West Dakota here we come; we can't wait to make you home."

   Mrs. Pendergast died tragically on the roads of East Dakota when Mr. Pendergast swerved off the highway to avoid hitting a horse. After the accident Mr. Pendergast completed his move to West Dakota. There he has been named defendant in a wrongful death suit brought by the estate of Mrs. Pendergast, which alleges he caused her death negligently.

   Both South Jersey and East Dakota recognize spousal immunity and would bar the lawsuit. West Dakota rejects spousal immunity. What law will the West Dakota courts apply?

Explanations

Bad Faith

1. If Pam's claim is classified as a tort, then section 145 applies. If her claim is classified as a personal injury, then there is an additional special rule (section 146) that directs the application of West Carolina law, where the injuries resulting from Defensco's bad faith occurred, unless another state has a more significant relationship to the occurrence and the parties. If the claim is classified as arising from an implied obligation in the contract, then section 188 applies, directing application of East Carolina law, where the place of negotiation and performance may have been.

   The "correct" answer will be more complicated under the Second Restatement, of course, because the specific tort rule in section 146 can be displaced by the law of the place with the most significant relationship. And section 188 states that the law of the place of negotiation-performance "usually" applies. But the general rules for torts and contracts themselves list different contacts, and it is possible that they would select a different law to apply.

   A Second Restatement court that emphasizes interest analysis considerations under section 6 would not avoid the need for characterization because the purpose of the laws will affect the strength of different interests and policies.

   The proper answer depends on proper characterization. What characterization is proper is properly problematic.

In a Jam

2. The outcome will depend on whether the Jungalia defense is characterized as loss-shifting (designed to prevent recoveries against Jungalia defendants) or conduct-regulating (designed to encourage risky hunting activity). If loss-shifting, then the case is a false conflict: all courts should apply Marmaland's law because Marmaland has the sole interest in applying its compensation policies in a case between parties domiciled in Marmaland. If the rule is conduct-regulating, then both jurisdictions have an interest in applying their law. Pure interest analysis would direct application of forum law. Modified forms of interest analysis might seek to accommodate different governmental interests.

Promises, Promises

3. The example is taken from Bernkrant v. Fowler, 360 P.2d 906 (Cal. 1961). First, we'll consider how interest analysis would treat the case. Applying interest analysis, the California court was able to avoid characterizing the issue as one of substance or procedure. It turned its attention to

the purposes of the state laws in conflict. It found that California's statute served to protect estates administered in California from fraudulent claims based on oral promises. It also found that Nevada and California shared a strong interest in enforcing the justified expectations of parties.

Ganrud's residence at the time he made the oral promise was unclear from the record, so the court considered two possibilities. If Ganrud resided in Nevada at that time, the court concluded that it would be unreasonable to frustrate the expectations of the parties by applying the forum's statute of frauds. If Ganrud resided in California, the court concluded that it would still be unreasonable to apply the forum's statute of frauds to frustrate the expectations of parties because the parties would not know at the time of contracting where the promisor would die domiciled.

The court concluded that the dispute presented a false conflict, so it disregarded the California's statute of frauds and enforced the oral promise under Nevada law. It basically converted the conflict into a false conflict by narrowly construing the purposes of forum law and then applying the law of the only interested state, Nevada.

This was not the only possible solution applying interest analysis. A court could just as easily have concluded that there was a true conflict between the forum's administrative interest served by the statute of frauds and the foreign state's interest in enforcing the oral promise. Pure interest analysis would then apply the forum statute and bar the claim. In contrast, comparative impairment would proceed to consider the effect of disregarding each jurisdiction's laws. Comparative impairment might well conclude that the foreign state's powerful interests would have been most significantly impaired by the nonapplication of its law.

Second, we'll consider how the Second Restatement would treat this case. For the Second Restatement, statutes of frauds, like other formalities, are substantive and governed by the law of the place with the most significant relationship in the absence of an effective choice of law by the parties. The Second Restatement's preference for validation is expressed in a subrule that formalities meeting the requirements of the place of execution will usually be acceptable. Second Restatement §199(2).

The outcome of a consideration of policies and interests under section 6 of the Second Restatement is not entirely clear because the purposes of the statutes and also the domicile of defendant at the time of contracting were uncertain. But several factors favor enforcement, including the parties' justified expectations. Section 188 contacts are similarly divided. But it is likely the court would emphasize place of negotiation and plaintiffs' performance in reliance on the oral promise. These contacts would support a finding that Nevada had the most significant relationship to the issue.

How Long, How Long?

4. Under the Second Restatement, each jurisdiction would apply its own statute of limitations. Under the original version of the Second Restatement, each jurisdiction applies its own statute of limitations, whether longer or shorter. Under the 1988 revised version, a forum still would apply its own shorter statute unless it was an unusual case and there was something unreasonable about applying its own shorter statute. There is nothing unusual or unreasonable here, and the forum has strong reasons for dismissing stale claims.

    In Nelson v. International Paint Co., 716 F.2d 640 (9th Cir. 1983), the court applied California's interest analysis to similar facts, and concluded that California had an interest in applying its statute of limitations to protect California residents and courts from stale claims.

5. Under the Second Restatement, each jurisdiction would apply its own statute of limitations. Under the original version of the Second Restatement, forum law applied to statutes of limitations whether they were shorter or longer. Under the 1988 revision, a forum will almost always apply its own shorter statute (see Example 4). The forums with longer limitations periods will also apply their own longer statutes unless (1) the forum has no substantial interest; and (2) the claim is barred by a state with a more significant relationship to the parties and occurrence. Here the jurisdictions have a substantial interest because claims are asserted that arose in their territory or are asserted against parties affiliated with the states. California (the state where the claim is time-barred) does not have a more significant relationship to the occurrence based on the fact that the plaintiff is from that state.

    In a case with similar facts, a federal court applying California's interest analysis permitted the claim. Ledesma v. Jack Stewart Produce, Inc., 816 F.2d 482 (9th Cir. 1987). It reasoned that a main purpose of the short statute was to protect California residents. The court concluded Arizona had an interest in applying its longer statute of limitations (assuming, without saying, that the rule was conduct-regulating). While California had an interest in barring stale claims, its interest was limited to judicial economy because no California defendants were present. The court then applied comparative impairment and determined that Arizona's interest in deterring injurious conduct would be more significantly impaired by not applying its law.

6 Confused? Welcome to the club. The facts and names are lifted from a real case from California. The trial court held that Oklahoma law applied and dismissed. The court of appeals unanimously reversed. The state supreme court unanimously reversed the reversal. See McCann v. Foster Wheeler LLC, 225 P.3d 516 (Cal. 2010).

This would not be an easy case under the First Restatement or the original version of the Second Restatement. Both direct a forum to apply a foreign statute of repose because it is "substantive" and cuts off the right as well as the remedy. But they would apply the substantive statute only if the cause of action arose in the foreign state. There is much uncertainty about where the plaintiff suffered the injury that would establish the place of wrong under the First Restatement.

Similar uncertainty explains why the California courts did not read their borrowing statute (with its exception) to require application of Oklahoma's statute of repose. Instead, they concluded that the borrowing statute did not (or rather might not) apply. This required them to choose between California and Oklahoma law under the state's version of comparative impairment.

The court of appeals determined that Oklahoma's statute of repose advanced loss-shifting policies. The court concluded that the state's interest was not advanced by applying the defense in favor of the defendant, a New York corporation acting in New York. In contrast the court found that California had an interest in providing a remedy in favor of a long-term California resident. In other words, the court of appeals classified the case as a false conflict and reasoned that California's statute of limitations should apply because only California had an interest in the application of its law.

The court of appeals also considered the possibility that there was a true conflict. It concluded that California law should still apply because California's remedial policy would be more seriously impaired if it were not applied than would Oklahoma's policy of limiting liability.

The Supreme Court of California reversed. First, it found there was a true conflict. It found that Oklahoma had a state interest in applying its statute of repose to limit the liability of both in-state and out-of-state businesses. Second, it found that California's state interest would be less seriously impaired by not applying it because the conduct giving rise to the claim occurred in Oklahoma.

The supreme court attributed to Oklahoma the interest of protecting non-resident corporations. It reasoned that applying the statute of repose to out-of-state businesses encouraged them to engage in the construction activity in Oklahoma. This reasoning is questionable under the facts of the case because parties don't usually rely on a statute of repose and because the Oklahoma statute was enacted decades after the conduct giving rise to liability. The reasoning is also troubling insofar as it can transform just about any loss-shifting rule into a conduct-regulating one.

The supreme court also restrictively construed California's remedial interest. It reasoned that the place of conduct has primary authority for regulating the consequences of the conduct and that a person entering another state should reasonable expect to be bound by that state's law. 225 P.3d at 535, 536.

Going in Circles

7. Neither the Second Restatement nor interest analysis applies renvoi to torts or contracts. No modern approach will apply the law of Neverland solely because Indian Country's choice of law rule applies the law of Neverland. Nevertheless, the decision of which local law to apply under both the Second Restatement and interest analysis can be influenced by the fact that Indian Country would not apply its own law.

Addressing these facts, the Second Restatement unhelpfully restates the consequences of the general torts rule: a court should apply the law of Indian Country (the place of injury and plaintiff's domicile) if the court determines that is the state with the most significant relationship. But the Second Restatement adds that courts may consider whether Indian Country would apply its own local law in deciding whether that is the state with the most significant relationship. See Second Restatement §145 illus. 3. The Second Restatement does not indicate the outcome and plainly suggests that it is possible for courts to reach different outcomes, since it is possible for a Second Restatement court to conclude that Indian Country is the state with the most significant relationship even though Indian Country would not apply its own law.

A court applying interest analysis could similarly consider Indian Country's choice rule for possible evidence of Indian Country's governmental interest in applying its law. This consideration could affect the classification of the conflict as a false conflict and lead interest analysis to apply the local law of the only state with an interest in applying its law.

The reasons for Indian Country's choice rule could be important. If Indian Country adopts interest analysis, its decision not to apply its law expresses its conclusion that Indian Country lacks an interest in applying its law. This would mean the case is either a false conflict or an unprovided-for case. If, however, Indian Country applies the law of the place of the injury for some reason other than lack of interest in applying its law, then its choice of law rules may not be good guides to the governmental purpose of its law.

8. The law that would be chosen is not certain partly because the reasons behind the strict liability rule are not known. But the analysis under both the Second Restatement and interest analysis approaches could be affected by Walloonia's choice of law rule, which limits its enforcement of its own tort rule to injuries sustained in Walloonia. This would be especially true if Walloonia limited its application of its fault rule because of a finding that it had no governmental interest in applying its tort rule extraterritorially.

First, we'll consider the Second Restatement. The Second Restatement applies the local law of the state with the most significant relationship to the occurrence and parties, and it specifies the law of the place of injury (Leberwurst) for personal injury actions unless another state has a more significant relationship. The most significant relationship is determined by considering policies and interests. And "in judging a state's interest . . . the forum should concern itself with the question whether the courts of that state would have applied [their own law]." Second Restatement §145 cmt. h.

Courts following the Second Restatement could find that Walloonia's choice of law rule indicates that Walloonia has no interest in applying its law in this case. *See, e.g.*, Phillips v. General Motors Corp., 995 P.2d 1002 (Mont. 2000) (finding North Carolina's interest in applying its law was weak based on fact North Carolina would not apply its own law because it was not the law of the place of the injury); Griggs v. Riley, 489 S.W.2d 469 (Mo. App. 1972) (refraining from applying foreign guest statute where co-domiciliaries' home court would not apply defense to accident occurring in another state). For example, courts applying the Second Restatement might conclude that the rule advances a conduct-regulating purpose that is limited to reducing injuries in Walloonia. Courts that conclude Walloonia has no interest will disregard most of the listed contacts under section 145 and find that the place of the injury is the most relevant contact. They will apply Leberwurst local law, the law of the only state with an interest, as the law of the state with the most significant relationship.

Other courts applying the Second Restatement might find that Walloonia's choice rule is not a guide to that state's interest, especially if Walloonia follows the traditional *lex loci* and does not address the force of the state's interest in the outcome of the decision. For example, in Pfau v. Trent Aluminum Co., 263 A.2d 129 (N.J. 1970), the New Jersey court concluded that Connecticut had a governmental interest in the application of its tort law, even though Connecticut still followed traditional conflicts rules and would not have applied its tort laws to an accident occurring outside the state. The New Jersey court, applying interest analysis, observed that the traditional choice rules do not identify a state's governmental interests in applying its local law.

If the Walloonia choice rule does not indicate that state's interests, then its local tort law does. If, for example, the requirement of fault is loss-shifting, designed to reduce costs of business, then the most relevant contacts are the parties' common domicile. Looking at such interests, Walloonia might be the state with the most significant relationship to the parties and occurrence with respect to the issue even though Walloonia would not apply its own law.

Second, we'll consider interest analysis. A court applying interest analysis would begin by determining whether the conflict between the tort standards is true or false. This requires an evaluation of whether each state has governmental policies that would be advanced by the application of its local law. In determining Walloonia's governmental interest, interest analysis could consider the fact that Walloonia would not apply its own law in this case.

Walloonia's choice rule might indicate that Walloonia has no interest in applying its law. This would be the case if Walloonia decisions apply interest analysis. If Walloonia decisions were based on traditional conflicts rules, then an interest analysis court would be less likely to find that the Walloonia decision expresses a lack of governmental interest in applying its law.

If Walloonia has no interest, then Leberwurst would apply its own forum rule under interest analysis either because the case is either a false conflict or an unprovided-for case.

Policy Odysseys

9. Northern California will almost certainly refuse to recognize the claims here, but it will not necessarily rely on the public policy exception. Under a variety of modern choice of law approaches, it could conclude that the forum's interest in applying its own law supports application of forum law, that contacts point decisively in favor of applying forum law, or even that forum law is the better law.

   The example illustrates how the public policy escape device may be less important for modern approach jurisdictions, where it will affect outcomes only when the modern approaches select the other state's law. Here the public policy exception might provide an additional reason for refusing to apply East Carolina law, but it is probably unnecessary.

   A case where public policy would make a difference would be a situation where all the parties were living in a state that recognized claims for criminal conversation and alienation of affections, and the wrongful acts occurred in that state. Even in such a case, a forum state's policy against such claims might support a choice of forum law without needing to refer to the public policy exception. But public policy would be available to permit a forum to avoid recognizing the foreign law if it deemed it sufficiently offensive.

10. This is a clear case for dismissing a cause of action offensive to the strong public policy of the forum. Liquidated damages of this sort surely fall within anyone's definition of "contrary to public policy." Here the offensive law supports the cause of action. It is not a defense. Even though the forum does not have an obvious interest to be advanced by applying its own law, it can dismiss the claim as contrary to its public policy.

The Second Restatement and treatises emphasize that courts should dismiss under such circumstances and not apply their own law. The better law approach provides some authority for a court to apply its own, better law. If a court merely dismisses under the doctrine of forum non conveniens, then the action can be commenced elsewhere. If the forum applies its own law and dismisses on the merits, then the judgment will preclude relitigation.

The case is easy because the facts are so outrageous. But more realistic cases are far less certain. Suppose, for example, Able agrees to sell Baker an Ipod in the country of Einsland, and their written contract provides that Able will pay Baker $1 million in the event of a breach. Einsland enforces all liquidated damages clauses as written under the theory of freedom of contract. Zweiland, however, refuses to enforce liquidated damages agreements that bear no reasonable relationship to the parties' anticipated or actual damages.

If Able and Baker are from Einsland and the contract was executed and to be performed there, then Einsland law would govern under most choice of law approaches. Nevertheless, the Zweiland forum might invoke public policy to explain its refusal to enforce, though it is uncertain why it would care to do so because the adverse consequences of enforcement would be felt exclusively in a country that welcomes them. The forum's lack of interest is a strong reason not to allow litigation, but that should be protected by the doctrine of forum non conveniens.

Moving Home

11. This example illustrates both technical domicile and changing domicile. At the time of the accident, both spouses remained domiciled in South Jersey even though they had left it forever. They were not yet domiciled in West Dakota because their intent to make West Dakota their new home had not (yet) coincided with physical presence in that jurisdiction. This leads to the odd result that South Jersey's law will apply to a loss-shifting issue even though that state no longer has any interest in applying its law based on any connection with the parties, except for their past domicile.

The defendant's post-accident move should not change the result, but you don't need to address the problem of changing domicile rules to reach this conclusion. The new home state would have no interest in applying its pro-recovery loss-shifting rule in favor of the nondomiciliary decedent.

PART V

Choice of Law
in Federal Courts

24 The *Erie* Doctrine

INTRODUCTION

The *Erie* doctrine requires federal courts to apply state law in certain cases. This chapter reviews the *Erie* doctrine and explains how to solve *Erie* problems.

The bad news is that almost 80 years after the *Erie* decision, there are still unanswered questions about when federal courts must apply state law—and even why they must do so. The good news is that the Supreme Court has consistently held that choice of law rules are "substantive" for purposes of *Erie*. This means federal courts in diversity cases must apply state choice of law rules. Generally, federal courts in diversity cases will apply the same conflicts rules as the state in which they are sitting.

There is one exception. When a case was transferred from a federal court in one state to a federal court in another state pursuant to section 1404(a), then the second federal court will apply the state conflicts law that the original federal court would have applied.

THE BIG PICTURE

Federal Laws as Supreme   The U.S. Constitution created a federal court system. The Supremacy Clause declares that the Constitution, laws, and treaties are the supreme law of the land. U.S. Const. art. VI. These laws are binding on both federal and state courts.

For example, if Congress passes a federal statute barring personal injury claims by pedestrians walking along railroad tracks, then that statute will be binding on all courts. Of course, the statute must be valid. Constitutional ideas have changed over time. Such a statute would probably have been considered unconstitutional in 1889 but constitutional in 1989.

Diversity and Judge-Made Law   The jurisdiction of federal courts extends to many cases that do not involve federal laws. They include some diversity and alienage cases between citizens of one state and citizens of another state or foreign country.

An early federal statute, the Rules of Decision Act, directed federal courts to apply the laws of the several states as rules of decision. This statute is still alive and well. 28 U.S.C. §1652 ("The laws of the several states . . . shall be regarded as rules of decision in civil actions in the courts of the United States, in cases where they apply.").

Swift and Federal General Common Law up to 1938   The Supreme Court held in Swift v. Tyson (1841) that the word "laws" in the Rules of Decision Act did not include state judge-made common law. The Court concluded that federal judges could and should make their own common law rules of decision in diversity cases when there was no state statute or state constitutional provision on point.

This practice of federal judges making rules of decision in diversity cases is called federal general common law. It meant that two different legal rules could apply in the same case. For example, if Donna Defendant injured Pat Plaintiff in Pennsylvania, Pennsylvania judge-made law might require Pat to prove gross negligence in order to recover. But if Pat were a citizen of Pennsylvania and Donna a citizen of New York, Pat might bring the action in federal court under diversity — or Donna might remove the action from state to federal court.

Federal courts deciding the same dispute would not apply a Pennsylvania judge-made rule. Instead, creating federal general common law, federal courts would require Pat to prove only ordinary negligence in order to recover.

Things were not as bad as they might sound. First, not all state law claims could be brought in or removed to federal court. Second, federal courts applied state procedure in olden times even when they applied their own general common law. Third, if state lawmakers hated a federal general common law rule of decision, then they could enact a state statute that would be binding on federal judges under the Rules of Decision Act. Fourth, if Congress hated the federal common law on some issue, it could pass a federal statute binding under the Supremacy Clause.

The* Erie *Revolution   In 1938, the Supreme Court overruled *Swift* and held that federal courts have no authority to make federal general common law. Erie Railroad Co. v. Tompkins, 304 U.S. 64 (1938). In diversity cases, federal courts must apply state judge-made common law as well as state statutes.

The Big Three

Erie   In *Erie*, Tompkins was injured in Pennsylvania by a train operated by the Erie Railroad. Tompkins could have sued in state court, but he sued in federal court because federal judges applied federal general common law and would permit recovery for ordinary negligence. In contrast, Pennsylvania common law required proof of willful or wanton negligence, which Tompkins could not prove.

The Supreme Court reversed the decisions of the lower federal courts, which had applied the federal general common law rule of decision. First, the *Erie* opinion reinterpreted the word "laws" in the Rules of Decision Act. It held that the statute covers state judge-made common law. Second, the opinion declared that *Swift* was unconstitutional because federal courts lacked constitutional authority to create federal general common law. "There is no federal general common law."[1]

Guaranty Trust v. York   The meaning of the *Erie* decision was unsettled at first. Some federal courts thought it was restricted to traditional common law cases like torts and contracts. Others thought it prohibited federal courts only from creating rules of decision like standards of care that deviated from state law.

This explains why the lower courts did not apply state law in Guaranty Trust Co. v. York, 326 U.S. 99 (1945). That lawsuit was in federal court based on diversity jurisdiction but the claim was for breach of trust—a traditional matter of "equity," not "common law." The exact issue was whether the federal judge must apply the state statute of limitations or should instead apply the judge-made equitable defense of laches. The lower courts concluded even after *Erie* that federal courts could apply the federal judge-made defense. They reasoned that the issue was one of "procedure" and "equity."

The Supreme Court reversed. It clarified that *Erie* requires federal courts to apply state statutes of limitations. More important, the Court explained

---

1. The bulk of the opinion addresses policy and philosophical problems with federal general common law. This discussion can be hard to follow but is purely icing on the cake. Even if federal general common law was nifty, the Court concluded that it was unconstitutional. Justice Reed concurred with the result but questioned the constitutional basis of the holding. For him the statutory and policy issues were decisive. I think Justice Reed was right, but the Court has not yet recognized this. That is why this discussion is in the footnotes, which you can skip.

that the *Erie* doctrine's repudiation of federal authority to make judge-made laws in diversity cases broadly extends to many issues that might be called procedural, and it is not limited to traditional common law claims. The Court emphasized that the goal of *Erie* was to achieve the same outcome in federal or state courts "so far as legal rules determine the outcome of a litigation."

Guaranty Trust acknowledged that federal courts were not required to apply all details of state "procedure." The Court announced the general rule that federal courts must apply state law to matters of substance. The test for whether a matter is substantive is: "[D]oes it significantly affect the result of a litigation for a federal court to disregard a law of a State that would be controlling in an action upon the same claim by the same parties in a State court?" It does not matter how a state classifies its own rule. A state might call its statute of limitation "procedural," yet the state statute of limitations is a matter of substance under the *Erie* doctrine because it significantly affects the result of litigation.

One problem with the outcome-determination test is that it is almost always satisfied. Even a rule regulating the size of staples can affect the outcome of litigation if the clerk will not accept papers stapled with the wrong-sized staple. The Supreme Court later[2] suggested two additional considerations that help in applying the test. First, consider whether a different federal rule would affect the result in a way that would encourage forum shopping and frustrate equitable administration of the laws. Second, consider whether the effect on the result is significant or substantial — whether applying a different federal rule would have a direct and certain impact on the result or whether the impact would be indirect and speculative. For example, a rule requiring different-sized staples would not affect results in a way that would promote forum shopping, and the impact of such a difference on outcomes is speculative.

Byrd   For years after *Guaranty Trust*, the Supreme Court applied the result-of-litigation test to invalidate federal practices whenever they made a difference in the outcome. The Court signaled a shift in Byrd v. Blue Ridge Rural Electric Cooperative, 356 U.S. 525 (1958). The issue in that case was whether a federal trial judge must follow the law of the state in which the court was sitting that required the judge to decide a particular fact question or whether the federal court could follow its own policy of sending the question to the jury. *Byrd* held that federal courts should follow their own federal practice and leave the factfinding on this issue to the jury. The Supreme Court went out of its way to clarify and readjust the scope of the *Erie* decision. The Court's analysis indicates the need for classifying cases.

---

2. It did this in dictum in Hanna v. Plumer, which is discussed in the next section.

First, Byrd clarified that *Erie* held that federal courts must enforce state-created rights and liabilities — and matters bound up with such rights and liabilities. It concluded that the state law in *Byrd* that required factfinding by the judge was merely a form and mode for enforcing the defense, not a rule bound up with the rights and liabilities.

Second, Byrd explained that *Erie* also advanced a broader policy of federal-state uniformity in diversity cases. This policy was advanced by *Guaranty Trust's* significantly-affects-result-of-litigation test. The Court conceded that a rule that directed a judge rather than a jury to decide a disputed fact might affect the result, and the *Erie* uniformity policy might indicate that federal courts should follow the state practice — if outcome were the only consideration.

Third, Byrd announced for the first time that considerations other than outcome uniformity could lead a federal court to disregard state law even when doing so significantly affected the result of litigation. The Court found such countervailing considerations in federal judicial control over the division of functions between judge and jury. It concluded that this control was an essential characteristic of federal courts that should not be disrupted by different state rules.

The Court found a federal policy favoring jury decisionmaking and further found that this policy was more important than the *Erie* policy of uniformity. One source of confusion is the opinion's reference to a federal preference for jury decisionmaking under the "influence" of the Seventh Amendment. The Court specifically refused to hold that the Seventh Amendment applied. Obviously, if the Constitution required jury decisionmaking, then the decision would be an easy one, and there would be no room for the Court to carve out a balancing test.

"Guided *Erie*": Rules Enabling Act Cases

The Supreme Court follows a different approach for diversity cases covered by federal rules adopted under the Rules Enabling Act. This approach is sometime called "guided *Erie*" analysis because the analysis is guided by reference to the Act.

Rules Covered The Rules Enabling Act gives the Supreme Court authority to promulgate rules of "practice and procedure and rules of evidence" so long as the rules do "not abridge, enlarge or modify any substantive right." 28 U.S.C. §2072(a) & (b). Rules created under the Rules Enabling Act include the numbered rules set forth in the Federal Rules of Civil Procedure, Federal Rules of Appellate Procedure, and Federal Rules of Evidence. Not all federal procedural rules are adopted under this authority. For example, the federal procedural rule allocating factfinding to the jury in *Byrd* was a judge-made rule, not a rule adopted under the Rules Enabling Act.

Hanna v. Plumer The Court announced the guided-Erie approach in Hanna v. Plumer, 380 U.S. 460 (1965). State law required personal delivery of service of process. In contrast, Federal Rule of Civil Procedure 4 authorized residence service.

The lower federal courts applied the outcome-determination test and required federal courts to follow the state service rules. The Supreme Court reversed. The Court emphasized that the validity of a Rules Enabling Act rule was not governed by the "unguided" application of Erie policies. On the contrary, a Federal Rule of Civil Procedure was valid so long as it (1) applies to the matter at hand and (2) "really regulates procedure—the judicial process for enforcing rights and duties recognized by substantive law and for justly administering remedy and redress for disregard or infraction of them."

Problem of Interpreting Scope of Particular Rules The greatest uncertainty in applying *Hanna*'s guided Erie approach is deciding whether a particular rule actually applies to a specific issue in litigation. The Supreme Court has sometimes (but not always) narrowly interpreted a Federal Rule of Civil Procedure. An example is Walker v. Armco Steel Corp., 446 U.S. 740 (1980), where the Court decided that "commencing" a lawsuit under Federal Rule 3 does not mean an action is commenced for purposes of satisfying a state statute of limitations. In narrowly construing the scope of rules, the Supreme Court sometimes relies on precedent and sometimes on a sort of federalist policy of avoiding clashes with state laws.

In contrast, in other cases the Court has given broad scope to the federal rules, reasoning that one of their chief goals is to make federal practice uniform, even when doing so causes deviations from state practices. An example is Burlington Northern Railroad Co. v. Woods, 480 U.S. 1 (1987), where the Court construed a Federal Rule of Appellate Procedure's grant of authority to award damages for frivolous appeals as vesting such broad discretion in federal appellate judges that it conflicted with and thus displaced a state rule that imposed mandatory sanctions.

In Shady Grove Orthopedic Associates, P.A. v. Allstate Insurance Co., 130 S. Ct. 1431 (2010), plaintiffs wanted to bring class action in federal court combining thousands of individual claims for statutory penalties under New York law. But New York prohibited consolidating such claims. The Supreme Court held that combining claims was permitted by Federal Rule of Civil Procedure. But four Justices dissented, urging a more restrained reading of Rule 23 in order to avoid frustrating the New York policy of limiting the potential exposure imposed by multiple statutory penalties.

Trust me, these seeming inconsistencies bug your Conflicts teacher as much as they bug you. The best you (or they) can do when faced with an Enabling Act rule is to recognize the possibility that the Supreme Court may narrowly construe the rule so as to avoid it trumping state law. And when some members of the Court narrowly construe a rule, they say they are giving it its plain meaning.

Test for Procedure The Supreme Court applies a different test to whether Federal Rules of Civil Procedure are authorized as "procedure" under the Enabling Act. Such rules are procedural when they regulate how issues are presented to and decided by courts. This is a much broader and more forgiving definition of "procedure" than *Guaranty*'s significantly-affects-result-of-litigation test. Many things that are "substantive" under the unguided *Erie* cases would be "procedural" under the guided *Erie* test. For example, federal rules providing for discovery and class actions decisively affect results of litigation and have a huge impact on forum selection. But they regulate how issues are presented to and decided by courts. An unguided *Erie* analysis would conclude that federal judges could not establish such practices on their own. But a guided analysis of the rules promulgated under the Rules Enabling Act would conclude that the rules are valid because they are procedural. It is unclear how far the guided *Erie* definition of "procedure" stretches. At the extreme, even statutes of limitations might be considered procedural.

Choice of Law

Supreme Law of the Land A few conflicts cases are governed by a federal constitutional provision, an act of Congress, or a treaty. When they are, those federal rules are the supreme law of the land in both federal and state courts. For example, in a lawsuit against the U.S. government brought under the Federal Torts Claim Act (an act of Congress), claims must be brought in federal court, and the courts must apply the whole law (including the conflicts rules) of the state or other place where the act or omission occurred. Richards v. United States, 369 U.S. 1 (1962). This is because the Act provides for governmental liability "under circumstances where the United States, if a private person, would be liable to the claimant in accordance with the law of the place where the act or omission occurred." 28 U.S.C. §1346. The Supreme Court held that the word "law" in the Act means "whole law of the State where the act or omission occurred." The federal statute (as interpreted by the Supreme Court) is valid and applies.

Congress can enact rules for federal courts that are different from state law. Of course, there can sometimes be a question about what a federal statute actually means, and the Supreme Court has the final word (until the statute is amended). For example, Congress authorizes a federal district judge to transfer a case to another district where it might have been brought when the transfer is for the convenience of parties and witnesses and in the interest of justice. 28 U.S.C. §1404(a). The Supreme Court held that federal judges granting transfers can enforce forum selection agreements even when the agreements are void and unenforceable under state contract law. Stewart Organization, Inc. v. Ricoh Corp., 487 U.S. 22 (1988).

Klaxon   Most conflicts cases that are in federal court due to diversity jurisdiction are not governed by any provision of the Constitution, act of Congress, or treaty. In Klaxon Co. v. Stentor Electric Mfg. Co., 313 U.S. 487 (1941), the Supreme Court applied unguided *Erie* analysis and found that state choice of law rules affect the result of litigation and are "substantive" for purposes of *Erie*. Federal courts sitting in diversity must apply the conflict of laws rules that would be applied by the state. This is necessary to achieve *Erie*'s goal of having state and federal courts in the same state decide cases the same way.

The Court has refused to deviate under the press of modern theories, holding that federal courts in diversity must apply state choice of law rules even if the case is a false conflict. Day & Zimmermann, Inc. v. Challoner, 423 U.S. 3 (1975) (holding that federal court in Texas was obligated to apply law of place of the injury under Texas choice of law even though the place of injury had no conceivable interest in preventing recovery).

Klaxon *Critics*   The *Klaxon* Court's refusal to develop federal choice of law rules in diversity cases has been unpopular with Conflicts gurus.[3] These scholars argue that *Erie*'s federalist concerns do not apply in conflicts cases because the federal government is expressly empowered and uniquely situated to resolve conflicts between state laws under the Full Faith and Credit Clause. They also argue that *Erie*'s hostility to judge-made substantive laws has less application in conflicts cases, where courts are just selecting between rules of decision and where this selection process has been traditionally exercised by judges.

The argument for special federal choice rules is strongest in a federal interpleader case, where federal courts have jurisdiction but no state court does. In such a case, there could be no incentive to forum shop. Nevertheless, the Supreme Court has ruled that federal courts must apply state choice of law rules even in interpleader actions. Griffin v. McCoach, 313 U.S. 498 (1941).

Which State's *Conflicts Law?*   The goals of federal-state uniformity make it obvious which state's conflicts laws must apply in almost all cases. Unless there is a transfer, the federal court must apply the state conflicts rules of the state in which the court is sitting. When the action was properly pending in

---

3. E.g., Richman et al., Understanding Conflict of Laws §107 at 346–47; Hay et al., Conflict of Laws §3.36 at 182; Weintraub, Commentary on the Conflict of Laws §10.8 at 767.

one district but transferred to another more convenient district under section 1404(a), the federal court will apply the state conflicts rules of the state from which the case was transferred. Ferens v. John Deere Co., 494 U.S. 516 (1989). When an action is brought in the wrong federal court and federal statutes authorize transfer to cure defects in jurisdiction or venue or when a federal court transfers an action to enforce a mandatory forum selection clause, then the federal court after transfer will apply the conflicts law of the state in which it is sitting. (See Chapter 5.)

Solving *Erie* Cases

A few pointers will help avoid the most common problems in Erie situations.

Look *Before* You Leap   Identify the sources of the state and federal laws in conflict. After Erie it does not matter whether the state rule of decision comes from a state statute or common law decision. But it still matters whether the federal law comes from the Constitution, laws, or treaties of the United States. For example, a valid and applicable federal statute is the law of the land, and a conflict between it and state law is not governed by the Erie doctrine but by the scope of the constitutional authority of Congress and the scope of the federal statute.

Consider Your Options   The solution to Erie cases depends on how the cases are classified. Be sure to consider alternatives. For example, if your problem seems to be governed by the specific language of a Federal Rule of Civil Procedure, then apply the guided Erie analysis. In doing so, consider the possibility that the specific language of the rule might be given a narrower interpretation so as to avoid a conflict between the rule and state law. If you find that the federal rule might not apply, then you should also consider how the case would be treated under the unguided Erie analysis.

Don't Look a Gift Horse in the Mouth[4]   Supreme Court decisions have authoritatively resolved many specific Erie problems. For example, *Guaranty Trust* leaves no question that federal courts in diversity cases must apply state limitations on claims even if the federal judges think the state limitations are substantively unfair. The Supreme gift for Conflicts students is *Klaxon's* holding that choice of law rules are substantive for purposes of unguided Erie analysis.

---

4. But *see* Virgil, Aeneid 2.51 (quoting Laocoon as opining that Trojans would have been better advised to reject large gift horse left by Greek adversaries without first checking contents).

What *Erie* Does Not Mean: The Survival of Federal Common Law

The *Erie* doctrine spelled death only for federal *general* common law. It did not abolish all federal judicial lawmaking. Federal courts retain authority to develop substantive rules of decision in a number of areas. In addition to interpreting and applying federal law found in the U.S. Constitution and federal statutes, these areas include:

1. disputes between states as parties
2. admiralty jurisdiction
3. federal government's rights and duties
4. international affairs

When cases in these areas require a choice of law, federal courts are not required to apply state choice of law rules, though they may choose to do so. For example, in admiralty cases, federal courts have adopted choice of law rules similar to the Second Restatement. (See Chapter 25.)

Clearfield Trust *Doctrine* The poster child for federal special common law is Clearfield Trust Co. v. United States, 318 U.S. 363 (1943). After paying a check that had been forged, the government discovered its error and sued the bank that had accepted and processed the forged check. Under state law the government's claim would have been barred because it was unreasonably delayed. But the Supreme Court held that the government's claim was not governed by state law. Instead the Court announced a special rule that government claims of this kind would be barred only if the defendant could show that the government's delay caused prejudice to the defendant.

Clearfield Trust was not governed by Erie. The case was not brought under federal diversity jurisdiction but rather under federal jurisdiction over claims by the U.S. government. The Supreme Court emphasized that the government was specifically authorized by Congress to engage in commercial activity and that the government issued a huge number of checks. The Court reasoned that the government's rights and liabilities in this area should be governed by uniform federal rules.

Clearfield identifies key ingredients for special federal common law. First, federal jurisdiction must not be based on diversity of citizenship. Second, there must be a need for a uniform federal rule. (The Supreme Court's conclusion that there was a need for a uniform federal rule in *Clearfield* is debatable. After all, huge financial institutions issue commercial paper in large quantities and are not greatly inconvenienced by the fact that Erie requires the application of different state law to different claims.)

Later cases make clear that federal courts will not automatically assume there is a need for federal uniformity that requires a special federal law different from the states' laws. In Kamen v. Kemper Financial Services, Inc., 500 U.S. 90 (1991), the Supreme Court held that state law governed aspects of a claim authorized by federal statute. The Court announced a presumption in favor of applying state law even in non-diversity cases and cautioned that special federal common law rules should be fashioned only when intended by Congress or "when the scheme in question evidences a distinct need for nationwide legal standards." The federal preference for state rules is not compelled by the Rules of Decision Act; it is itself a federalist value adopted in the course of special federal common lawmaking.

Examples

Misfire

1. Why does the following answer earn low scores during final exam season?

> Bugs sued Elmer for personal injuries sustained during the course of a hunting trip. Bugs brought the action in federal court based on diversity of citizenship jurisdiction. State law in this jurisdiction required the filing of a certificate of good cause by an attorney. The certificate required the attorney to certify that he or she had investigated the complaint, that there was good cause to proceed with litigation, and that reasonable efforts to settle the dispute out of court had not been successful. The *Erie* doctrine requires federal courts to apply state substantive law and federal procedural law. The state certificate requirement is substantive because a failure to file it in state court leads to dismissal of the claim. Dismissal will significantly affect the outcome of the lawsuit, so a federal court must apply the state law.

A Punishing *Erie* Problem

2. In the time of tort reform, the state of Confusion adopted the Freedom Fairness Act. Under the state act punitive damages can be recovered only upon proof that a defendant acted willfully and wantonly. The act further provides that the total amount of punitive damages that can be recovered is no more than twice the amount of compensatory damages recovered.

Priya, a citizen of New York, was injured by a truck operated by Dev, a citizen of the state of Confusion. Priya sues Dev in federal court in Confusion under federal diversity jurisdiction. The complaint alleges that Dev caused the injury willfully and wantonly. It demands compensatory damages in the amount of $50,000 and punitive damages in the amount of $1 million.

Dev moves for summary judgment on the claim for all punitive damages that exceed twice the amount of compensatory damages. Rule on the motion and explain.

Bright Lights . . .

3. The state of East Dakota does not permit class actions. As a result its court system has been flooded with individual lawsuits against tanning bed manufacturers and tanning salons in connection with claims that the products and services have caused skin cancer. To relieve the congestion, the state legislature enacted the Tanning Litigation Fairness and Freedom Act. The preamble to the Act explained that its purpose was to encourage the settlement of tort claims against tanning bed manufacturers and tanning salons, to expedite the litigation of unsettled claims, and to reduce the burden on state judges. The Act provided for the creation of special panels of three state judges to which all such lawsuits are transferred for settlement hearings and trial.

    Coco Skinker, a citizen of East Dakota, commences a diversity case in federal court for the District of East Dakota against Sunshine Haven Corp., a Delaware corporation with its principal place of business in Kentucky. Skinker seeks damages for personal injury stemming from the sale and marketing of tanning beds.

    The defendant moves to transfer the case from federal court to the state three-judge panel designated to hear such suits. Rule on the motion and explain.

4. Same facts. Will the federal court permit consolidation of Skinker's claim with other claims to form a class action, or must the court follow the state law barring such class actions?

Jury Justice

5. The West Carolina state constitution guarantees the right to trial by jury on all issues. The West Carolina courts have consistently construed this state constitutional right as prohibiting the granting of motions for summary judgment and motions for a directed verdict. Instead, state courts leave all disputed facts to the jury.

    In a diversity action pending in federal court in West Carolina, the defendant, Acme Co., moves for summary judgment under Federal Rule of Civil Procedure 56. The plaintiff argues that the federal court must deny the motion pursuant to the state constitutional right to jury trial. Rule on the motion and explain.

Eerie Choices of Law

6. Stella, a citizen of the state of New York, visited the state of Tradition. There she offered a ride to Luna, a citizen of the state of Tradition. Luna suffered serious personal injuries when Stella lost control of the car and hit a brick wall. Luna has brought a diversity action against Stella in federal court in New York.

   Stella moves to dismiss under a state statute in force in Tradition at the time of the accident. The statute bars all claims for personal injuries by passengers who refuse to wear seatbelts. Luna was not wearing a seatbelt at the time of the accident. Assume that in a previous case brought in New York state court, the New York Court of Appeals held that New York courts must apply the Tradition statute because it is conduct-regulating. Rule on the motion and explain.

7. The Akron Day School is a private school in Akron, Ohio, operated by Akron Day School, Inc., an Ohio corporation. The school hired Coach Pedovile, an Ohio citizen, to coach its girls' basketball team. The school did not conduct a thorough background check, which would have disclosed that Pedovile had been fired by previous employers for improper sexual advances toward students. Nor did the school conduct a search of criminal records, which would have revealed that Pedovile had pleaded guilty in Texas to a misdemeanor charge of disorderly conduct, which also stemmed from improper sexual conduct with a 14-year-old girl.

   Under Pedovile's coaching, the girls' basketball team was undefeated. The team was invited to participate in a tournament in New York. Pedovile traveled with the team. One night in New York he sexually assaulted Jamie Jameson, a student member of the team.

   After the assault, Jameson's parents moved to New Jersey. After becoming citizens of New Jersey, they commenced a diversity action against Akron Day School, Inc., in federal court for the Southern District of New York. Their complaint alleges that the school negligently hired and supervised Pedovile, and that the school's negligence caused damages to Jamie and to the parents.

   The defendant moves to dismiss based on the defense of charitable immunity. Assume that New Jersey and Ohio recognize a defense of charitable immunity but that Ohio does not apply the defense to cases alleging negligent hiring and supervision. New York does not recognize the defense of charitable immunity, but New York state courts apply the defense in cases where the law of the parties' common domicile provides a defense of charitable immunity. Assume that in this case New York and New Jersey state courts would dismiss under the law of charitable immunity but that Ohio courts would not do so.

You are the federal judge in New York. Rule on the motion to dismiss and explain.

Limitation Irritation

8. Drake served Ham Burger a bad sausage in the state of Endurance. At the time of the sausage serving both Drake and Burger were citizens of the state of Endurance. Endurance has a four-year statute of limitations on personal injury claims.

   After the accident, Burger moved to and became a domiciliary of Mississippi. Three and one-half years after the accident Burger sued Drake in Mississippi state court, demanding damages in the amount of $1 million. Drake removed the action to federal court and then moved to dismiss under the Mississippi three-year statute of limitations. Mississippi state courts characterize statutes of limitations as procedural and would apply the shorter forum statute of limitations. Rule on the motion and explain.

9. June and her infant son Teddy, citizens of the state of Northern California, flew to the state of South Florida, where Teddy had a life-saving operation performed by Doctor Whom. Unfortunately, a bottle cap was left inside Teddy during the operation.

   Fifteen years later, the bottle cap shifted location, causing pain and requiring additional surgery. Teddy brings a diversity action against Doctor Whom in federal court in Northern California. Teddy gets personal service of process on the defendant while he is attending a medical conference in Northern California.

   Doctor Whom moves to dismiss under a statute of repose in force in South Florida that extinguishes all claims for medical malpractice after 12 years. In past cases, the Northern California courts have acknowledged that statutes of repose are substantive, but they have refused to apply them in medical malpractice cases, holding that such claims are tolled indefinitely until the negligence or resulting injuries are discovered.

   You are the federal judge. Do you apply the statute of repose or the tolling rule?

Revenge of Renvoi

10. Tex, a citizen of the state of South Texas, was injured in the country of Mordor when a piece of shrapnel penetrated his body armor, causing serious personal injuries. Tex brings a civil action in federal court in South Texas against American Thrifty Armament Corp., a Delaware citizen. Assume that South Texas state courts still follow the First Restatement and would apply the law of Mordor to a claim seeking

damages for personal injuries. Under the law of Mordor, manufacturers of military goods are absolutely immune to all civil actions. The defense is not recognized in either South Texas or Delaware, and South Texas has no governmental policy that requires the application of Mordor's defense. Nor would Mordor apply its own law in this case. May the federal court in South Texas apply South Texas substantive tort law and permit recovery?

Lukewarm Air Balloon

11. Fergus, a citizen of Scotland, was injured in Scotland when the hot air balloon in which he was traveling suddenly lost altitude and collided with a tree. Fergus commenced a diversity action in federal court in California against two defendants: Hot Air Tours, Inc., a New York corporation with its principal place of business in New York, and Great Rubber Ball Corp., a Delaware corporation with its principal place of manufacturing in New York. Fergus alleges that the defendants jointly designed and manufactured a defective product, the heating mechanism for the balloon.

Hot Air Tours engages in systematic and continuous tourism marketing services in the state of California. It is, accordingly, subject to personal jurisdiction and venue in the district in which Fergus brought the action. In contrast, Great Rubber Ball Corp. is not engaged in business in California, and it is not subject to personal jurisdiction under that state's long-arm statute.

The defendants jointly moved the trial court to dismiss the action for improper jurisdiction over both defendants or, in the alternative, for an order transferring the action to federal court for the Southern District of New York. The federal judge in California agreed that the court lacked personal jurisdiction and venue over Great Rubber Ball, but rather than dismissing, she transferred the case to the Southern District of New York pursuant to 28 U.S.C. section 1406 (authorizing transfer from federal district without venue to district where case could have been brought) and section 1631 (authorizing transfer to federal district with jurisdiction).

The federal judge in California concluded jurisdiction and venue were proper in the civil action against Hot Air Tours. But the judge also transferred that action to the Southern District of New York under 28 U.S.C. section 1404(a), reasoning that more of the evidence and parties were in New York, the action could have been brought in the Southern District of New York, and trial there would be more convenient for parties and witnesses and would serve the interest of justice.

After transfer, the defendants move to dismiss under the statute of limitations. Assume the claims are time-barred under the statute of limitations in Scotland, that California state courts would apply a longer California statute of limitations and find that the claims are not time-barred, and that New York state courts would apply that state's borrowing statute and hold the claims time-barred under Scotland's statute.

What law applies to the statute of limitations?

Explanations

Misfire

1. This answer scores in the low, low land for misstating the law and for misapplying the *Erie* doctrine. In fact, it commits three *Erie* errors calculated to most inflame the passions of reasonable Civ Pro and Conflicts professors and cause them to lash out in anger. First, it wrongly states that a federal court must apply federal procedural law. Even when federal courts are not required by *Erie* to apply state law, they may still apply state law and often do so. Federal courts will apply federal procedural law when directed to do so by a valid statute or Enabling Act rule. They will establish federal practices different from state practices by judicial lawmaking only when there is an identifiable countervailing federal interest, such as the interest in controlling the division of labor between judge and jury and the federal preference for jury decisionmaking identified in *Byrd*. If there is no need for a federal wide policy, federal courts will apply state law. Moreover, some Enabling Act rules direct federal courts to apply state procedure even though valid federal rules might have created a federal-wide policy. For example, Federal Rule of Evidence 501 provides that state law governs privilege in civil actions concerning a claim or defense based on state law.

   Second, the answer makes the common mistake of saying that *Erie* requires federal courts to apply state substantive law. This is true only in a highly qualified sense, and from the first Supreme Court decisions announcing the policy of deferring to state law on matters of substance, the Supreme Court has cautioned that cases cannot be solved just by classifying a rule as one of substance or procedure. On the contrary, the Court employed in Guaranty Trust v. York a functional analysis that asks whether the law in issue significantly affects the result of litigation in a way that promotes forum shopping and frustrates equitable administration of the laws. In *Byrd* the Court amplified this by also requiring consideration of countervailing federal interests in cases where such interests existed.

   Third, the answer makes the mistake of concluding that the outcome determination test is satisfied simply because applying state law would in fact have changed the result. Even the most trivial differences can sometimes change the outcome. The question is whether the difference is substantial enough that it would attract litigants to federal court so as to violate the policies behind Erie.

There is a further problem with the answer: it assumes the applicability of the state procedure is governed by an unguided Erie consideration of whether the state certificate requirement is substantive. On an unguided Erie approach, my best guess is that the state certificate would not be binding in federal court because it is not likely to substantially affect the outcome in a way that would violate Erie's policies. At the same time, federal courts might well require compliance with the state policy.

But the case is probably guided by the analysis set forth in Hanna v. Plumer. The goal of the state certificate appears to be to require pretrial investigation of claims. This requirement is imbedded in federal practice in Federal Rule of Civil Procedure 11, adopted pursuant to the Rules Enabling Act. This rule specifies pre-filing obligations to investigate the factual and legal merits of a claim and provides that compliance is manifested by a lawyer's signature on a pleading. Rule 11 seems to completely cover the issue. Rule 11 also sets forth sanctions for noncompliance. The rule seems to specifically cover the issues treated by the state certificate.

Rule 11 is a valid exercise of authority under the Enabling Act because it is procedural in the sense of regulating how issues are presented to and decided by courts—even though it may impose substantive liability as a means of achieving its procedural goal. If Rule 11 is valid and applies, federal courts will follow it, not the state certificate requirement.

A Punishing *Erie* Problem

2. Grant the motion. The state statutory limit on punitive damages is binding on federal courts in diversity cases. There is no federal statute, and federal courts lack general common law power to create substantive rules regarding damages in diversity cases. After Erie it makes no difference whether the source of the state rule is a state statute or state judge-made rule of decision. The important thing is that federal courts are required to apply state laws defining rights and scope of liability.

Bright Lights . . .

3. The motion to transfer to the special state panel is denied. Don't forget the big picture! Federal courts' jurisdiction and venue are governed by federal statutes, and states cannot directly interfere with federal jurisdiction. Federal courts are not deprived of jurisdiction or venue by the state law requiring state litigation in the special state court.

The state procedure may also violate the Seventh Amendment if it requires factfinding by judicial panels rather than juries. The Seventh Amendment preserves the right to trial by jury in civil cases in federal court.

4. The federal court would permit consolidation into a class action if the cases satisfied the requirements of Federal Rule of Civil Procedure 23. This requires a guided *Erie* analysis. Rule 23 explicitly authorizes class actions. It covers the issue. The rule providing for class actions is procedurally valid under the Rules Enabling Act because the rule regulates how issues are presented to and decided by courts.

Jury Justice

5. Acme Co.'s motion for summary judgment will be granted by the federal court even though such a motion would be denied by the state court because of a state constitutional right. This is a guided *Erie* situation because the issue is regulated by Federal Rule of Civil Procedure 56. Rule 56 specifically governs the issue, and it is procedurally valid under the Rules Enabling Act because it controls how issues are presented to and decided by federal courts. It does not abridge a "substantive" right but a procedural one.

   This example and Example 2 demonstrate that the outcome in *Erie* problem cases depends on the source of the federal law. In both these examples, the federal rules were adopted pursuant to the Rules Enabling Act and were valid and procedural under the test applied to such rules. Similar practices adopted by federal judges without such a Rule of Civil Procedure would flunk the unguided *Erie* analysis test set forth in *Guaranty Trust* because the federal practices would significantly affect the result of litigation in ways that would promote forum shopping.

Eerie Choices

6. The federal court in New York must grant Stella's motion to dismiss and apply the law of Tradition because New York state courts would apply the law of Tradition. Having decided that Tradition's rule was conduct-regulating, New York courts would apply the law of the place of the conduct to the case regardless of where the parties were domiciled. There is no federal statute or Rule Enabling Act rule regulating general choice of law. Under the unguided *Erie* analysis, federal courts must apply state choice of law rules because they lack authority to develop a federal general common law of conflicts and because choice of law rules significantly affect the result of litigation.

7. This case is a version of Schultz v. Boy Scouts of America, Inc., 480 N.E.2d 679 (N.Y. 1985), but is pending in federal rather than state court. The answer is easy. The federal court in New York must apply New York's choice of law rules and decide the case as a New York court would. The example says New York state courts would apply the defense of charitable

immunity and dismiss, so that is exactly what a federal court sitting in New York would do.

Limitation Irritation

8. Drake's motion to dismiss is granted. The federal court in Mississippi applies the statute of limitations that would be applied by the state court of the state in which it is sitting because federal judges do not have authority to create separate limitations rules and because applying a different federal rule to limitations would significantly affect the result of litigation in a way that would promote forum shopping. This was the precise issue in Guaranty Trust v. York. As this example points out, authoritative Supreme Court decisions often settle whether particular issues are governed by state law under *Erie*. *Guaranty Trust* has ruled that statutes of limitation are substantive for purposes of *Erie* regardless of the fact that states may characterize them as procedural for other purposes such as choice of law. *Klaxon* has held that choice of law rules are substantive, and federal courts must apply the conflicts law of the state in which they are sitting.

9. The federal judge will apply the conflicts law of the state in which he or she is sitting and not bar the claim under the statute of repose. Regardless of how states characterize the limitations law in issue, it is a matter of substance for purposes of *Erie*. It cuts off a right to recover and decisively affects the outcome of litigation in ways that encourage forum shopping. In diversity cases federal courts must apply the limitations law applied by the state in which they are sitting (unless there has been a section 1404(a) transfer) in order to respect the scope of state rights and in order to achieve the *Erie* goals of avoiding creating incentives for forum shopping and avoiding the unequal administration of justice.

Revenge of Renvoi

10. No, the federal court may not apply South Texas substantive law and permit recovery. The federal court must apply Mordor law because that is what South Texas courts would do. The result may be stupid from the standpoint of modern choice of law theory, but federal courts are not authorized to improve state conflicts rules. The *Erie* doctrine requires federal courts to apply state choice of law rules, even if they are dated and outmoded, so long as they would be applied by state courts.

This was made clear by the Supreme Court in Day & Zimmermann, Inc. v. Challoner, 423 US. 3 (1975). The plaintiffs brought a diversity action in federal court in Texas for death and personal injury in Cambodia allegedly caused by defective artillery shells manufactured in Texas. The Fifth Circuit employed a form of interest analysis and concluded that the Texas place-of-the-wrong rule should not apply because Cambodia had no interest in applying its law. The Supreme Court reversed, holding that in a diversity case the federal court must apply the Texas choice of law rule.

When state choice of law rules are in flux, then federal courts are in the difficult position of trying to guestimate what approach the state courts would currently follow. In doing so, federal courts must make an informed prediction about what rule of decision would be adopted by the state supreme court. This can be difficult in practice, but this difficulty is no different in conflicts cases from others where state law is changing.

Lukewarm Air Balloon

11. The California law on limitations applies to the case against Hot Air Tours, which was transferred pursuant to section 1404(a) because that is the limitations law that would have been applied by the California federal court where the case was properly filed. (The California federal court would have applied the California limitations law because that is what the state courts in California would have done.) A transfer under section 1404(a) is treated like a mere change of courtroom and does not change the law that would be applied. Even after transfer the plaintiff gets the benefit of whatever law would have been applied by the original federal court. This is so regardless of who moves for the transfer.

In contrast, New York limitations law applies in the action against Great Rubber Ball Corp. The transfer occurs under section 1631, and the original forum was not authorized to hear the lawsuit. Transfer under this statute is an administrative alternative to dismissal, not a change from one proper courtroom to another. Following such transfers, *Erie* requires the federal court to apply the state law of the state in which it is sitting rather than the state law that would have been applied by the federal court from which the case is transferred.

Give yourself bonus points for recognizing that the facts were inspired by the procedural history in Piper Aircraft Co. v. Reyno, 454 U.S. 235 (1981). In that case, the personal representative of the estates of Scottish subjects brought a wrongful death action in California state court against the manufacturers of an airplane and the manufacturer of its propeller when the plane crashed in Scotland.

The action was first removed to federal court in California. The airplane manufacturer was subject to personal jurisdiction in California, but the judge transferred the action to the Middle District of Pennsylvania pursuant to section 1404(a) for the convenience of witnesses and parties and in the interests of justice. The federal court in

California concluded that it lacked personal jurisdiction over the propeller manufacturer, but it also transferred that case pursuant to section 1631 to the Western District of Pennsylvania, where the propeller manufacturer did business.

After the transfers in *Reyno*, the Middle District of Pennsylvania granted a motion to dismiss on the ground of forum non conveniens. The Supreme Court affirmed. One of the factors favoring forum non conveniens dismissal was the fact that different state choice of law rules would apply against the two defendants. The case against the airplane manufacturer would be governed by California's choice of law rules, because it was transferred from the federal court in California under section 1404(a). But the case against the propeller manufacturer would be governed by Pennsylvania's choice rules, because it was transferred under section 1631. The complexity of applying different choice rules was one of the factors that favored dismissal and litigation in Scotland.

PART VI

International
Conflicts

CHAPTER 25

International Scope of Federal Laws

INTRODUCTION

This chapter discusses the international scope of federal laws. The question of whether a particular federal law applies to events or persons outside the United States is itself a matter of federal law. Federal courts apply different standards to determine the international reach of different kinds of federal law. This chapter considers the international application of acts of Congress, rules of admiralty, and constitutional provisions.

CONGRESS CONTROLS THE GLOBAL REACH OF FEDERAL STATUTES

Congress controls the legal effect of federal statutes including where they apply. If Congress directs the application of its law in a particular place outside the United States, then courts must so apply it unless doing so violates the Constitution. Head Money Cases, 112 U.S. 580 (1884). But courts also assume that Congress does not want federal statutes to be applied unreasonably in ways that conflict with international law. As Chief Justice Marshall wrote, "[A]n act of Congress ought never to be construed to violate the law of nations if any other possible construction remains." Murray v. The Schooner Charming Betsy, 6 U.S. 64, 118 (1804).

Problem Areas   Problems arise either when Congress does not indicate whether a statute applies internationally or when Congress indicates that the statute applies in some international situations but does not necessarily mean for the statute to preempt all conflicting foreign law.

When Congress Speaks to the Issue

Many federal statutes expressly apply internationally to impose civil and even criminal liability on persons acting outside the United States. *See* Hay et al., Conflict of Laws §3.63 at 229. In contrast, some federal statutes expressly provide that they do not apply internationally. Here are two examples.

Federal Tort Claims Act   The Federal Tort Claims Act provides an example of how Congress can restrict the application of its legislation outside the United States. The Act authorizes private persons to recover tort damages from the U.S. government "under circumstances where the United States, if a private person, would be liable to the claimant in accordance with the law of the place where the act or omission occurred." 28 U.S.C. §1346(b).[1]

You might think the Act gives Berta a claim when she is injured in Mexico by the careless driving of a U.S. government employee acting in his official capacity when a private person would have been liable for such conduct according to Mexican law. But no, Congress has expressly provided that the Federal Tort Claims Act "shall not apply to . . . any claim arising in a foreign country." 28 U.S.C. §2680. In figuring out where the Act does not apply (where the claim arises), the Supreme Court has interpreted the place where a claim arises for purposes of this territorial limitation as the place of the injury, not the place of the conduct causing the injury. In other words, even if the government negligence occurs in California, when Berta suffers the injury in Mexico, she is out of luck. Sosa v. Alvarez-Machain, 542 U.S. 692 (2004).

Foreign Sovereign Immunities Act   The Foreign Sovereign Immunities Act (FSIA) gives foreign countries immunity from jurisdiction in both federal and state court unless some exception applies. 28 U.S.C. §1604. One exception involves certain claims for damages for personal injury, death, and property damages "occurring in the United States." 28 U.S.C. §1605(5). Another exception involves commercial activity by foreign countries in three situations: (1) a claim based on commercial activity in the United States by the foreign country; (2) a claim based on an act by the foreign

---

1. The "law" of the place of act or omission includes that place's choice of law rules. See Chapter 24.

country in the United States in connection with commercial activity outside the United States; and (3) a claim based on an act by the foreign country outside the United States in connection with commercial activity outside the United States and which causes a direct effect in the United States. 28 U.S.C. §1605(a)(2). Most of the exceptions to immunity that authorize claims against foreign countries require an act in the United States, but the Act also authorizes jurisdiction over claims outside the United States in connection with commercial activity that has certain effects in the United States. *See* Republic of Argentina v. Weltover, Inc., 504 U.S. 607 (1992).

The FSIA provides that when an exception to immunity exists, the foreign state "shall be liable in the same manner and to the same extent as a private individual under like circumstances." 28 U.S.C. §1606.[2] The FSIA does not contain choice of law rules. Federal courts are divided over the need for a uniform federal choice of law rule in claims against foreign countries. Some apply a special federal conflicts rule modeled on the most significant contacts approach of the Second Restatement. Others follow *Klaxon* and apply the choice of law rules of the state in which they are sitting. (See Chapter 24.) *See* Hay et al., Conflict of Laws §10.19 at 492.

Congressional Silence

Confusing History The standards adopted by federal courts for determining the reach of federal statutes have changed over time. In the glory days of the traditional territorial approach, the Supreme Court refused to apply federal legislation to conduct that occurred in a foreign country. Justice Holmes announced an extreme territorial principle: "The general and almost universal rule is that the character of an act as lawful or unlawful must be determined wholly by the law of the country where the act is done." On this theory, the Court concluded that applying a statute extraterritorially would be unjust and interfere with another sovereign's sphere of authority. American Banana Co. v. United Fruit Co., 213 U.S. 347 (1909).

With the decline of territorial thinking, federal courts adopted different approaches for different types of cases. The approaches tended to move away from a rigid application of traditional rules and toward considering factual connections, the purposes of federal legislation, and the interests of the U.S. government in the application of U.S. law. E.g., Spector v. Norwegian Cruise Line Ltd., 545 U.S. 119 (2005); Lauritzen v. Larsen, 345 U.S. 571 (1953). Lower courts increasingly assumed that Congress meant to reach much international activity when it had effects in the United States. *See* Hay et al., Conflict of Laws §§3.68 at 242. By 1990 federal courts were

---

2. Warning: the FSIA also provides a separate level of immunity to execution of judgments against foreign countries.

regularly applying various versions of the effects doctrine to determine the international scope of different types of federal statutes when Congress was silent. *Id.*

The Aramco Presumption   In 1991 the Supreme Court resurrected territorialism as a rule of construction. In EEOC v. Arabian American Oil Co. [*Aramco*], 499 U.S. 244 (1991), the Court held that the Civil Rights Act of 1964 did not apply to claims by a U.S. citizen against Delaware corporations that allegedly fired him because of his race, religion, and national origin. Because the alleged discrimination occurred in Saudi Arabia, the Court referred to "a long-standing principle" that a federal statute "is meant to apply only within the territorial jurisdiction" of the United States. The Court justified the presumption against extraterritorial application of federal legislation on two grounds. First, the presumption conforms to the unexpressed intent of Congress.[3] Second, the presumption avoids unintended clashes between federal law and other countries' laws.

For years the effect of the *Aramco* presumption remained unsettled. The Supreme Court did not adhere to it in all cases, and lower courts continued to apply the effects test in some areas, especially federal securities law. In 2010 the Supreme Court forcefully asserted the general application of the *Aramco* presumption. It did so in a case involving federal securities laws, making clear that the presumption applies even in areas where lower courts had long applied different tests for determining congressional intent. *See* Morrison v. National Australia Bank Ltd., 130 S. Ct. 2869 (2010). Unless a contrary congressional intent is "clearly expressed," federal statutes are presumed to concern conditions in the United States. "When a statute gives no clear indication of an extraterritorial application, it has none."

Good News — and Bad   The good news is that the *Aramco* presumption is easy to state. It is also easy to apply when conduct and effects take place in the same country. The presumption displaces some messy balancing tests. And it probably implements Congress's intent in most situations.

The bad news is that the presumption is controversial and may result in bad law. First, despite what the Court says about its pedigree, the presumption is inconsistent with prior Supreme Court and lower federal court decisions. Second, the presumption does not accurately express the "intent" of Congress, because it is employed in situations where Congress did not think about the territorial reach of its legislation, and it produces outcomes

---

3. Whatever the general merits of the presumption against extraterritoriality, it did not conform to Congress's policy goals at the time of the decision. Congress promptly enacted legislation that expressly applied the protections of the Civil Rights Act to Americans employed abroad by Americans. 42 U.S.C. §§2000e(f), 2000e-1.

that surprise Congress.[4] Third, the principle of territorialism (either as way of dividing up spheres of lawmaking power or as a method for determining legislative intent) runs counter to the choice of law approaches of most states and many foreign countries. Fourth, the presumption applies even when there is no need to avoid clashes with other countries' laws.

The presumption forces Congress to specify the territorial reach of its legislation. This may result in better law to the extent it makes Congress think about the scope of its statutes and encourages Congress to provide detailed rules for construing the scope of its enactments.

Overcoming the Presumption The *Aramco* presumption is based on the premise that Congress usually enacts laws for the purpose of regulating domestic matters. The presumption can be overcome by clear expressions of Congress's intent that a statute be applied to people, conduct, or events outside the United States. Evidence of such intent may be found in remedial provisions that assume the application of the law outside the United States and, perhaps, in legislative history. For example, the federal Longshore and Harbor Workers' Compensation Act provides compensation for work-related injuries suffered on "navigable waters of the United States." Workers brought claims for injuries suffered on the high seas, and the defendants argued that the presumption limited the statute to U.S. waters. On appeal, the Second Circuit first observed that the *Aramco* presumption applied in construing the reach of the statute. But the court next decided that the presumption was overcome by a provision elsewhere in the Act that establishes a compensation district for injuries and deaths on the high seas. Kollias v. D & G Marine Maintenance, 29 F.3d 67 (2d Cir. 1994). Also helping to overcome the presumption was the fact that Congress's purpose was to fill gaps left by state compensation programs, and this purpose would be frustrated by limiting the Act's effect to territorial waters of the United States.

Comity as a Principle of Restraint

The *Aramco* presumption applies when Congress is silent. Problems still arise when Congress has indicated that federal legislation has some international effect but does not spell out exactly what effect the legislation should have.

---

4. The British courts apply an almost identical presumption that "Parliament did not intend to legislate beyond the territorial limits of the United Kingdom," and an English scholar points out that the presumption "is just not true." Adrian Briggs, *The Principle of Comity in Private International Law*, 354 Collected Courses of the Hague Academy of International Law 65, 96 (2011).

Federal courts apply additional principles to restrain the unreasonable extra-territorial application of federal law. The Supreme Court justifies these principles of restraint on mixed grounds of comity and congressional intent.

In F. Hoffman-La Roche v. Empagran, S.A., 542 U.S. 155 (2004), the Supreme Court confronted the issue of the international reach of federal antitrust legislation. Congress wanted to cut back on the broad international reach of antitrust laws. So it enacted a statute that prevented the application of antitrust law to certain nonimport foreign commerce. But Congress also provided an exception to this limitation when the foreign conduct had certain effects. Lower courts were divided on the meaning of this congressional exception.

The *Aramco* presumption provides no guidance because Congress was not silent: the legislation specifically addressed the international application of federal law. In construing the statute, the Supreme Court adopted a rule of construction that "ordinarily construes ambiguous statutes to avoid unreasonable interference with the sovereign authority of other nations." *Id.* The rule reflects principles of customary international law. The Court reasoned that Congress itself ordinarily means to follow the principle of avoiding unreasonable interference with foreign sovereigns. This led the Court to conclude that applying U.S. antitrust law to a claim based on foreign conduct that caused a foreign harm would be unreasonable. It noted that federal antitrust law clashed with the law of many foreign countries, and applying federal law could interfere with the legal-economic environments in foreign countries regulated by their own antitrust laws.

In Microsoft Corp. v. AT&T Corp., 550 U.S. 437 (2007), the Supreme Court applied a more territorially defined rule of restraint. Unlike antitrust law, federal patent laws originally prohibited infringements only in U.S. territory. Congress expressly provided for extraterritorial application in one area: the export of "components" that could be combined outside the United States into an infringing product. The Supreme Court was faced with the issue of whether copying computer code onto computers was assembling "components." The Supreme Court applied the presumption against extraterritoriality and held that the ambiguous provision was not violated. The Court observed that the presumption operated on two levels. First, as in *Aramco*, it limited the scope of federal legislation to domestic matters when Congress was silent. Second, the presumption applied to limit the *extent* of the international application of a statute when Congress was not silent but when the international scope was uncertain. *Id.*

Finally, in Hartford Fire Ins. Co. v. California, 509 U.S. 764 (1993), the Supreme Court decided that principles of comity or restraint did not prevent the application of antitrust law to a conspiracy in London. In that case the Court found that federal antitrust law reached the conduct in England.

It also found that compliance with federal law would not have violated British law. Consequently, it refused to refrain from applying federal legislation solely on grounds of comity. In finding that comity did not restrain the application of federal law, the Court emphasized that U.S. law did not require the London-based insurers to act in violation of British law.[5] The decision appears to disfavor comity as a principle of prudential judicial restraint when Congress has otherwise directed the application of federal law. This seems inconsistent with decisions like *Hoffman-La Roche v. Empagran* that attribute comity-like intentions to Congress in construing ambiguous legislation. Professor Spillenger concludes, "[W]e simply have to acknowledge that the Court has been erratic in its recognition and deployment of the 'presumption against extraterritoriality.'" Clyde Spillenger, *Principles of Conflict of Laws* 397 (2010).

Difference from Choice of Law

Decisions from federal courts construing the international scope of federal legislation look like choice of law cases in which courts apply traditional territorial rules for resolving conflicts between laws of different states and countries. But there is a major difference. When the Supreme Court decides that federal legislation does not govern, it concludes that there is no claim. In other words, it does not choose between federal law and some other law.

Conflicts gurus are baffled by why federal courts don't engage in choice of law in cases involving the scope of federal statutes — at least in cases other than admiralty. Maybe federal courts assume Congress never wants courts to engage in such a choice of law. Maybe courts assume they lack authority to engage in choice of law or that Congress lacks authority to direct the application of foreign rules of decision.[6] In cases involving patents and antitrust, there are substantive legal reasons for assuming no other law could apply, state or foreign. But the courts do not discuss those reasons. And in a case like *Aramco*, there is no obvious reason why federal courts could not apply Saudi Arabian law or the law of Delaware if the federal statute does not apply.

---

5. British law did not prohibit the conspiracy but it also did not require the conspiracy, so it did not prevent compliance with U.S. law. For this reason, the Supreme Court opinion said there was no "true conflict." Every Conflicts scholar points out that this is not the normal meaning of either conflict or "true conflict."
6. Some older federal cases dismissed for lack of subject matter jurisdiction when they found that a federal statute did not apply extraterritorially. The Supreme Court clarified that federal courts have subject matter jurisdiction over claims based on federal legislation and should dismiss for failure to state a claim when the statute does not apply. Morrison v. National Australia Bank Ltd., 130 S. Ct. 2869 (2010).

ADMIRALTY

Admiralty jurisdiction over claims that arise on or in connection with navigable waters is vested in the federal courts. U.S. Const. art. III, 28 U.S.C. §1333. Admiralty is a three-credit course, with two of its credits devoted to the mysteries involved in the overlapping jurisdiction between federal and state courts. In cases within admiralty jurisdiction, federal courts have long created and applied general maritime law — a salty version of special common law. But in making maritime law, the federal courts sometimes borrow from state law to fill gaps. Thomas J. Schoenbaum, *Admiralty and Maritime Law* 92–103 (5th ed. 2012).

In admiralty cases federal courts may adopt state laws when there is no clear need for a uniform federal rule. For example, federal courts apply state wrongful death laws to the measure of nonpecuniary damages available in admiralty actions that arise in state waters (when the person who died was not a seaman[7]). When a conflict exists among the applicable state laws in such a case, the admiralty court will apply a most significant relationship approach to determine which state's law governs. *See* Yamaha Motor Corp., U.S.A. v. Calhoun, 516 U.S. 199 (1996), Hay et al., Conflict of Laws §17.63 at 920, Weintraub, Commentary on the Conflict of Laws §3.2C5 at 100.

For many issues in admiralty, federal courts apply the uniform federal maritime law. This law is developed by Congress and federal judges. The rules of maritime law can differ dramatically from state statutes and common law. For example, in torts maritime law employs its own form of comparative negligence that differs from most states. In contracts, maritime law has its own rules and may find an oral contract valid that does not satisfy the requirements of state statutes of frauds.

Federal courts have crafted special choice of law rules for admiralty cases. These rules incorporate elements of the most significant relationship approach of the Second Restatement and elements of interest analysis. The Supreme Court announced these choice of law rules in construing the scope of the Jones Act, which gives seamen a right to recover for injuries on navigable waters. The Jones Act does not specify where it applies. In limiting the reach of the Jones Act, the Supreme Court requires a consideration of eight factors: (1) place of the wrongful act, (2) law of the flag, (3) allegiance or domicile of the injured person, (4) allegiance of the defendant ship owner, (5) place of contract, (6) inaccessibility of foreign forum, (7) law of the forum, and (8) base of operations. Hellenic Lines Ltd. v. Rhoditis, 398 U.S. 306 (1970); Lauritzen v. Larsen, 345 U.S. 571 (1953), Schoenbaum, *Admiralty and Maritime Law* §3-24 at 214-218. The Court applied these factors

---

7. Seaman's claims are governed by the Jones Act. The Act is named for its sponsor Senator Wesley L. Jones, not Davy Jones.

to deny a recovery when a foreign seaman was injured on a foreign ship in foreign waters. It also denied recovery when a foreign seaman was injured on a foreign vessel in American waters. Romero v. Int'l Terminal Operating Co., 358 U.S. 354, 384 (1959) (characterizing place of the injury as a "wholly fortuitous circumstance"). As with the Second Restatement, there is a potential for a split between courts that mechanically count contacts and those that evaluate governmental interests.

The Supreme Court's choice of law decisions in Jones Act cases influenced the evolution of modern approaches to choice of laws. None of the decisions applied a rigid presumption against extraterritoriality. It remains to be seen whether the *Aramco* presumption will displace the approach that has prevailed in Jones Act cases. In any event, the *Aramco* presumption will not apply to admiralty cases requiring a construction of the scope of judge-made admiralty rules or requiring a choice among conflicting state laws.

CONSTITUTIONAL PROTECTIONS

Most Conflicts casebooks include one or two cases dealing with the extraterritorial application of protections provided directly by the U.S. Constitution. The truth is: these cases are out of place because their issues fall far beyond the private rights that are the core concern of Conflict of Laws. Instead, these cases concern matters of government powers, criminal law, and liberty interests that are regulated by principles studied in courses on Constitutional Law and International Law. I am tempted to skip these cases, but since they are in the curriculum, they might be on the final exam.

The Supreme Court in United States v. Verdugo-Urquidez, 494 U.S. 259 (1990), held that the Fourth Amendment does not apply to U.S. government searches and seizures of property located in a foreign country and owned by an alien. The Court's opinion relied on both territorial and status factors. It concluded that the amendment was aimed principally at restricting searches in U.S. territory, and it focused on language in the amendment that declared the goal of "the right of the people" to be secure from unreasonable searches, suggesting that this limited the protection to people affiliated with the United States and thus need not apply to a nonresident alien. The opinion also noted the practical difficulty (impossibility?) of getting a search warrant for a search in a foreign country.

In contrast, the Supreme Court has held that aliens enjoy many constitutional rights in U.S. territory, and it has held that provisions of the Fifth and Sixth Amendments apply to U.S. prosecutions of U.S. citizens in tribunals outside the United States. See Reid v. Covert, 354 U.S. 1 (1957). These decisions can be distinguished on a number of grounds, including the degree to which the government is acting in a governmental capacity. When the government is acting like a government, establishing tribunals for trying Americans abroad, more constitutional protections apply than when its agents are merely acquiring evidence with the cooperation of foreign police officers.

Be careful not to overapply these cases to other areas of law. What the Supreme Court says about territorial limits of constitutional protections does not tell us anything about the territorial reach of other federal or state laws. When the Supreme Court limits a constitutional protection to the territorial limits of the United States, it does not do so in order to avoid conflicts with the laws of foreign countries. Instead territoriality in such cases expresses a policy of judicial abstention that cedes control to the executive or legislative branches.

The Constitution itself places some limit on the Court's policy of abstaining. The Constitution acknowledges the privilege of habeas corpus and restricts the circumstances under which the writ can be suspended. In Boumediene v. Bush, 553 U.S. 723 (2008), the Court held that enemy aliens held by the United States at a navy base at Guantanamo Bay were entitled to file petitions for habeas corpus to challenge the legality of their detention, including the determination of their status as enemy combatants, notwithstanding an act of Congress that tried to eliminate federal jurisdiction over habeas petitions from aliens determined to be enemy combatants. First, the Court noted that the United States maintained both de facto jurisdiction and plenary control over the site of detention since 1898. Second, the Court observed that the Constitution's guarantee of habeas corpus and the limits on its suspension provided "an indispensable mechanism for monitoring the separation of powers." If habeas corpus was not available to people detained in such territory outside the United States, then the executive and legislative branches could create regimes around the world subject to their exclusive control but without any legal review. "[I]t would be possible for the political branches to govern without legal constraint."

THE OUTER LIMITS

The U.S. Constitution provides modest limits on the application of federal and state law in conflicts cases. (They are discussed in Chapter 27.) For example, the Due Process Clause requires a forum government to have a significant contact or significant aggregation of contacts creating governmental interests so that the application of its law is not arbitrary or fundamentally unfair. This prevents courts from applying either federal or state law to a case with no connection to the federal government or the state. For example, New York may not apply its tort law and disregard an Ontario guest statute in a case stemming from a car accident in Ontario involving only Ontario domiciliaries. Similarly, if Congress enacted a statute that created a cause of action for car accidents in Paris, the Due Process Clause would prevent federal courts from applying the statute to a case involving French citizens and no other connection to the United States.

Some Conflicts scholars think customary international law should provide additional limits on federal or state choice of law in international cases. Under international law, the power of a country or state to apply its law to a case is called legislative jurisdiction. International law recognizes five traditional bases for legislative jurisdiction: (1) The territorial principle authorizes a country to apply its law based on events occurring in or relationships based in the country. (2) The nationality principle authorizes a country to apply its law to persons who have a national affiliation with the country. (3) The protective principle authorizes a country to apply its law to protect itself from a direct, specific threat to its national security. (4) The universality principle authorizes a country to apprehend and prosecute perpetrators of particular heinous offenses such as crimes against humanity, piracy, and torture. (5) The passive personality principle authorizes a country to apply its law based on the nationality of the victim. Courts in the United States sometimes refer to these principles when they support the extension of U.S. laws to persons or events outside the United States. *See* United States v. Yunis, 681 F. Supp. 896 (D.D.C. 1988). Legislative jurisdiction based on territoriality and nationality are widely recognized, but the other principles are more controversial and subject to limitations. The passive personality principle, even when hedged with limitations, remains controversial.

When a ground of legislative jurisdiction permits a country to apply its law, principles of international law may still caution against a country applying its law when applying its law unreasonably interferes with the law of a foreign country. Restatement (3d) of Foreign Relations Law of the United States §403(1). When it would not be unreasonable for more than one country's law to apply, a country "should to defer to the other state if that state's interest is clearly greater." Id. §403(3). The Supreme Court has cited this authority when it restrained the application of antitrust law, reasoning that Congress meant to avoid unreasonable applications of its law.

Examples

Killer Toys

1. Suppose Congress enacts the Tiny Tots Toy Protection Act. The Act provides: "No person shall manufacture or sell baby toys that contain detachable parts smaller than one inch in diameter." The statute defines baby toys to include objects primarily for the entertainment of children under age five.

   The preamble to the Act explains that Congress's purpose is to protect babies and young children from being exposed to toys that present the risk of choking. The Act creates a private cause of action for persons who suffer injuries by toys that are manufactured or sold in violation of the statute. The statute does not contain any language that explains where it applies.

Pedro Infante is a two-year-old citizen of Mexico who has never left his hometown of Mazatlán. For his second birthday, his grandmother gave Pedro a toy she bought at the local market. The toy consisted of a barn with two horses in it. The horses were less than one inch in diameter. Pedro immediately placed a toy horse in his mouth, choked, and suffered personal injuries. The seller and manufacturer of the toy are lifelong citizens of Mazatlán.

Does Pedro have a valid claim against the seller for violating the federal statute?

2. Same facts. Cal and his four-year-old daughter are both citizens of California. During a vacation in Japan, Cal buys a toy baby doll for his daughter. Cal gives the doll to his daughter in Japan. She promptly removes its tiny hat (less than one inch in diameter), puts it in her mouth, and chokes. The doll was manufactured in China by Microdollco, a Delaware corporation.

Cal and his daughter commence a civil action against Microdollco under the Tiny Tots Toy Protection Act. The defendant moves to dismiss. How should the court rule on the motion?

3. Suppose the preamble to the Tiny Tots Toy Protection Act provides, "The goal of this Act is to secure the worldwide elimination of certain toys that injure and kill young children. The protections afforded by this Act apply to conduct and injuries sustained anywhere in the world." Would that change the answers to the Examples 1 and 2?

Bad Medicine

4. Malfortunata Jacinta, a citizen of the country of Patagonia, was treated at a Veterans Administration Hospital in the state of Northern California. Punctilio, a hospital employee, filled a prescription for Jacinta in the hospital pharmacy. Punctilio carefully followed all instructions. Unfortunately, the manufacturer's labels were incorrect. As a result, instead of filling Jacinta's bottle with Zextipep®, the stimulant prescribed, he filled it with Dormtotale®, a powerful tranquilizer.

Jacinta ingested the first pill after returning to Patagonia. As a result she became disoriented and walked in front of a bus in downtown Patagonia City. She was killed instantly.

Jacinta's estate commenced a civil action against the U.S. government under the Federal Tort Claims Act. A Northern California state case with similar facts held that a pharmacist who followed manufacturer's labels was not liable. But Northern California applies the law of the place of the wrong in wrongful death actions. In contrast, Patagonia imposes strict liability on pharmacists for distributing mislabeled drugs. Patagonian courts adhere to the traditional approach to choice of law in such cases.

The government moves to dismiss for failure to state a claim. Does Jacinta have a good claim against the government under the Federal Torts Claim Act under these facts?

Fishy Cases

5. Nelson and Nemo, citizens of the state of West Carolina, entered into a contract under which Nemo agreed to transport five barrels of fish heads across the Tarheel River. They shook hands and agreed to the contract while seated in a boat on the Tarheel River. The Tarheel River is a body of navigable water that forms the border between the states of East Carolina and West Carolina. Nemo and Nelson were on the East Carolina side of the border when they shook hands.

   According to their agreement, Nemo promised to make five trips. On each trip he was to pick up a barrel at Nelson's facility located near the center of the state of West Carolina. Nemo agreed to transport the barrels to a barge on the East Carolina side of the Tarheel River, to retrieve the barrels after they had been emptied, and to return the empty barrels to Nelson's facility in West Carolina. Nelson promised to pay Nemo $12,000 in cash at the facility in West Carolina after the return of the last empty barrel.

   After Nemo made the first delivery, he called Nelson and announced that he had changed his mind because the fish heads had an offensive odor. Nelson arranged for someone else to perform the service at a cost of $27,000.

   Nelson brings a suit against Nemo in federal court asserting admiralty jurisdiction. Under West Carolina's statute of frauds, the agreement is unenforceable because it was not in writing. Under East Carolina contract law, the oral contract is enforceable because of Nemo's part performance. East Carolina applies the law of the place of contracting. West Carolina applies interest analysis.

   The action is pending in federal district court for the District of West Carolina. Nemo's answer raises the defense that the contract claim is barred by the statute of frauds. Nelson's lawyer calls you for advice about what law will apply to the issue of the statute of frauds.

6. Farragut and Jones, citizens of East Carolina, went fishing on the Tarheel River in Farragut's motorboat. While drifting on the West Carolina side of the state line, Farragut did not pay attention to the current. The boat struck a concrete pier supporting a road bridge. The impact caused Jones to fall into the river and drown.

Jones's estate commences a wrongful death action against Farragut in federal court for the district of East Carolina, asserting admiralty jurisdiction. The East Carolina wrongful death statute permits damages for the value of the loss of enjoyment of life. West Carolina law does not permit damages for loss of enjoyment of life. What law of damages will apply?

A Bruising Question

7. Fredonia Air Lines flight 13013 departed as scheduled from Southern California International Airport. Unfortunately, Captain Fidget carelessly activated the dethernambulator at the time of takeoff, resulting in a crash landing in the state of West Texas. Elle Woods was not harmed. But her little dog Bruiser was traveling in her purse. Bruiser escaped during the crash landing and was never found. Miss Woods is a citizen of the state of Southern California. Fredonia Airlines is owned by the foreign country of Fredonia.

   Woods commences a civil action against Fredonia in federal court in Southern California under the Foreign Sovereign Immunities Act. Under case law in Southern California, damages recoverable for the injury or destruction of a companion animal are limited to the fair market value of the animal. Under case law in West Texas, compensatory damages for the destruction or loss of a companion animal may include damages for the emotional suffering experienced by the owner resulting from the loss of the animal. In conflicts cases, Southern California applies the law of the place of the wrong. West Texas follows interest analysis. What damages are available against Fredonia in a claim under the Foreign Sovereign Immunities Act?

Explanations

Killer Toys

1. The statute does not apply to create a valid claim. Even if Congress's power to regulate interstate and foreign commerce gives it authority to enact such statute, there is a question about whether Congress has in fact exercised its power by making the statute apply in foreign countries. Because there is no clear expression of a contrary intent, the *Aramco* presumption requires that the statute be applied only to domestic U.S. matters. Accordingly, Pedro's claim should be dismissed for failure to state a claim on the ground that the federal statute does not apply to the events in Mexico.

2. I would dismiss the case. The *Aramco* presumption that Congress did not mean to legislate with respect to conduct or injuries in foreign countries still applies.

3. I would still dismiss Pedro's claim but for different reasons. Because Congress expressed its intent that the statute apply in foreign countries, the Act obviously has some extraterritorial application. But despite its broad language, there still may be a question as to whether Congress meant the statute to apply to parties and conduct in Mexico. There does not appear to be any recognized basis for legislative jurisdiction under principles of international law. Applying the Charming Betsy presumption would require a construction that the statute does not apply so as to avoid a violation of international law. Similarly, because the scope may be uncertain, the presumption against extraterritorial application may still guide the construction of the *extent* of its application outside the United States.

   Notice that nothing in this example suggests that the U.S. statute conflicts with Mexican law. If it did, and if the reach of the statute was uncertain, then courts might additionally employ the presumption from *Empagran* that the statute should be restrictively construed so as to avoid unreasonable interference with foreign sovereigns.

   If Congress really intended for the statute to apply to the purely foreign tort and none of the limiting constructions prevent its application, then I would still not apply the statute. Under such circumstances, the application of the statute would appear to violate Due Process. There is no significant contact or significant aggregation of contacts with the United States creating a governmental interest in applying the statute, so applying U.S. law appears to be arbitrary and unfair.

   In contrast, I would not dismiss Cal's and his daughter's case. The statute expressly applies extraterritorially. The citizenship of all the parties in the United States gives the U.S. government an interest in regulating foreign commerce to protect its citizens. While the extraterritorial application of the statute may be unusual, I don't see how it is arbitrary or fundamentally unfair. Principles of legislative jurisdiction under international law support the application of U.S. law: the nationality principle supports regulating conduct of citizens abroad. (The passive personality principle is more controversial and is limited in ways that do not authorize broad application of laws to protect citizens abroad.)

Bad Medicine

4. Jacinta does not have a valid claim under the Federal Torts Claim Act. The Act does not apply to claims that arise in foreign countries. The Supreme Court has explained that a claim "arises" for purposes of this limitation where the injury occurs. Thus the claim arises in Patagonia, the Federal Torts Claim Act does not apply, and the court must dismiss.

Fishy Cases

5. Welcome to admiralty! This example raises two problems. The first problem is whether there is admiralty jurisdiction, which depends on whether the contract is a maritime contract. There is no easy mechanical test. The fact that the agreement was concluded on navigable waters does not make it a maritime contract. It is a mixed contract because the transportation of the cargo takes place over land and water. Although most of the distance covered is on land, I think the contract should still be considered primarily maritime because of the importance (and potential cost) of the final transportation over water, the offloading onto vessels and, perhaps, the fishy contents of the cargo. *See* Norfolk Southern Railway Co. v. Kirby, 543 U.S. 14 (2004) (setting forth the conceptual analysis for determining whether a contract is maritime).

   Although this fishy case definitely has a maritime odor, it is not absolutely clear that it has a sufficient maritime flavor to be in admiralty — but it probably does. If it does not, the federal courts lack subject matter jurisdiction. If refiled in state court, the state courts would apply state law, including its own conflicts rules.

   The second problem raised by the example is whether federal courts will develop a distinct rule governing oral contracts for cases within admiralty jurisdiction. The answer in theory requires a consideration of whether there is need for a uniform federal rule and the strength of local interests. In the absence of the need for a uniform rule, federal courts may borrow state law. The Supreme Court has concluded that "oral contracts are generally recognized as valid by maritime law." Kossick v. United Fruit Co., 365 U.S. 731, 734 (1961). Consequently, if this is found to be a maritime contract, the federal court will not apply any of the state rules but will recognize a valid oral contract under the maritime law.

6. I may be all wet, but I think the admiralty court should apply East Carolina's wrongful death law to permit recovery for loss of enjoyment of life. First, there is a question as to whether this tort claim is maritime. I believe it is because it occurred in navigable waters, because it involves a vessel and concerns traditional maritime activity, and because this type of incident has the potential to interfere with commercial activity on the river. If I am wrong, then the case must be dismissed because there is no other basis for federal jurisdiction. The plaintiff could then commence an action in state court, which would apply state law. In this case, the plaintiff has a choice of two states. But East Carolina provides a more favorable state forum because its choice of law rules will lead it to apply the more generous recovery permitted by West Carolina's tort law.

   If the claim falls within the federal court's admiralty jurisdiction, then the court must decide whether it should be governed by the general maritime tort law. The right of non-seamen to recover wrongful death damages in admiralty was clarified by the Supreme Court in Yamaha Motor Corp. U.S.A. v. Calhoun, 516 U.S. 199 (1996). The Court rejected the argument that because nonpecuniary damages were traditionally not available under general maritime law, this policy of nonrecovery pre-empted the right to recovery under state wrongful death statutes. It held, on the contrary, that there was no need for a uniform admiralty rule on the remedy, and admiralty courts should borrow and apply state wrongful death remedies in deaths of non-seamen that occur in territorial waters.

In subsequently determining what state's law to apply, the Third Circuit did not employ any state's choice of law rules. It applied an admiralty choice of law rule — the law of the state with the most significant relationship to the incident and the dominant interest in the application of its law. Calhoun v. Yamaha Motor Corp., U.S.A., 216 F.3d 338, 345 (3d Cir. 2000). The court concluded that the place of an accidental injury was unimportant for compensatory damages and applied the tort law of the plaintiff's domicile. (In contrast, it found that the law of the place of the accident had a dominant interest in deterring misconduct and applied that place's law to punitive damages.)

Applying the admiralty choice of law rule to the example, East Carolina has a powerful interest in applying its measure of compensatory damages to compensate the plaintiff. East Carolina also has an interest in applying the loss-shifting rule to a case between parties domiciled in the state. West Carolina does not seem to have any interest other than that of deterring accidents in its territory, and its deterrent interest is adequately served by applying East Carolina's measure of damages. The location of the place of the accident seems fortuitous and gives neither state a stronger interest in applying its law. For these reasons, I would apply East Carolina's law permitting recovery for loss of enjoyment of life.

A Bruising Question

7. The Federal Sovereign Immunities Act answers some questions about damages. For example, it generally prohibits punitive damages in claims against a foreign government but not against a government-owned corporation. In general, the FSIA does not direct what law governs claims or damages. It provides only that the foreign country is liable "in the same manner and to the same extent" as a nongovernmental defendant "under like circumstances." Federal courts must thus decide which state's substantive law determines the liability of a defendant under the circumstances.

There is a split among the federal courts applying the FSIA. Some federal courts apply the conflicts law of the state in which they are sitting.

Under this approach, the federal court applying Southern California's place of the wrong rule would select West Texas law and allow recovery of damages for emotional distress. *See* Barkanic v. General Administration of Civil Aviation of the People's Republic of China, 923 F.2d 957 (2d Cir. 1991) (applying the choice of law rule of state in which FSIA court is sitting). This is what the plaintiff would prefer.

Other federal courts apply a uniform federal choice of law approach in FSIA cases. They select the law of the state that has the most significant relationship. With respect to the issue of damages, the defendant has a strong argument that the state with the most significant relationship is the plaintiff's home state, especially as that is also the place of the conduct. Consequently, the federal court following this approach would apply the damages law of Northern California, despite the fact that Northern California would itself apply another state's law. This is what the defendant would prefer. Cf. Schoenberg v. Exportadora de Sal, 930 F.2d 777 (9th Cir. 1991) (applying federal choice of law rule in FSIA litigation).

Under neither approach would federal courts sitting in Northern California apply the choice of law rules of West Texas in a claim brought under the FSIA. But if the plaintiff commenced the action in federal court in West Texas, then the West Texas conflicts rules might govern if the federal court in West Texas followed those federal courts that apply forum state conflicts rules in FSIA cases. The split creates incentives for forum shopping in FSIA cases.

Choice of Law
in Europe

26

INTRODUCTION

This chapter discusses European approaches to conflict of laws and summarizes the choice of law rules adopted in the European Union (EU) that govern contracts, torts, wills, and inheritance.

EUROPEAN TRADITIONS

Overview In European practice, conflict of laws is called Private International Law. Each European country developed its own rules of Private International Law, borrowing from shared legal and academic sources. In England, choice of law rules evolved from judicial decisions. In contrast, civil law countries experienced a long tradition of rational codes and accordingly sought to reduce conflicts rules to statutory form. European countries embraced various forms of the traditional territorial approach combined with a parallel tradition of applying the law of the seat of the parties' relationship.

The European Union has adopted regulations that now govern most contract and tort cases. Some but not all EU countries have also adopted a regulation that governs the administration of estates of people affiliated with the EU. And the EU is working toward common choice of law rules to govern other areas like marriages. National Private International Law regimes still govern in countries like Switzerland that are not part of the EU and in EU countries when matters that are not covered by EU rules.

European Union   Building on a series of cooperation pacts among Western European countries, the European Union was established under that name in 1993. The EU has grown into a confederation of over 25 countries. The EU includes most of the countries in Europe but not Norway, Russia, Switzerland, or Turkey. Territory of EU countries can extend far outside Europe. Parts of France are in South America and the Pacific Islands.

The EU operates through permanent executive, legislative, and judicial organs. It can promulgate regulations binding on member states, and member states can also be bound by treaties and conventions.

ROME I AND II

Short History   Rome I establishes choice of law rules for contracts. It was first adopted as a convention before the formation of the EU and has been reissued as a regulation binding on EU countries. Rome II establishes rules for torts and was promulgated under EU authority as a regulation.[1]

EU countries will apply the rules in Rome I and II to all conflicts cases, not just those involving EU country law or parties. For example, suppose Meena injures Kumari in a car accident in Delhi, India. Meena and Kumari were lifelong residents of Delhi, but after the accident, both move to Paris. There Kumari sues Meena in a French court. Suppose India requires proof of fault but France does not. In determining what law to apply, French courts will apply Rome II rules and select the law of India (either because that is where the injury occurred or because that was the parties' common habitual residence at the time of the tort).

Effect and Scope   Rome I and Rome II preempt choice of law rules in member countries to the extent they apply. But they do not provide rules for many conflicts problems. They do not apply to claims against states, claims involving taxes, obligations arising from marriage and family relationships, trusts, negotiable instruments, corporate law, nuclear damage, and defamation and invasions of privacy rights. For example, suppose Jean and Marie

---

1. To impress your teacher and make friends with classmates, call Rome I and II by their official citations: Regulation (EC) No. 593/2008, Regulation (EC) No. 864/2007.

The rules apply to all EU members except Denmark. Go figure. The United Kingdom did not originally sign Rome I, but it adopted its provisions through an act of Parliament, and the United Kingdom has agreed to be bound by the recent promulgation of Rome I as an EU regulation. *See* Nils Willem Vernooij, *Rome I: An Update on the Law Applicable to Contractual Obligations in Europe*, 15 Colum. J. Eur. L.F. 71 n.4 (2009).

got married in Belgium and then move to France. A dispute later arises about who owns property that Jean acquired during the marriage. If there is a conflict between the laws of Belgium and France, Rome I and II do not apply. So unless some other convention or regulation applies, French and Belgian courts will determine what law applies under their own choice of law rules.

Habitual Residence   Many of the rules select the law of a party's habitual residence. Habitual residence is determined as of the time of the conclusion of the contract or the time of the tort.

One trap and pitfall to watch out for is the way the regulations define "habitual residence." Habitual residence sure sounds a lot like domicile. A corporation or unincorporated body has its habitual residence in "the place of central administration." And this sounds like the "nerve center" test for principal place of business. (See Chapter 24.) But when the corporation has a local branch and contract was made or damage caused in the course of the operation of the branch, then its habitual residency is the place where the branch is located. This means a business could have hundreds of habitual residences. Similarly, for torts, a person's habitual residence is not his or her personal residence but the principal place of business where he or she is acting in the scope of his or her employment. Rome II art. 23.

For example, Carlos Camionero ran over Pedro Peatón in Liverpool, England. Camionero is a citizen of Spain but is employed driving a truck out of a depot in Marseilles, France. He was making a delivery at the time of the tort. Accordingly, his habitual residence will be France because that is his principal place of business. A different analysis would apply if the lawsuit were against the trucking company for which Camionero worked. Its habitual residence would be where its central administration was located. That might be Frankfurt, Germany. But if Camionero's acts were in the course of the operation of its branch in Marseilles, then the company's habitual residence would become France, and if his acts were in the course of the operation of the company's business in Liverpool, its habitual residence would become England.

Depeçage

American approaches tend to look separately at each issue in litigation. For example, courts applying interest analysis might apply the standard of care from the state where the accident occurred but select the charitable immunity law from the home state of both the plaintiff and defendant when they share a common domicile.

European practice generally avoids splitting different issues. EU rules typically provide that one country's law applies to the entire tort. But the policy of promoting party autonomy for contracts trumps the policy against splitting issues, and Rome I permits parties to choose one country's law to govern only part of their contract. Parties could choose French law to govern interpretation and the scope of duties but Hong Kong law to govern the sufficiency of performance.

No Renvoi for Contracts and Torts

Rome I and II exclude renvoi by providing that the law selected by their provisions does not include the chosen country's choice of law rules.

ROME I: CONTRACTS

The Contract Rules   Rome I endorses party autonomy in its main rule: "A contract shall be governed by the law chosen by the parties." Rome I art. 3(1). The choice must be "made expressly or clearly demonstrated."[2] No reasonable basis or other connection to the chosen law is required. If John from the United Kingdom and Marta from Bulgaria expressly choose Saudi Arabian law to govern their contract, their choice is valid.

There are some exceptions and limits on party choice. When all relevant elements are in a country and under that country's law the law cannot be derogated by agreement, then parties cannot dodge the effect of the law by choosing foreign law. Protections for consumers and employees cannot be voided by choosing foreign law when those protections cannot be derogated by agreement.

Absent party choice, Rome I provides a series of rules. First, it provides specific rules for specific kinds of contracts. Contracts of sales, services, and franchise agreements are governed by the law of the country of habitual residence of the seller, provider of services, or franchisee.[3] Contracts relating to rights in immovable property are governed (except for leases up to six months) by the law of the situs; auctions are governed by the law of the place where the auction occurs; employment contracts are governed by the law of the country in which, or from which, the employee habitually carries out his work.

---

2. Although a nonexpress choice of law must be demonstrated clearly, courts may consider a forum-selection agreement as one factor in determining whether the choice is clearly demonstrated. Rome I declaration 12.

3. The black letter rules modify the prior approach of the Convention that prescribed applying the law of the country with which the contract is "most closely connected" and set forth certain presumptions about the places of "characteristic performance."

Second, for contracts not covered by a specific rule, Rome I provides a fallback rule: such contracts are governed by the law of the country of the habitual residence of the "party required to effect the characteristic performance of the contract." Rome I art. 4(2).

Third, if a contract is not covered by any of the other rules, it applies the law of the country "with which it is most closely connected." Rome I art. 4(3)-(4).[4] Rome I also directs courts to disregard most of its other choice rules for contracts when under all the circumstances the contract is "manifestly more closely connected" with another country.

Finally, there are escape devices that permit a court to disregard all the choice of law rules. A court may apply its "overriding mandatory provisions" that it regards as crucial for safeguarding public interests, and a court may refuse to apply a provision of the law of a country that is manifestly incompatible with its public policy.

Scope   The law chosen by Rome I applies broadly to interpretation, performance, and even remedies.

An additional rule eases the requirements for formal validity. A contract between persons who are in the same country at the time of the conclusion of the contract is valid if it satisfies either the formal requirements of the law selected by Rome I rules or the law of the place where the contract was concluded. Rome I art. 11(1).

ROME II: TORTS AND MORE

Terminology and Coverage   Rome II applies to "noncontractual obligations," which include claims for damages arising from torts. Civil law systems typically use the term "delicts" for torts, and the English version of Rome II calls them "torts/delicts." Rome II also applies to some nontort obligations such as unjust enrichment.

The Three Big Rules

Rome II provides three rules that will apply to most torts:

1. Place of the Injury   The first general rule states that an obligation arising from a tort "shall be the law of the country in which the damage occurs irrespective of the country in which the event giving rise to the damage

---

4. This was originally the main rule under the Convention. It is now a fall-back provision for cases not governed by specific rules.

occurred and irrespective of the country or countries in which the indirect consequences of that event occur." Rome II art. 4(1). Professor Symeonides observes that this is basically the First Restatement's old "place of the wrong" rule. He gives the example of a Swiss mining company that sets off an explosion in the Swiss Alps that causes an avalanche in the French Alps that injures English tourists. France is the country where the damage occurs and England is the country where the indirect consequences occur.[5]

2. Common Habitual Residence   Rome II provides a second general rule that displaces the first: "[W]here the person claimed to be liable and the person sustaining damage both have their habitual residence in the same country at the time when the damage occurs, the law of that country shall apply." Rome II art. 4(2).

These two rules seem to create opportunities to manipulate outcomes in situations where plaintiffs are injured by more than one person or where one person's fault may be legally attributed to another. I don't have a clue how European systems deal with these situations.

3. Place with a Manifestly Closer Connection   Rome II provides a third rule that can displace both first-injury and common habitual residence rules. When the tort is "manifestly more closely connected with a country," then that country's law applies. The text explains that such a manifestly closer connection "might be based" on a preexisting relationship like a contract. This rule aims to make sure that some tort or breach of trust claims arising from a contract are governed by the law that applies to the contract.

Exceptions or Escape Devices

Two escape devices authorize deviations from the choice of law rules. First, a forum may apply its own "mandatory" law. Second, it may refuse to apply a foreign country's law that is "manifestly incompatible" with the public policy of the forum. Rome II arts. 16, 26. Rome II offers the example of "excessive" punitive damages as a law that may violate a forum's public policy. Rome II recital 32.

A third provision in Rome II states that courts should take account of "rules of safety and conduct" where the event giving rise to liability occurs. Rome II art. 17. This sounds like it authorizes application of conduct-regulating rules of safety, but its effect is uncertain.

---

5. Symeon C. Symeonides, *Rome II and Tort Conflicts: A Missed Opportunity*, 56 Am J. Comp. L. 173 (2008).

Special Applications

Rome II has special rules for products liability, unfair competition, environmental torts, intellectual property, and industrial action (strikes).

Products Liability   For products liability, courts apply the law of common habitual residence if there is one. If not, they apply the law of the plaintiff's habitual residence at the time of injury if the product was marketed in that country. Failing that, they apply the law of the country where the product was acquired, if the product was marketed in that country. Failing that, they apply the law of the country where the damage occurred, if the product was marketed in that country.

There are two escapes from these rules. If the defendant could not reasonably foresee the marketing of the product in any of the countries whose law applies under these rules, then courts apply the law of defendant's habitual residence. And if the tort is manifestly more closely connected with another country, they apply that country's law. Rome II art. 5.

Environmental Torts   For environmental damages, a plaintiff can elect either the law of the place of the first injury or the law of the country where "the event giving rise to the damage occurred." Rome II art. 7. For example, when toxic emissions from Brennan's belch furnace in Switzerland poison Fischer's fish ponds in Austria, Fischer may elect to apply either the law of Switzerland or the law of Austria. (It doesn't matter where the parties are habitually resident.)[6]

Unjust Enrichment   Claims for unjust enrichment are governed by the law that governs the contract or relationship between the parties when it concerns that relationship. For example, if Big Bank Gesellschaft deposits 1 million Euros in the account of Frida Frugal, its claim for repayment will be governed by the law that governs the contract between them. In cases where the law cannot be determined in this way, the obligation is governed by the law of common habitual residence. When there is no common habitual residence, the obligation is governed by the law of the country where the unjust enrichment took place. All these rules can be displaced by the law of a country with which the obligation is "manifestly more closely connected." Rome II art. 10.

---

6. I'm hoping this example works. Rome II defines an environmental tort as a change in a natural resource such as water, land, or air, or impairment of function by that resource, or impairment of variability among living organisms. Huh?

Scope

The law selected under Rome II applies both to substantive matters and to matters traditionally classified as procedural. It applies to liability, defenses, and vicarious liability.

Party Choice for Torts

Rome II allows parties to choose what law applies after a claim has arisen. This is not much different from U.S. practice where parties enjoy broad freedom to waive rights, settle claims, and stipulate to matters (including governing law) during litigation.

Rome II takes party autonomy a bold step further. It allows parties to select the law that governs a tort prior to the tort. Such pre-tort choice is limited to parties "pursuing a commercial activity" and to agreements that are "freely negotiated." Rome II art.14(b).

Succession of Property at Death

Overview The EU encourages the free movement of persons and property within the EU. As a result more and more people are moving from one EU country to another and dying owning property in more than one country. Conflicts then arise concerning the proper court to administer the estate, the power of executors or administrators, the rules that govern the validity of wills, and the rights and priority of beneficiaries and other claimants. After years of efforts, the EU adopted a regulation designed to establish clear jurisdiction in one court and to reduce conflicts. Regulation (EU) No. 650/2012 (effective 2015).

The regulation does not apply to some of the most common succession problems. It excludes certain marital property rights, joint property, and trusts. *Id.* art. 1(d), (j).[7]

---

7. The regulation expressly excludes trusts. Period. But the recital says: "This should not be understood as a general exclusion of trusts. Where a trust is created under a will . . . the law applicable to the succession under this regulation should apply with respect to the devolution of the assets and the determination of the beneficiaries." Regulation (EU) No. 650/2012 (13). A similar disconnect between recitals and implementing rules appears when Recital (57) demands renvoi to assure uniformity, but art. 34(2) eschews renvoi in applying the law of the country with which the decedent was manifestly more closely connected.

I told you that you can skip the footnotes. But if you got this far and understand what the regulation is doing, please email me.

Details Courts of the EU country where a person had his or her habitual residence at death get jurisdiction to rule on the succession as a whole even if the property is elsewhere. Id. art. 4. But estate plans that select a different EU country court can be enforced, and rules aim to locate the administration in the country whose law will apply to the substantive issues of succession. Id. art. 5.

The regulation contains clear choice of law rules. First, a person may choose the law of his or her nationality (determined either as of the time of the choice or as of the time of death) to govern. Id. art. 22(1). Second, when there is no such choice, the general rule designates the law of the country where the decedent had his or her habitual residence at death. Id. art. 21(1). Third, in exceptional cases, when the deceased was manifestly more closely connected with another country, then that country's law applies. Id. art. 21(2).

The law selected under the general rule is the whole law of the decedent's habitual residence, including its choice of law rules. But when the law is chosen by the decedent or in the exceptional case, then it is the local law, and there is no renvoi. Id. art. 34.

The chosen law applies to substantive matters including the powers of administrators and the rights of persons to the estate assets. Id. art. 23. In contrast, a disposition in writing will be valid so long as it complies with the law of the place where the disposition was made; where the decedent was a national, domiciliary, or habitual resident (either at death or at the time of the disposition); or where immovable property is located. Id. art. 27. (Age, nationality, and personal condition restrictions are disfavored and governed by the rule for formal requirements.)

The regulation seems to require that courts strictly apply the law chosen under the regulation. Thus, it provides that chosen law may be refused only when it "is manifestly incompatible with the public policy" of the forum. Id. art. 35. At the same time, the regulation provides special protection for creditors by authorizing the forum to apply its own law (in disregard of chosen law) for their enhanced security. Id. art. 29(2).

The regulation seeks to promote the enforcement of EU succession decisions throughout the EU. It creates a European Certificate of Succession that will make it easier for heirs and beneficiaries to enforce their rights in other countries where the estate had assets. See Chapter 6.

How It All Works Pedro, a Spanish national, moves to Paris and becomes a habitual resident of France. He dies on vacation in New York. He had signed a written document indicating that he wanted all his property to go to Fernando. His property includes bank accounts in France and Germany and a farm in France. He is survived by an adult daughter who is not provided for in the document.

Problem There may be conflicts between the law of Spain, France, and New York regarding the validity of the document as a will and whether Pedro can exclude his daughter.

Solution The written will is valid if it satisfies the formal requirements of the law of either France (habitual residence at death) or Spain (nationality). Because Pedro did not choose another forum, France will have jurisdiction over the entire succession. And because Pedro did not choose another law, French courts will apply the law of his habitual residence at death (French law). The French decision must be respected by other EU countries. And Fernando can eventually get a certificate specifying his rights that will be enforceable in all EU countries.

Not So Fast The regulation promises to make it easier to administer estates with property in more than one EU country. Its solution avoids creating a new EU law of succession and instead requires application of the local succession laws of the EU countries involved—the country where the decedent died domiciled or was a national. But the regulation also makes some substantive changes. For the sake of convenience, it subjects all property to a single law of succession even though some EU countries like England apply different rules to different types of property. And the regulation implements a value preference for enforcing written estate plans and for protecting creditors.

It is unclear exactly how the regulation will work in practice and whether its rules will be flexible enough for large estates and its procedures cheap enough for smaller ones. Special concerns were raised about whether transfers during the decedent's life should be taken into consideration in disposing of the assets that remain at death.

England, Ireland, and Denmark have opted not to be bound by the regulation. Regulation (EU) No. 650/2012 (82)-(83).

WHAT'S NOT TO LOVE?

Rome I and II offer appealing, rigid rules. The rules seem easy to apply and offer satisfactory results in most situations. Are they a viable model for U.S. reform?

For all their apparent rigidity, the EU rules include residual escape devices that would provide creative common law judges enough wiggle room to reach results comparable to those supported by the wishy-washy Restatement Second.

Codifying rigid rules can produce problems. These problems can be quickly remedied in the EU, where regulations are periodically revisited and amended. In contrast, U.S. statutes are forever.

Despite their black-letter form, the EU rules are not as perfect or complete as they seem. They don't define habitual residence, explain what "most closely connected" means, or indicate when they should be displaced by mandatory law or public policy.

Some rules are bad as written. Protection for weaker parties is inadequate — and too often left to the uncertain judicial application of overriding mandatory provisions or nonderogatable law. Party autonomy is not appropriate for torts and, if it is, the EU rule does not adequately protect the weak and stupid.

Some tort rules express pro-defense and anti-immigrant bias. For example, applying the lower standard of the place of first injury in cross border torts favors tortfeasors for no good reason. Applying the plaintiff's habitual residence in claims against European manufacturers benefits Europeans and hurts third-world plaintiffs whose home-country law will be less favorable.[8]

The wills and inheritance rules offer greater predictability after death, but enforcing local claw-back provisions may create more uncertainty about transfers of property before death. The policy preference for enforcing informal written wills promotes values of autonomy but may encourage fraud and frustrate policies designed to protect family wealth.

Examples

Bollywood Blues

1. Raj, a citizen of India who is a habitual resident of London, operates a retail DVD store in London. He regularly orders merchandise wholesale from Kumar, a lifelong resident of Mumbai. Raj and Kumar have a written agreement that provides among other things that "the law of England shall govern all disputes under this agreement."

   Raj claims that Kumar sent him 100 defective copies of "Bollywood Blues," the latest megahit from India. He claims the disks were injured in transit because Kumar improperly prepared them for shipping in Mumbai. Kumar argues that all risk of damage passed to Raj after the disks left his custody and control.

   Assume that under the law of India, the shipper bears the risk of damage until received unless the contract expressly provides to the contrary. Assume that the law of England provides that a commercial purchaser assumes the risk of damage during shipment and bears the obligation to obtain insurance.

   What law applies and why?

---

8. Professor Symeonides raises these criticisms in his article (p. 182).

2. Same facts. What law would apply if the parties had not chosen English law?

Tell's Tale

3. William Tell, a habitual resident of Switzerland, takes careful aim at an apple in Switzerland. Unfortunately, he misses and his arrow crosses into Austrian territory where its strikes and injures Gessler, a habitual resident of Austria.

   Assume that under the law of Switzerland an archer in a sporting event is not liable for injuries when he or she takes all appropriate and due care. Assume that Austrian law imposes strict liability on archers for injuries caused by arrows they discharge.

   What law will Austria apply? What law will Switzerland apply?

Blame in Spain

4. Cola Cola, a corporation that manufactures and distributes beverages, is incorporated in Delaware and has its principal place of business in Atlanta, Georgia. Cola Cola also has a local branch office in Madrid, Spain.

   The Madrid branch is responsible for operating and maintaining the delivery trucks that serve a large area in central Spain. To save money, the branch manager failed to replace worn tires on 20 delivery trucks.

   One of the trucks experienced a blowout, veered out of control, and struck and killed Pedro, a habitual resident of Madrid.

   Assume the law of Delaware and Georgia require proof of negligence but that Spanish law imposes strict liability. In a lawsuit in Madrid, will the Spanish court require proof of negligence? Explain.

Scuttled Scooter

5. Hubert and Wilma are married to each other and have lived their entire lives in the U.S. state of West Dakota. One day they take their dream vacation to Rome. They rent a car at the airport. While Hubert is driving from the airport to the hotel, a motor scooter suddenly pulls into his lane of traffic. To avoid hitting the scooter, Hubert swerves to the right and collides with a parked car. Wilma is injured.

   Assume that West Dakota provides a defense of spousal immunity for torts but that applicable Italian law does not. If Wilma's case were litigated in Italy, what law would apply to the tort?

A Bloody Mess

6. Fran, a citizen and habitual resident of the U.S. state of West Dakota, and Jan, a citizen and habitual resident of the U.S. state of East Carolina, are visiting Belgium to attend a conference sponsored by their church. It is a

fundamental principal of their church that believers should never receive blood transfusions.

While Fran and Jan are in their hotel room, Jan falls through a glass door, loses consciousness, and begins to bleed profusely. Fran attempts to stop the bleeding but is unsuccessful. She refuses to call for medical attention because she is convinced that treatment would involve involuntary blood transfusion. As a result Jan dies.

The legal representatives or next of kin entitled to bring a wrongful death action differ in West Dakota, East Carolina, and Belgium. Whose law applies to determine the legal representative?

7. Assume that under the law of Belgium Fran had a duty to summon medical attention and is civilly liable for preventable damages.

Assume that under the law of both West Dakota and East Carolina, a patient may refuse life-saving blood transfusions. Moreover, in both states a third person is immune to civil liability for failing to provide medical attention that she otherwise has a duty to provide when that person believes in good faith that the patient would refuse the medical attention. In other words, Fran has a defense to liability under the law of both her home state and Jan's home state, but not under the law of Belgium.

Whose law applies and why?

Hunting Dilemma

8. Scar and Simba are habitual residents of Kenya. Scar injures Simba in a hunting accident in Sherwood Forest in England. Assume that under the facts English law provides for actual damages in the amount of $200,000. But assume that a statute in Kenya limits damages for hunting accidents to $1,500. The preamble to the statute states that the purpose of the limitation is to promote tourism in Kenya. Assume further that Kenya choice of law rules would apply English law in this case.

What damages are recoverable in an action brought in England?

Explanations

Bollywood Blues

1. The law of England applies because the parties expressly chose it. So, under the hypothetical English law, the commercial purchaser, Kumar, bears the risk of damage in shipment.

2. If the parties had not expressly chosen English law, the contract would have been governed by the law of India. Under Rome I, contracts of sales are governed by the law of the habitual residence of the seller. In this case, the seller's habitual residence is India.

Although Rome I also directs courts to disregard specific choice rules when under all the circumstances the contract is "manifestly more closely connected" with another country, in this case, the contract is not manifestly more closely connected to England. No escape devices prevent applying Indian law: no mandatory provision requires application of English law, and applying Indian law does not violate any English policy.

Tell's Tale

3. Austria is a member of the EU. It will apply Rome II under which the tort is governed by the law of the place of the first injury—Austria—and strict liability applies.

   This result is not displaced by any other rule. The common habitual residence rule does not apply because Tell and Gessler have different habitual residences. And the tort is not manifestly more closely connected with Switzerland than with Austria.

   Switzerland is not a member of the EU. It will apply Swiss choice of law rules, and I don't know what those are. The point of the question is to remind you that EU countries will apply EU choice rules to claims with elements outside the EU, and also to remind you that not all countries in Europe are in the EU.

Blame in Spain

4. The Spanish court, applying Rome II, will apply Spanish law. Spain is the law of the place of the first injury. It is also the law of the parties' common habitual residence. Pedro is a habitual resident of Spain. For purposes of the tort arising from the negligent operation of the corporation's branch in Spain, the corporation is also a habitual resident of Spain. This is not a case where Spanish law would be displaced, because the tort is not manifestly more closely related to Delaware or Georgia than Spain.

Scuttled Scooter

5. Give yourself bonus points if you see the preliminary problem about whether Rome II applies to this case even in the EU. Rome II excludes "obligations" arising from marriage and family relationships. Since this case raises a potential defense to an obligation arising from a car accident, I think Rome II applies.

   Under Rome II, even though damages were first experienced in Italy, the tort is governed by the law of the parties' common habitual residence, so Hubert has a valid defense of spousal immunity under West Dakota law. The tort does not seem to be manifestly more closely connected to Italy so as to prevent applying the parties' home state law.

You might share my lack of complete confidence in this analysis and be worried by the potential claims of the scooter driver. After all, the tort is supposed to be governed by one country's law, and the Italian court would surely not apply West Dakota law so as to frustrate an Italian party's claims or defenses. There are two main points to note here. First, the formal application of the rules does not require a consideration of policy. Second, it is a complete mystery how the rules apply in multi-party situations.

A Bloody Mess

6. Fran and Jan are both citizens of the same country, the United States. But when a country has multiple units with their own tort law, each unit is treated as a separate country. Rome II art. 25. Because they are habitual residents of different states, and states are the source of tort law, they do not share a common habitual residence. Accordingly, under Rome II the tort is governed by the law of the place of first injury (Belgium), and Belgian law will decide who is the proper legal representative or next of kin.

   Professor Symeonides argues that this result makes no sense because Belgium has no interest in deciding who should be the proper party or claimant, while the dead person's home state has a big interest.

7. Apply Belgian law to the tort for the same reasons set forth in Explanation 6. Under Belgian law Fran had a duty to summon medical attention and is civilly liable for preventable damages.

   This result is also questioned by Professor Symeonides. Notice that if Fran and Jan shared a common habitual residence, then their home law would apply under Rome II, and Fran would have a defense.

   Here West Dakota and East Carolina are different states, but their law is identical, and Fran has a valid defense under both. There does not seem to be any good reason to view this case as involving any greater conflict. But rules are rules, and identical home-state law does not equal common habitual residence. Thus, Rome II would apply the law of the first injury, and the tort does not have a manifestly closer connection to another country.

Hunting Dilemma

8. I think the short right answer is: apply the law of the parties' common habitual residence under which Simba's damages are limited to $1,500.

   Maybe this is a case where you could persuade the court that the tort is manifestly more closely connected to England than Kenya, but good luck. You might have more luck persuading the court in England to disregard the Kenyan limitation on the ground that it violates forum public policy of fair compensation for injuries. Rome II gives excessive damages as an example of a law that violates public policy, and inadequate damages may equally violate public policy.

The fact that Kenya would apply English law is irrelevant because Rome II rejects renvoi. The rejection of renvoi is great provided there is a real conflict to resolve. But the failure to consider the territorial application of the Kenyon law seems counterproductive to the extent that, barring its application in England, there is no conflict.

This example illustrates how the EU effort to establish formal rules can produce bad results. The underlying difficulty arises from the fact that Rome II rejects territorial principles and adopts the law of common habitual residence while discouraging a consideration of state policies and interests. In this case, the policies behind the Kenya law make clear that it was not designed to have extraterritorial effect. But Rome II's choice rules and anti-renvoi provisions create a conflict and then require that it be resolved by applying the one country's law that makes the least sense.

PART VII

Constitutional Limits

Constitutional Requirement of Significant Contacts

INTRODUCTION

The Due Process Clause and Full Faith and Credit Clause place outer limits on the application of a state's law in certain cases. These limits are different from the limits imposed by the same clauses on a state's power to exercise personal jurisdiction and on a state's power to refuse to recognize judgments from other states.

Due process and full faith and credit require that a state must have a significant contact or significant aggregation of contacts creating state interests in order for the state's law to apply. In contrast, due process requires that a person have only minimum contacts with a state in order for the state to be able to exercise personal jurisdiction (Chapter 3).

Constitutional limits on choice of law are sometimes called constitutional limits on legislative jurisdiction. Legislative jurisdiction refers to the power of a state to make law (either by legislation or common law) as opposed to judicial jurisdiction, which refers to the power of the courts to decide a dispute.

The fact that the Constitution limits state choice of law means that every conflicts case requires two analyses. First, you need to consider what states' laws will apply under their choice of law approaches. Second, you need to consider whether a state's choice of law is permitted by due process and full faith and credit.

A SHORT HISTORY OF CONSTITUTIONAL LIMITS ON STATE CHOICE OF LAW

The Mother Case   In Home Insurance Co. v. Dick, 281 U.S. 397 (1930), the Supreme Court held that the Due Process Clause prevented Texas from applying its law so as to enlarge the obligations of parties to a Mexican contract that had nothing to do with Texas. The case firmly established constitutional limits to states' choices of law and rooted the limits in the Due Process Clause. The Full Faith and Credit Clause was not an issue because the case involved a foreign country's law.

The case stemmed from an insurance policy with a Mexican insurance company covering a Mexican tugboat used in Mexican waters. The policy owner was living in Mexico, and the claim was for a boat destroyed by fire in Mexico. The contract expressly provided that no lawsuit could be brought on the contract after one year from the date of the loss.

The plaintiff commenced the action more than one year after the loss. Defendants raised the one-year suit clause as a defense. The Texas courts rejected the defense because a Texas statute prevented parties from limiting the time in which to sue to less than two years and provided that any agreement to a shorter period of time was invalid.

The Supreme Court reversed, holding that the application of the Texas statute deprived defendants of property without due process. The Court emphasized that nothing in the contract related to Texas and that Texas state policies did not justify the application of Texas law to abrogate the rights of persons beyond its boarders who have done nothing in Texas and have no relation to anything in Texas.

The facts in Dick were extreme. The only Texas contact was the fact that the assignee of the person who originally bought the insurance was a citizen of Texas, and even he was residing in Mexico, though he remained a legal citizen of Texas.[1]

Years of Confusion   During the heyday of substantive due process, the Supreme Court flirted with the idea that legal rights vested under the law of the place of the wrong or contract and that disregarding such rights could amount to a taking in violation of due process. Some of the most extreme substantive due process conflicts cases predate Home Insurance Co. v. Dick, and the Supreme Court has not referred to them with approval for many years. See Weintraub, Commentary on the Conflict of Laws §9.2A at 658.

---

1. The Texas court did not even have personal jurisdiction over the Mexican insurance company. Instead, the plaintiff obtained quasi in rem jurisdiction over two New York corporations that insured the insurance company. Such quasi in rem jurisdiction would not be constitutionally permissible today.

By the late 1930s the Supreme Court rejected any notion of vested rights and held that more than one state's law might constitutionally apply to a dispute. As the Court wrote in Pacific Employers Insurance Co. v. Industrial Accident Commission, 306 U.S. 493 (1939), "[T]he full faith and credit clause does not require one state to substitute for its own statute, applicable to persons and events within it, the conflicting statute of another state, even though that statute is of controlling force in the courts of the state of its enactment with respect to the same persons and events."

In the decades following World War II, the Supreme Court repeatedly upheld state court decisions applying their own law. Watson v. Employers Liability Assurance Corp., 348 U.S. 66 (1954), held that Louisiana had "legitimate interest," which permitted the constitutional application of the state's direct action statute to a claim by a Louisiana resident injured by a hair-curling product manufactured out of state. Clay v. Sun Insurance Office, Ltd., 377 U.S. 179 (1964), held that Florida had "ample contacts" permitting the constitutional application of Florida law to a claim by a Florida resident for an insured loss occurring in Florida.

These cases signaled an unmistakable loosening of restrictions on state choice of law. Some Conflicts gurus even thought the Supremes might be charting a path toward overruling Home Insurance Company v. Dick or toward limiting that case to its unique, unrepeatable facts. Others thought the Court might be moving toward consolidating constitutional limits on personal jurisdiction and choice of law. It just goes to show how wrong you can be.

The New Standard   In the 1980s the Supreme Court decided three cases that clearly established several important points. First, the Court made clear that the Constitution provides limits on state choice of law that can be more restrictive than constitutional limits on personal jurisdiction. Second, the Court adopted a single standard for the limits on choice of law imposed by both the Due Process and Full Faith and Credit Clauses. Third, the Court limited the constitutional restriction to state choice of substantive law and permitted states to apply their own forum law to matters that are historically considered procedural under the Full Faith and Credit Clause.

SIGNIFICANT CONTACT OR SIGNIFICANT AGGREGATION OF CONTACTS CREATING STATE INTERESTS

The New Rule

In Allstate Insurance Co. v. Hague, 449 U.S. 302 (1981), a supermajority of the Supreme Court agreed on a new basic rule: "[F]or a State's substantive law to be selected in a constitutionally permissible manner, that State must have a significant contact or significant aggregation of contacts, creating state interest, such that choice of its law is neither arbitrary nor fundamentally unfair." The supermajority agreed that this test was required by both the Due Process and Full Faith and Credit Clauses.

The language of the significant contacts test is deliberately similar to the minimum contacts test required for personal jurisdiction. The Court's verbal formula indicates several things. The rule applies to the selection of a state's "substantive law." The requirement that the contact or aggregation of contacts be "significant" suggests that the test is different from the minimum contacts test and further suggests that minimum contacts may not be enough to permit the selection of a state's law. Finally, the contact or aggregation of contacts must create a state interest in the application of its law.

Applying the Rule to a Close Case The Supreme Court was divided on how to apply the new rule to the facts in the case where it was adopted. But everyone agreed it was a close case.

In Allstate Insurance Co. v. Hague, a Wisconsin resident was killed in Wisconsin when the motorcycle on which he was a passenger was rear-ended by a car. The drivers of the car and the motorcycle were also Wisconsin residents.

The drivers were uninsured, so a claim was made on the victim's own insurance policies. He had three policies for three cars, and each policy provided $15,000 for uninsured personal injury damages. The question was whether such coverage was cumulative. Wisconsin disallowed "stacking" of uninsured motorist coverage in separate policies and would limit recovery to $15,000. In contrast, Minnesota would allow "stacking" and permit a total recovery of $45,000.

Minnesota courts applied Minnesota law. The Supreme Court affirmed. While all members of the Court except Justice Stevens agreed on the new rule, only a plurality found that the new rule was satisfied by the facts. The plurality counted three separate contacts with Minnesota. First, the dead motorcycle passenger had been a longtime member of Minnesota's workforce and had commuted across the state line into Minnesota for 15 years. Second, the defendant insurance company was present and doing business in Minnesota. Third, the plaintiff, who had been married to the dead man and living in Wisconsin at the time of his death, later moved to Minnesota and married a Minnesota resident.

The plurality conceded that none of the three contacts was "significant" enough by itself to support the constitutional application of Minnesota law. Instead it found that the three contacts added up to being a significant aggregation creating state interests. The dissent agreed with the new rule. The dissent also agreed that none of the three contacts alone was significant, but the dissent disagreed that there was a significant aggregation.

Although divided, the Court's decision provided much clarity. First, a supermajority agreed that the state's jurisdiction over the defendant insurance company by itself was not enough for the state to apply its law. This makes clear that the significant contact test will require more than minimum contacts or even continuous and systematic contacts by the defendant that support personal jurisdiction when the claim is unrelated to the jurisdictional contacts. Second, the supermajority agreed that a plaintiff's post-event change of residence to the state does not by itself establish a significant contact permitting the constitutional selection of the state's law.

Giving Teeth to the New Rule

Allstate Insurance Co. v. Hague provided mixed signals. It created a new rule. Yet by upholding the application of Minnesota law under such skimpy contacts, the decision might have been signaling that significant contacts would exist in all but the most extreme situations. Four years later, in Phillips Petroleum Co. v. Shutts, 472 U.S. 797 (1985), the Court gave teeth to the test. It reached substantial agreement that a state's choice of its own law was unconstitutional.

Shutts was a class action brought in Kansas state court on behalf of persons entitled to interest for delayed royalty payments from gas leases. About 28,000 class members asserted claims averaging about $100 per claimant. The Kansas courts applied Kansas equity law to pick a fair rate of interest.

The Supreme Court reversed. It found no significant contact or significant aggregation of contacts permitting application of Kansas law to all claims when fewer than 1,000 of the class members were residents of Kansas, and only one-fourth of 1 percent of the gas leases were located in Kansas.

The Court's opinion added one more factor to consider in determining whether a state choice of law is constitutionally permissible: when considering fairness under the significant contacts test, "an important element is the expectation of the parties." This test had been first proposed by the dissent in Allstate.

The Court avoided explaining the practical consequences of the Shutts holding. While Kansas law could not be applied to all the claims, the Court observed that sometimes more than one state's law could be applied constitutionally. This left open the question of whether the law of a state like Texas where many of the claims arose might be applied to all claims. On the one hand, it might be fairer to apply the law of a state with a strong connection to many claims and claimants. On the other hand, the application of any single state's law to unrelated claims might run afoul of language in Shutts, quoted from Home Insurance v. Dick, that a state "may not abrogate the rights of parties beyond its borders having no relation to anything done or to be done within them."

One thing clearly emerged from *Shutts*: the significant contacts test had teeth. For plaintiffs with an average claim of $100, the significant contacts bite could be just as bad as its bark.

The Procedure Exception

Sun Oil v. Wortman   In a case with facts almost identical to *Shutts*, the Kansas courts applied the Kansas statute of limitations to all class members' claims even though the vast majority of claimants and gas leases were outside Kansas. The Supreme Court affirmed the application of Kansas procedural law despite the lack of a significant contact. Sun Oil Co. v. Wortman, 486 U.S. 717 (1988).

The Court's decision was unanimous but was supported by different opinions. The majority concluded that nothing in the Constitution prevents a state from applying its own statute of limitations. This is true even when the Constitution mandates that the substantive laws of another state govern the claims. The majority relied heavily on the historical practices under the Full Faith and Credit and Due Process Clauses. Under both clauses, states had long applied forum statutes of limitations to foreign claims. The majority also found that forum states had an interest in regulating their court dockets, and this interest supported application of forum statutes of limitations. Finally, the majority emphasized that the application of forum statutes of limitations would not cause unfair surprise because that was the traditional rule.

The majority opinion clarifies that the new significant contacts rule does not apply to matters traditionally deemed procedural for full faith and credit and due process purposes. In contrast, the concurrence maintained that the application of procedural laws like statutes of limitations must also satisfy the significant contacts standard. But the concurrence found that the test was satisfied under the facts.

Now . . . the Bad News   *Wortman* declared an absolute rule that should make life easy. Forums may constitutionally apply forum procedure in conflicts cases. This rule creates a new problem of characterization. The Court provides little guidance about how to differentiate substance and procedure for constitutional purposes. It refers to historical practice. But even in some older cases the Court itself avoided characterization. For example, in Home Insurance Co. v. Dick the Court looked to the effect of disregarding the contractual provision limiting claims, emphasizing that disregarding the provision enlarged obligations rather than classifying the matter as one governed by Texas limitations law. The distinction between substance and procedure, though rooted deeply in time, has bedeviled generations of courts and Conflicts gurus. Even on statutes of limitations, as two separate concurrences noted in *Wortman*, there can be uncertainty because some statutes of limitations are traditionally considered "substantive."

Finally, the majority's heavy reliance on history is not logically limited to matters of procedure. The opinion has been read as supporting a twofold approach to conflicts. Older, established rules (including procedural rules) may be constitutional based on continuing tradition, while the choice of law under some newer theory must meet the significant contacts test. Richman et al., Understanding Conflict of Laws §97[d] at 322. While this is farther than the Court has gone, it hints at remaining areas of uncertainty for constitutional limits on state choice of law.

Problem Spotting

Most state choice of law decisions will not exceed the constitutional limits on state choice of law or legislative jurisdiction. The significant contacts requirement will be met by traditional territorial rules, because the occurrence of the accident, the place of contracting, or location of property will establish a significant contact in the jurisdiction that gives the state an interest in applying its law. Significant contacts will likewise be met in decisions applying the approach of the Second Restatement because that approach directs the application of the law of the state with the most significant relationship to the issue.

The most obvious sources of constitutional problems will be decisions applying extreme forms of the better law approach and interest analysis. For example, under the better law approach, a forum might apply the better (forum) law in the absence of any contact. Under governmental interest analysis, a disinterested forum would resolve a true conflict between two other states' laws by applying forum law. Such applications of forum law are unconstitutional unless there is a significant contact or significant aggregation of contacts creating forum state interests in applying forum law.

Examples

Snare for the Unwary

1. What's wrong with this exam answer? "The Constitution requires minimum contacts for a state to exercise personal jurisdiction, but the Constitution requires significant contacts for a state to apply its substantive law. In other words, for a state's law to apply, there must always be more contacts than are required for personal jurisdiction. Minimum contacts are never enough for a state to apply its substantive law."

Phony Contact

2. Dr. Pamela Pinkerton is a physician living and practicing medicine in East Dakota. She is also executive director of the East Dakota Hospital. After assembling the members of the East Dakota hospital board for its annual meeting in Dakota City, East Dakota, Dr. Pinkerton connected the speakerphone and then pressed the preset code for Dr. Hennypenny, the consulting expert scheduled to brief the board on the first agenda item.

   Unfortunately, Dr. Pinkerton entered the wrong code and was connected with her former spouse, Dr. Andy Anti, a resident of the sovereign country of Zanti. When Dr. Anti picked up his phone in Zanti and heard his former spouse's voice, he became enraged. Before Pinkerton could terminate the connection, he accused her of assaulting him and abusing their daughter. The statements were false. Nevertheless, they embarrassed Dr. Pinkerton.

   Pinkerton sues Anti in state court in East Dakota for defamation. She alleges no economic injury but demands damages for emotional distress. Under the law of East Dakota, a false accusation of criminal conduct, including assault and child abuse, is defamatory per se and supports a right to recover damages for emotional distress. Under the law of Zanti, false accusations of this sort establish a legal right to recover only if economic damages can be proven.

   Dr. Anti has never been to East Dakota. He was married to and lived with Dr. Pinkerton in New York. Despite lacking connections to East Dakota, he answers the lawsuit and moves for summary judgment. He argues that the lawsuit is governed by Zanti law because Zanti was the place of his conduct. He also argues that applying East Dakota's tort standard would violate the U.S. Constitution.

   East Dakota follows the traditional territorial approach to torts. In defamation cases, its courts have held that the place of the wrong is the place of communication and that the place of communication is the place where the statement was heard by others. Accordingly, the trial court denies Anti's motion. Anti appeals the constitutional issue to the state supreme court. What's the court to do?

Stacking Students

3. Minnie, a citizen of Minneapolis, Minnesota, attended the University of Wisconsin. While in college, she bought a car in Wisconsin. During her senior year, she also bought a motorcycle. She bought two insurance policies for the vehicles from Cheesemakers Insurance Corp., a Wisconsin corporation. The day before graduation, Trucker ran a light and collided with Minnie while she was riding her motorcycle in Wisconsin. Trucker is a citizen of Wisconsin. Trucker is uninsured and insolvent.

Minnie seeks to recover the maximum amount of uninsured motorist coverage under both of her policies with Cheesemakers Insurance Co. Assume Wisconsin law does not permit such stacking but Minnesota does. Assume also that the corporation is qualified to do business in Minnesota and is subject to personal jurisdiction in that state. The insurance company calls you for advice. Should it pay on both policies?

4. Same facts. The corporation's counsel asks whether it will make any difference if it includes an express provision in insurance contracts that all claims under the contract are governed by Wisconsin law. Please advise.

5. Madison, a citizen of Wisconsin, attends the University of Minnesota. During spring break, while driving her father's car in Wisconsin, she is injured by Trey Trinker, a drunk driver. Trinker is uninsured, but Madison's father owns three cars, all insured by Cheesemakers Insurance Co., a Wisconsin corporation.

Madison sues Cheesemakers Insurance Co. in Minnesota seeking to recover the maximum amount of uninsured motorist coverage available under all three of her father's policies. The defendant moves for partial summary judgment, arguing that the Minnesota court is constitutionally barred from applying its own rule on stacking and must apply Wisconsin law. Rule on the motion.

Contract Contacts

6. Thomas orally agreed to haul cargo for Gordon between two warehouses in the country of Sodor. The parties to the contract were citizens of Sodor, and the contract specified that it was to be governed by the law of Sodor. The parties agreed to limit damages to $500. Unfortunately, Thomas dropped a box containing a Grecian Urn, causing property damage in the amount of $20,000.

Gordon sues Thomas in West Carolina and gets personal jurisdiction over Thomas while Thomas is vacationing in the state. The limitation on liability is valid under Sodor law but invalid under the contract law of West Carolina. West Carolina follows the better law approach.

Thomas has already paid $500 and moves for summary judgment, arguing that the court must apply Sodor law to the issue of damages. Rule on the motion and explain.

7. Same facts. Gordon commenced the action after the time prescribed by the applicable Sodor statute of limitations. Thomas moves the court to dismiss under the Sodor statute of limitations. Gordon argues that the court should apply the longer West Carolina statute, under which the claim is not time-barred. Who wins?

8. Same facts. Thomas and Gordon's oral agreement is enforceable under the law of Sodor. But the West Carolina statute of frauds provides that a contract to limit liability for loss is "void unless evidenced by a writing signed by the person bound thereby." May the West Carolina courts constitutionally apply the statute of frauds so as to exclude Thomas from limiting his liability?

Ugly Duckling

9. Bucky Duckling, a citizen of New York, learned in an airline magazine about Fountain of Youth Surgery Center in the state of East Carolina. Bucky traveled to the Center to have plastic surgery performed. Unfortunately, the surgery was not successful, and Bucky is uglier than ever.

   Assume Bucky sues the Surgery Center three years after the surgery in New York state court and gets personal jurisdiction over the defendant based on its solicitation of business in the state. Assume the action is timely under New York statutes of limitations and that East Carolina has a statute requiring medical malpractice claims to be commenced within two years. Assume further that under East Carolina law, the expiration of two years extinguishes all substantive rights as well as remedies.

   The defendant moves to dismiss under East Carolina law and under the Due Process and Full Faith and Credit Clauses. Rule on the motion and explain.

Explanations

Snare for the Unwary

1. The Supreme Court's deliberate formulation of the significant contacts test in language similar to the minimum contacts test invites error. It is certainly true that minimum contacts sufficient for personal jurisdiction are not necessarily sufficient for the selection of the state's law. This is true as a matter of logic. After all, if the constitutional limits on personal jurisdiction adequately limited choice of law, there would be no need for a separate limit. This is also obvious from the line of cases from *Dick* to *Hague*, because the courts' personal jurisdiction in those cases never prevented a further consideration of constitutional limits on choice of law.

   But the important point is that the conclusion of whether a contact is "minimum" or "significant" is not quantitative. Applying the tests requires a consideration of the purposes of the constitutional limits. The minimum contacts test serves to restrict the unfair expansion of state personal jurisdiction and protects defendants from the burden of litigating in constitutionally inconvenient forums. Accordingly, minimum contacts analysis focuses on the defendant's purposeful conduct in or directed toward the forum state and the reasonableness of the exercise of jurisdiction. In contrast, requiring significant contacts serves to prevent the unfair application of state substantive law to disputes in which the state has no interest in applying its law. Accordingly, the significant contacts test focuses on contacts by any person or other circumstances that create a state interest in applying its law.

Sometimes the significant contacts test requires more than minimum contacts. For example, a supermajority of Justices in *Hague* agreed that personal jurisdiction was not a significant contact. In that case personal jurisdiction was even supported by extensive business contacts that permitted the exercise of general jurisdiction rather than merely minimum contacts. Nevertheless, the extensive contacts did not establish a significant contact because they did not have anything to do with the issues in litigation and did not establish a state interest in applying the state's stacking rule.

From this it does not follow, however, that the significant contacts test always requires more than the contacts required for general jurisdiction. On the contrary, a minimum contact will in some cases also be a significant contact permitting application of a state's law. For example, where a nonresident motorist causes a tort in the forum state, the single tortious act establishes a minimum contact permitting exercise of long-arm jurisdiction. The same single act will be a significant contact creating a state interest in applying the forum's tort law.

Moreover, a significant contact may be established by a contact that does not count as a minimum contact because it was not a purposeful act by the defendant directed at the forum state. The residence of the plaintiff in a state would normally establish a significant contact permitting the application of that state's substantive law because states have an interest in protecting their residents. This is true even when conduct giving rise to the claim by or against the resident occurred elsewhere and might not support the exercise of personal jurisdiction over the defendant.

Phony Contact

2. The court should affirm. The facts that the plaintiff is domiciled in the state and that the defendant's words were heard there establish significant contacts creating state interests so that the application of East Dakota's tort law does not violate the Due Process or Full Faith and Credit Clauses.

   This example makes several important points. The first point is that, because the court has merged the due process and full faith and credit limits on choice of law, the significant contacts limit on state choice of law also applies whether the conflicting law is from a sister state or foreign country. In this example the Full Faith and Credit Clause does not really apply since the competing law is from a foreign country rather than a sister state.

The second important point is that the due process limits on the state court's exercise of personal jurisdiction differ from the due process limits on the application of the state's law. Under these facts, the exercise of personal jurisdiction is probably unconstitutional. But the defendant has not raised that defense.

Personal jurisdiction limits the exercise of state power in order to protect the defendant from being seriously inconvenienced. Accordingly, the necessary minimum contacts required for the exercise of personal jurisdiction over a nonresident defendant focus on the defendant's contacts with the state. Minimum contacts require purposeful activity by the defendant directed toward the forum state. Here such contacts are lacking, and the plaintiff's contacts with the state do not establish minimum contacts. But because the defendant has waived the defense, the court obtained valid personal jurisdiction.

The significant contacts required for the application of a state's law differ from the contacts needed for personal jurisdiction. Allstate Insurance Co. v. Hague makes clear that minimum contacts sufficient to establish personal jurisdiction are not necessarily enough for significant contacts. But the contacts the plurality found to be significant related less to the defendant than to the tort victim's past relationship with the forum and the plaintiff's post-accident residence in the forum state. Contacts by persons other than the defendant were sufficient to establish an identifiable forum interest in applying forum law to permit a larger recovery. Similarly, in the example, Dr. Pinkerton's residence in East Dakota gives that state an interest in applying its law to promote its residents' interests in being free from emotional distress.

The third important point is that the contacts evaluated for purposes of determining whether there is a significant contact or significant aggregation of contacts are not necessarily the same facts considered under the state's choice of law rule. For example, the plaintiff's residence in the forum state may establish a significant contact, but that fact is not considered in the forum's application of its place of the wrong rule.

The fourth important point is the need for caution in relying on historical conflicts rules as a safe harbor. Traditional rules may not automatically satisfy significant contacts requirements. The First Restatement contains rules formulated from principles of vested rights that did not always have strong case law authority. Its rule that the place of the wrong for defamation is where the words were heard may be an example of such a rule. For traditional conflicts rules, the safe course will be to apply the significant contacts test, identifying factual connections with the forum state and showing, if possible, how application of the traditional choice rule will not cause surprise. The lack-of-surprise argument is not too persuasive in a situation like that described in the example where the rule results in an odd, unforeseen law being applied. While a radio broadcaster might expect to be heard in distant jurisdictions and might not be surprised to find those countries applying their laws, Anti had little reason to expect the words spoken in Zanti to be overheard by third persons in a foreign country.

The final important point is that constitutional limits on choice of law can be pretty loose. The significant contacts test does not prevent bad choice of law decisions.

Stacking Students

3. I would advise my client to pay under both policies. Minnie can get personal jurisdiction over the insurance company in Minnesota, and that state will permit stacking. The application of Minnesota law will not be unconstitutional because Minnie's legal residence in the forum state is a significant contact that gives that state an interest in applying its law.

   The facts in the example are distinguishable from *Hague*, where the victim of the tort and claimant on the insurance policy were not residents of Minnesota at the time of the injury and where the plaintiff became a resident of Minnesota only after the accident.

4. Adding the contractual choice of Wisconsin law in Wisconsin insurance contracts will probably not make it unconstitutional for Minnesota to apply its law to claims by Minnesota residents, though the contractual language might persuade it or other states to apply Wisconsin law. The plaintiff's residence in Minnesota would still be a significant contact creating a state interest in applying Minnesota law.

   Adding the choice of Wisconsin law makes the case look more like the facts in Home Insurance Co. v. Dick, where the Supreme Court held that enlarging the party's obligations beyond the terms of the contract violated due process. And adding the choice of law clause strengthens the defendant's argument that it would be unfairly surprised by the application of Minnesota law.

   Nevertheless, I think these arguments will be losers. *Dick* involved a plaintiff who had no legal relationship with the forum state except for a technical residence. Perhaps more important, the insurable loss was physically located in Mexico and could not be removed from Mexico. In contrast, cars are mobile; insurance companies expect to cover losses in other states; and they expect the law of other states to govern. Clay v. Sun Insurance Office Ltd. held that there were "ample contacts" to apply Florida law and to void the one-year suit clause in a contract where the insured property was mobile and the plaintiff resided in Florida. Even more obviously, an insurance company may expect to have its anti-stacking provisions disregarded by other states, and an insurance company's protest that it is "shocked, shocked"[2] to find its contract governed by Minnesota's stacking rule is hardly credible after Allstate Insurance Co. v. Hague.

5. I would deny the motion and hold that Minnesota was not constitutionally prevented from applying its law. But the answer is not certain, and the example illustrates the issues on which the Supreme Court split in *Hague*.

On the one hand, the plaintiff's residence in Minnesota would establish a significant contact. On the other hand, if the plaintiff had no connection with Minnesota, then there would be no significant contact. The facts in the example may fall in the middle and present two questions. First, they raise the question of whether enrollment as a student establishes a meaningful contact — either one that is significant or one that can be aggregated with others. Second, they raise the question left open by the plurality in *Hague* as to whether two of the three contacts — the plaintiff's ongoing relationship with the forum state and the defendant's business activity in the forum state — form a significant aggregation of contacts creating state interests that support application of forum law.

I would find that the plaintiff's enrollment as a student in Minnesota was a significant contact analogous to domicile that created a state interest in applying its stacking law. This stems from my view that the state has a strong interest in applying its law for the protection of young people who come into the state for prolonged periods of time, many of whom eventually become residents or enter other formal legal relationships with residents. It also stems from the reality that states derive identifiable economic and other benefits from out-of-state students and actively solicit attendance by such students. In sum, like the plurality in *Hague* I would emphasize the variable relationships with a state that give the state a real interest in applying its law. The relationship of the nonresident student is arguably even more significant than that of the commuter-worker. If forced to, I would probably find that two of the three *Hague* contacts were a significant aggregation. Like the plurality, I am inclined to see some long-term relationships as equal to or even more important than legal domicile.

The contacts might be evaluated differently by other judges. The dissenting Justices in *Hague* might construe the contacts more narrowly. They insisted on a careful consideration of the ways in which the contacts logically supported the application of state interests. "The State has a legitimate interest in applying a rule of decision to the litigation only if the facts to which the rule will be applied have created effects within the State, toward which the State's public policy is directed." 449 U.S. at 334

---

2. *See Casablanca* (1942).

(Powell, J., dissenting). This standard might not support application of Minnesota law, because it is difficult to show how long-term presence in the state is tied to a policy requiring stacking.

Contract Contacts

6. I would grant the motion on the ground that there is no significant contact or significant aggregation of contacts creating state interests for the application of the West Carolina's law. This is a case like *Dick*, where disregarding the limits on liability, valid where the contract was entered and to be performed, would surprise the defendant and substantially enlarge obligations. Under these facts, applying forum law would constitute a taking in violation of due process.

7. Gordon wins. If West Carolina wants to apply its longer statute of limitations, then it is not prohibited by due process. Sun Oil v. Wortman is directly on point. *Wortman* held that the forum's application of its own statute of limitations was not unconstitutional because statutes of limitations are procedural, forums traditionally applied forum procedure, and the significant contacts test does not apply so as to prevent a forum from applying its procedural rules.

8. Aargh. This example illustrates the new problems created by *Wortman's* exception for "procedure." In the absence of contacts creating state interests, due process prevents a state from applying its substantive contract law so as to enlarge the obligations of parties to an out-of-state agreement. But according to *Wortman*, a state may apply its own procedural rules.

   The question is whether statutes of frauds "voiding" a foreign oral agreement limiting liability are procedural. *Wortman* indicates that whether an issue is procedural for this purpose is largely historical. The duration of the practice is relevant to the Framer's intent and helps remove the element of unfair surprise. The problem is that the characterization of statutes of frauds as substantive or procedural was a source of much confusion and uncertainty. For example, statutes that merely prevented oral evidence might be procedural while statutes that imposed formal requirements for a valid contract might be substantive.

   While the answer is uncertain, I would hold that due process prevents West Carolina from applying its statute of frauds. First, I would argue that the statute is substantive and emphasize that it speaks of voiding a contract rather than excluding evidence. Applying the significant contacts test to this substantive law, I would find there is no significant contact or significant aggregation of contacts creating an interest in applying the statute. This, too, is uncertain. The forum may arguably have an interest in applying its "substantive" rule of formal validity in order to promote certain procedural or evidentiary goals such as requiring corroborative proof of oral promises.

Second, I would draw on the Court's opinion in *Dick* to adopt a more functional approach to the characterization problem. The disregard of the oral promise would have the practical effect of enlarging liability — regardless of how the rule was characterized. I would argue that such an effect should not be permitted absent a significant contact. Although *Wortman* seemed to indicate that no contact creating a state interest was required for traditional procedural rules, the majority also noted that the forum had an interest in applying its statute of limitations. No similar state interest supports applying the statute of frauds under the facts.

Ugly Duckling

9. Motion denied. New York may constitutionally apply New York's longer statute of limitations. This example is a reminder that splits on the court and legal confusion do not necessarily prevent certainty in a particular fact situation.

First, *Wortman* makes clear that New York may apply its statute of limitations in disregard of a foreign statute of limitations, because forums traditionally applied forum procedural law. The problem is that the East Carolina statute may be a "substantive" statute of repose. Concurring Justices in *Wortman* expressly left open the question of whether a forum could disregard a substantive limitation in a foreign law when the state lacked significant contacts supporting the application of its substantive law. A strong case could be made, for example, that a state could not apply a longer forum statute of limitations and permit a trespass action by a former owner in disregard of a foreign statute of limitation that has the effect of transferring title by adverse possession. Although East Carolina's statute extinguishing medical malpractice claims may be a statute of repose, it seems to serve the same purposes of finality as a normal statute of limitations. Such a statute does not seem to have substantive effects similar to a statute conferring title to property, so New York might be permitted to apply New York's longer limitations under the traditional rule in *Wortman*.

Second, even if the issue is substantive, New York may constitutionally apply its law. The facts establish several significant contacts supporting New York's interest in applying its law. The plaintiff is a resident of New York, and the harmful consequences of the conduct were felt in New York. Moreover, the defendant solicited business in the state and encouraged people to leave the state to obtain medical services elsewhere that were not subject to the direct control of New York public health law. Each one of these contacts may have been significant because they created state interests in applying forum law. Together the contacts certainly add up to a significant aggregation of contacts.

In conclusion, sometimes the answer is easy even when the law is confusing. Here New York can apply its longer statute of limitations. If the statute is procedural, then there is no constitutional problem with applying it according to *Wortman*. If it is substantive, it is constitutional for New York to apply it because there are probably one or more significant contacts creating state interests, and there is certainly an aggregation of contacts creating state interests in applying New York's law.

CHAPTER 28

Other Constitutional Limits on State Choice of Law

INTRODUCTION

This chapter considers three more situations where the Constitution may limit state choice of law. First, it considers state "door closing" statutes where a state attempts to deprive its own courts of jurisdiction to hear claims that arise in other states. Second, it considers "reverse door closing statutes" or "localizing statutes," where one state creates a cause of action and attempts to restrict all litigation to courts of that state. Third, the chapter considers whether states must respect sovereign immunity defenses raised by sister states.

DOOR CLOSING

Closing Door to Judgments We will see (in Chapter 29) that a state may not refuse to give full faith and credit to a judgment from a sister state just because the other state's law offends the forum state's public policy. The Supreme Court has also held that a state may not escape its obligation to enforce a sister state's judgment by removing jurisdiction from its state courts to enforce such judgments. Kenney v. Supreme Lodge of the World, 252 U.S. 411 (1920).

Closing Door to Claims In Hughes v. Fetter, 341 U.S. 609 (1951), a Wisconsin statute removed jurisdiction from the state courts to hear wrongful death claims arising in other states. The state did not have a public policy against wrongful death actions. On the contrary, a Wisconsin statute permitted recovery for wrongful deaths that occurred in the state.

The Supreme Court held that Wisconsin could not refuse to recognize the wrongful death action that arose under Illinois law when Wisconsin had no objection to the claim except for the fact that it arose in another state. The Supreme Court rooted Wisconsin's obligation to open its door to the claim in the Full Faith and Credit Clause. Because the Full Faith and Credit Clause imposes obligations on states to respect other state laws, the decision has no application to claims based on the law of foreign countries.

The Supreme Court reached its conclusion in *Hughes* by balancing the Full Faith and Credit Clause policy of recognizing sister state laws against the Wisconsin policy against enforcing death actions from other states.

Despite a well-reasoned dissent that won four votes, *Hughes* appears to be settled law. But it applies only in the narrow situation where a state seeks to close its door to sister state laws for no good reason other than that they are sister state laws. Such door-slamming is rude, unsisterly — and unconstitutional.

REVERSE DOOR CLOSING

Extraterritorial Effect of Local Venue Rule Once upon a time, the Alabama legislature enacted a statute that established a cause of action for certain work-related injuries. The new statute created rights that were not recognized at common law. And it required all claims under the statute to be brought in Alabama state courts "and not elsewhere." This attempt to force litigation in the home state courts is called a reverse door closing statute because it tries to close the doors of other jurisdictions. It is also called a localizing statute because it tries to localize the place of litigation.

The Supreme Court held in Tennessee Coal, Iron & Railroad Co. v. George, 233 U.S. 354 (1914), that a sister state was not prohibited from hearing a lawsuit based on the Alabama statute. The defendant argued that the Full Faith and Credit Clause required respect for the limits imposed by the Alabama statute. The Supreme Court rejected the argument. It reasoned that states cannot control the enforcement of rights they create in other states. Of course, the Constitution does not *prohibit* other states from respecting such restrictions on grounds of sisterly comity. It just does not require such respect.

The Supreme Court has similarly held that states need not enforce special venue or procedural requirements imposed by the state whose law creates a claim. In Crider v. Zurich Insurance Co., 380 U.S. 39 (1965), the Court held that a state may enforce a claim created by a sister state's law and need not give full faith and credit to a requirement imposed by the sister state that the claim must be brought before a particular administrative tribunal. The lesson is clear: a state may create a new cause of action and control the litigation in home state proceedings. But it loses control over such claims in other states, because sister states do not have to give full faith and credit to another state's attempt to control litigation outside the state.

SISTER STATE SOVEREIGN IMMUNITY

In Nevada v. Hall, 440 U.S. 410 (1979), a person was injured in California by a car owned by the state of Nevada and operated by a Nevada state driver. In a tort action in California state court against the state of Nevada, the California courts rejected Nevada's defense of sovereign immunity. The lawsuit could not have been brought in or removed to federal court because the Eleventh Amendment provides, "The judicial power of the United States shall not be construed to extend to any suit in law or equity, commenced or prosecuted against one of the United States by Citizens of another State, or by Citizens or Subjects of any Foreign State." U.S. Const. amend. XI.

The Supreme Court held that the Constitution does not require state courts to respect sovereign immunity defenses of sister states. The Court rejected federalism arguments based on history, the Full Faith and Credit Clause, and the structure of the Constitution. Three Justices dissented. They argued that sovereign immunity was universally accepted by the Framers and implied by the structure of the Constitution.

Tit for Tat In Franchise Tax Board of California v. Hyatt (Hyatt I), 538 U.S. 488 (2003), a Nevada citizen sued the state of California in Nevada state court, claiming that California's tax authorities had committed various intentional torts in attempting to collect state taxes. The Nevada[1] courts rejected California's defense of complete sovereign immunity for acts in pursuit of official duties. The Supreme Court affirmed. The Court found no basis for distinguishing torts stemming from car accidents and tax collection. 538 U.S. at 498.

---

1. Yes, the *same* home of the mustangs that was so outraged by Nevada v. Hall that it petitioned for a constitutional amendment banning states from disregarding other states' sovereign immunity.

Almost Overruled A growing number of Justices now question whether Nevada v. Hall was rightly decided. After remand in *Hyatt I*, the plaintiff recovered a judgment for $1 million damages against the state of California. California challenged the judgment in the U.S. Supreme Court on two grounds in *Hyatt II*, 136 S.Ct. 1277 (2016). First, California asked the Court to overrule Nevada v. Hall and to declare that the U.S. Constitution requires state courts to respect the sovereign immunity of sister states. At the time the Court decided *Hyatt II*, there were only eight Justices on the Court. Four Justices wanted to overrule Nevada v. Hall. This was one vote short of the majority needed reverse the decision below.

Parity for Sister States In *Hyatt II* California also asked the Supreme Court to reverse the $1 million judgment on the ground that California should get the benefit of the $50,000 cap on damages that the state of Nevada enjoyed when it was sued in its own courts. A majority of the Supreme Court agreed. Failing to give sister-states the same immunity that the forum state enjoys expresses "a constitutionally impermissible 'policy of hostility'" that violates the Full Faith and Credit Clause. 136 S. Ct. 1277, 1282 (2016). The new parity requirement means that a forum state must give other states at least as much immunity as it gives its own state when it is a defendant.

Comity Not Prohibited Nothing in the Constitution requires states to reject the defense of sovereign immunity raised by sister states. Some states on grounds of comity continue to respect the defense of sovereign immunity raised by sister states. *See* Schoeberlein v. Purdue University, 544 N.E.2d 283, 287 (Ill. 1989).

Examples

Meandering Mother

1. Caddy fled the state of West Florida, leaving behind her daughter, Quentin, who was raised in West Florida by Caddy's brother Jason. Jason stole money that Caddy sent to Quentin. Jason also refused to let Caddy see her daughter when she visited town.

   Caddy commences a civil action against Jason in the state of East Carolina for alienation of Quentin's affections based on Jason's conduct in West Florida. The law of West Florida recognizes a cause of action for alienation of affections under these circumstances. Although the East Carolina courts follow the traditional territorial rules of the First Restatement of Conflicts, the East Carolina legislature has recently passed a statute that eliminates causes of action for the tort of alienation of affections. The statute specifically provides: "No action shall be brought seeking damages for alienation of affections or criminal conversation." The East Carolina supreme court has construed this statute as depriving state courts of subject matter jurisdiction over claims for alienation of affections.

The trial court dismisses Caddy's claim. She appeals on the ground that the East Carolina refusal to recognize the alienation of affections claim is prohibited by the Full Faith and Credit Clause. Rule on the appeal and explain.

Tort Jam Door Slam

2. Assume the California state court system has become flooded with medical malpractice claims. Some of the claims are based on medical services provided in other states and even foreign countries. Plaintiff's lawyers have been drawn to California because of its plaintiff-friendly laws and because physicians frequently travel to the state for medical conventions where they can be served with process.

   The judiciary committee of the state legislature has proposed several bills aimed at curing the state's woes. The committee is currently considering a proposed bill that provides: "The subject matter jurisdiction of the courts of California shall not extend to medical malpractice claims that arise outside the state." You are on the committee, and all heads turn to hear your sage advice about the efficacy of the proposed measure. Please advise.

Injury Worse Than the Insult

3. The state of Confusion has passed a statute prohibiting "actionable insult." The law defines the cause of action to include the use of certain offensive words and gestures and permits any person insulted by such conduct to recover damages fixed in the amount of $50.00. The law creating the cause of action provides expressly that "all actions to enforce claims under this act must be brought before a competent Justice of the Peace in the state of Confusion and Justices of the Peace have exclusive jurisdiction to enforce said claims."

   Patrick commences a civil action in Utah state court asserting a claim against Donna under the Confusion statute for an actionable insult that occurred in Confusion. Donna moves to dismiss on the ground that Utah is constitutionally obligated to respect the Confusion requirement that claims be litigated exclusively before Justices of the Peace in Confusion. Rule on the motion and explain.

Jury Worry

4. The state legislature in East Dakota is considering adopting a state tort claim act that would partially waive the state's defense of sovereign immunity to personal injury tort actions. The legislature wants to require that all claims under the act will be litigated in a new special state claims court, which will sit without a jury. Dotty Dooright, a state legislator, asks you whether the state requirements will be binding in other states, or whether other states might permit tort claims against the state of East Dakota to be tried to a jury. Please advise.

Sorority Sister State Conflict

5. Sissie Carrie is a member of the Sigma Iota Sigma sorority at the University of East Dakota, a state university. Carrie went on an official university-sponsored event to California. She traveled with four sorority sisters in a private car operated by Professor Blinky Nod, the sorority's faculty advisor. After entering the state of California, Professor Nod fell asleep at the wheel and crashed into a brick wall. Carrie suffered serious injuries in the accident.

   Carrie brings a civil action in California state court against Professor Nod. The state of East Dakota retains a complete defense of sovereign immunity. Under the law of East Dakota, faculty members at the state university are deemed state actors and have a complete defense of sovereign immunity to tort liability for acts committed in the scope of their employment. Case law in East Dakota establishes that falling asleep on the job is an act in the scope of employment.

   California courts reject the defense of sovereign immunity and enter judgment against the professor. Your nomination to the Supreme Court has been confirmed. This is your first case. Do you vote to affirm or reverse?

6. Same facts. Sissie Carrie is rushed to the state hospital in Los Angeles by Officer Kali Berkeley, a California state police officer. On the way to the hospital, Officer Berkeley slams on her brakes to avoid hitting a dog, skids, and hits—yep—another brick wall. Sissie Carrie suffers additional personal injuries as a result.

   Assume that Officer Berkeley has a complete defense to personal injury liability under California's doctrine of sovereign immunity. Carrie waits until Berkeley travels through East Dakota and then serves her with process in a tort action seeking damages for the accident in California. Berkeley moves to dismiss, arguing that disregarding the defense of sovereign immunity is unconstitutional. Is it?

Explanations

Meandering Mother

1. The trial court's dismissal of the alienation of affections claim is affirmed. There is no full faith and credit problem because the forum statute applies to all claims, including those that arise in the forum state. The blanket prohibition of jurisdiction over such claims evidences a forum policy against enforcing such causes of action wherever they arise. A forum can refuse to recognize claims that conflict with its own policies and can likewise refuse to exercise jurisdiction over such claims. The case is different from Hughes v. Fetter, where the forum had no policy against wrongful death claims and denied jurisdiction solely to claims that arose in other states.

Tort Jam Door Slam

2. Aside from the fact that the bill would probably be bad law with unintended consequences, there would also be constitutional problems with enforcing the jurisdictional exclusion in certain situations. Full faith and credit prevents California from refusing to exercise jurisdiction over a claim that arises under the law of another state just because it arises elsewhere. Because Full Faith and Credit imposes an obligation to respect only sister state laws, the bill might be applied to claims that arise in foreign countries.

Injury Worse Than the Insult

3. The motion is denied. Full faith and credit does not require one state to recognize the jurisdictional limits imposed on causes of action created in another state. This example is indistinguishable from Alabama's unsuccessful effort to restrict employee claims to Alabama courts in Tennessee Coal, Iron & Railroad Co. v. George, 233 U.S. 354 (1914).

Jury Worry

4. The venue restriction and exclusion of the jury will not be binding in other states. Other states need not give full faith and credit to such venue and procedural conditions even when they are enforced in the courts of the state that created the cause of action.

Sorority Sister State Conflict

5. You vote to affirm unless you want to overrule Nevada v. Hall. California is not required by the Constitution to recognize the sovereign immunity

defense available under another state's law—at least not when it has a substantial interest in applying its law and when its disregard of foreign law is not based on hostility to the law of a sister state. Here California has a substantial interest in providing full compensation to persons injured on its highways.

The only facts in the example that distinguish it from Nevada v. Hall are that the individual defendant claims the benefit of the defense and the injured plaintiff is not a resident of California. These differences do not alter the outcome. California has a substantial interest in providing full compensation to persons injured on its highways. Its interest in compensating nonresidents is legitimate for constitutional purposes even if it is not accorded much respect by interest analysis theorists. Moreover, the state has an interest in imposing liability on the individual driver in order to deter negligent driving on its highways. The fact that the judgment runs against the individual driver rather than the sovereign state of East Dakota makes the case even easier than Nevada v. Hall because the interests of the sister state are not involved as directly.

6. Is this the hard case meeting bad law? It makes sense for the individual police officer protected by her home state defense of sovereign immunity to enjoy the same protections in other state courts that her sovereign would. And it seems hard to impose East Dakota's liability standards on the police officer doing her job back home. The fear of this kind of case may lead the Supreme Court to overrule Nevada v. Hall and declare that states must respect sovereign immunity defenses of sister states. But so far the Court's decisions provide limited authority for preventing East Dakota from applying its own tort law and rejecting the defense of sovereign immunity.

First, Officer Berkeley is subject to general personal jurisdiction in East Dakota, where she was physically present and served with process.

Second, the fact that an East Dakota citizen was injured normally would probably establish a significant contact so that East Dakota's application of its own law would not violate due process or full faith and credit.

Third, in the absence of a constitutional limitation on East Dakota's choice of law, the Supreme Court does not (yet) require East Dakota to respect California's defense of sovereign immunity. *Hyatt I* did not distinguish between core sovereign functions and other state activities.

After *Hyatt II*, East Dakota courts must give California at least as much immunity as they give to East Dakota when it is sued in its own state courts. If East Dakota has a complete defense of sovereign immunity in East Dakota courts, then so will California (and its officer). And if East Dakota's damages are capped at $10,000, then so will California's (and its officer's).

Equal Protection and Privileges and Immunities

INTRODUCTION

The legal rules applied in conflicts cases sometimes treat parties differently based on their place of residence, domicile, or citizenship. This chapter considers constitutional challenges to such unequal treatment based on the Equal Protection Clause and the Privileges and Immunities Clause of the Constitution.

CHAPTERS AND VERSES

Equal Protection The Equal Protection Clause of the Fourteenth Amendment provides, "[N]or shall any State . . . deny to any person within its jurisdiction the equal protection of the laws." U.S. Const. amend. XIV §1.

Privileges and Immunities The Constitution contains two different Privileges and Immunities Clauses. The main Privileges and Immunities Clause is in the original body of the Constitution: "The Citizens of each State shall be entitled to all Privileges and Immunities of Citizens in the several States." U.S. Const. art. IV §2. Also called the Comity Clause, this provision creates no rights but helps forge a unified nation by requiring that important rights created by state laws be applied equally to all citizens.

After the Civil War, the Fourteenth Amendment was added to correct the outrageous Dred Scott decision. It provides, "All persons born or naturalized in the United States and subject to the jurisdiction thereof, are citizens of the United States and of the State wherein they reside." U.S. Const. amend. XIV §1. The Fourteenth Amendment contains its own Privileges and Immunities Clause: "No State shall make or enforce any law which shall abridge the privileges or immunities of citizens of the United States." Id.

Scope of Protection The Equal Protection Clause applies broadly to all legal persons, including corporations and citizens of foreign countries. The main Privileges and Immunities Clause applies only to "citizens" of "states." It does not apply to citizens of foreign countries or to corporations. Blake v. McClung, 172 U.S. 239 (1898) (holding corporations are not "citizens" for purposes of the Privileges and Immunities Clause).

OVERLAP AND UNCERTAINTY

The Supreme Court has set forth different tests for the Equal Protection and Privileges and Immunities Clauses, but there is much overlap. A state law flatly prohibiting citizens of other states from marrying would violate both clauses. But the Supreme Court has not yet found that ordinary choice of law rules offend either clause just because they may disadvantage out-of-state residents. Lower courts have rejected such challenges. E.g., Skahill v. Capital Airlines, Inc., 234 F. Supp. 906, 908–909 (S.D.N.Y. 1964). See generally Weintraub, Commentary on the Conflict of Laws §9.4 at 720.

JUDICIAL TESTS FOR EQUAL PROTECTION

Strict Scrutiny The Supreme Court applies a sliding scale for different equal protection claims. At one extreme are state laws that treat persons differently based on race. Such unequal treatment is not absolutely prohibited, but it is entitled to no deference and is subject to strict scrutiny. State laws that treat persons differently based on race violate the Equal Protection Clause unless the state can show that such unequal treatment is necessary to achieve a compelling state interest.

Strict scrutiny review usually results in a finding that the challenged law is unconstitutional. But the application of the test is not purely logical and reflects historical context and the values of the Court. In 1944 a divided Court approved the forced relocation and internment of a disfavored racial minority, Japanese Americans and Japanese. Korematsu v. United States, 323

U.S. 214 (1944). In 2003 a divided Court disapproved a state university's admissions program that gave a numerical preference to racial minorities. Gratz v. Bollinger, 539 U.S. 244 (2003). In a similar case, a still divided Court held that an individualized consideration of race was permitted by a state law school in order to achieve the compelling state interest of admitting a diverse student body. Grutter v. Bollinger, 539 U.S. 306 (2003).

Aliens   Older Supreme Court decisions allowed states considerable leeway in discriminating against aliens. In 1923 the Court upheld state alien land laws that prohibited the sale or lease of farm land to aliens. Terrace v. Thompson, 263 U.S. 197 (1923). Later cases applied strict scrutiny to state classifications that targeted discrete and insular minorities, including aliens. In re Griffiths, 413 U.S. 717 (1973) (holding state statute prohibiting aliens from practicing law violates equal protection).

There are exceptions to strict scrutiny of legal classifications based on alienage. Federal laws discriminating on the basis of alienage are not subject to strict scrutiny review owing to Congress's plenary power over immigration. Federal laws will be upheld so long as they do not "arbitrarily subject all resident aliens to different substantive rules from those applied to citizens." Hampton v. Mow Sun Wong, 426 U.S. 88, 100 (1976). State laws discriminating against undocumented aliens are not generally subject to strict scrutiny, but those that discriminate against their children are. Plyler v. Doe, 457 U.S. 202 (1982). State laws preventing aliens from voting or participating in positions "intimately related to the process of democratic self-government" are not subject to strict scrutiny. Bernal v. Fainter, 467 U.S. 216 (1984). Such laws need only satisfy the rational basis review applied to nonsuspect classes.

Fundamental Rights   The Court has also applied something like strict scrutiny to review laws — even laws that do not discriminate on their face — that have an unequal impact on different persons when those laws affect fundamental rights. Fundamental rights tend to be narrowly construed. They include the right to vote and to marry. The Court recognized a fundamental right of same-sex couples to marry. Obergefell v. Hodges, 135 S. Ct. 2584 (2015). There is a fundamental right of access to the courts only where fundamental rights are affected as a result of the process. M.L.B. v. S.L.J., 519 U.S. 102 (1996) (equal protection violation where state fee prevented mother from appealing termination of parental rights), United States v. Kras, 409 U.S. 434 (1973) (no equal protection violation where $50 fee prevented debtor from filing in bankruptcy).

Rational Basis Review   Most state conflicts rules do not discriminate on the basis of suspect classifications like race or alienage and do not affect fundamental rights. Courts defer to nonsuspect state classifications and presume their constitutionality. A nonsuspect classification that treats different persons differently will be upheld when it satisfies a two-part test. First, the legal classification needs to serve some legitimate interest or policy goal. Second, the legal classification needs to be rationally related to achieving the state interest. The state law does not have to be the best possible way to achieve the interest, and the law can be rationally related even if it is broader or narrower than necessary. In other words, rational basis review tends to permit classifications that are not completely irrational or arbitrary. Courts applying the rational basis standard tend to find that the challenged laws are constitutional.

JUDICIAL TESTS FOR PRIVILEGES AND IMMUNITIES PROTECTION

Protected Interests Privileges and immunities protected by the Constitution must be sufficiently important to bear on the vitality of the nation as a single entity. Protected rights include the right to travel to and reside in a state, the right of access to state courts, the right to obtain medical services, the right to practice law, and the right to be employed and practice a trade. In contrast, recreational hunting and fishing are not a privilege and immunity that bears on the vitality of the nation as a whole. Baldwin v. Fish & Game Commission of Montana, 436 U.S. 371 (1978).

Standard for Violation The test for whether a state law violates the Privileges and Immunities Clause is similar to the test for nonsuspect class equal protection violations. When states tax or place other burdens on their own citizens, it is often impossible for states to treat citizens of other states in exactly the same way. But states are nevertheless required to accord citizens of other states substantial equality of treatment. When a state treats nonresidents differently, it must show (1) there is a substantial reason for the difference in treatment and (2) the different treatment bears a substantial relationship to the state's objective. Lunding v. New York Tax Appeals Tribunal, 522 U.S. 287, 298 (1998).

A higher level of scrutiny may apply to preferential tax treatment of home state residents because a core goal of the Privileges and Immunities Clause was to eliminate tax burdens on citizens of sister states. The Supreme Court held that a state commuter tax on income earned only by nonresidents violated privileges and immunities where the state did not similarly tax income earned by residents. Austin v. New Hampshire, 420 U.S. 656 (1975). In contrast, the Supreme Court has approved special taxes imposed on nonresidents when residents pay local property or other taxes not imposed on nonresidents. Such special taxes are constitutional so long as they reflect an attempt to distribute tax burdens fairly.

DISCRIMINATING AGAINST FOREIGN LAWS?

In Watkins v. Conway, 385 U.S. 188 (1966), the plaintiff brought a lawsuit in Georgia to enforce a judgment in Florida. The claim was dismissed under the Georgia statute of limitations, which required claims on foreign state judgments to be brought within a shorter period of time than claims on Georgia judgments. The Supreme Court affirmed. It held that Full Faith and Credit did not prevent the application of forum limitations law. The Court reasoned that the shorter time for enforcing Florida's judgment did not violate equal protection because the plaintiff could have revived the judgment in Florida, and the revived claim would not have been barred under the forum's statute of limitation. It observed that any denial of recovery was due to the failure to revive in Florida, and requiring revival in Florida neither violated the Full Faith and Credit Clause nor subjected plaintiff to invidious discrimination. The opinion has mystified generations of readers. The Court failed to consider the absence of any possible reason for the law other than hostility to foreign claims or claimants. Deference has its limits, and a completely arbitrary classification should flunk the rational relationship test.

DURATIONAL RESIDENCY DISCRIMINATION

Some state laws treat persons differently based on how long they have resided in the state. For example, all states require a party seeking a divorce to reside or be domiciled in the state for a certain period of time, often one year. State universities may require students to reside in the state for a fixed period of time before qualifying for in-state tuition.

Rules requiring residence for a certain period of time do not discriminate against nonresidents per se. Instead they create different classes of persons based on duration of residence, and they impede persons' right to travel by disabling or delaying persons from obtaining benefits available to longer-term residents.

The Supreme Court has held that a variety of durational residency requirements are unconstitutional. Older decisions relied on equal protection reasoning. The Court held that a one-year residency requirement for eligibility to vote was unconstitutional, but a 50-day requirement was not; a one-year residency to receive welfare benefits or free medical care violated equal protection, but one-year residency requirements for in-state college tuition did not. *See generally* Norman Redlich et al., Understanding Constitutional Law 487-490 (3d ed. 2004), Weintraub, Commentary on the Conflict of Laws §2.10 at 28-29. The Supreme Court similarly held that equal protection was violated by a state scheme that authorized the payment of money to state citizens based on how long they had resided in the state. Zobel v. Williams, 457 U.S. 55 (1982).

More recently, the Court has relied on the Privileges and Immunities Clause of the Fourteenth Amendment in holding unconstitutional a durational residency requirement for welfare benefits. Saenz v. Roe, 526 U.S. 489 (1999). The Court reasoned that the Constitution guarantees the rights of citizens to establish citizenship in a new state and that the new state must extend to all bona fide citizens the same legal rights. The clause relied on by the Court surprised gurus (and provoked a dissent) because it differs from the main Privileges and Immunities Clause in article IV and had not been the basis for a Supreme Court decision since 1872.

Examples

Equine Equality

1. The state of Mississippi enacts a statute that establishes immunity against personal injury claims for persons who offer horse-riding instruction or recreational services. Yorkie, a citizen of New York, owns a farm in Mississippi and lets neighbors and friends ride her thoroughbred stallion, Bone Crusher.

   One day Yorkie lets Cindy and Peter ride Bone Crusher without a saddle. Bone Crusher injures both riders. Cindy is visiting from New York, where she is domiciled. Peter is domiciled in Mississippi.

   Cindy sues Yorkie in New York court. Yorkie raises the defense of the immunity provided by the Mississippi statute. The New York court rejects the defense and applies New York tort law. The court reasons that New York has a strong interest in compensating New York plaintiffs and also has an interest in deterring dangerous conduct outside New York that injures New York residents. It concludes that the Mississippi statute is a loss-shifting rule designed to protect Mississippi defendants. Accordingly, it applies New York law.

   Peter learns of Cindy's decision and sues Yorkie in New York. Again the defendant raises the Mississippi statute as a defense. Peter argues that the court must reject the defense in his case as it did in Cindy's. He further argues that the failure to extend him the benefit of New York tort law will violate the Equal Protection Clause of the Constitution.

   The New York court applies Mississippi law, reasoning that it has no interest in applying New York tort law. Peter appeals to the appellate court, which assigns the case to you to draft the opinion on the Equal Protection issue.

Borrowing Trouble

2. Missie and Tex are injured in a car accident in Texas. They sue the tort-feasor in Mississippi state court. The claim is barred by the Texas statute of limitations but not by the Mississippi statute. Applying the Mississippi borrowing statute, the court dismisses the claim against Tex because the cause of action is barred by the law of the place where the action arose. However, the court refuses to dismiss Missie's claim because Missie is a resident of Mississippi, and the borrowing statute contains an exception that gives Mississippi resident plaintiffs the benefit of the forum's longer statute of limitations. Does the application of a borrowing statute violate equal protection?

Property Restrictions

3. The state of East Dakota passes a law that prevents ownership of real property in the state of East Dakota by any citizen of a foreign country except for citizens of Lebanon. Connie, a citizen of Canada, wants to buy land in East Dakota and asks you if the statute is legal.

4. The state of Northern California is considering adopting a will-borrowing statute that will permit the recognition of foreign wills when they are valid under the law of the state of the decedent's domicile. Legislator Phoebe Katz objects that Northern California should recognize another state's law only if the other state recognizes Northern California's wills. She proposes an amendment to the borrowing statute that will limit the effect of the statute to validating wills of nonresidents only when the law of the nonresidents contains a borrowing statute. Her amendment has been referred to the judiciary committee, which asks your advice about whether the amendment violates equal protection.

The Uncollegial College

5. Dr. Athena Minerva, the wise new president of West Carolina College, a college owned and operated by the state of West Carolina, has ambitious plans to improve the academic quality of the college and to enhance the quality of campus life. She proposes a rule that will require all faculty members to live on campus or within 20 miles of campus. She reasons that proximity to the campus will facilitate interaction with students and improve collegiality.

   Jefferson, a citizen of Virginia, is applying for a teaching job at the college. His current home in Virginia is 25 miles from the college. Jefferson was planning to commute to work if he got the job. He asks you whether the proposed residency requirement violates the Privileges and Immunities Clause. Please advise.

Over a Pork Barrel

6. For many years the city of Porkopolis, Ohio, admitted visitors to the city-owned Pork Museum[1] without charging an admission fee. Over the years, the operating costs rose sharply, and the city population declined, as did the city tax revenues. During the same time, the number of visitors to the Pork Museum who were residents of Boomburb, Ohio, and various communities in northern Kentucky increased.

    To raise funds to help defray the operating costs of the Pork Museum, the city authorized the museum to begin charging $5.00 admission to nonresidents of the city.

    Boone Wildcat, a litigious lawyer from northern Kentucky, writes a letter to the city complaining that the $5.00 fee violates the Privileges and Immunities Clause and threatens to sue. The city has asked you to write a letter in response. What do you say in the letter?

Respect Your Own Elders

7. Al Gator is running for the Florida legislature. He thinks too many people are retiring to the Sunshine State to take advantage of its advantageous estate tax laws. He makes two proposals for changing the Florida estate tax law. First, he proposes that the state tax any person who dies within one year of moving to the state at the estate tax rate that would have been applied under the law of the decedent's previous domicile. Second, he proposes a new tax credit for estates of people who died in Florida. The tax credit would reduce the taxes payable by the amount of $1,000 for each year that the decedent resided in Florida. Is either proposal constitutional?

Explanations

Equine Equality

1. The discrimination is probably not an equal protection violation. This example modifies the dram shop hypothetical discussed by Conflicts gurus. *See* Weintraub, Commentary on the Conflict of Laws at §9.4 at 717. Professor Weintraub suggests that a forum court's refusal to extend the benefit of forum law would violate equal protection if its only reason was lack of interest in nonresidents, but this is debatable.

---

1. This example is not based on the Krohn Conservatory in Cincinnati.

So far, the Supreme Court has reviewed challenges based on residency by the deferential rational-basis test. Under this level of review the law will not violate equal protection as long as it rationally relates to some legitimate state interest.

Legitimate interests are not limited to the policy goals that motivated the original law. The fact that the forum disclaims an interest under interest analysis does not necessarily mean that the forum does not have a reason (or interest) or that the law is completely arbitrary. For example, the forum state may have strong interests in conserving judicial resources for cases where identifiable forum policies are affected. This interest will be advanced by a choice of law rule that results in the routine dismissal of cases involving nonresidents in which the compensatory policies served by the state's tort laws are not promoted. As Justice Holmes observed in sustaining a state statute permitting dismissal based on nonresidency, "There are manifest reasons for preferring residents in access to often overcrowded Courts, both in convenience and in the fact that broadly speaking it is they who pay for maintaining the Courts concerned." Douglas v. New York, New Haven & Hartford Railroad Co., 279 U.S. 377, 387 (1929).

Similarly, dismissing the case under the law of the place of the wrong may also advance other legitimate forum interests even though, in this case, the jurisdiction that is the place of the accident may not have an interest in applying its own law according to interest analysis. First, applying the law of the place of the accident will have the benefit of discouraging forum shopping. (This is recognized as a legitimate goal in many contexts.) Second, applying the law of the place of the wrong may advance some policy goals of the foreign jurisdiction — for example, the goal of applying law equally regardless of residency of parties.

Such legitimate goals are probably enough under a deferential rational-basis review to persuade the courts that the choice of law rule is not so arbitrary that it violates equal protection. But a more searching review that disfavors rules that discriminate against nonresidents may not be so easily satisfied.

Borrowing Trouble

2. There is probably no equal protection violation. The analysis is similar to the explanation in the "Equine Equality" example. The outcome will depend ultimately on what level of scrutiny the Supreme Court employs and on the continued validity of Douglas v. New York, New Haven & Hartford Railroad Co., 279 U.S. 377 (1929).

Under a deferential rational-basis review, the state need only have legitimate interests that are rationally related to the legal classification. The legitimate interests need not be those that motivated the law. This is important, because the motivation for the law was (probably) a legislative compromise between plaintiff and defense advocates that reflected nothing other than home-state favoritism for home-state residents. The borrowing statute deters forum shopping by nonresidents but preserves the traditional rule for residents that the forum courts will apply the forum statute of limitations. Legitimate interests may include conserving limited judicial resources for state residents and discouraging forum shopping by a group (nonresidents).

The differential treatment in the state law may promote other, less obvious, policies. Applying the limitations law of the place where the cause of action arose will require nonresidents to litigate in the place of the accident or in their home states. It may be fairer for nonresidents' claims to be governed by the laws of states with a closer connection to the dispute. And the statute may encourage other states to reciprocally respect forum laws in cases where forum parties are involved.

The Supreme Court of Texas rejected equal protection challenges to the selective retroactive application of its borrowing statute to nonresidents, finding that the legislature "reasonably believed that Texas's resources were better spent on cases having a more substantial relation to Texas, and that Texas residents were being denied access to their own courts because of a backlog of cases." Owens Corning v. Carter, 997 S.W.2d 560, 582 (Tex. 1999).

There are two reasons for lack of confidence that such discrimination will survive Equal Protection challenges. First, it is uncertain how far the Court will go in entertaining speculative and after-the-fact rationalizations for state laws that discriminate against nonresidents. Second, the rationalizations for the state discriminatory law tend to restate in various ways the forum state's goal of giving preferential treatment to its residents. It remains uncertain whether the Court will defer to rules that discriminate openly against nonresidents.

The Supreme Court has held that the preferable treatment of forum residents in a borrowing statute does not violate the Privileges and Immunities Clause. Canadian Northern Railway Co. v. Eggen, 252 U.S. 553 (1920). This, of course, is an older case, and addresses Privileges and Immunities, not Equal Protection issues. See Pryber v. Marriott Corp., 296 N.W.2d 597 (Mich. App. 1980), aff'd without op., 307 N.W.2d 333 (Mich. 1981) (upholding constitutionality of borrowing statute exception for residents). See generally Weintraub, Commentary on the Conflict of Laws §3.2C2 at 70 n.59 (discussing cases).

Property Restrictions

3. This example raises a problem because of the tension between general rules disfavoring discrimination on the basis of alienage and older decisional law permitting state limitations on aliens owning property.

I would first apply strict scrutiny. A state has compelling interests in controlling many aspects of property law, including qualifications for ownership. In an older case permitting the exclusion of aliens from owning agricultural land, the Supreme Court observed, "The quality and allegiance of those who own, occupy and use the farm lands within its borders are matters of highest importance and affect the safety and power of the State itself." Terrace v. Thompson, 263 U.S. at 221. This observation is not further explained, and it is not clear what compelling interest requires a ban on all alien ownership of land.

The state interest in controlling land ownership stems from the fact that land is a finite resource. Perhaps the state may claim a compelling interest in controlling the market by restricting potential owners to U.S. citizens. This interest would be more clearly established if, for example, the legislation responded to an increase of land sales to aliens that reduced the land available to citizens. But it is not clear how the prohibition is closely related to such a goal.

Even if a prohibition on alien ownership is sustained, the further distinction between different groups of aliens made by some states, cf. Miss. Code Ann. §89-1-23 (prohibiting nonresident aliens from inheriting land but providing exceptions for citizens of Syria and Lebanon), creates groups of specially disfavored aliens. These groups may be discrete insular minorities.

The formal application of strict scrutiny review would suggest that alien land laws should be found to violate the Equal Protection Clause. But older decisions (generally applying rational basis review) permitted discriminatory land laws. Terrace v. Thompson, 263 U.S. 197 (1923). Moreover, they did so even when the practical effect of the state law was to prohibit land ownership by particular aliens of particular races or national origins. Id. (sustaining state law barring East Asians). Consequently, the answer to the example may depend on whether the Supreme Court relies on precedent or applies strict scrutiny. I would strike the law unless someone comes up with a compelling state interest. But then I'm not on the Supreme Court.

4. This is probably not a violation of equal protection. A similar reciprocity requirement is imposed by a number of state versions of the Uniform Foreign Country Money Judgment Recognition Act (Chapter 30). The reciprocity requirement may be bad law, but it here serves to promote the state interest of encouraging other states to recognize Northern California wills. This retaliatory rule is permitted by the holding in Western & Southern Life Insurance Co. v. State Board of Equalization of California, 451 U.S. 648 (1981), where the Court held there was no equal protection violation by a California retaliatory tax that applied only to those foreign insurance companies whose home states taxed California corporations.

The Uncollegial College

5. The right to pursue a common calling is protected under the Privileges and Immunities Clause, and the residency requirement may have the practical effect of discriminating against persons from other states. Nevertheless, the policy will not be unconstitutional if the state has a substantial reason for it and if the rule substantially advances the goal. Here the state college appears to have a substantial goal of establishing a residential community of faculty and students living in close physical proximity. The distance requirement seems substantially related to achieving that goal. This should be enough to avoid a privileges and immunities violation.

Over a Pork Barrel

6. I would write a letter apologizing for the regrettable need to raise funds for operating costs and inviting a generous donation. Then I would explain that the city would never deliberately violate any law and that it is not violating the Privileges and Immunities Clause for at least two reasons. First, admission to the Pork Museum is not a right that bears on the vitality of the nation as a single entity. Access to cultural or recreational experience is similar to equal access to hunting that the Supreme Court held was not protected by the Privileges and Immunities Clause. Second, the higher fee for noncity residents may be defended as imposing substantial equality of treatment. City residents already defray costs through city taxes. Noncity residents who visit the Pork Museum cause increases in operating expenses but do not defray costs through city taxes.

   Did you assume there was no privileges and immunities problem because the city discriminated against noncity residents, including most of the citizens of Ohio, and not just citizens of other states? Welcome to the club. But in United Building & Construction Trades Council of Camden v. Mayor and Council of the City of Camden, 465 U.S. 208 (1984), the Supreme Court held that a Camden, New Jersey, ordinance requiring 40 percent of construction workers to be Camden residents could violate privileges and immunities even though it similarly disadvantaged in-state citizens who did not reside in the city. The Court emphasized that residency and citizenship are largely interchangeable and that the nonstate citizen was excluded from employment. While the in-state residents outside Camden were also excluded, they could at least seek relief through the New Jersey political process. Only Justice Blackmun dissented on the ground that the pro-city preference was not a discrimination against citizens of other states. Having found a potential violation of the Privileges and Immunities Clause, the Court remanded for a determination of whether there was a "substantial reason" for the discrimination.

Respect Your Own Elders

7. Gator's proposals are dead in the water. The first proposal imposes a durational residency requirement: Florida residents only get the benefit of Florida tax law after living in the state for one year. It imposes exactly the sort of unwelcome treatment on recently arrived residents that the Supreme Court held violated privileges and immunities in Saenz v. Roe. Such disparate treatment effectively penalizes nonresidents who exercise the right to travel and seek to relocate to another state. The *Saenz* opinion emphasized that states may not seek to deter persons from moving to the state, nor may they create different levels of citizenship rights.

   The second proposal is also unconstitutional, doing in the form of tax credits what *Zobel* held states may not do in the form of direct cash payments—conditioning a benefit on duration of residence. Though *Zobel* was decided on equal protection grounds, the reasoning in *Saenz* suggests that the creation of different levels of citizenship also violates privileges and immunities rights.

PART VII

Enforcing Judgments

30

Foreign Country Judgments

INTRODUCTION

The law on enforcing foreign country judgments is an extension of the law of res judicata that governs the enforcement of judgments within a single jurisdiction. There are a few special requirements designed to make sure the foreign court system provides for basic fairness. In addition, foreign judgments based on laws that violate a forum's strong public policy need not be recognized. And some courts refuse to enforce judgments from a foreign country when the foreign country itself does not recognize the judgments of the forum court.

RES JUDICATA REVIEW

Need for Finality In order for law to be law, as opposed to nonbinding moral pronouncements, legal rights must become enforceable at some point. After that point, there can be no "wrongly decided" exception. Permitting a defendant to avoid judgment day by continually raising defenses would ultimately eliminate the rule of law. So would allowing plaintiffs to sue repeatedly after losing. Losing parties often think their case was wrongly decided, and if "wrongly decided" were a ground for preventing enforcement of judgments, then judgments would never be enforceable. Or they would not become enforceable as long as parties had resources to continue to litigate.

Fairness, Justice, and Economy   Res judicata rules serve other important values. They can promote legal consistency, discourage multiple lawsuits, and save resources.

Terminology   The field of res judicata is full of jargon. To make matters more complicated, during the last century law professors invented new terms for the old terms. Not all judges and lawyers use the new terminology. So now you need to know twice as much jargon. Knowing the terms is important because they stand for different kinds of problems that are subject to different rules. You get to the right rule only if you make the proper classification.

Old Term	New Term
res judicata (broad meaning)	finality or preclusion
res judicata (narrow meaning)	claim preclusion
collateral estoppel	issue preclusion

Res Judicata (Broad Meaning)   "Res judicata" is Latin for things that have been decided. It has two overlapping legal meanings. In the broad sense, it means the rules governing the finality of judgments in general — both res judicata in the narrow sense (also called claim preclusion) and collateral estoppel (also called issue preclusion).

Res Judicata (Narrow Meaning): Claim Preclusion   Res judicata in the narrow sense (also called claim preclusion) means the law that prevents the relitigation of claims that have been reduced to judgment. For example, if Madea sues Tyrone for a particular claim and loses, res judicata prevents Madea from suing Tyrone again for the same claim.

Collateral Estoppel: Issue Preclusion   Collateral estoppel (also called issue preclusion) prevents parties from relitigating facts or issues that have previously been litigated. Facts or issues that may qualify for collateral estoppel range from detailed facts (like Madea's blood type) to big legal issues that start to look more like claims (like whether Tyrone was speeding, negligent, or even liable). Liability would be an issue rather than a claim (governed by claim preclusion), because liability is only part of what is necessary to establish a claim. In addition to liability, a party must prove damages.

BASIC REQUIREMENTS: VALID, FINAL JUDGMENT ON THE MERITS

For a prior decision to be given any preclusive effect, the decision must be (1) a valid judgment, (2) a final judgment, and (3) a judgment on the merits.

Validity To be valid, the judgment must be enforceable by the court that entered it. Defects in personal jurisdiction or subject matter jurisdiction may prevent a judgment from being enforceable. If so, the judgment is not valid and will not preclude litigation in other proceedings.

Finality To be final, the judgment must be ripe for enforcement in the jurisdiction that rendered it. A judgment is final after appeals have been exhausted or the time for appeal has lapsed. Judgments can become enforceable at an earlier stage—for example, if Madea wins at trial and Tyrone appeals but does not take affirmative steps to delay execution of the judgment by posting a supersedeas bond or obtaining an order suspending enforcement from the trial court.

On the Merits A judgment must be on the merits to preclude relitigation. Default judgments are on the merits even though they are entered automatically and there was no actual judicial determination of disputed facts. Dismissals for lack of personal jurisdiction, subject matter jurisdiction, improper venue, defective service, and forum non conveniens are not judgments on the merits. Courts are divided over whether some judgments are on the merits, including dismissals for failure to state claims upon which relief can be granted, dismissals under statutes of limitations, and dismissal of claims that were not raised as compulsory counterclaims in previous litigation.

THE RULES

Res Judicata (Claim Preclusion) There are two requirements for res judicata or claim preclusion: (1) identity of parties (or privity) and (2) identity of claim.

Same Parties The identity of parties is usually easy to determine. But res judicata also precludes relitigation by persons in "privity" with the original parties. Sometimes privity is a matter of substantive law. A property owner may be in privity with previous owners and bound by judgments against them involving the property. Privity also may exist when someone is closely related to a party and controlled the course of litigation or under other circumstances where it is fair to bind a person by the judgment.

Same Claim   The identity of claim requirement contains a trap for the unwary. It applies to the same claim that was actually litigated in a previous lawsuit. It also applies to claims that are so closely related that they are deemed part of the same claim under the law of res judicata. For example, if Driver sues Trucker and wins $10,000 for a broken arm, claim preclusion will prevent Driver from later suing Trucker for more damages for a broken leg suffered at the same time. All these damages are deemed part of the "same claim." It can sometimes be difficult to determine whether claims are separate or the same, and rules vary from jurisdiction to jurisdiction.

Bar and Merger   A party is barred from relitigating claims that were actually lost. A party is also precluded from seeking additional damages or raising related claims that form part of the "same claim." Such omitted claims are said to merge in the original judgment. There is older authority that merger does not apply to foreign country judgments. The reasons for this are unclear. Conflicts gurus think merger should prevent a plaintiff from raising claims that merged in the judgment under the law of the foreign country.[1]

Collateral Estoppel or Issue Preclusion   There are four (or five) requirements for the operation of collateral estoppel or issue preclusion:

(1) The same issue or fact must have been actually litigated and determined.
(2) The determination was necessary to the judgment.
(3) The party against whom collateral estoppel is asserted must have had a day in court.
(4) There must have been similar incentives and opportunities to litigate the contested issue in the prior proceedings.
(5) There must have been mutuality of parties.

The mutuality requirement is similar to the identity of parties requirement for claim preclusion. It requires that a party seeking the benefit of collateral estoppel was either a party in previous litigation or was in privity with a party. Mutuality was based on the idea that a party should only get the benefit of issue preclusion if he or she would have been precluded if the

---

1. Hay et al., Conflict of Laws §24.3 at 1382; Weintraub, Commentary on the Conflict of Laws §11.6 at 790.

earlier case had gone the other way. The mutuality requirement has been abandoned or relaxed in most jurisdictions for most kinds of cases.

Offensive and Defensive   Collateral estoppel is offensive when it is raised by a plaintiff to prevent a defendant from relitigating some issue. It is defensive when it is raised by a defendant to prevent a plaintiff from relitigating an issue. Normally, the same rules apply whether issue preclusion is raised by a plaintiff or a defendant. Some jurisdictions require mutuality for offensive collateral estoppel by plaintiffs but not for defendants. (Such jurisdictions require mutuality for plaintiffs in order to encourage plaintiffs to join together in litigating similar claims.)

PARTIES BOUND BY JUDGMENT

The rules of issue and claim preclusion and due process limit the effect of judgments on persons who were not joined as parties to the action. A person will not be adversely affected by proceedings in which the person did not participate as a party or was not in privity with a party. For example, if Flem claims he owns a mule and sues Mink for damages or for a court order for recovery of the mule, the court's judgment will be binding on Flem and Mink—if it is valid, final, and on the merits. It will not bind Eula unless she was a party or in privity with a party.

In Rem Actions   In an action in rem, the court exercises jurisdiction over the thing ("res") by actually or constructively exercising control over the thing. The judgment in an action in rem is binding on the world, parties, and nonparties, to the extent of their interests in the thing.

HELPFUL HINTS

You are not alone in your confusion about res judicata. The trick is to work separately through the possible classifications. When you are not sure about the proper classification, consider the alternatives. For example, if you are not sure whether something is a claim or an issue, then consider how the case should be treated under both claim and issue preclusion. If you are not sure whether a closely related claim merges, consider what happens if it does and does not. You are likely to get full points for seeing the problem and considering the consequences of applying all relevant rules. Avoid rushing to the conclusion that collateral estoppel is unavailable because one requirement is not satisfied. You could be wrong, so consider all the other requirements and identify any others that may not be satisfied.

Examples

Speedy Blue Roadster

1. Nancy took Beth for a ride in her speedy blue roadster. She stopped at a stop sign behind a red convertible driven by Ned. The two cars collided. Nancy argues that Ned put his car in reverse and backed into her stopped roadster.[2] Ned argues that Nancy drove into his stopped convertible.

   Nancy sues Ned for damage to her front bumper. The case goes to trial, and the jury returns a judgment for the defendant. Nancy is outraged and sues again for the damage to her front bumper. Ned moves to dismiss on the grounds of res judicata. Rule on the motion and explain.

2. Same facts. But some time after losing the first lawsuit, Nancy discovers she is suffering from degenerative pendadigitatis resulting from the collision and commences a lawsuit against Ned seeking damages for her personal injuries. Ned moves for summary judgment. Rule on the motion and explain.

HILTON v. GUYOT

The traditional American rule for enforcing foreign judgments was set forth in Hilton v. Guyot, 159 U.S. 113 (1895). In that case, the Supreme Court rejected its older approach under which foreign judgments were merely prima facie evidence of obligations. "Prima facie" may sound tough, but it meant that foreign judgments just provided some evidence of a debt and could be countered by other evidence on the merits. The older approach did not preclude relitigation because it permitted the argument that the foreign judgment was wrongly decided.

Hilton declared that a foreign judgment should be given full preclusive effect if (1) there was an opportunity for a full and fair trial before a court of competent jurisdiction; (2) it was the product of regular proceedings; (3) it was decided after due citation or voluntary appearance; and (4) the foreign system of justice was likely to secure the impartial administration of justice between citizens of different countries. This precluded relitigation

---

2. This actually happened to my mother when she was a teenager, but no one believed her.

except when the foreign judgments were challenged on grounds of lack of jurisdiction, fraud, clear mistake or irregularity, or invalidity of the judgment under the law of the place where rendered.

Judgments from Different Systems   Hilton rejected the argument that the French judgment was not enforceable because the French court had relied on unsworn testimony, considered hearsay evidence, and provided no opportunity for cross examination. The Court's rejection of this argument was important. Most jurisdictions in the world do not have common law rules of evidence and procedure. The Hilton decision makes clear that significant differences in legal systems such as lack of trial by jury and common law rules of evidence will not prevent enforcement of a foreign country's judgment.

Fraud   Hilton recognized fraud as a possible defense but did not reach the issue in that case.

Public Policy   A court may refuse to enforce a foreign country judgment that is based on law that is contrary to the public policy of the forum. An example is Telnikoff v. Matusevitch, 702 A.2d 230 (Md. 1997), where the Maryland high court held that public policy prevented recognition of a British libel judgment. The court concluded that British defamation law was so contrary to U.S. standards that it was repugnant to public policy. This decision was controversial among Conflicts gurus, who point out that the libel occurred in England and that U.S. jurisdictions have no authority to export U.S. free speech standards to foreign countries. They argued there is no good reason to disregard a valid final judgment from a British court in such a case. The SPEECH Act (discussed below) now prohibits U.S. courts from enforcing foreign country judgments that are inconsistent with First Amendment rights.

The scope of the public policy ground for refusing recognition to foreign country judgments is uncertain. The statements of the rule do not require that the foreign country judgment be contrary to strong or fundamental policy of the forum. This contrasts with the traditional public policy exception for causes of action that have not been reduced to judgment, which must offend a strong public policy. (See Chapter 15.) Though Telnikoff involved important constitutional values, other decisions have refused to enforce foreign country judgments that involve differences that are more procedural. See Andes v. Versant Corp., 878 F.2d 147 (4th Cir. 1989) (refusing to enforce English judgment against guarantor of a loan on the ground that the English law prevented the guarantor from joining other obligors, and this was repugnant to public policy because it violated "normal

American notions of litigation"). No doubt many international laws and procedures violate normal American notions of litigation. But *Hilton* taught that mere difference in laws is not supposed to prevent enforcement of an otherwise valid final judgment.

Reciprocity Requirement   The Supreme Court in *Hilton* ultimately denied enforcement of the French judgment on the ground that French courts would not enforce judgments from courts of the United States. The Court was closely divided over the reciprocity requirement.

CODIFYING HILTON v. GUYOT: THE GOOD OLD UFCMJRA

The *Hilton* approach (except the reciprocity requirement) has been widely followed by courts. It has been codified by a majority of states in the form of the Uniform Foreign Country Money Judgment Recognition Act (UFCMJRA). This Uniform Act provides that foreign country money judgments preclude relitigation and have the same effect as judgments from sister states. There are two sorts of exceptions.

Judgments That Cannot Preclude Relitigation   The Uniform Act provides that foreign judgments are *not* conclusive when entered by: (1) a system that did not provide impartial tribunals compatible with due process or (2) a foreign court that lacked subject matter jurisdiction or personal jurisdiction. UFCMJRA §4(a), 13 U.L.A. 39.

Judgments That May Not Preclude Relitigation   The Uniform Act provides that judgments "need not" be recognized for certain grounds. The meaning of "need not" is not absolutely clear, but some courts read it to mean that courts have discretion to refuse enforcement to foreign judgments on the following grounds:

(1) The defendant did not receive notice in time to defend.
(2) The judgment was obtained by fraud.
(3) The foreign cause of action was repugnant to public policy.
(4) The foreign judgment conflicts with another final judgment.
(5) The foreign proceedings violated an arbitration or forum-selection agreement.
(6) The foreign forum was seriously inconvenient for the defendant.

Id. §4(b).

THE SPEECH ACT

Few if any foreign legal systems recognize all the free speech protections built into U.S. federal and state law. Foreign countries may not recognize truth as a defense; may not require proof of malice for claims by public officials; may shift the burden of proof to the defendant; and may impose ruinous damages designed to stifle certain forms of speech. As a result, people with complete loser cases under U.S. law began to take their lawsuits to foreign countries and win judgments. This practice was called "libel tourism" to emphasize that in extreme cases the plaintiffs were legal tourists visiting foreign countries just for the purpose of bringing libel lawsuits.

After a few outrageous cases, Congress enacted the SPEECH Act.[3] The Act prohibits a federal or state court from recognizing a foreign defamation judgment unless the court determines either: (A) that "the defamation law applied in the foreign court's adjudication provided at least as much protection for freedom of speech and press in that case as would be provided by the first amendment to the Constitution of the United States and by the constitution and law of the State in which the domestic [federal or state] court is located"; or (B) that the party "would have been found liable for defamation by a domestic court" applying federal and state law. 28 U.S.C. §4102(a)(1). The party who wants to enforce the foreign judgment bears the burden of showing the judgment meets these requirements. Id. §4102(a)(2).

The Act imposes on the party who wants to enforce a foreign defamation judgment the burden of showing that the foreign court's personal jurisdiction comported with the due process requirements imposed on U.S. courts. Id. §4102(b). A defendant does not waive jurisdictional defenses by appearing in the foreign lawsuit. Id. §4102(d). The Act is binding on state courts and authorizes defendants to remove actions to enforce foreign country judgments from state court to federal court based on minimal diversity of citizenship. Id. §4103. The Act authorizes federal declaratory judgment actions to declare foreign defamation judgments unenforceable by U.S. citizens, permanent residents, corporations, and persons who were legal residents in the United States at the time they researched, prepared or disseminated the speech that is at issue. Id. §4104.

Just because the Act does not apply does not mean a foreign country judgment is enforceable. It still may still be unenforceable as a matter of public policy. For example, suppose Cal from California visits Paris, takes a photograph, and posts it on his website. The photograph depicts Yvette singing in the rain. Yvette is enraged when she learns of the posting and

---

3. 28 U.S.C. §§4101–4105. SPEECH stands for Securing the Protection of our Enduring and Established Constitutional Heritage.

sues Cal in Paris where she recovers a 100,000 Euro judgment for invasion of privacy and interference with her right to publicity. She then seeks to collect the judgment in California. The SPEECH Act defines "defamation" broadly as any action or proceeding "for defamation, libel, slander, or similar claim alleging that forms of speech are false, have caused damage to reputation or emotional distress, have presented any person in a false light, or have resulted in criticism, dishonor, or condemnation of any person." Id. §4101(1). This definition might cover the claim for invasion of privacy — if a photograph is speech. But it may not cover the claim based on the interference with Yvette's right to publicity. The point is that even if the Act does not apply, a U.S. court would be free to refuse to enforce the French judgment if it finds that the French law is repugnant to federal or state public policy.

Example

Harmful Words

3. Flash Gordon, a citizen of New York, was traveling in Europe. At the border of Caledonia, he was treated rudely by a guard, and the guard damaged his luggage during inspection. Later that day at a bar in Caledonia, Gordon told the bartender that he believed the guard was racist and was harassing him because of his appearance. The bartender told the guard what Gordon said, and the guard sued Gordon for defamation in Caledonia.

   Under the law of Caledonia, accusing someone of being "racist" is considered defamatory per se. Truth is not a defense. Moreover, the law authorizes the prevailing plaintiff to recover statutory damages in the amount of $200 plus all attorney fees. Fees for successfully prosecuting a defamation lawsuit are set by statute at $7,000. Gordon ignored the lawsuit. As a result the guard recovered a judgment against him from the Caledonia court in the amount of $7,200.

   Gordon has received a letter from the guard attaching a certified copy of the Caledonia judgment. The letter demands payment. Gordon has come to you for advice. What do you advise?

OTHER EXCEPTIONS

Penal and Tax Judgments Add two more traditional grounds for refusing to recognize foreign country judgments. Courts refused to enforce penal judgments and judgments for taxes from other jurisdictions.

Injunctions Traditionally, only foreign money judgments were enforceable. Injunctions and decrees for specific relief other than money damages were not recognized. This limitation has been affected in a few areas by statutes. For example, some states apply their versions of the Interstate Family Support Act to enforce support orders from foreign countries as well as from sister states.

RECIPROCITY TODAY

States are divided over reciprocity. The Uniform Foreign Country Money Judgment Recognition Act does not include reciprocity as a ground for non-recognition. Nevertheless, some state versions of the Uniform Act add reciprocity as a requirement.

The reciprocity requirement was controversial from the get-go. Many recent decisions reject reciprocity. Conflicts professors hate it.

There are two criticisms of reciprocity. First, refusing to enforce a judgment on grounds of reciprocity frustrates forum policies against unnecessary, duplicative litigation. The immediate losers are litigants in U.S. courts, the courts themselves, and U.S. taxpayers, who pay for the privilege of hosting duplicative litigation. Second, the judge-made reciprocity requirement is an ill-advised judicial effort to influence foreign policy. The executive and legislative branches are arguably more appropriate authorities for influencing legal change in foreign countries.

Hilton's adoption of reciprocity may not be binding today in federal courts. The decision was an exercise of federal general common law in the days before *Erie* declared such authority unconstitutional. States were never bound by *Hilton's* reciprocity requirement, and in cases where federal courts must apply state law, most will also apply state law on the issue of the preclusive effect of foreign country judgments. E.g., Tahan v. Hodgson, 662 F.2d 862 (D.C. Cir. 1981).[4]

Examples

Wild Ponies

4. Brien sued Patrick in the country of Connemara for capturing wild ponies on his land. The action was dismissed for failure to comply with

---

4. In federal question cases, federal courts are not required to apply state law under *Erie*. They may continue to regard *Hilton* as authoritative. But it is questionable whether the federal courts will still require reciprocity under federal common law principles today. *See* Weintraub, Commentary on the Conflict of Laws §11.6 at 789.

Connemara's notice requirements. Brien later sued Patrick in state court in New York. Patrick moved to dismiss, arguing the claim was res judicata. Rule on the motion and explain.

Celebrity Bash

5. The international celebrity, Ladonna, owns condominiums in four different countries where she spends a few months each year. While she was staying at her condominium in the country of Lazulia, she was sued in Lazulia courts by her agent, Primo Prince. Prince is a citizen of Lazulia. In the complaint, Prince alleges that Ladonna owes him $2 million, representing 2 percent of her net income derived from the film *Goatkillers' Bible*. Ladonna was served personally with the complaint at her condominium.

    Ladonna appeared and disputed the claim. She denied that she owed Prince the money and demanded trial by jury.

    The Lazulia court denied the demand for a jury and tried the case to a three-judge panel. Over Ladonna's repeated objections, the judges admitted testimony about what people said out of court. The judges based their decision in large part on photocopies of documents that were not authenticated, ruling that the burden was on Ladonna to show inaccuracies in the documents. Although Ladonna was permitted to address the court, she was not permitted to take an oath as to the veracity of her testimony.

    After deliberating for two days behind closed doors, the three-judge panel announced its unanimous decision in favor of Prince. The court explained that it found Prince's explanations to be "much more believable" than Ladonna's.

    Ladonna left the country in disgust. Her condominium property in Lazulia was seized and sold for $500,000 to satisfy part of the judgment. But Prince has come to the state of East Virginia, where Ladonna owns additional real property. Prince has commenced a lawsuit in East Virginia state court seeking to recover a new state judgment for the amount of $1.5 million that remains unsatisfied on his judgment from Lazulia. Ladonna appears and denies liability on the ground that the foreign country judgment is unenforceable.

    Your client, Big Bank Co., is trying to decide whether to extend more credit to creditors of Ladonna and wants to know whether East Virginia is likely to recognize the claim on the foreign judgment. Please advise.

A Rose by Any Other Name

6. In 1985 Fern and Fritz Bush, domiciliaries of East Dakota, named their baby girl George Bush for the then-Vice President of the United States. Many years later, George was on vacation, visiting the country of Barataria.

There she was served with legal papers by a uniformed member of the Baratarian Constabulary. The documents were written in Baratarian, and George could not understand them. The documents were sealed with a red official looking seal.

She ignored the documents. Sometime after returning to East Dakota, George learned that a default judgment in the amount of $100,000 was entered against her in Barataria. The papers were a complaint in a lawsuit commenced by Kristof Kristerson. The complaint alleged that the defendant, George Bush, as President of the United States, committed intentional torts upon Kristerson in the year 2003. Pursuant to Barataria law, when George did not answer the complaint, a hearing was held solely on the issue of damages. Judgment was entered by the court for an amount of damages that it found to be reasonable based on Kristerson's testimony at the hearing.

Kristerson has now sued George in federal court for the district of East Dakota. Kristerson attaches a certified copy of the default judgment from the Barataria court and moves for summary judgment based on the foreign country judgment. George opposes, arguing that the foreign judgment should not be given any weight because the plaintiff sued the wrong person, because the complaint was in Baratarian, and because she did not do anything wrong. Rule on the motion and explain.

Cyberspace Service

7. Spock visited the country of Tralfamadore for a rest cure. While he was lounging in the sanatorium, he was unaware that a lawsuit had been filed against him for a personal injury he allegedly caused while driving from the spaceport to the sanatorium. Service was obtained pursuant to Tralfamadore Rule of Civil Procedure 4(i) by posting notice of the lawsuit on the Tralfamadore Judicial blog.

Default judgment was entered while Spock was still recovering at the sanatorium. The plaintiff is now attempting to enforce the judgment in the state of West Carolina, where Spock owns real property. Spock has come to you for advice about whether the foreign country judgment will be enforceable. Please advise.

Buked and Scorned

8. After President Woody's violent seizure of power in the country of Bananaland, he installed loyal members of the Bananaland Liberation Front in public office, including as judges of the country's judicial system. Because the United States refused to recognize the new government, President Woody denounced America in numerous public speeches and called on all public officials to eliminate all traces of American influence in Bananaland.

During the height of anti-American fervor, Harry Bligh, a Bananaland citizen, commenced divorce proceedings in Bananaland court against his U.S.-born wife Wynona. Wynona appeared in the proceedings and contested all claims. The court entered a decree of divorce. It awarded all property to Harry. It also entered a judgment against Wynona in the amount of $40,000, which was the amount that Harry claimed she owed him under an oral contract. Wynona disputed the claim.

Harry has commenced an action in the state of Confusion to enforce the foreign country money judgment. Wynona comes to you for advice and asks if she has any good defenses. Please advise.

Study Abroad

9. Eddie, a citizen of East Dakota, started a travel agency in the country of Albion for the purposes of serving the needs of American students who study abroad. Eddie reserved bus tickets for six students with Bingo Busco, an Albion corporation. The students never completed the purchase of the tickets, and Bingo Busco sued Eddie in Albion court for the value of the tickets. Eddie appeared and defended, arguing that the bus company should not be able to recover because it did not mitigate damages by trying to resell the bus tickets to other passengers after learning that the students would not buy them.

The Albion court rejected the defense and entered judgment for Bingo Busco for the purchase price of the tickets. Eddie appealed the decision to the Albion Supreme Court, which affirmed in a lengthy opinion, explaining why it was fair to hold Eddie liable for tickets that he had reserved for others.

Eddie returned to his home state, where the foreign plaintiff has commenced an action to enforce the foreign country judgment. Eddie moves to dismiss the action, attaching a certified copy of an Albion statute that prohibits the enforcement of foreign country money judgments in Albion. What will the court do?

Explanations

Speedy Blue Roadster

1. Res judicata (claim preclusion) bars the second action. Nancy raised the exact same claim in a prior lawsuit involving the same parties. The prior court had jurisdiction, and its judgment is final and on the merits.

2. This one is trickier. The personal injury claim being raised was either part of the same claim as the property damage claim in the earlier litigation or a different claim. In most jurisdictions, it would be considered part of the same claim, and the plaintiff gets only "one bite of the apple."

So res judicata would bar the second claim. This rule can have harsh results when a plaintiff recovers a judgment or settles a lawsuit and later discovers more serious injuries — like a slipped disk that worsens and causes permanent disabilities. For this reason, plaintiffs' lawyers must take great care in evaluating injuries and settling claims.

In some jurisdictions, the personal injury claim might be separate — or there may be an exception for injuries that manifest themselves later. In such jurisdictions, the defendant could still argue that collateral estoppel should apply and prevent the plaintiff from relitigating facts or issues that were actually litigated and decided in the first lawsuit.

The difficulty with applying issue preclusion to the first action, however, is that it may be uncertain exactly why the plaintiff lost previously. Sometimes the record contains jury answers to interrogatories or other indications of exactly what the factfinder decided. But the record may not allow the second court to conclude that the issue was actually determined. Moreover, even if the issue was actually litigated and determined against Nancy, she will have a strong argument that that she did not have the same incentive to litigate the issue of liability in a claim for damage to her bumper that she now has in an action seeking damages for a lifetime disability. For example, it probably would not have been cost-efficient to hire expert witnesses in the first case, but it would in the second.

Harmful Words

3. The foreign country judgment is not enforceable in any U.S. court. The guard will be unable to establish either of the prerequisites for enforcing the defamation judgment. First, the law applied in the foreign adjudication did not afford Gordon at least as much protection as is available under federal and state law. Truth is a defense under U.S. law. And I'm no First Amendment scholar but I'm guessing the statutory fine and fees recoverable in Caledonia without regard to harm or ill will also violate First Amendment protections. Second, the guard cannot show that he would have recovered the judgment if U.S. laws applied.

In this case, the guard could probably satisfy his jurisdictional burden of showing that the Caledonia court's exercise of personal jurisdiction comported with due process. Gordon made the statements in Caledonia where the defendant lives, and the legal claims arose out of his purposeful acts in Caledonia and establish minimum contacts.

Gordon has two options. He can wait for the guard to bring an action to enforce the judgment in a U.S. state or federal court. This has some advantages. The guard will have the burden of establishing that the foreign country judgment is enforceable. If the guard brings the action in a state court, Gordon may remove. Whether or not he removes, the

Act provides for attorney's fees to the party who successfully opposes recognition of the foreign judgment "absent exceptional circumstances." 28 U.S.C. §4105.

Gordon's second option is to take the offensive and sue the guard before he tries to enforce the judgment. The Act authorizes Gordon as a "United States person" to bring a declaratory judgment in federal court to have the foreign defamation judgment declared unenforceable for failure to comply with the requirements of the Act. There are some disadvantages with seeking a declaratory judgment. Gordon will have to establish personal jurisdiction over the guard. (The Act provides for nationwide service of process. Id. §4104(b).) Gordon will bear the burden of establishing the nonenforceability of the judgment under the Act. And the statute does not authorize the recovery of fees if he prevails in obtaining a declaratory judgment.

Wild Ponies

4. The motion to dismiss is denied. To be enforceable, foreign judgments must always meet the general prerequisites for res judicata. The judgment in this case fails to qualify because it is not a valid final judgment on the merits. Dismissal based on lack of notice or personal jurisdiction does not decide the merits of the case; rather, it is based only on the court's lack of authority to decide the dispute between the parties. The plaintiff's failure to commence the action properly in Connemara does not preclude him from commencing an action again—either in Connemara or in another court.

Celebrity Bash

5. East Virginia is likely to recognize the foreign country judgment, although a more detailed analysis would be possible if we knew more about East Virginia's law on point—whether, for example, it codifies a version of the Uniform Foreign Country Money Judgment Recognition Act.

The general requirements for res judicata are all satisfied. There was a valid final judgment on the merits involving the same claim and same parties. There do not appear to be any grounds for challenging it under the rule in Hilton v. Guyot or the Uniform Act. The different procedures followed in the Lazulia court are similar to the differences that the Supreme Court observed in Hilton would not prevent recognition of the French judgment.

A Rose by Any Other Name

6. This is a toughie. But first, the easy part. It is not a valid defense to the judgment that the plaintiff sued the wrong person, that the complaint

was in Baratarian, or that the defendant did not do anything wrong. These defenses are all variations of the argument that the judgment should not be enforced because it was wrongly decided. There is no wrongly decided exception to res judicata, and no wrongly decided exception for recognizing foreign country judgments. Tahan v. Hodgson, 662 F.2d 862 (D.C. Cir. 1981), specifically held that an individual defendant who claimed he was wrongly sued in his individual capacity for a corporate debt — that is, he was the wrong person — could not raise that defense when he could have raised it along with other defenses on the merits but chose not to do so by taking a default judgment.

Tahan also rejected the argument that a judgment was unenforceable when the pleadings were written in Hebrew, the official language of the foreign jurisdiction. And *Tahan* also illustrates that default judgments are enforceable. *See also* Somportex Ltd. v. Philadelphia Chewing Gum Corp., 453 F.2d 435 (3d Cir. 1971) (holding English default judgment enforceable).

The thing that makes this case a toughie is the possible existence of other grounds for nonrecognition. The easy way out is to say that they have not been raised as defenses. But it is worth considering them. First, in *Hilton*, the Supreme Court observed that "clear mistake or irregularity" could provide a defense to a foreign judgment. The scope of this defense is uncertain, though it requires something more than factual error. Perhaps a court could be persuaded that the administrative blunder of suing a private person instead of the former President rises to the level of a clear mistake or irregularity. Second, a foreign country judgment will not be enforced if it is repugnant to public policy. If the intentional tort claims against a President would be unenforceable, then our George may have a good defense against enforcing the judgment against her, too.

Cyberspace Service

7. I would advise Spock that the foreign judgment is unenforceable because it was not obtained after due citation, as required by *Hilton*, or proper notice, as required by the Uniform Foreign Country Money Judgment Recognition Act. The lack of notice prevented Spock from having an opportunity for full and fair litigation abroad. At a more basic level, the judgment did not satisfy the basic requirements for res judicata. It is not a valid judgment because the foreign legal system's blog notice is not a method reasonably calculated to notify the parties of the pendency of the proceedings and afford them an opportunity to appear and be heard. Reasonable notice is required as a matter of due process.

Buked and Scorned

8. Differences in substantive law and procedure do not prevent the enforcement of a foreign country money judgment. But the foreign system must

be one likely to secure the impartial administration of justice. Here it appears that Bananaland's courts are not able to administer justice impartially in a case involving U.S. citizens' interests. Accordingly, the money judgment for $40,000 should not be recognized and enforced.

Study Abroad

9. The right answer is: it depends. The Albion judgment qualifies for recognition except for the problem of reciprocity. The answer to the question thus requires you to recognize the reciprocity problem and explain its current status. Jurisdictions are divided over reciprocity. Although reciprocity was required by the Supreme Court in Hilton, that part of the decision has been criticized and rejected by many courts. As a product of federal general common law, Hilton was never binding on states, and it is probably not binding on federal courts after Erie. The majority of U.S. states do not require reciprocity, and it is not required by the Uniform Foreign Country Money Judgment Recognition Act. But we don't know what East Dakota's statute or case law provides regarding reciprocity.

CHAPTER 31

Sister State Judgments

INTRODUCTION

The Full Faith and Credit Clause mandates: "Full faith and credit shall be given in each state to the public acts, records, and judicial proceedings of other every other state." U.S. Const. art. IV, §1.

The Full Faith and Credit Clause requires all states to give another state's judgment the same effect that the judgment would be given by the state that entered the judgment. In Hampton v. McConnel, 16 U.S. (3 Wheat.) 234, 235 (1818), Chief Justice Marshall formulated the black letter rule that is still good law:

> [T]he judgment of a state court should have the same credit, validity, and effect in every other court in the United States, which it had in the state where it was pronounced, and . . . whatever pleas would be good to suit thereon in such state, and not others, could be pleaded in any other court of the United States.

The policy of looking to the law of the judgment state is expressed by the Full Faith and Credit Clause implementing legislation enacted in 1790: judgments "shall have the same full faith and credit in every court within the United States . . . as they have by law or usage in the courts of such State . . . from which they are taken." 28 U.S.C. §1738.

NUTS AND BOLTS

To enforce a judgment from a foreign country, a party must commence a new cause of action on the judgment in a state or federal court that has jurisdiction. If the foreign country judgment is entitled to preclusive effect, then the plaintiff should be able to recover a summary judgment. In contrast, judgments from sister states can be directly enforced by following the state procedures in many states, and federal judgments are enforceable in other federal districts simply by registering them there.

JUDGMENTS AND JUDICIAL PROCEEDINGS GIVEN FULL FAITH AND CREDIT

Judgments   Judicial proceedings that must be given full faith and credit include money judgments and declaratory judgments.

Injunctions   For many years there was uncertainty about whether full faith and credit applied to equitable decrees like injunctions and court orders. Unlike money judgments, such orders were not traditionally recognized when they were issued by foreign country courts. In Baker v. General Motors, 522 U.S. 222 (1998), the Court considered the effect in other states of a Michigan state court injunction that banned an engineer from testifying against his former boss. The Court held that states must give full faith and credit to injunctions. But the Court then performed a balancing act and found that Michigan's decree exceeded that state's authority to the extent it sought to prevent testimony in other states because other states have exclusive authority over their own judicial processes. We now know full faith and credit applies to injunctions and court orders, but the practical scope of the mandatory enforcement of sister state injunctions remains to be seen.

Administrative Proceedings   Full faith and credit applies only to state "judicial proceedings," not quasi-judicial functions of state administrative agencies. This means full faith and credit must be given to state agency proceedings that have been reviewed by a state court; it does not apply to unreviewed agency proceedings. University of Tennessee v. Elliott, 478 U.S. 788 (1986). For example, a state agency finding that an employee was fired based on her race would only be binding in other states if the agency finding was appealed to and reviewed by a state court.

VALID, FINAL, AND ON THE MERITS

To be given preclusive effect, all judicial decisions must be valid, final, and on the merits (Chapter 29). The Full Faith and Credit Clause requires some refinements of the analysis of these three requirements that are designed to secure greater respect for sister state decisions, including decisions about their own decision's validity, finality, and scope.

Personal and Subject Matter Jurisdiction   A judgment entered by a court without a constitutionally sufficient basis for personal jurisdiction is void. Enforcing such a judgment even in the state that entered it violates the defendant's right to due process, and it is thus not valid for full faith and credit purposes anywhere.

Traditionally, a judgment entered by a court without subject matter jurisdiction was also void and would not be recognized by other jurisdictions.

Lack of personal jurisdiction and subject matter jurisdiction remain grounds for refusing recognition to a foreign country judgment. But full faith and credit limits challenges to judgments from sister states. In Durfee v. Duke, 375 U.S. 106 (1963), the Supreme Court limited challenges to a state judgment when the parties had appeared before the state court and the court found it had subject matter jurisdiction. The Court announced the rule that "a judgment is entitled to full faith and credit — even as to questions of jurisdiction — when . . . those questions have been fully and fairly litigated and finally decided in the court which rendered the original judgment." This is true for both subject matter jurisdiction and personal jurisdiction. *See* Aldrich v. Aldrich, 378 U.S. 540 (1964).

Could Have, Should Have Policy   Parties that could have raised valid objections to personal jurisdiction and subject matter jurisdiction in a federal court are normally required to do so or the judgment will be binding after it becomes final. Though subject matter jurisdiction is not waived in federal court and can be brought up at any time in the federal trial court or on appeal, once the judgment becomes final, it is valid and enforceable and cannot be attacked collaterally in other courts for lack of subject matter jurisdiction if the party appeared and failed to raise the issue. *See* Chicot County Drainage District v. Baxter State Bank, 308 U.S. 371 (1940). Full faith and credit requires a judgment to be given the effect it has in the state where rendered. State law varies, so you need to look to the law of the state where a judgment was entered to determine the effect in other courts of any defects in subject matter jurisdiction in the original state court. If the judgment is now valid and enforceable in the original state, it is valid and enforceable in all states.

Bankruptcy Exception? In Kalb v. Feuerstein, 308 U.S. 433 (1940), farmers sued a sheriff and others in Wisconsin state court claiming they had been illegally evicted and assaulted. The evictions had occurred in earlier Wisconsin foreclosure proceedings against the farmers. The farmers had not raised the issue of subject matter jurisdiction in the Wisconsin foreclosure proceedings, but they had filed for bankruptcy, and the bankruptcy statute mandates a stay of all state court foreclosure proceedings.

The sheriff and other defendants in the state tort lawsuit argued that the earlier foreclosures were lawful because the farmers had appeared and had not challenged subject matter jurisdiction. The Supreme Court disagreed and ruled that the automatic stay in bankruptcy has the effect of depriving state courts of jurisdiction and permitting later attacks on jurisdiction by persons who did not raise the issue of the court's jurisdiction before the original court. The Court based the decision on the supposed intent of Congress.

Many law professors hate *Kalb*. The decision is in tension with the general rule that parties cannot collaterally challenge jurisdiction when they appeared and did not raise the issue. And the *Kalb* opinion does not do a good job of explaining why permitting collateral attacks is necessary to advance the goals of bankruptcy protection.

Final Normally a judgment is final when it is enforceable. Judgments can become enforceable in many states even while they are on appeal. So finality must be determined by looking to the law of the state that rendered the decision. For example, if in Rhode Island an appeal suspends the enforceability of a judgment, then other states will not give full faith and credit to a Rhode Island judgment while it is being appealed in that state.

On the Merits You might expect that whether a judgment is "on the merits" would also be determined by reference to the law of the state that entered the judgment. The problem is that you cannot tell whether a decision is on the merits by asking whether the state that entered it would permit relitigation. California might dismiss a claim for lack of personal jurisdiction. Its decision would bar relitigation in California. But the decision would not prevent another state from exercising personal jurisdiction.

Examples of judgments that are on the merits are default judgments, dismissals with prejudice, and compulsory counterclaims. Examples of judgments that are not on the merits are dismissals for lack of jurisdiction. In general, a decision is on the merits if a party had an opportunity to litigate the merits. Hay et al., Conflict of Laws §24.1 at 1377.

FRAUD EXCEPTION — OR NOT

The Supreme Court opinions have repeatedly stated that state judgments are entitled to full faith and credit in the absence of fraud. This might suggest a wide fraud exception for Full Faith and Credit. Do not be deceived! The status of the fraud exception to full faith and credit is surprisingly unclear, and its application is even less clear. Most of the discussions of the fraud exception address situations that do not qualify for the exception. Treatises distinguish "extrinsic" from "intrinsic" fraud and assert that only extrinsic fraud exempts courts from the obligation to give full faith and credit to another state's judgment. E.g., Hay et al., Conflict of Laws §24.17 at 1404. Extrinsic fraud is something like bribery of a judge that prevents a court from being a fair forum. Perjury and cheating that occur during the course of proceedings are "intrinsic" and do not provide a basis for refusing to enforce the judgment if it is enforceable under the law of the state that entered the judgment.

PUBLIC POLICY

No General Public Policy Exception States may refuse to enforce foreign country judgments that offend their policy. But there is no public policy exception to the obligation to give full faith and credit to sister state judgments. This is so firmly established that the only controversy is whether there is room for even a narrow policy exception in extreme cases. The Supreme Court has never found such an exception, but law professors search dicta for clues.

The lead case is Fauntleroy v. Lum, 210 U.S. 230 (1908). The parties had entered a contract for cotton futures in Mississippi, where the contract was void and the conduct was criminal.[1] The plaintiff got a judgment in Missouri based on the contract and then took the Missouri judgment to Mississippi to enforce it. The Mississippi courts refused to enforce the sister state judgment. The Supreme Court reversed and held that Mississippi was required to give the judgment the same effect that the judgment would have under the law where it was rendered. The fact that the underlying claim violated Mississippi law and was offensive to its public morals was not an exception.

---

1. Selling cotton futures was considered a form of gambling. Bad. The case predates legalized riverboat gambling. I mean gaming.

Workers' Compensation Exception   In 1946 the Supreme Court held that full faith and credit does not preclude a supplemental workers' compensation award in a second state even though the injured worker had already recovered an award in another state and the first state's award barred an additional award. This is at odds with the normal rule that requires a judgment to be given the same effect it would have under the law where rendered.

The Court reaffirmed the workers' compensation exception in Thomas v. Washington Gas Light Co., 448 U.S. 261 (1980). Three members of the court thought the exception was illogical but voted to preserve it because it was well established. Four Justices joined a plurality opinion that tried to rationalize the exception.

The four-Justice opinion permitted a supplemental award by balancing the interests of the first state in limiting liability, the shared interests of both states in compensating the injured worker, and the interest of the first state in the integrity of its decisions. This balancing test is controversial. The Court has not expanded the balancing approach in later opinions. In fact, it has reasserted that there is no "roving" public policy exception for full faith and credit. Baker v. General Motors Corp., 522 U.S. 222, 233 (1998).

The workers' compensation exception is narrow. It applies only to workers' comp claims. And it applies more narrowly to supplemental awards where the second court's additional award is not inconsistent with any facts determined in the first state.

LAST-IN-TIME RULE

The Full Faith and Credit Clause requires a second state to enforce a prior state court judgment. This should prevent a second state from entering an inconsistent judgment. But mistakes happen. Parties and judges are human, and multiple inconsistent state court judgments can exist in real life. They can exist even more often on Conflicts final exams.

When faced with conflicting state judgments, the Supreme Court has directed courts to enforce the most recent judgment entitled to full faith and credit. Treinies v. Sunshine Mining Co., 308 U.S. 66 (1939).

For example, suppose Roseanne and Johnny were involved in a car accident in Nashville, Tennessee. Each claimed the other was to blame. Roseanne sued Johnny in Tennessee state court, where he counterclaimed. The Tennessee court found in favor of Roseanne and entered final judgment for her in 2009. Meanwhile, in 2010 Johnny sued Roseanne in a Kentucky state court for the same accident. Roseanne raised the defense of res judicata. The Kentucky court erroneously rejected her defense and entered judgment for Johnny. Because both are valid, final, and on the merits, states would normally be required to give them full faith and credit. But because they conflict, *Treinies* requires that the 2010 judgment be given full faith and credit. This means that Johnny can enforce his judgment in all states, including Tennessee. If Roseanne tries to bring a third lawsuit, the court should dismiss it and give res judicata effect to the 2010 judgment.

The last-in-time rule for state judgments contrasts with the treatment of foreign country judgments, where neither judgment need be recognized when they are in conflict.

The last-in-time rule means that the latest state court decision is binding, even if erroneous, if it meets the requirements for full faith and credit (it is valid, final, and on the merits). The last-in-time rule applies even if the second court erroneously refused to give full faith and credit to a prior judgment. In practice, this means a party must raise full faith and credit issues in the second court and appeal any error.

HOW LONG?

Time Period for Enforcing Judgment Judgments, like all other legal claims, are subject to statutes of limitations. A state court is free to apply its own forum statutes of limitations to judgment claims. This is consistent with the traditional rule that courts apply their forum statutes of limitations to foreign causes of action, but it is an exception to the general rule that requires the effect of foreign judgments to be determined by reference to the law of the place where the judgment was entered.

Revival States provide procedures for reviving their own courts' judgments prior to the expiration of the statute of limitations for enforcing the judgments. These procedures permit diligent plaintiffs to continue to attempt to satisfy their claims. After a judgment has been revived by one state, the question can arise in a second state as to whether the revival merely continues an existing judgment or establishes a new judgment. This makes a difference because the second state can apply its own statute of limitations, and the claim on the original judgment may be time-barred.

The Supreme Court held in Union National Bank v. Lamb, 337 U.S. 38 (1949), that whether a revived judgment is a new judgment or merely extends the time for enforcing the old judgment is governed by the law of the state where the judgment was revived. If the state where the revival occurred treats the revival as a new judgment, then all other states must give full faith and credit to the revived judgment. States can still apply their own statutes of limitations, but the clock starts over if it is a new judgment.

Dismissals of Time-Barred Claims A state court decision dismissing a claim as barred by the statute of limitations is not considered on the merits and is not binding on other states under the Full Faith and Credit Clause. Hay et al., Conflict of Laws §24.24 at 1413.

GREATER FAITH AND CREDIT?

States must give a state court judgment at least the preclusive effect that it has in the state where it was entered. If the claims or issues are precluded under the law where the judgment was entered, then other states must preclude them even if their own res judicata law is more lenient. Richman et al., Understanding Conflict of Laws §110[c][1] at 362–63.

State Courts It is unclear whether other states may give a sister state judgment more preclusive effect. An example of the problem is Hart v. American Airlines, Inc., 304 N.Y.S.2d 810 (Sup. Ct. 1969). Lawsuits stemming from an airplane crash were filed against American Airlines by various parties in several states. Texas entered judgment against the airline in one case. Under Texas law, this judgment did not prevent the airline from relitigating its liability in cases brought by other injured persons. But when one of these injured persons sued in New York, the New York court prevented the airline from relitigating its liability. The New York court reasoned that all the requirements for issue preclusion were satisfied under New York law and that it did not violate full faith and credit to give greater preclusive effect to the Texas judgment than Texas courts would.

Federal Courts Federal courts may not give state judgments greater preclusive effect than they have under state law where entered. Marrese v. American Academy of Orthopedic Surgeons, 470 U.S. 373 (1985). This reasoning may extend by equal force to state courts. Richman et al., Understanding Conflict of Laws §110[c][2] at 366. If so, Hart v. American Airlines is wrongly decided.

FULL FAITH AND THE FEDS

Enforcing State Judgment in Federal Court The Full Faith and Credit Clause does not literally require federal courts to give full faith and credit to state judgments, but the federal statute implementing the clause makes this obligation explicit. 28 U.S.C. §1738.

Enforcing Federal Judgment in State Court   Though not explicitly covered by the Full Faith and Credit Clause or by federal statute, state courts are obligated to give full effect to federal court judgments. They must give the same effect to the judgment as federal courts will. In federal cases based on diversity of citizenship, the preclusive effect of federal judgments is generally governed by the law of the state in which the federal court entering the judgment sat. Semtek International, Inc. v. Lockheed Martin Corp., 531 U.S. 497 (2001).[2]

Examples

Three Office Visits

1. You and Ali grew up together in South Jersey, where you both still live. One day Ali comes to you for legal advice. Ali hands you crumpled up pieces of paper. These contain a summons and complaint from a state court in Hawaii that Ali received one year ago by certified mail. In the complaint, the plaintiff Lee Park alleges that Ali assaulted him. The complaint demands compensatory damages in the amount of $5,000 and punitive damages in the amount of $5,000 plus fees and costs.

   Also included with the crumpled paper is a letter to Ali from Park enclosing a photocopy of a judgment entered by the Hawaii court against Ali in the amount of $14,397. The letter demands that Ali pay the judgment.

   Ali is confused. He insists he never assaulted Lee Park and has never been to Hawaii. He asks whether the judgment is enforceable. Please explain.

2. Ali comes back to your office. He has had an email exchange with Lee Park. In one email Park reminded Ali that Ali dropped his suitcase on Park on an airplane while the plane had stopped to refuel. Ali believes that the plane was stopped in Japan, not Hawaii. He asks if this changes anything. Please advise.

3. Ali comes back to your office. He triumphantly shares all the documents related to the flight and lawsuit. His ticket and itinerary reveal that the plane traveled far north of Hawaii and refueled in Japan, where the alleged tort took place. While looking in the documents, you also find a photocopy of a letter that Ali sent the Hawaii court when he received the original complaint. The letter reads, "Dear Judge, I have never been

---

2. The Court in *Semtek International* emphasized that federal principles of finality would apply in exceptional cases where the state law of finality was incompatible with federal interests, such as where a federal court dismissed an action with prejudice for willful violation of federal court orders but a similar state court dismissal would not bar relitigation.

to Hawaii, though I have always wanted to visit your beautiful state. The complaint is full of lies. Please make it go away." The copy of the letter was stamped "motion denied" by the Hawaii court and mailed back to Ali by the court's clerk. Does this change anything?

Amazing Expanding Jurisdiction

4. Kate sued Big Farm Corp. in Justice of the Peace Court in the state of Confusion. The complaint alleged that the defendant's patented feed corn had stunted the growth of her cows, causing her sales to lag and leading to insolvency and a loss of lifetime earnings in the amount of $5 million. The complaint was duly served on the defendant's corporate counsel during the annual meeting of the corporation in Confusion. The corporate counsel did nothing with the complaint because she determined that Justice of the Peace Courts in the state of Confusion had a maximum civil jurisdiction of $1,000.

   The Confusion Justice of the Peace Court entered judgment in the amount of $5 million. Kate now seeks to enforce the judgment in the neighboring state of Bewilderment. Under Confusion state law, a Justice of the Peace Court's jurisdiction is limited, but a party must raise such limits to the court. If the court enters a final judgment in excess of its jurisdiction, a party must appeal the judgment. Otherwise the judgment is enforceable in the state of Confusion. In contrast, under Bewilderment state law, judgments from its courts of limited jurisdiction are void and unenforceable for any amount in excess of the jurisdictional limits.

   Kate garnishes the corporation's bank account in the state of Bewilderment in the amount of $5 million. The corporation appears and moves to quash the execution of any amount over $1,000. You are the judge. Rule and explain.

Clash of Policy

5. The state of East Dakota has legalized prostitution and recognizes contracts to perform sexual acts in exchange for money. In contrast, in West Dakota prostitution is a crime, and contracts to perform sexual acts for money are void as violations of West Dakota public policy.

   John Doe, citizen of West Dakota, travels to East Dakota, where he agrees to pay Terry Nemo $500 to perform certain sex acts.

   After Doe returns to West Dakota, Nemo sues him in East Dakota state court and recovers a judgment for breach of contract in the amount of $500. The complaint alleges that plaintiff agreed to and did perform sexual acts for money pursuant to the agreement and that defendant did not pay.

   Doe ignored the complaint, and default judgment was entered in East Dakota. Will the judgment be enforceable in West Dakota courts?

Workers' Comp

6. Hans Culotte, a worker employed in Virginia by Savage Grinding Wheels Co., was injured on a job in the state of Maryland. Culotte filed a workers' compensation action in Maryland, where the state workers' compensation agency awarded him a total of $5,000 for permanent partial disability resulting from the severing of part of his ear and partial hearing loss. It rejected his claim that he is entitled to permanent total disability, and its findings were affirmed upon review by the Maryland state courts.

   Culotte then commenced a second workers' compensation action in Virginia. He seeks to introduce expert medical evidence that he suffers from brain damage as a result of his injury that renders him permanently disabled. The employer moves to dismiss, arguing that the Maryland workers' compensation proceedings must be given full faith and credit. Rule and explain.

Good Law After Bad

7. Roche recovered a judgment against McDonald in a Washington state court. Years later the Washington statute of limitations that governed actions to enforce judgments had expired. Moreover, the judgment could no longer be revived under Washington law.

   Roche commenced an action in Oregon state court to enforce the Washington judgment because the Oregon statute of limitations for actions on the judgment had not yet expired. Does the Full Faith and Credit Clause require Oregon to dismiss the action under the Washington statute of limitations?

8. Same facts. Oregon enters a new final judgment on the Washington judgment. The plaintiff now takes the Oregon judgment back to Washington and seeks to enforce it there. Must the Washington court give the Oregon judgment full faith and credit?

Explanations

Three Office Visits

1. The Hawaii judgment must be given full faith and credit by all state courts, including the courts of New Jersey, provided it is a valid final judgment on the merits. But a default judgment entered by a court that lacks personal jurisdiction over the defendant is void. The court that entered the judgment cannot enforce it without violating the defendant's right to due process, and such a judgment is not binding on other state courts.

The key issue will be whether Ali was properly subject to the personal jurisdiction of the Hawaii state courts. If he has never been to the state, has done no acts purposely directed toward the state, and has not consented to jurisdiction or entered an appearance, then the court will lack personal jurisdiction, and the judgment will be unenforceable.

2. Ali is the kind of client who demonstrates why it is a good idea to give full legal advice rather than yes or no answers. Indeed, whether the alleged tort occurred in Hawaii changes everything. Ali's physical presence in the state would establish a constitutionally sufficient basis for the exercise of jurisdiction over him by the courts of that state for claims arising from his activity in the state. Ali may have good defenses on the merits to the tort claim, but he is required to present those in the Hawaii action if the court has jurisdiction. Because he failed to present the defenses, he will be prevented from raising them as defenses to enforcement of the judgment. The only defense to full faith and credit enforcement of the judgment on these facts will be lack of personal jurisdiction. If the New Jersey courts find that Ali was present in Hawaii and the claims arose from his presence, then they must enforce the judgment.

3. Ali probably does not mean to be a problem client, but like many clients he does not know what events and documents are legally significant. The good news is that the Hawaii court may not have personal jurisdiction based on the tort having occurred there. The bad news is that Ali may have entered an appearance by sending the letter to the court. The court's action in response to the letter indicates that the court considered it some sort of motion (perhaps a motion to dismiss for lack of personal jurisdiction). The court denied the motion (possibly erroneously). But the Hawaii court probably obtained jurisdiction over Ali either because Ali appeared without challenging its personal jurisdiction or because he raised the issue, lost, and failed to appeal it. The judgment will now be a valid final judgment on the merits. All states must give it full faith and credit, including New Jersey. States must give the judgment the same effect it would have in Hawaii. If Hawaii would allow a defense to the judgment, then other states may. Attacking default judgments under any state's law is an uphill battle.

Amazing Expanding Jurisdiction

4. Kate looks like a winner. The subject matter jurisdiction of state courts and the effect of filing in the wrong court is complicated and varies from state to state. But for full faith and credit purposes, the validity and effect of a judgment, including defects in subject matter jurisdiction, are governed by the law of the state where it was entered. The Justice of the Peace Courts were not given original subject matter jurisdiction,

but their judgments are nevertheless valid and enforceable under the law of the place where rendered because the defendant did not appear and challenge the court's jurisdiction. In other words, the Justice of the Peace Court effectively acquired subject matter jurisdiction as a result of the defendant's acts. All states must now give full faith and credit to the Confusion judgment.

Clash of Policy

5. The state court judgment reducing the offensive cause of action to judgment will be enforceable in all other states. The important thing to recognize is that the Full Faith and Credit Clause does not include any general public policy exception. The judgment is otherwise a valid final judgment on the merits.

Workers' Comp

6. The Virginia court must give full faith and credit to the fact findings of the Maryland decision that Culotte was not permanently disabled and dismiss his claim.

It is important that the other state's agency proceedings were reviewed by a court, because unreviewed agency actions are not entitled to full faith and credit. The example is distinguishable from the supplemental award permitted in Thomas v. Washington Gas Light Co. In that case the Court permitted a supplemental award for the same injuries, reasoning that the second state was not doing anything legally inconsistent with the proceedings in the first state other than permitting a more generous measure of recovery. But in Culotte's case, the worker is asking the second court to provide a recovery based on facts that are inconsistent with the facts found by the first state. Even in the area of workers' compensation, the state must respect the factual determinations of the first state and deny additional recovery based on a theory that has been considered and rejected by the first state.

Good Law After Bad

7. A state may apply its own statute of limitations, so Oregon may enter a new judgment under Oregon law even though the claim on the judgment is time-barred under the law of the state that originally rendered the judgment. This is what happened in the case on which this example is based. See Roche v. McDonald, 275 U.S. 449 (1928).

8. The Washington court must give the same full faith and credit to the Oregon judgment that Oregon courts would give it. This is what happened in Roche after the plaintiff got the new judgment in Oregon. Id. Since the judgment is valid and enforceable in Oregon, the Washington

courts must enforce it too, even though the second judgment could not have been entered by a Washington court. Washington must treat the judgment as a new judgment, but it may apply its own statute of limitations to the (new) judgment and refuse to enforce it after it becomes time-barred under the Washington statute.

Domestic Relations Judgments: Divorce, Support, and Alimony

INTRODUCTION

This chapter deals with domestic relations *judgments*. Marriages and civil unions are not judgments, and the rules governing them are covered in Chapter 10. For lots of unromantic reasons, there is greater need for certainty and uniformity in matters regarding divorce than marriage. For example, if a marriage is not valid, the parties may go through another ceremony and still get married. In contrast, if a divorce is not valid, then a subsequent remarriage becomes bigamy — a strict liability crime.

"D-I-V-O-R-C-E"

An old-time song referred to divorce just by spelling it. Divorce was considered immoral and legally disfavored. Divorce was not always available as a legal right in all states, though wealthy individuals could get private legislative relief to terminate their marriages.

Today courts in all states grant divorces, and states recognize no-fault grounds for divorce. Nevertheless, the availability, procedures, and effects of divorce vary. Some jurisdictions now prefer the term "dissolution" for divorce. "Dissolution" is also the term of choice for judgments terminating civil unions. Annulments are like divorces except they are based on the theory that a valid marriage never existed.

The important thing is that divorces, dissolutions, and annulments are judicial judgments or decrees. The general jurisdictional requirements for divorces, dissolutions, and annulments are the same.

DOMICILE FOR DIVORCE

A Short History of Marital Domicile   Divorce jurisdiction was traditionally a form of in rem jurisdiction. A valid divorce judgment required jurisdiction over the "thing" of the marriage. Such jurisdiction was available only in the courts of the marital domicile. The divorce court would apply its own forum law, but this was also the law of the marital domicile.

The historical rules are still the starting point for international enforcement. Foreign country divorces are generally recognized when granted by a court of the marital domicile. And it is still the rule that divorce courts apply forum law in deciding whether to grant a divorce.

Common Domicile   The marital domicile was the place where both parties were domiciled or the last place where they were both domiciled. First Restatement §§110 & 113(b).

Domicile of One Spouse Plus Consent or Personal Jurisdiction   If one party left the marital domicile and moved to a new state, the new state did not automatically acquire jurisdiction to enter a valid divorce even if the party made the new state his or her domicile. But the new state where one party was domiciled could enter a valid divorce decree if the nondomiciliary spouse either consented or was subject to personal jurisdiction. This tended to give nonconsenting spouses a veto over divorce in foreign courts. It forced spouses to seek divorce in the original state of common domicile. If divorce was not available there, then too bad.

To some extent, these old rules permitted states to control the termination of marriages of their domiciliaries. But the rules also encouraged deceptive, manipulative, and coercive behavior designed to induce consent or establish domicile.[1]

---

1. Anyone who longs for the good old days should know that there was an additional ground for jurisdiction that anticipated all the later problems: the state where only one party was domiciled could enter a valid divorce when the nonconsenting absent spouse's misconduct caused him or her to "cease[] to have the right object to the acquisition of" the new domicile. First Restatement §113(a)(ii).

DOMICILE OF ONE SPOUSE FOR U.S. DIVORCES

In Williams v. North Carolina, 317 U.S. 287 (1942), the Supreme Court revolutionized national divorce law by holding that a state where only one spouse was domiciled had jurisdiction to enter a valid divorce decree binding on all other states under the Full Faith and Credit Clause. This means an ex parte divorce—a divorce granted when only one of the parties to the marriage was before the court—is valid and entitled to full faith and credit, provided that one party was domiciled in the state.

This rule drastically changes the normal due process requirement that a court may adversely affect the rights of a defendant only if the defendant is subject to the court's personal jurisdiction. An absent spouse without any minimum contacts in Nevada will be bound by a Nevada divorce decree so long as one spouse was domiciled in Nevada.

Williams requires that the party obtaining the divorce be domiciled, not merely present. This prevents a spouse from getting a quickie divorce merely by traveling to another state. To further discourage fraudulent claims of domicile, most states impose additional residency requirements on parties seeking divorces. The Supreme Court held in Sosna v. Iowa, 419 U.S. 393 (1975), that such additional requirements are constitutional so long as they are reasonable.

DOMICILE AS JURISDICTIONAL FACT NOT BINDING ON NONPARTY

The Williams case went to the Supreme Court twice. Williams I held that in a bigamy prosecution the state of North Carolina could not refuse to recognize a Nevada divorce that was based on the domicile of only one party. After that decision North Carolina reprosecuted for bigamy on the theory that the spouse did not get a valid divorce because the spouse was never really domiciled in Nevada. In Williams II, 325 U.S. 226 (1945), the Supreme Court affirmed the second conviction. It held that another state's ex parte determination of the jurisdictional fact of domicile is not entitled to full faith and credit and is not binding on nonparties.

BILATERAL DIVORCE—CONSENT AND FRAUD

An action where both parties appear is called a "bilateral" divorce. Some bilateral divorces are bitterly contested, but others are not. The Supreme

Court held in Sherrer v. Sherrer, 334 U.S. 343 (1948), that when the spouses appeared and had the opportunity to raise the issue of domicile in divorce proceedings in one state, they could not later challenge the validity of the divorce elsewhere by arguing that one of them was not domiciled there. This may be fair to the parties, but what about others affected by a divorce decree? In Johnson v. Muelberger, 340 U.S. 581 (1951), the Court held that nonparties, too, are precluded from later challenging a state divorce decree on the theory that neither spouse was domiciled in the state when the spouses appeared and either litigated or had the opportunity to litigate the issue of domicile.

FOREIGN COUNTRY DIVORCES

Williams's modification of the marital domicile requirement was motivated by federalism concerns. Neither its holding nor its rationale requires the recognition of international divorces, where a foreign country enters a judgment based exclusively on the domicile of one party.

Foreign divorces, even if valid where entered, are not entitled to full faith and credit. Most states refuse to recognize foreign "quickie" divorces even when both spouses appear and waive jurisdictional defenses. The New York decision Rosenstiel v. Rosenstiel, 209 N.E.2d 709 (N.Y. 1965), is famous as an extreme case where a state court recognized a bilateral divorce based on personal jurisdiction and one-day "residence" in a foreign country whose law did not require domicile. Even when consensual, such foreign "quickie" divorces are not recognized many places. They are not valid anywhere when they are ex parte and based on only one spouse's presence.

"DIVISIBLE DIVORCE" — DIVORCE vs. ALIMONY, CHILD CUSTODY, AND EVERYTHING ELSE

The term "divisible divorce" refers to the fact that in evaluating the validity of a court's legal decision, it is necessary to divide the issue of divorce from all other legal decrees and judgments. The Williams one-party-domicile rule applies only to the narrow issue of divorce. All other decrees must meet normal jurisdictional requirements. Court orders involving everything other than divorce are valid only if the court had personal jurisdiction over the defendant. Personal jurisdiction is required for valid decrees affecting property, alimony, support, and child custody.

A state court has jurisdiction to grant a divorce sought by a person domiciled there even without personal jurisdiction over the other spouse, but its decree in the same case regarding alimony is void and unenforceable against a defendant who did not appear and was not subject to the court's personal jurisdiction. Estin v. Estin, 334 U.S. 541 (1948). Similarly, even if a court has the constitutional authority to enter a valid divorce decree based on one parent's domicile, it cannot enter a valid custody decree affecting the other parent's rights to custody of children without personal jurisdiction over the parent. May v. Anderson, 345 U.S. 528 (1953).

FULL FAITH AND CREDIT FOR SUPPORT AND CUSTODY DECREES

Nonmodifiable Lump Sum Decrees — Weird, Rare, and Troubling

Bad Bad Case In Yarborough v. Yarborough, 290 U.S. 202 (1933), the Supreme Court held that the Full Faith and Credit Clause requires other states to give the same effect to a nonmodifiable lump sum award of child support that the award has under the law of the state where it was entered. The *Yarborough* decision has not been overruled and is a leading case in all but one Conflicts casebook. Its practical consequences are bad. The lump sum award was consumed within two years, yet the child's home state was powerless to require additional support from her father.

I have never understood why the Georgia judgment was valid to begin with. The Georgia court never acquired personal jurisdiction over the daughter, so I don't understand why precluding her from challenging that judgment in Georgia or any state was not a taking without due process.[2]

Zombie Case The most important thing to realize about the nonmodifiable-lump-sum-awards case is that it is a Zombie — the living dead. It is living because it has not been overruled. But it is dead because it has little or no application in real life. The rule was always limited to nonmodifiable support orders. Such nonmodifiable awards have gone the way of the extinct

---

2. The court discusses this in part of the opinion omitted from some casebooks and concludes that the termination of rights in the child is enforceable because it is a "legal incident" of divorce under Georgia law. If you are getting even more confused, join the club.

dodo bird. Today, child support awards are modifiable in all states. Symeon C. Symeonides, Conflict of Laws: American, Comparative, International 721 (2d ed. 2003). Of course, even dodos can fly in the alternative universe known as Final Exam World.

Modifiable Decrees — Normal and Troubling

The Full Faith and Credit Clause did not require enforcement of support and custody decrees from sister states when they were modifiable. Courts reasoned that either full faith and credit did not apply because modifiable decrees were not final decisions or that, if full faith and credit applied, it did not require strict enforcement because such decrees could be modified consistent with the law where entered. The result was that losers could relocate to a new state and challenge the custody or support decree. Passions run high in these disputes, and this became a huge problem.

The Solution — Alphabet Soup

Solutions Beginning in 1950, states responded to the problem by enacting uniform laws requiring enforcement of custody and child support decrees from other jurisdictions. A long series of acts closed loopholes in earlier acts. For example, the URESA (Uniform Reciprocal Enforcement of Support Act) was promulgated in 1950, amended in 1968, and replaced in 1992 by UIFSA (Uniform Interstate Family Support Act), which was later amended. Similar states' acts — UCCJA (1968), UCCJEA (1997) — require recognition of custody decrees from other jurisdictions.

Congress also enacted federal legislation requiring states to enforce custody and support decrees rendered by other states. These require parties seeking modification to return to the original states. PKPA (Parental Kidnapping Prevention Act), 28 U.S.C. §1738A (requiring states to enforce and not modify custody decrees from other states); Full Faith and Credit for Child Support Orders Act (1994), 28 U.S.C. §1738B (requiring enforcement of valid child support orders from sister states).

The state and federal acts are detailed and comprehensive. The uniform state laws are broader and may cover foreign country judgments and spousal support, which are not covered by the federal acts. Where the federal acts apply, they federalize obligations to enforce custody and child support decrees. In the event of conflicts, the federal law prevails and assures nationwide uniformity. But the federal acts do not create federal claims or confer jurisdiction on federal courts.

Enforcing Foreign Country Support Awards Neither the Full Faith and Credit Clause nor any federal statute or treaty requires states to recognize support decrees from foreign countries. But states have begun to enter into reciprocal enforcement agreements with foreign countries with the encouragement of Congress. Richman et al., Understanding Conflict of Laws §128 at 434.

Hague Convention on the Civil Aspects of International Child Abduction (1980) Federal law requires "the prompt return of children abducted to or wrongfully retained in a country when both that country (in this case the United States) and the country of the child's habitual residence . . . are parties to the Hague Convention and for so long as the child is under age 16." Sheikh v. Cahill, 546 N.Y.S.2d 517 (Sup. Ct. 1989). The federal law applies to children who are wrongfully abducted or retained. It is not limited to custody disputes involving the enforcement of a court order or custody decree. The law can be enforced in both federal and state court.

JUDGMENTS RESPECTING SAME-SEX MARRIAGES

Before 2015 some states enacted laws that prohibited any recognition of same-sex marriages even when they were valid in other states. Some of these state laws also prohibited enforcing judgments that respected same-sex marriages or granting divorces to same-sex married couples. To add to the confusion, Congress enacted a "Defense of Marriage Act" that seemed to permit states to evade their normal obligations to give full faith and credit to judgments from sister states when the judgments respected same-sex marriages.

Now same-sex marriages are valid in all states. (See Chapter 10.) State laws to the contrary are void. And no state has a valid reason to resist sister-state judgments respecting such marriages. Obergefell v. Hodges, 135 S. Ct. 2584 (2015).

For example, if Ira and Jan got married in Massachusetts, the Full Faith and Credit Clause would require Texas to recognize the validity of their same-sex marriage. They have the same rights to divorce as other married couples. Similarly, if Jan died, and a Massachusetts probate court entered a decree declaring that Ira was entitled to Jan's personal property as the surviving spouse, then Texas and all other states would be required to give full faith and credit to the decree.

Examples

Unhappily Married

1. Elizabeth and Richard were U.S. citizens domiciled and residing in East Carolina. They got married in East Carolina and enjoyed a short but tempestuous marriage. One day, Elizabeth announced she had had enough, boarded the red-eye shuttle for the country of Vespugia, and hired a divorce lawyer. Following the advice of the Vespugia lawyer, she resided in Vespugia for one week and filed a formal document declaring Vespugia to be her residence and domicile. At the end of the week, she commenced a divorce action. Richard received notice of the divorce proceedings but refused to respond. Three weeks later the Vespugia court entered a divorce decree. The decree is valid under the law of Vespugia.

   Elizabeth remained in Vespugia for one more month. During that time, she fell in love with her lawyer and married him. The marriage was valid under the law of Vespugia.

   She then returned to East Carolina to retrieve some of her property. There she was arrested and charged with criminal bigamy. While sitting in jail, she was served with process in a divorce action filed in East Carolina state court by Richard. Elizabeth raises her Vespugian divorce as a defense in both the criminal and civil proceeding. Is it a good defense?

Sanctuary

2. Flem and Eula, citizens of the state of Mississippi, got married in Mississippi. Two years later Flem ran off to West Dakota and filed for divorce one day after his arrival on the ground that Eula beat him. Eula received a copy of the complaint and became enraged. She traveled to West Dakota, where she contested the divorce, arguing that Flem was not entitled to a divorce because he was the one who beat her. She also argued that the court lacked jurisdiction because Flem was not a resident of West Dakota as required by state law. The trial court granted a divorce, and Eula did not appeal.

   After the divorce, Flem returned to Mississippi. Six years later he went through a marriage ceremony with Victoria. Eula then filed an action for divorce in Mississippi state court. The district attorney has also charged Flem with criminal bigamy. Victoria comes to you and asks whether she is validly married and whether Flem is guilty of criminal bigamy. Please advise.

The Katz Spats

3. Hubert and Wilma Katz were married and living in West Virginia, where they had three children. One day Hubert ran off to Sin City, Nevada and

got a job as a bartender. After living in Nevada for two years, Hubert commenced a civil action seeking a divorce and alimony from Wilma. He arranged for service of process both by certified mail and by personal delivery on Wilma at her home in West Virginia.

Wilma tore up the papers and took no action. As a result, the Nevada court entered a decree of divorce and also entered a decree ordering Wilma to pay Hubert alimony in the amount of $500 per month until he got remarried.

After one year, Hubert traveled back to West Virginia to collect the alimony that was due him pursuant to the Nevada decree. He filed a civil action in West Virginia to collect the alimony. Wilma files a motion to dismiss on the ground that they are still married and that the Nevada judgment is unenforceable. Please rule on the motion and explain.

4. Same facts. While Hubert is visiting West Virginia, Wilma commences a separate action in West Virginia court seeking a divorce, alimony, and child support. She arranged for personal service of process on Hubert while he was in West Virginia. Hubert does not answer the lawsuit. He returns to Nevada. The West Virginia court enters a decree ordering Hubert to provide monthly alimony and child support. Must Nevada now recognize the West Virginia judgment?

Custodial Confusion

5. Abe and Beth were married and lived for 20 years in the state of East Carolina. They had two children, Sonny and Babe. The last years of the marriage were marked by substance abuse by Abe and Beth, violent conflicts, arrests, and public accusations of wrongdoing.

East Carolina entered a no-fault divorce decree, but Abe and Beth were not able to agree on custody. Each insisted that the other was an unfit parent. The young children were traumatized and gave conflicting evidence that partially supported the claims by each parent that the other parent abused the children. The trial judge agonized over the decision because she was not sure whom to believe. She decided to grant temporary custody to Abe, concluding that the physical evidence was more consistent with his version of the facts than with the testimony of the young children.

Beth learned of the judge's decision from a cell-phone call from her lawyer while she was taking the children to Church School. Fearing for the life of her children, Beth drove directly with the children to her mother's house in the neighboring state of West Carolina. That afternoon she filed an action for a temporary restraining order in West Carolina seeking emergency interim relief from the East Carolina custody decree. Abe has appeared in the West Carolina court and insists that it must enforce the sister state decree granting him temporary custody. Beth argues that the decree is not entitled to full faith and credit because it is a modifiable temporary order. She also argues that the lives of the children are at issue and that the court has inherent emergency power to grant her temporary custody.

The trial judge never took Conflicts and calls you, an old school friend, for advice. The judge tells you he believes the mother and asks whether he can grant her relief. Please advise.

Policy Prohibitions

6. Bari's spouse, Terri, was injured in a car accident in Massachusetts when she was struck by a car driven recklessly by James Bond. Terri settled her claim with Bond's insurance company. Bari then presented a claim for her own loss of consortium resulting from the loss of companionship and support caused by the personal injuries suffered by her spouse. Bond's insurance company refused to settle the loss of consortium claim because Bari and Terri are the same sex. Bari sued Bond and recovered a judgment in the amount of $1 million.

   Bond has not satisfied the judgment. But Bari has located a safe deposit box owned by Bond in the state of Tradition. She believes the box contains personal property assets that may be used to satisfy part of the judgment against Bond. Accordingly, she commences a civil action against Bond in the state of Tradition, seeking enforcement of the judgment from Massachusetts. Tradition enacted a state constitutional amendment in 2004 that limits marriage to persons of different sexes and prohibits giving any recognition to same-sex marriages even when they are valid elsewhere. Does full faith and credit require the Tradition state court to enforce the money judgment from Massachusetts?

Explanations

Unhappily Married

1. The short answer is that the divorce decree from Vespugia is not valid and will not be recognized in East Carolina. Because the divorce judgment is not from a sister state, it is subject to the traditional requirement that a valid divorce must be granted by the court of the marital domicile, the jurisdiction in which the parties lived together in marriage. Vespugia did not have the power to render a valid divorce that would have been traditionally recognized elsewhere. Hence the remarriage will not be recognized in East Carolina, and Elizabeth does not have a good defense to the criminal prosecution for bigamy (assuming East Carolina follows the common law view that bigamy is a strict liability crime). Nor does her attempted divorce end the marriage, and Richard may obtain a valid divorce in East Carolina.

The longer answer gets into areas of factual and legal uncertainty. Full faith and credit does not apply since Vespugia is not a sister state. Nevertheless, it is conceivable that a U.S. state like East Carolina might want on grounds of comity to apply the same rules to foreign country divorces that it does to sister state divorces. The question then is whether Elizabeth became domiciled in Vespugia. Changing domicile requires only physical presence plus subjective intent to make the place the person's legal home. Elizabeth's subjective intent is a fact question. But courts would be extremely reluctant under these facts to find that her brief presence, initially for the purpose of obtaining a divorce, satisfies the necessary intent.

Even if Elizabeth was domiciled in Vespugia, a further question arises as to whether a state under these facts could constitutionally give comity to the resulting divorce decree without violating Richard's due process rights. Some gurus suggest that most U.S. courts will recognize foreign national divorces based on domicile, Richman et al., Understanding Conflict of Laws §123[f] at 426. But the authority for this is not certain when only one party is domiciled in the foreign country.

The conclusion is clear that in international divorce situations, it is possible that divorces — and later remarriages — may be valid in some countries but not recognized in others. The Full Faith and Credit Clause helps avoid the inconsistent treatment of divorces from sister states.

2. My advice is that Victoria is validly married and that Flem is not guilty of criminal bigamy. West Dakota did not originally have jurisdiction to grant a valid divorce because Flem was not domiciled there. He also did not satisfy any additional residency requirement imposed by state law for a divorce. The court should have dismissed the action, and it erred in denying Eula's motion. Unfortunately, Eula did not appeal the erroneous decision, and it is final. Moreover, because she had the opportunity to raise the jurisdictional issue — in fact she actually did raise it and lost due to error! — the judgment is also valid and binding on both Eula and third parties under the rule in Sherrer v. Sherrer, 334 U.S. 343 (1948), and Johnson v. Muelberger, 340 U.S. 581 (1951).

Although these Supreme Court decisions make clear that the bilateral divorce cannot be collaterally attacked by parties to the divorce or third-party individuals, some Conflicts gurus have argued that they leave open the possibility that the state itself might not be prevented from disregarding a bilateral divorce entered by a sister state without jurisdiction in a prosecution for bigamy. I myself don't understand how a divorce could be constitutionally valid for all purposes except a subsequent bigamy prosecution.

The Katz Spats

3. Wilma is half right. She is right that the alimony award is unenforceable. But she is wrong that the parties are still married. The case illustrates the "divisible divorce" and the need for separately analyzing the validity of the divorce and the validity of other judgments such as support and custody. The divorce is valid and binding on all states because one of the parties to the marriage (Hubert) was domiciled in the state that rendered the divorce. Personal jurisdiction is not required for the divorce to be valid.

    In contrast, personal jurisdiction over the defendant is required for the alimony or support decree to be entitled to full faith and credit. Indeed, in the absence of personal jurisdiction, such a decree is void and unenforceable even in Nevada, where the decree was rendered. Wilma has no contacts with Nevada, was not served in the state, and did not appear or consent to the state's exercise of personal jurisdiction over her. Accordingly, the alimony judgment is void and unenforceable against her anywhere. The West Virginia court must grant her motion to dismiss.

4. Hubert is a loser. Again, it is necessary to divide the analysis of the divorce and the other claims. The Nevada divorce is valid and must be accorded full faith and credit. The Nevada alimony award was void because that state lacked personal jurisdiction over Wilma, and West Virginia properly refused to enforce it.

    In contrast, the West Virginia support judgment was valid. West Virginia could have exercised long-arm jurisdiction over the defendant, who left the state for obligations stemming from his activity in the state. But long-arm jurisdiction is unnecessary since Wilma got personal jurisdiction over Hubert while he was physically present in West Virginia. Its support orders are thus valid and enforceable. The child support order must be enforced according to its terms without modification in other states, pursuant to the federal Parental Kidnapping Prevention Act. The spousal support award also appears to satisfy the requirements for interstate enforcement under the Uniform Interstate Family Support Act.

Custodial Confusion

5. The judge may not grant relief inconsistent with the decree awarding custody to Abe. The Uniform Child Custody Jurisdiction Act and the federal Parental Kidnapping Protection Act require the enforcement even of modifiable and temporary custody decrees from sister states according to the terms of the decree, obligating the parties to return to the court that entered the original decree to seek modification. Those acts were designed to prevent just the sort of parental forum shopping present in the example.

The sister state judgment must be valid to be entitled to enforcement. It is valid here because the court had personal jurisdiction over the parent domiciled in the state. The rendering court is also granted jurisdiction to award custody by the Uniform Act because it is in the state where the children were living for six months prior to the commencement of the action.

Policy Prohibition

6. The outcome of this case was uncertain before Obergefell v. Hodges, 135 S. Ct. 2584 (2015). The old federal Defense of Marriage Act attempted to relieve states of the obligation to enforce certain judgments that were previously binding under the Supreme Court's interpretation of the text of the Full Faith and Credit Clause. Scholars debated whether Congress had the authority to reduce the full faith and credit due to sister state judgments.

   After *Obergefell* it is clear that the state of Tradition constitutional amendment is void. All states must recognize the same-sex marriage that is valid under the law of a sister state. Likewise, states now can have no legitimate public policy reason for refusing to give full faith and credit to judgments based on rights created by such marriages.

PART IX

Practice and Procedure

Proving Foreign Law

INTRODUCTION

This is the end.[1] This last chapter covers how to prove what foreign law is in a case where it applies. It also covers what happens when a party fails to make proper proof of foreign law at trial.

ESTABLISHING THE CONTENT OF FOREIGN LAW

Danielle is driving a car in Paris and injures her passenger, Pierre. For some reason, Pierre sues Danielle in Chicago. The parties are both French citizens, and all the facts relevant to the claim occurred in France. Under both traditional and modern approaches, French law would govern most of the issues. But how does Pierre or Danielle raise the issue of French law and show what French law is?

The Bad Old Days—Foreign Law as "Fact"   Traditionally, common law courts treated the content of a foreign jurisdiction's law as a question of "fact." This fact had to be asserted and established like any other fact, subject to rigorous rules of evidence. Remember hearsay? Even published copies of statutes might be inadequate because of problems establishing their

---

1. *The End*, The Doors (1967).

authenticity. Satisfactory proof might require testimony by a properly qualified (and expensive) expert witness. *See* First Restatement §621 cmt. a.

The Trend—Foreign Law as "Law" The trend is for courts to treat the
content of foreign law as a matter of law rather than fact. Doing so frees
courts to consider all the sources of information they consult in determining local law—from photocopies of statutes to the Internet. Treating foreign law as "law" rather than "fact" also means a trial judge's determination
of foreign law, like other matters of law, will be reviewed de novo by appellate courts.

This trend has been more complete for findings of sister state law than
for foreign country law. Federal courts and most, if not all, states will take
judicial notice of the law of sister states without requiring proof of the law
under rules of evidence. Federal courts treat the determination of foreign
country law as "a ruling on a question of law" rather than fact. Fed. R. Civ.
P. 44.1. Over half the states also take judicial notice of foreign country law.
Hay et al., Conflict of Laws §12.17 at 553.

In some cases a foreign government may submit an official statement
of the meaning and application of its law. Federal courts "should accord
respectful consideration" to such submission but are not bound by it and
may consider all other relevant sources. Animal Science Products, Inc. v
Hebei Welcome Pharmaceutical Co., 138 S. Ct. 1865 (2018).

Notice In federal court and some states, parties must provide notice in the
pleadings or in some other form if they intend to rely on a foreign country's law. Federal Rule of Civil Procedure 44.1 requires a party who wants
a federal court to apply a foreign country's law to give notice in writing.
Rule 44.1 follows the trend of treating the determination of foreign law as
a matter of law by providing that federal courts may consider "any relevant
material or source," whether or not admissible as evidence, and by declaring that the trial judge's "determination must be treated as a ruling on a
question of law."

Old Fashioned Presumptions

Older authorities presumed the identity of common law rules when the
foreign jurisdiction was a common law jurisdiction. They did not presume that foreign statutes were the same as local statutes and required
actual evidence of foreign statutes. *See* First Restatement §§622–623. The
presumption of identity of common law would help a plaintiff when the
forum's law was pro-recovery. But it could prevent a plaintiff from recovering under a foreign judge-made rule.

The Case of Presumption Gumption

In Coon v. The Medical Center, 797 S.E.2d 828 (Ga. 2017), a pregnant woman from Alabama drove to Georgia where she delivered a stillborn baby. The hospital carelessly sent the wrong remains to Alabama, causing the woman great distress. Alabama courts applying the common law recognize a cause of action for negligent infliction of emotional distress under the facts. But Georgia courts applying common law would not recognize a claim of negligent infliction of emotional distress because there was neither physical impact nor pecuniary loss.

When the case was litigated in Georgia, most of the lower court judges thought the big issues were what state's law applied and whether there was a public policy exception to applying Alabama law. No! The Supreme Court of Georgia explained that the choice of law was easy: Georgia still follows *lex loci delicti*, so the governing law would be Alabama where the injury was suffered. But in looking to Alabama law, the court noted that there was no statute. Even though everyone agreed that Alabama common law recognized a claim, the Georgia court held that "a Georgia court will apply the common law as expounded by the courts of Georgia [not Alabama]." It reached this result by applying Alabama common law and then presuming Alabama common law was identical to the common law of Georgia (even though it knew it was not).

Admitting that its approach "may seem anachronistic," the court explained that the presumption of identity stems from an era when judges believed there was a single common law that applied everywhere, not multiple common laws in different states. When asked to reject this old-fashioned presumption of common law identity, the Georgia court explained that it preferred to retain the doctrine, observing that "a precedent's antiquity is a factor that weighs in favor of adhering to it."[2]

Newfangled Presumptions

Given how easy it is to prove foreign law today, there shouldn't be many cases where a party fails to submit some information to support a judicial finding as to the content of foreign law. But such cases do arise.

Absent proof of the content of foreign law, cases follow a variety of approaches. These are summarized in Tidewater Oil Co. v. Waller, 302 F.2d 638 (10th Cir. 1962). In that case a worker brought a personal injury action

---

2. But see Robert Rantoul Jr., *An Oration Delivered Before the Democrats and Antimasons* 37 (July 4, 1836) ("Sin and death are older than the common law. Are they, therefore, to be preferred to it?").

in Oklahoma stemming from an airplane accident in Turkey. The worker failed to make any showing at trial about what the law of Turkey was. The appellate opinion discussed three possible ways to respond to this failure of proof. Each has some authority.

1. Courts could dismiss a party's claim when the party relies on foreign law but fails to show what it is.
2. Courts could presume that foreign law is identical to the law of the forum.
3. Courts could presume that the foreign country's law adopts certain universally followed fundamental legal principles.

In *Tidewater*, the court followed the third option. The court reasoned that Turkey, a civil law jurisdiction, would allow recovery of actual damages for fault. But the court concluded that it would not be reasonable to assume that Turkey had enacted a form of comprehensive workers' compensation legislation identical to Oklahoma's that barred tort claims by workers against employers.

Certification

Even after the legal sources are studied, there may remain uncertainties as to what the law of a particular jurisdiction is. Almost all U.S. state courts have procedures that authorize courts from other systems to certify questions of law, asking for clarification about the state's law.

Certification can be helpful, especially for federal courts required to apply state law under the *Erie* doctrine. But certification is not the solution to all uncertainties about a state's law. First, state certification procedures do not usually permit certification from foreign country courts.[3] Some states limit certification to federal courts. Some restrict certification to federal appellate courts.

Second, the certification procedures are doubly discretionary. They permit but do not require a court to ask. And they permit but do not require a state court to answer. Under uniform procedures adopted in most states, there are additional restrictions: the question of law must be determinative of an issue in litigation, and there must be no controlling authority from the state whose law is in issue.

---

3. The uniform act or rule proposed in 1995 provides alternative language [in brackets] that allows states to answer questions from Mexican and Canadian courts. Uniform Certification of Questions of Law Act Rule (1995). So far only a few states have adopted this more expansive alternative formulation.

Examples

Tragic Ending

1. Don José stabbed Carmen to death outside a bull ring in Seville, Spain. After Don José becomes a U.S. citizen, the estate of Carmen brings a wrongful death action against Don José in federal court in New York. Suppose Carmen's estate wants to rely on some aspect of Spanish law such as a rule imposing strict liability on persons causing death by stabbing. What steps must the estate's lawyer take to raise the issue?

Office Field Trip

2. Two office co-workers in Scranton, Pennsylvania, drive to Ontario, Canada, to attend a convention. After entering Ontario, while Dwight is driving, he loses control of the car and hits a brick wall. Pam Passenger sues Dwight in Pennsylvania state court for personal injuries resulting from the accident. Dwight makes an oral motion to dismiss, arguing that the accident happened in Canada and that there might be complete defenses to liability under Canadian law. What should the court do?

Think[4]

3. Aretha is a fourth grader in Memphis, Tennessee. One day she goes on a class field trip to a circus in Mississippi. At the circus, Aretha rides on a pony, Dynamite. The pony ride concession is owned and operated by Bub Snopes, a citizen of Mississippi.

   Aretha suffers an injury when Dynamite rears and throws her into a brick wall. Snopes had not provided a helmet, and the lack of the helmet aggravated Aretha's injuries.

   Aretha sues Snopes in federal court in Mississippi. Snopes raises a defense under a Mississippi statute that establishes immunity for personal injuries caused by persons engaged in equine activities. The immunity does not extend to willful and wanton disregard of safety.

   Aretha's lawyer contends the Mississippi statute should not apply to a child noncitizen of Mississippi and that failing to provide a helmet shows willful and wanton disregard. A lengthy and expensive trial would be a waste of time if an appellate court ultimately decides that the statute provides a complete defense.

   Can the federal trial judge certify the questions of law about the applicability and scope of the Mississippi statute to the Mississippi Supreme Court?

---

4. Aretha Franklin and Ted White, Think (1968) ("You better think about what you're trying to do to me.").

Explanations

Tragic Ending

1. To raise an issue of foreign country law, the estate must provide advance notice in writing under Federal Rule of Civil Procedure 44.1. This would also apply to the defendant. For example, if Don José wanted to rely on a defense under Spanish law such as a statute of limitation or cap on damages, then he must provide notice in writing.

   The procedure regulating proof of foreign law determines only how a party must raise an issue of foreign law and bring the content of foreign law to the attention of the court hearing the case. The trial judge must still decide what law to apply under the applicable choice of law rules.

Office Field Trip

2. The court should deny the motion. There are two different issues. First, there is the question of who must show what law applies. Second, there is the question of what happens if there is no sufficient showing. Each of these issues will be treated differently under traditional and more recent authority.

   Under traditional rules, the law of the place of the wrong would apply to substantive issues such as the standard of care and damages. Moreover, under older authority, the plaintiff would have to show that the law supported her claim, and a forum might require her to plead and prove the "fact" of foreign law supporting her claim. However, presumptions available under older authority would also allow some facts to be found without any proof. For example, under the First Restatement, Pennsylvania could presume that Ontario, a common law jurisdiction, had common law rules of liability identical to those of Pennsylvania. (The presumption would not work if the accident happened in Québec, because it is not a common law jurisdiction.) The common law rules that could be presumed would include negligence, recovery for actual damages, and the doctrine of respondeat superior. In contrast, the court could not presume the identity of statutory law. Consequently, the plaintiff's tort claim would go forward based on the presumed identity of Ontario's negligence law. The court would not presume the identity of any statutory defense like the guest statute, and a party seeking to rely on such a defense would bear the burden of making proper proof.

   Under newer authority, the correct answer would require jurisdiction-specific research into forum law. Many courts, including federal courts, require a party seeking to raise the issue of a foreign country's law to raise the issue in the pleadings or other written notice. (Pennsylvania is one of these, 42 Pa. C.S.A. §5327(a), though you wouldn't be expected to know that without further research.)

Under modern choice of law approaches, the choice of law determination would depend on the issue and might require more information. For example, most modern approaches would apply Ontario's conduct-regulating rules (including speed limits and standards of care) but would tend to apply the law of the parties' common domicile to loss-shifting rules (like spousal immunity or guest statutes). There are not enough facts to tell what law would apply under any modern approach. And, of course, the example doesn't say what the law of Ontario might be.

In such a situation, modern courts will tend to apply their own law unless a party makes a sufficiently persuasive case for them not to do so. E.g., Tucker v. Whitaker Travel, Ltd., 620 F. Supp. 578 (E.D. Pa.), aff'd, 800 F.2d 1140 (3d Cir. 1985) (following Fed. R. Civ. P. 44.1 and applying Pennsylvania state law in tort case arising in Bahamas where parties neither argued foreign law should apply nor made any showing of the content of the foreign law). Courts rationalize their application of forum law either by the presumption of the identity of foreign and forum law or by the theory that parties "acquiesce" in the application of forum law when they fail to challenge its application or fail to make a sufficient factual showing about the other jurisdiction's law. These rationalizations may not be completely convincing, but they produce acceptable results in most cases. Nevertheless, as *Tidewater* suggests, courts may be reluctant to apply their own law in all its details when they know the local law is not something that is universally adopted.

Think

3. This is a situation where certification might be a good idea. Some state certification procedures authorize their state courts to answer such an unresolved issue of state law. First, the questions of law will likely be determinative of the issue in litigation. If the statute applies to the pony ride, then the defendant wins. If it does not, the case will probably settle. Second, there is no controlling authority from the state. The issues are ones that can be authoritatively settled only by the state's supreme court.

Of course, certification is never required. A federal court might prefer to make its own determination rather than certify. It is also possible that the state's supreme court would refuse to answer. For example, in this case, the federal trial judge might recognize that deciding the helmet issue would require evidence about standards at pony rides. For this reason, he or she might refuse to certify. If the issue was certified, the state supreme court might refuse to answer because the record lacked evidence about standards, costs, and benefits of providing helmets.

If you have gotten this far, you get a near-perfect score. But you should also know that states differ in what courts they allow to certify questions. Mississippi might or might not permit federal trial courts to certify. Now you have a perfect score. (My students in Mississippi would also know that Mississippi only authorizes certification of questions from federal appellate courts. Miss. R. App. P. 20.)

And in the end,[5] certification is like most law. As the old joke goes: the correct 1L answer to all legal questions is "I don't know." The correct 3L answer is "It depends."

You have mastered the law when you know that most states have some form of certification and recognize that the unsettled questions of law in the example present an arguable case for certification under the general requirements in most states. But the correct answer to whether a lower federal court can certify "depends." The complete answer requires you to hit the books. Your Conflicts class and this book aim to get you to the point where you know what you don't know — what the answer depends on, and what to look up. Good luck.

---

5. John Lennon and Paul McCartney, The End, Abbey Road (1969).

Table of Cases

Table of Cases

Table of Cases

Table of Cases

Index

Index

Index